UNDERMINING
INTERSECTIONALITY

Barbara Tomlinson

UNDERMINING INTERSECTIONALITY

The Perils of Powerblind Feminism

TEMPLE UNIVERSITY PRESS
Philadelphia • *Rome* • *Tokyo*

TEMPLE UNIVERSITY PRESS
Philadelphia, Pennsylvania 19122
tupress.temple.edu

Paperback edition published 2020
Cloth edition published 2019

Library of Congress Cataloging-in-Publication Data

Names: Tomlinson, Barbara MacMichael, 1946– author.
Title: Undermining intersectionality : the perils of powerblind feminism /
Barbara Tomlinson.
Description: Philadelphia : Temple University Press, 2018. | Includes
bibliographical references and index. |
Identifiers: LCCN 2018018510 (print) | LCCN 2018033632 (ebook) |
ISBN 9781439916520 (E-book) | ISBN 9781439916506 (hardback : alk. paper)
Subjects: LCSH: Feminism—History—21st century. | Feminism—Social aspects.
| Race—Social aspects. | BISAC: SOCIAL SCIENCE / Feminism & Feminist
Theory. | SOCIAL SCIENCE / Women's Studies.
Classification: LCC HQ1155 (ebook) | LCC HQ1155 .T665 2018 (print) |
DDC 305.4209—dc23
LC record available at https://lccn.loc.gov/2018018510

ISBN 9781439916513 (paperback)

071020P

CONTENTS

ACKNOWLEDGMENTS

I am grateful for the frequent, diverse, and plural instances of convening, conversing, and collaborating about social justice issues on campuses and in community settings that helped bring this book into existence. Special thanks and recognition are owed to my wonderful colleagues in the Department of Feminist Studies at the University of California, Santa Barbara (UCSB): Edwina Barvosa, Jacqueline Bobo, Eileen Boris, Grace Chang, Mireille Miller-Young, Laury Oaks, Leila Rupp, and Jennifer Tyburczy. My research, writing, and teaching have all been enhanced by working with them. I also greatly appreciate my students and the work of our departmental staff, Christina Toy, Sonya Baker, and Crystal Carlos.

Campus faculty outside the department, especially my dean, Melvin Oliver, and Felice Blake, Mary Bucholtz, Esther Lezra, and Glyn Salton-Cox, have been supportive colleagues and generative interlocutors. Claudine Michelle and Maria Herrera-Sobek graciously welcomed me to the UCSB faculty. It has been a special delight to learn with—and from—a new generation of scholars, particularly Denise Gill, Katrina Kimport, Joan Budesa, Jason Pfeifle, Angela Baez, Darlene Craviotto, Chloe Diamond-Lenow, Leigh Dodson, Chelsea Jones, Rachel Rhys, Anita Stahl, Laura Tanner, Liza Munk, and Anna Wald.

My research has been informed at every stage by my work with the African American Policy Forum (AAPF), especially its executive director, Kimberlé Crenshaw, and its co-founder, Luke Harris. Like everyone who writes about intersectionality, I have been educated and inspired by Crenshaw's clarity, courage, and critical acumen. My experience working with her as a co-editor of scholarly collections and observing her many splendid contributions to the Forum's Social Justice Writer's Workshop has been an education in itself. In his own research and in his principled commitment to nurturing the scholarship of others, Harris provides the power of a good example, a way of working that is well worth emulating. Participating in the work of the Forum has also enabled me to interact with and learn from the brilliant scholars involved with it. I am especially grateful to Devon Carbado for his careful reading and for his thoughtful comments and suggestions. Work with the AAPF has also connected me to extremely valuable conversations with Sumi Cho, whose thinking about neoliberalism has been especially useful to my framing of struggles at the scene of argument. I have profited as well from AAPF discussions featuring Dorothy Roberts, Kristie Dotson, Cheryl Y. Harris, Daniel HoSang, Duncan Kennedy, Paul Butler, and Brittany Cooper.

Scholars across the disciplines, across the continent, and around the world have been generous with comments, criticisms, and questions that have helped me hone and refine my ideas. I have benefited greatly from dialogues in person and in print with Sarah Banet-Weiser, Celeste-Marie Bernier, Amy Farrell, Rosa Linda Fregoso, Susan Gillman, Kathy Glass, David Theo Goldberg, Neil Gotanda, Herman Gray, Paula Ioanide, Robin D. G. Kelley, Claire Jean Kim, David Kim, Vivian May, Susan McClary, Charles McGovern, Marzia Milazzo, Jonathan Munby, Chandan Reddy, Alan Rice, Tricia Rose, Jackie Stacey, Cecelia Tichi, Valerie Walkerdine, Rob Walser, and Wendy Walters. I am indebted in many ways for the insights and ideas ensconced in the scholarship of Sara Ahmed, Judith Butler, Elizabeth Spelman, Angela McRobbie, Gail Lewis, Stuart Hall, Ghassan Hage, Sirma Bilge, Bronwyn Davies, Sue Saltmarsh, and Gloria Wekker.

I appreciate the comments and suggestions I received from audience members and respondents at the following conferences, workshops, and seminars: Art, Politics and Performance in the Black Atlantic, Institute for Black Atlantic Research, University of Central Lancashire, UK; American Studies, University of Regensburg, Germany; Center for the Study of Intersectionality and Social Policy, Columbia University Law School; Critical Race Studies Workshop on Intersectionality, University of California, Los Angeles (UCLA) School of Law; Fourth Annual Critical Race Studies Symposium, UCLA School of Law; Countering Colorblindness across the Disciplines, University of Oregon School of Law; Colorblindness across the Disciplines, UCLA School of Law; American Studies, Mount Holyoke College; American Studies, College of William and Mary; American Studies, University of Wyoming; Antiracism Inc. and Antiracism Inc. Presents: The Intervention, an Anticonference sponsored by the American Cultures and Global Contexts Center, UCSB; the

Interdisciplinary Humanities Center, UCSB; and the Social Justice Writer's Retreat at Negril, Jamaica, sponsored by the AAPF.

I am particularly appreciative of the fantastic advice offered by anonymous reviewers for Temple University Press, *Signs, Meridians, Social Identities, Feminist Theory*, the University of California Press, and Punctum Books and the expertise of Sherri Barnes of Moonlight Indexing and copyeditor Virginia Perrin. I owe great thanks for the work of Ann-Marie Anderson, Sara Jo Cohen, Gary Kramer, Kate Levy, and Joan S. P. Vidal of Temple University Press.

Thanks for years of amusement and mutual appreciation go to George Lipsitz, Kerry Tomlinson, Matthew Tomlinson, Lisa Choy Tomlinson, Rebecca Tomlinson, Emily Tomlinson, Kevin Tomlinson, Patrick C. Miller, Coen Miller, and Joel Miller.

Some of the material in this book has been revised in whole or in part from my previous publications. I gratefully acknowledge these sources below:

In Chapter 1: "To Tell the Truth and Not Get Trapped: Desire, Distance, and Intersectionality at the Scene of Argument," *Signs: A Journal of Women in Culture and Society* 38.4 (Summer 2013): 993–1017. Copyright © The University of Chicago Press.

In Chapter 2: "Review of *Fatal Invention: How Science, Politics, and Big Business Re-create Race in the Twenty-First Century*, by Dorothy Roberts," *Kalfou* 4.1 (Spring 2017): 123–128. Copyright © 2017 Regents of the University of California.

In Chapter 5: "The Vise of Geometry: Distorting Intersectionality at the Scene of Argument," *Meridians: feminism, race, transnationalism* 16.1 (2017): 1–36. Copyright © Indiana University Press. Reprinted with permission from Indiana University Press.

In Chapter 7: "Category Anxiety and the Invisible White Woman: Managing Intersectionality at the Scene of Argument," *Feminist Theory* 19.2 (2018): 145–164. Copyright © 2017 Barbara Tomlinson. Reprinted by permission of SAGE Publications. DOI:10.1177/1464700117734735.

In Chapter 8: "Colonizing Intersectionality: Replicating Racial Hierarchy in Feminist Academic Arguments," *Social Identities: Journal for the Study of Race, Nation and Culture* 19.2 (2013): 254–272, www.tandfonline.com. Copyright © 2013 Routledge.

UNDERMINING
INTERSECTIONALITY

1

INTERROGATING CRITIQUES
OF INTERSECTIONALITY

Feminists face many problems that we know about all too well. We know that we live in a thoroughly misogynistic society. All around the world women still experience gender as an axis of exclusion, domination, and subordination. We know that sexism is a crucible where the logics of racism, coloniality, class domination, anti-immigrant nativism, homophobia, transphobia, and many other cruelties are learned and legitimated. Phobias and fantasies that are enabled and encouraged by exaggerated notions of gender difference make inequality and injustice appear to be natural, necessary, and inevitable. Feminists are well aware that the institutions that shape women's lives are structured in dominance—in the economy and the educational system, in reproductive health care and housing, in the images circulated by advertising and entertainment.

But feminists also have some problems that we know all too little about. I argue that the very terrains of feminist analysis, activism, and argument are infused with neoliberal social pedagogies, with cultural training programs that normalize structures of power and hierarchy. The articles and books that we read, the classes that we take and teach, and the activist organizations that we join and support often reproduce and reinforce the categories and conditions that feminism has been committed to contesting. Feminism is a collective oppositional social movement and a critical intellectual practice, but it is also an entity that holds power inside institutions that parcel out individual rewards and promote interpersonal competition.

Within its core realms of interest and expertise, feminism has long been aware of how exclusion and subordination can become encoded in and transmitted by ordinary activities and practices. Feminist writings have justifiably chronicled a long history of overt misogyny, of socially sanctioned assaults on women's bodies, denials of access to property and voting, and exclusion from employment and education. Yet feminists have also recognized that these overt exclusions have been enabled, augmented, and exacerbated by microsocial practices honed through cultural training programs promoting the devaluation of women in many seemingly small ways—through the identification of men as watchers and women as those being watched in the cinematic gaze (Mulvey 1975; Johnston 1976); through the conventions of language use and protocols about who gets to speak and when (Lakoff 1975; Tannen 1990); and through the assumptions encoded in therapeutic advice, counseling, and self-help literature (Buhle 1998; Mitchell 1974; Samuels 1992). Like the hegemonic sexism that feminists find to pervade so many aspects of social life, hegemonic racism does not require a conscious intention or an originating action, but rather becomes absorbed organically through many different cultural practices, unless it is challenged by a clear and fully conscious oppositional culture and politics.

Feminists are well aware of the power that is deployed against us. Many of our analyses and arguments identify the causes and consequences of the power imbalances that pervade the gendered structures of society. Yet we have been less critical of—even oblivious to—the power that we ourselves wield in our roles as gatekeepers and managers of an academic field, as writers, reviewers, editors, and interlocutors, as embodied subjects unified by a common field of inquiry but deeply divided by differences in social experiences, understandings, and aspirations.

Recognizing that things are wrong in the world does not lead automatically to rectifying them. Knowing that we work within sexist institutions does not clarify what we need to do to negotiate the challenges of working within them honestly and honorably. Most important from my perspective—and most central to the evidence, ideas, and arguments advanced in this book—is that merely recognizing and condemning gendered, racialized, classed, and sexualized power does not protect us from unwittingly deploying terms and tools that are saturated with power and structured in dominance. The result is that feminism too often betrays its social justice imperatives not because of bad faith, ill will, or incompetence, but because it fails to acknowledge how often the work we do at quotidian scenes of argument unwittingly reflects dominant ideologies and epistemologies that should be deliberately countered.

This book uses tools of critical and poststructuralist discourse analysis to examine the disturbing racial politics running through more than two

decades of widely cited white feminist commentary on the intellectual production of women of color, specifically white feminist critiques of intersectionality, an interdisciplinary concept developed by Black feminists and other
women of color. The argumentative strategies and rhetorics of these white
feminist critiques, I argue, are replete with "powerblind" discursive practices
that reinforce racial hierarchies and undermine feminism's stated commitment to social justice.

In this chapter, I explain the project of intersectionality, identify the problem of powerblind discourses prevalent in white critiques of it, situate powerblindness at the scene of argument as part of the shared social agreement
about what counts as acceptable feminist academic argument, and consider
challenges that feminist argumentation might take up to move away from
powerblind discourses. I conclude the chapter by identifying the premises of
my argument and the plan for the book.

THE PROJECT OF INTERSECTIONALITY

The radical critique posed by intersectional thinking—originating in attempts by women of color feminists to fuse gender justice with racial justice—gained traction in feminist academic discourses particularly from the
1970s to the 1990s, when Black women as well as other women of color were
actively intervening in scholarly discussions. The generators of intersectional
thinking argue that entrenched social, legal, and academic practices of framing social categories as given, isolated, fixed, and static are pivotal to the reproduction of social dominance. They contend that categories such as gender,
race, and class are not stable and discrete but, rather, variable and changing
constellations that are *relational, interconnected, mutually constituted,* and *simultaneous* (see, for example, Bambara 1970; Carby 1982; P. Collins 1986,
1991; Combahee River Collective 1983; Crenshaw 1989; A. Davis 1981; Dill
1988; Giddings 1984; Higginbotham 1983, 1985; Mullings 1986; Rollins
1985; B. Smith 1983a). Other women of color in the United States developed
related arguments (for example, Anzaldúa 1987; Glenn 1985, 2002; Hurtado
1989; Lowe 1991, 1996; Matsuda 1991; Sandoval 1991, 2000), as did scholars
in Britain (for example, Anthias and Yuval-Davis 1992). (For overviews of
the development and debates about intersectionality, see Carastathis 2016;
Collins and Bilge 2016; Dhamoon 2011; Hancock 2016; May 2014, 2015.)

Intersectional thinking emerged from the theorizing of women of color
as a tool against structural subordination, an analytic to challenge structural
inequality and call for institutional transformation. It is a political and analytic concept; a sensibility or disposition; a heuristic for thinking in supple and
strategic ways about social categories, relations of power, and the complexities

of sameness/difference in terms of conceptions of *both/and* rather than *either/ or* (see P. Collins 1991; Crenshaw 1989, 1991).

Intersectional analysis reveals how single-axis theories of subordination inscribed in law but also utilized in self-defense by aggrieved groups can obscure shifting and multiple axes of power. As a conceptual framework that focuses attention on the degree to which all identities are multidimensional, intersectionality is a nexus of complex arguments about gender, race, ethnicity, sexuality, religion, nation, hierarchy, power, control, and value. Intersectional analysis—particularly the work of legal theorist Kimberlé Crenshaw (1989, 1991) and sociologist Patricia Hill Collins (1986, 1991)—has served as a catalyst for widespread use of intersectionality as a political and analytic tool. It has served as a major theoretical resource in the development of Critical Race Theory (Crenshaw 2010, 2011c), in feminist studies (McCall 2005), in an increasing number of academic disciplines, in discussions of social policy,[1] and in popular activism.[2] Intersectionality has become one of the most cited and deployed frames for speaking about all social identities and power.

An extraordinary body of work has provided original and generative deployments of intersectional thinking to demonstrate how *politics defines identities* rather than *identities defining politics.* Drawing on arguments about history, difference, flexibility, fluidity, specificity, and multiplicity, scholars argue that gender- and race-based antisubordination struggles do not flow organically from shared physical features but rather emerge in struggles that seek to imbue complex and complicated embodied identities with dynamic political meanings (see, for example, Barvosa 2008; Blackwell 2011; Cho 2009; Cohen 1997; Connolly and Patel 1997; Crenshaw 1992, 2011a; A. Davis 1997; Fregoso 2003; Fujino 2005; Hawkesworth 2003; Hernández 2010; James 1996; S. Lee 2008; Lowe 1996; Maira 2000; Maxwell 2006; McCall 2001; Reddy 2011; Roberts 2012; Rodríguez 2003; Rose 2008, 2013; Sandoval 2000; Shah 2001; A. Smith 2006; Tapia 2011; Valdes and Cho 2011; Wilkins 2012).

Intersectionality has been proposed not as an overarching grand theory but as a politically grounded mid-level theory for antisubordination and social change: in the terms that Stuart Hall used in describing the value of Antonio Gramsci's theories, a mid-level theory "complexifies" existing theories and problems by connecting large concepts to specific situations (1986, 5), exemplifying Gramsci's argument for a middle-range, protracted "war of position" to be waged across many different sites (see Chapter 2 for further discussion of Gramsci's war of position).

As a mid-level theory, intersectionality is appropriate to the vexed and vexing nature of its objects of study and the need to operate across many different sites: there are always racisms, always sexisms, but never the same over time and space. Racial, sexual, and gender projects are both local and global, so neither scholarship nor activism benefits from having to choose between parochial microsocial descriptions or overly general disembodied claims of universality. Different social arenas require different arguments: legal, literary, sociological, cultural, and ethnic studies need different forms of theorizing because they have different goals, methods, and objects of analysis (see, for example, P. Collins 1989, 1991; Crenshaw 1989; Lowe 1991; Sandoval 1991). Rather than focusing on ideal and abstract schematic formulations about what identities should be, "mid-level theorizing" attends to concrete struggles over power and social structures, over what identities are now and what they are capable of becoming. The situated but transferrable epistemology and ontology of intersectional women of color provide a revealing lens for theorizing society as a whole, enabled by, but not limited to, their experiences. Some critics claim intersectional thinking is merely the "parochial" and "embodied" concern of women of color. But since all views—including the view of the white middle-class heterosexual woman—are partial perspectives, the intersectional theorizing of women of color is already fit for universality. Though the point is usually ignored in white feminist critiques of intersectionality, mid-level theorizing is particularly suited to the tasks of feminist analysis.

Speaking to the National Women's Political Caucus in 1971, Fannie Lou Hamer asked her listeners to refuse any vision of racial justice that did not include gender justice and to reject any vision of gender justice that did not include racial justice (C. Lee 2000). The originators of intersectional analysis in academic writing and teaching echoed and elaborated on this vision. Nearly all of the core writings that established intersectionality as an activist and academic imperative emphasized its practical utility and programmatic commitment to confront and contest the ways in which sexism undermines antiracism and racism undermines antisexism. Yet, as I demonstrate throughout this book, this is not the intersectionality that has survived and thrived within feminism. A set of tools designed to address intersecting vectors of power has often been watered down into an enterprise aimed largely at ruminating about overlapping aspects of individual identity. The emphasis on the parameters of individual identity in feminist critiques of intersectionality works to occlude the workings of power.

THE PROBLEM OF PERVASIVE POWERBLINDNESS

The provocation of intersectional thinking challenged white feminism's dominant emphasis on gender as the primary axis or site of oppression and its emphasis on white women as the primary representatives of feminism, positions encouraging a concomitant suppression of the heterogeneity of race, class, and sexuality. Intersectional analysis provoked white feminism to go beyond a liberal acknowledgment of "difference" to examine *which differences make a difference.* Requiring the reformulation of dominant feminist theories of subjectivity, power, social structures, and subordination, intersectionality has proven to be a crucial tool for theorizing about subordination and for developing antisubordination arguments.

Despite its importance as a tool for antisubordination, intersectionality has also provoked a plethora of powerblind discursive practices that I delineate in this book. It is among the most misread, mischaracterized, and misunderstood concepts in scholarship about social justice. Few theories are as consistently misinterpreted.[3] Critics routinely misrepresent the history and arguments of intersectional thinking, treat it as a unitary entity rather than an analytic tool used across a range of disciplines, distort its arguments, engage in "presentist" analytics, reduce its radical critique of power to desires for "identity" and "inclusion," and offer a "de-politicized" or "de-radicalized" intersectionality as an asset for dominant disciplinary discourses. Critics tend to approach conceptions of intersectionality carelessly, through metacommentary and complaint, through recommendations to bring its radical critique under control by advocating recourse to specific and often deeply conservative disciplinary methods—without acknowledging that such methods may have long been criticized for their service to dominant discourses.[4] Critics repeatedly present arguments that have already been made by intersectional scholars as if they were the critic's own original, new, significant claim (May 2014, 2015).

A long line of critical commentary has consistently misrepresented the intersectional theorizing of women of color. As I demonstrate in this book, this extensive body of widely referenced commentary, articles, and books— often cited, taught, and imitated—accuses intersectionality of creating the very categories and social relations that it exposes and contests. This work portrays intersectionality as fixed when it is fluid and flexible. It relies on an extensive set of uninterrogated argumentative conventions and writing practices that subordinate the generative intellectual labor of women of color on the basis of casual claims of white feminist critics. Again and again, these powerblind critics declare the ideas of the feminists of color who developed intersectionality to be simplistic and merely experiential, while even the most superficial ideas of white scholars are treated as sophisticated and theoretical. In effect, many white scholars position themselves as "rescuing" the concept of intersectionality from the inadequate thinking of the women of color who developed it.

These positions might seem plausible to those who read them because powerblind critiques routinely rely on reviews of the research literature that are dramatically disproportionate with regard to race and scope. Powerblind critiques often buttress their own condemnations by citing a surfeit of previous critiques, the overwhelming majority by white feminists; the result is often not an analysis of intersectionality but simply a compilation of the negative things that white feminists have said about intersectionality. A few intersectional theorists of color are usually cited and discussed—though generally not analyzed—to ground the critiques of intersectionality, with particular emphasis on a few old texts, rather than close examination of contemporary arguments. The tendency to treat intersectionality as a unitary entity—rather than a cluster of flexible analytic tools used for various disciplinary and political purposes—encourages critics to position a comment of any intersectional scholar as representative of all of intersectional thinking. As a result, declaring deficient any particular argument of an intersectional scholar is treated as tantamount to proving "intersectionality" deficient. The apparent credibility of this argumentative structure is contrived through restricting its citations. Virtually never cited in such powerblind critiques of intersectionality are the myriad generative and insightful intersectional analyses connecting power, politics, race, gender, sexuality, and other categories written over the last several decades notably (but not solely) by scholars of color. Because this scholarship is rendered invisible, utterly inaccurate claims about the nature of intersectionality's limitations ("cannot be used to study experience," "fails to deal with concrete individuals") may seem tenable to uninformed readers.

Such powerblind discourses have been established as the prevailing and preferred mode for white feminist critiques of intersectionality. Critiques especially fail to acknowledge adequately intersectionality's metaphoricity and its disposition toward the *both/and* rather than the *either/or*. Instead they resort to judgments structured through conceptual binaries that have long been criticized by feminists for oversimplifying the complex, dialogic, flexible, and even contradictory relations inherent to arguments about antisubordination. As Kimberlé Crenshaw notes, critics constantly return to the terms of tired tropes: "strains of particularism versus universalism, personal narrative versus grand theory, identity-based versus structural, static versus dynamic, parochial versus cosmopolitan, underdeveloped versus sophisticated, old versus new, race versus class, US versus Europe, and so on" (2011b, 222–223).

Many contemporary scholars who want to draw on intersectional thinking seem to believe that they must make submissive gestures to distance themselves from commonplace representations of an "imaginary intersectionality" framed as deeply flawed. I argue that these submissive distancing gestures are a result of the distorted terms of debate established by more than two decades of powerblind white feminist critiques, reiterated, re-enforced, and continued into the present by their systematic repetition and problematic politics of citation. For many years these critiques have largely gone unchallenged; published rebuttals such as this book have appeared only in recent years (see, for example, Alexander-Floyd 2012; Bilge 2013, 2014; Carbado 2013; Cho 2013; B. Cooper 2015; May 2014, 2015; Tomlinson 2013a, 2013b). The constant repetition of such rhetorics distorts feminist studies' goals of social justice. It encourages feminist scholars to assume that their task should be *to condemn, reform, and appropriate intersectionality,* rather than *to foster intersectionality's ability to critique subordination.*

Intersectionality—perhaps feminism's most celebrated icon of inclusion—may strike some readers as an odd point of entry for an analysis of the currents of dominant racial discourses sedimented within white feminism. Yet as I show in these chapters, feminism's inclusion of the women of color who developed intersectionality has been of a significantly conditional kind, more a stripping of assets and an evisceration of radical critique than incorporation and development of a body of thought created by women of color. The incessant negativity of white feminist critiques reveals dominant feminism's resistance to identifying and interrogating its covert allegiances—and its continuing insistence on placing the interests of white women at the center of feminist analysis, argument, and activism.

Deployment of racially dominant discursive strategies by white women is not new, though many contemporary white feminists may not have noticed the ways that conventional powerblind academic rhetorics reinscribe racial hierarchy at the center of feminist discourse. The rhetorics examined in this book are a contemporary instantiation of a long historical pattern in which generative social critiques by Black women have been suppressed, ignored, and discounted. Work by intersectional analysts and other Black scholars often mentions historical figures whose arguments were ignored—for example, Sojourner Truth, Maria W. Stewart, Ida B. Wells, Fannie Barrier Williams, Anna Julia Cooper, and Mary Church Terrell (see, for example, the critiques of discursive racism in Carby 1982; P. Collins 1991; Combahee River Collective 1983; Cooper 1892; Giddings 1984; Green 2007; Guy-Sheftall 1995; King 1988; C. Lee 2000; Lorde 1984; Lugones and Spelman 1983; May 2012, 2015; Richardson 1987; B. Smith 1983a; Terrell 2005; F. Williams 1987). Thus contemporary feminist academic discourse replicates the very dynamic of being ignored and silenced that has characterized white reception of the intersectional thinking of Black women since its inception in the nineteenth and twentieth centuries (see particularly May 2015, and also Bambara 1970; Giddings 1984; Guy-Sheftall 1995).

The history of racialized critiques and their remarkable resurgence in the past two decades in feminist scholarship through powerblind discourses and problematic practices of citation offer women of color an inclusion in feminism—but of a subordinate kind. Women of color routinely find themselves implicated in discussions of intersectionality characterized by incessantly repeated falsehoods and denigration. They are expected to ignore more than two decades of white feminist argument systematically demeaning the ideas, the scholarship, the scholars, and the social formations that created intersectionality. They are expected to overlook the fact that for many years, despite their manifest problems of evidence and argument, these white feminist critiques have been valorized and seldom subjected to criticism by other white scholars. The result, I argue, is a picture of a neoliberal white feminism that may well be all but unrecognizable to most white feminists, but which is all too familiar to women of color.

Powerblindness is an unarticulated ideological commitment that structures the social imagination and circulates widely within feminist reading and writing practices. Through powerblind discourses, authors and activists present themselves as unaware of their own racial power, as independent of and isolated from the currents of racial power that permeate their societies and the institutional matrices in which they work. Powerblind rhetorics are used in feminist studies to erase racial specificity, to make white authors and readers feel that they are color-blind, to proclaim white innocence and register white injury, to devalue the research of women of color, to hoard academic resources (honors, awards, and recognition) for white scholars who purport to supersede the work of women of color, and—significantly—to disguise the neoliberal stripping of intellectual assets from women of color.

Such powerblind strategies are widespread and readily visible in white feminist critiques—"hidden in plain sight"—because white feminist scholars have not trained themselves to *read* intersectionally, to consider the intersectional *effects* created by the reinscription of social dominance at the scene of feminist argument. In this book I bring to light some of the specific strategies through which powerblindness is implemented. These include tactics of social amnesia, incorporation, appropriation, erasure, ventriloquizing, arguing with straw persons, adopting imaginary allies, treating inclusion as a one-way street, neoliberal asset-stripping, rhetorics of rejection and replacement, errors of attribution, chains of fallacious citations, decontextualizing metaphors, deploying the "mark of the plural," creating a gulf between the critic and the criticized, "fixing" the "essential" nature of women of color, rewriting the role of inclusiveness in the history of feminism, providing alibis for dominant white feminists, dissolving the concept of intersectionality into the history of white feminism, and reinscribing white feminism as the center of the field's social analysis. As I argue more fully in Chapter 9, these strategies do not operate separately or additively; their iteration, repetition, and citational legacy work together to create an "Epistemic Machine"—a discursive machine for invalidating the knowledge of intersectional scholars of color.

How do we explain the persistence and pervasive presence of patently false claims and racially condescending formulations in peer-reviewed feminist scholarship? Why do researchers from a field founded to advance gendered inclusion succumb to practices that promote racial exclusion? What is it about the hierarchies and rewards of academic and activist feminism that lead feminists claiming concern for social justice to craft and embrace a surfeit of arguments that appear blind to their own deployment of racial power?

Just as schools of fish take for granted the waters in which they swim, our schools of thought in academic and activist circles rarely allow us to recognize that we are swimming in a sea of neoliberal beliefs, incentives, structures, and cultural frames. Neoliberalism elevates individual experiences and aspirations over collective obligations and responsibilities. It promotes relentless competition for recognition and reward. It encourages people to strip assets from others and to view deeply political problems as susceptible to only apolitical, personal, or technical solutions. These powerblind white feminist misrepresentations of intersectionality imbibe the ideology of neoliberalism through practices of asset-stripping that delegitimize the intellectual production of women of color while effecting appropriation of the concept of intersectionality for management and ownership by an unmarked white feminism. Equally significant is the use of strategies that serve to subdue and depoliticize intersectionality's originating radical critique of structural power, often reducing the concept to little more than liberal acknowledgment of diverse personal identities. These strategies work to create a concept of intersectionality that is safe for power.

Powerblind strategies emerge in part from professional pressures, reward structures, and credentialing mechanisms that feminists do not sufficiently interrogate. Scholars are eager to publish. Displacing and supplanting previous knowledge conforms to the structures of professional reward. Scholars may exaggerate their criticisms of work by others to draw on the prestige of the appearance of novelty and innovation in ways that are destructive rather than constructive, competitive rather than contributive. Editorial decisions at the site of publication play an important role here. As Lauren Berlant argues, "To decide to publish something is to confirm that it has made a case for its worthiness as knowledge" (2007, 671). Journals and presses may fail to see that what appears to be a "lively" or "controversial" article in fact replicates widespread and systematic misrepresentations of intersectional thinking. Academic journals are part of a training "pipeline" that includes graduate student cultures, presentations at professional meetings, and prestige hierarchies that spread word-of-mouth approval and disapproval. These sites function to produce what counts as "critique" and what defines the safest and most satisfying ways to deliver it.

Other aspects of our academic training may produce the unwitting use of powerblind strategies. Graduate students learn to rely on reading practices that attack and disparage texts rather than analyze them. Unarticulated fears and social dangers pervade academic culture. The practices of consumption and connoisseurship that saturate social relations in this society teach people that it is dangerous and humiliating to be out of date and out of fashion. Consequently, expressing *dislikes* may appear safer than expressing *likes,* a preference that David Riesman long ago connected to consumption practices. In a study of consumers of popular music, he found that "enthusiasm would seem to be a greater social danger than negativism: The fear is to be caught liking what the others have decided not to like" (1950, 369). Scholars do not leave these practices behind when they leave graduate school. As a result, they may deploy inadequate modes of argument that do not contribute positively to feminist knowledge production focused on antisubordination.

Academic training may encourage powerblind strategies when specific disciplinary discourses are deployed to restrain, dismiss, and appropriate radical critique. The interdisciplinary, boundary-crossing focus of feminist studies as a whole exists in tension with the disciplinary training of many feminist scholars. As this book demonstrates, arguments in some disciplines may be so focused on how intersectionality meets disciplinary interests that they ignore or treat disrespectfully its significance for other disciplines. These arguments may frame intersectionality in narrow, discipline-bound ways, as if the entire value of the concept rests on its ability to meet strictures proposed as appropriate for a specific discipline. The ways of knowing characterizing a specific discipline are elevated to stand in for all feminist ways of knowing. Because discipline-bound strategies are taken for granted within disciplinary discourses, they can serve as potent tools of dominance, infusing the reading situation with strategies of racialized subordination that go unremarked because they are authorized by tradition and convention. As Aileen Moreton-Robinson notes, "Patriarchal whiteness surreptitiously works to support white feminists being racially disembodied as their thinking, knowing, and writing becomes more consistent with Western Male epistemology and disciplines. Patriarchal whiteness deludes women into thinking their epistemology is unaffected by this process because of 'academic freedom' and their positioning as subject/knowers" (2000, 351).

The managerial training that silently accompanies our disciplinary training may also unwittingly encourage the use of powerblind strategies. Because universities are class-based institutions that privilege managerial perspectives, critics of prevailing power relations trained in these academies can come to see their proper role as "managing" the opposition. Dominant power is secured through discursive practices at the scene of argument throughout the academy as well as through control of economic, political, and legal institutions. Dominant ideas are learned and legitimated through what Ranajit Guha calls the "prose of counter-insurgency," a shared social discourse that positions critics of the social order as complainers or "insurgents"—as illegitimate rebels against the sedimented authority of hegemonic ideas and actions (1988). At the scene of academic argument, the prose of counterinsurgency relies on taken-for-granted ways of framing issues that are complicit with subordination and exploitation. It contains what Mikhail Bakhtin describes as a "materials memory" inside language that assumes inequality is natural and normal and that delegitimizes arguments on behalf of social justice (cited in Terdiman 1993, 45). In scholarship, it elevates authority over equity, equilibrium over equality. Within this framework, gendered, raced, and nonnormatively sexed agonists are discredited in advance, their arguments dismissed before they even begin to speak (for "discredited in advance," see C. Mills 2007). Without rigorous interrogation, feminists in the U.S. and European academies who are racially dominant may frame racialized others as "insurgents" whose arguments should be dismissed or contained.

These political and intellectual problems are not resolved or overcome by intersectionality's current "success"—its centrality as a concept for contemporary feminism. The audit culture that preceded and now in a different way pervades the neoliberal academy exerts its power in perverse ways. Academic debates often focus on criticizing and "uncrowning" popular theories. In fact, there are numerous critiques attempting to "uncrown," "dethrone," discredit, confuse, and contradict conceptions of intersectionality, with no analysis of how jettisoning intersectional analysis would destabilize feminist cross-racial alliances and undermine feminist knowledge production concerned with race. There is also an enduring temporal dimension to these problems. The architecture of academic argument ensures continuing citation in the present of problematic critiques of the past. Because feminism has not yet even fully acknowledged, much less come to grips with its immersion in neoliberalism and its own discursive deployment of power—because it is "blind" to how racialized power undergirds its system of critique—it unwittingly reinforces the logic of domination that it purports to protest.

White feminists have obtained control over a whole area in the academy that has been of great value. Yet consistent with neoliberal notions of property and power, they have labored to maintain their privileged access to those resources, to proclaim their gendered inclusion in the academy as a victory for all, while zealously appropriating for themselves the right to determine the degree, nature, and pace of racial inclusion. This leads to the bizarre spectacle of white feminists belittling and demeaning the very intersectional ideas they proclaim as their own.

This view of feminism as a site where white privilege is produced and protected will likely come as a surprise to many feminists. As a field of inquiry and activism, feminism has long claimed commitments to social justice. To its credit, many of its key thinkers have honestly and honorably recognized feminism's organic affinities with antiracist ideas and actions. Both sexism and racism are inscribed on the body, exaggerating small differences in appearance to create large differences in treatment and opportunity. Overt declarations of racist intent are rarely present in feminist discourse. Yet under the terms of neoliberal social organization, economics, and culture, statements of racist intent are not needed to produce outcomes with racist effects. Neoliberal racism generally includes persistent denials and disavowals of racism, yet racial stratification still permeates nearly every area of human endeavor. Feminist social justice that includes a commitment to antiracism can become possible only through full awareness and presence of mind about the need to identify, analyze, and oppose the insidious ways in which feminism—as well as the larger society—contains practices that produce what Eduardo Bonilla-Silva aptly names "racism without racists" (2003).

THE SIGNIFICANCE OF THE SCENE OF ARGUMENT

It is the performative and social nature of feminist academic argument that creates the conditions of possibility for powerblind discourses that undermine feminism's commitment to social justice. While often criticizing larger cultural discourses, feminist scholars tend to view their own practices of reading and writing as conventional and transparent, frequently failing to acknowledge and examine how the arguments and scenes they construct are *always already* situated within fields of power and *always already* participate in forms of social domination. Framing academic and political discussions in commonsense ways treats writing conventions as parts of a neutral technology to be deployed or evaluated in isolation from their conditions of production, the situations of speakers, and the effects of social power. Yet as this book demonstrates, feminist arguments can absorb and convey uninterrogated and deeply hierarchical models of textuality, argument, authorship, and evidence.

Louis Althusser argues that concrete individuals become constituted as "subjects" through ideology, but the most powerful ideological influences do not come to us in the form of ideological pronouncements (1971). Such pronouncements would be visible, controversial, and refutable. Instead, he argues, the most powerful ideologies exist in "apparatuses," in practices, and these practices are always material. Reading, writing, and arguing are material social practices laced with ideologies of legitimacy and propriety so powerful and pervasive that we presuppose their value rather than examining their effects. If, as I argue, feminists become "arguing subjects" through material practices that they have not sufficiently examined, then we need to transform the terms of reading and writing to take responsibility for the ways that feminist discourses at the scene of argument can function as technologies of dominant power.

Examining how academic feminists become "arguing subjects" reveals that discourses at the scene of argument are part of what *constitutes* an academic feminist public (see Warner 2002, 16, on constituting publics). The texts we read and write—and our reading and writing of them—are material social practices that shape *what counts as* academic feminism. Feminist scholarship establishes itself not merely by circulation of prominent ideas but also by production of the most mundane conventions of argument, reiterated as commonplaces in texts that become widely read and cited. Under such circumstances, problematic conventional textual practices can go unremarked while serving to subdue radical praxis. Whether or not we desire it to be so, feminist academic discourses are nodes in a network of communications structured in dominance. Like other discourses, feminist academic discourses interpellate, "hail," or call out to us *as if* we are certain kinds of feminist subjects, their efficacy based on their citation of certain prior and "authoritative" practices (see Butler 1997). These discourses have indirect effects whether they are intended for us or not, whether we receive them or not, whether we resist them or not. Through this barrage of hailing, we come to understand what is "obvious," what "goes without saying," what counts as "coherent." Dominant readings are reinforced through their ideological intelligibility, even if a reader is critical (see S. Mills 1995). They subject and subjectify. Feminist knowledge practices and critical performances at the scene of argument serve as "socializing pedagogies" (Wiegman 2010, 83). In effect, feminism is *produced* through discourse.

We cannot escape being interpellated by the effects of the scene of argument. Our practices of writing proceed through patterned acts of argumentation, fully immersed in the social history of language, deploying words and forms that have been "completely taken over," as Bakhtin argues, "shot through with intentions and accents" (1981, 293). Feminists cannot escape using conventional patterns of language, claims, and arguments, but we can insist on looking more closely at the scene of argument in order to determine how conventionalized argumentative structures serve us badly when they gain purchase as convincing moves, yet undermine radical critique.

The long-standing pervasive practices of unacknowledged feminist powerblindness that appear in white critiques of intersectionality reveal the scene of argument to be a much more important site for feminist praxis than is often acknowledged, and one that is all too clearly neglected. The scene of academic argument is a discursive site, a textual stage, a platform for social contestation, a location for the rhetorical enactment of power (see also Tomlinson 2010; Tomlinson and Lipsitz 2019). The scene of argument is a social site where academic feminism is produced: articulated, modeled, learned, and legitimated. At the scene of argument we can examine what kinds of claims are being made, how and why these claims are justified, to whom they are attributed, how they are passed on and adopted by others, and how they serve to influence larger arenas of discussion. It is at the scene of argument that we can examine how the powerblind relationship between intersectionality and its critics has been formed, how it has *emerged from* the practical forms of articulation, exchange, and consumption that are already in place within the institutions we inhabit. The scene of argument reveals a great deal about who we are as feminist scholars: how we see the purpose of our arguments, our assumptions about the efficacy of conventional scholarly textual strategies, and the nature of the "metadiscursive regimes" that authorize what it is acceptable or desirable to argue in the field of feminist studies.

Metadiscursive regimes contain widespread, largely unarticulated ideologies of language, argument, and discourse. They shape and constrain the discursive practices that appear at the scene of argument. Academic argument is not an individual enterprise but a collaborative socially shared activity created with common tools wielded by a wide range of writers, reviewers, and readers. Academic authors seeking to intervene in ongoing scholarly conversations shape their arguments according to their perceptions of feminist studies' socially shared standards of research. They deploy argumentative and rhetorical conventions considered acceptable and desirable in feminist studies. Manuscripts undergo procedures of peer review in which reviewers and editors of journals and presses offer advice—again based on standards that are socially shared—advice that may drastically change the claims and evidence marshaled in particular texts. Once published, texts are read, cited, and commented on by other feminist scholars, extending the conversation and production of knowledge taking place through feminist argument. Under such circumstances, the powerblind argumentative decisions I examine in this book cannot be framed as individual issues—merely matters of private choice and personal style. They must be seen as evidence of socially shared understandings of the proper nature of feminist academic discourse enacted by a phalanx of scholars—colleagues, editors, reviewers, anthologizers, citers, readers—evaluating, sanctioning, and promoting particular texts and arguments according to the frameworks of feminist metadiscursive regimes.

Metadiscursive regimes frame our ways of thinking about broader notions of social power. Discursive technologies of power encourage affiliation with dominant discourses through complex means of identification and repudiation. General societal and disciplinary power relations give utterances friendly to prevailing power relations an overdetermined "reasonableness" while rendering most oppositional arguments automatically suspect. Even in feminist academic discourses, conventional social or disciplinary criticisms infused with such overdetermined "reasonableness" can serve to circumscribe and control the much-needed unruliness of oppositional critique. Richard Bauman and Charles L. Briggs argue that metadiscursive regimes are a foundational creation of modernity, formulating rules about the proper boundaries and relationships among language, tradition, science, and society, and providing "a basis for what could be thought, discussed, and enacted by modern subjects" (2003, 51). For example, the metadiscursive regimes of modernity we have inherited contain and constrain the imagination in ways that underpin feminist powerblindness: they valorize elite voices as "authoritative" while trivializing voices of the Other as "authentic" but illegitimate as sources of knowledge (312). If contemporary critical projects that frame themselves as opposing structures of inequality unwittingly deploy the metadiscursive regimes of modernity without interrogating their ideological grounding, efforts "to challenge racial and other structures of inequality will be sapped of their interpretive and political efficacy from the outset" (306). By sustaining privileged modes of thinking, uninterrogated metadiscursive regimes place dominant power, hierarchy, and exploitation at the heart of feminist argument.

Acknowledging the potent role of dominant metadiscursive regimes in shaping what is considered acceptable and desirable in feminist academic argument enables our understanding of powerblindness. Powerblindness is not an individual problem of politeness or etiquette but a problem of ideology, of politics and ethics. Michel Foucault argues that power is a mobile part of every relation; the rationality and logic behind power relations are not directed and controlled by specific individuals or groups but, rather, operate through *strategies* that can exercise power or counter it (1980a). Thus, I emphasize, the texts I examine in this book are *examples* but not the *target* of my analysis. The texts function as representative conventional uses of argument appearing in works that have been vetted by peers—edited, published, anthologized, and cited as authoritative by a chain of subsequent scholars. A host of feminist scholars has approved these texts according to shared standards of feminist research. My *target* here is exactly those shared standards and their complicity in reproducing unacknowledged and uninterrogated metadiscursive regimes of modernity and disciplinarity that feminist scholars both inherit and forge, regimes that, I argue, lead them to reinscribe social and racial hierarchies at the scene of feminist argument and thereby weaken the precision and productivity of feminist thought.

The ready acceptance and repetition of powerblind strategies can be overcome if feminist argumentation is no longer treated as a neutral technology but reframed as a site of political praxis requiring at least the same level of reflexivity as feminist theorizing and methodology. Powerblindness is fostered when feminist discourses address intersectionality *nonintersectionally*. Approaching feminist discourses intersectionally can prompt us to interrogate whether conventional discursive strategies and taken-for-granted ways of thinking about academic argumentation produce intersectional effects.

CHALLENGES FOR FEMINIST ARGUMENT

The problems of the discursive evidence that I examine in this book signal how vital it is for feminism to transform its terms of reading and writing. Transforming the affective, ethical, and conceptual life of feminist academic arguments concerning race requires feminists to reconfigure the metadiscursive regimes that shape what counts as acceptable or successful feminist academic argument or discourse. Altering taken-for-granted discursive strategies requires academic feminism to address a series of challenges.

The first challenge is to more satisfactorily incorporate race into the structure of feminist thought. The prevalence of powerblind critiques shows that feminism's failure to develop a fully theorized intersectionality makes the introduction of the realities of race function as an unwelcome disturbance rather than an organic component of antisubordination thinking. In effect, intersectionality pressures many white feminists to consider whether the nature of their subordination by gender must be rethought in order to also account for racial privilege. Yet such reconsideration is seldom evident in powerblind critiques of intersectionality, which tend to be written from the position of an unmarked white woman whose racial privilege is deployed but unacknowledged. Critics' racial privilege is particularly evident when they casually and confidently deploy dominant notions of race to denigrate the knowledge of race demonstrated in the arguments of intersectional scholars of color. This exhibition of undue authority about race based on white racial privilege is particularly significant because the great majority of critiques of intersectionality have inescapably racial stakes: the originating theories and metaphors of intersectionality are productions of women of color, yet most critiques are written from the subject position of the unmarked white woman, published in journals generally edited by white women, and addressed to audiences assumed to be primarily white. The structures of racial dominance that underpin the critiques are virtually never acknowledged.

This evidence of the continuing disturbance of race in feminism challenges feminists to revisit arguments about the stance of the feminist knower, particularly about the difficulty of recognizing the nature of one's own social power. As Elizabeth V. Spelman argues, race and class privilege often appear invisible to white feminist scholars who deploy them. She maintains:

> A measure of the depth of white middle-class privilege is that the apparently straightforward and logical points and axioms at the heart of much feminist theory guarantee the direction of its attention to the concerns of white middle-class women. . . . If we think of privilege simply as appearing in individuals rather than being *lodged in ways of thinking*, we focus on what privilege feeds *but not on what sustains it*. (1988, 4, emphasis added)

Spelman's argument suggests that the nature of privilege tends to make it imperceptible to individuals, who simply take for granted certain ways of selecting what problems might seem worthy of attention, how debates should be framed, who should be heard and how, what should count as compelling evidence, what must be explained or justified, and what may be assumed or taken for granted in constructing arguments. Countering powerblind strategies requires bringing into focus racial and class privilege that may be unnoticed by the feminist critic.

The second challenge is to process more satisfactorily the affective history stemming from the moment when many white feminists perceived that they were losing control of feminism because of the disturbance of race. I argue that the prevalence of powerblind strategies used against intersectionality by white feminists reveal the traces of an uninterrogated and unprocessed historical shock related to feminism's encounter with the disturbance of race, a shock with enduring consequences in the present. The distortions of race in critiquing intersectional thinking in the present represent the material residue of a moment in the 1980s and 1990s when white women seemed to perceive that they were losing control of feminism—when the universal category of "woman" around which the field initially cohered became complicated by uneven dynamics of social difference (see Hemmings 2011). Intersectionality became perceived as a marker of that moment, and it persists as a haunting that must be exorcised in order for white women to effect a revanchist return of feminism to its primary emphasis on gender and to restore for themselves what they may imagine to be their rightful place at the center of the field.

Enunciated initially in white feminist critiques during the 1990s, discursive devices aimed at distorting intersectionality have become central tropes in and techniques of feminist argument, relentlessly reproduced in later critiques through repetition and the politics of their citation (see also Bilge 2013, 2014; May 2014, 2015). The trauma of diminished overrepresentation experienced by white feminists in the 1980s and 1990s impacts adversely the work that all feminists do today, while continuing to inflict an ongoing historical assault on Black women knowers and other women of color in the name of repairing white feminism's perceived losses.

The third challenge is to eschew a consensual contemporary "social amnesia" that simply erases feminism's own problematic history of theorizing categories in order to present the intersectional theorizing of social categories by women of color as singularly inept. The history of feminism supplies abundant evidence of what is being erased. For example, Spelman (1988) provides an incisive critique of the racial and class politics of feminist theory dominant during the period of intersectionality's successful intervention. Her work reveals that various theoretical "flaws" often attributed to intersectional thinking were, in fact, central to the white middle-class feminist theory that intersectionality challenged (see also Sandoval 1991, 2000). For example, intersectional analyses are criticized for thinking of categories as "separable," yet feminism was built on this assumption. Spelman argues that white middle-class privilege "lodges at the very root of much feminist thinking—for example, in the assumption that gender identity exists in isolation from race and class identity" (1988, x). Spelman maintains:

> In the case of much [white middle-class] feminist thought we may get the impression that a woman's identity consists of a sum of parts neatly divisible from one another, parts defined in terms of her race, gender, class, and so on. We may infer that the oppressions she is subject to are . . . neatly divisible. . . . This is a version of personal identity we might call *tootsie roll metaphysics*: each part of my identity is separable from every other part, and the significance of each part is unaffected by the other parts. On this view of personal identity (which also might be called *pop-bead metaphysics*), my being a woman means the same whether I am white or Black, rich or poor. (136, emphasis added)[5]

When practiced by dominant white feminists, the isolation of the category of gender—specifically the focus on women as a unified category—was not criticized, but valorized. Yet when women of color promote intersectional analysis as a counter to isolating single categories, they are denigrated and accused of treating categories as "separable" at the very moment they are proposing that they are not.

Spelman argues that feminist theory's focus on women "as women" created a fixed category, one that actually encompassed the condition of only white middle-class women in industrialized countries (1988, 3); it was assumed that the meaning of sexism and one's experience as a woman was the same for all women (x). Differences from other women were downplayed and neglected (4). Aspects of identity other than gender were dismissed and ignored in favor of speaking "as a woman." In effect, Spelman asserts, "in feminist theory it is a *refusal* to take differences among women seriously that lies at the heart of feminism's implicit politics of dominance" (11, emphasis in original). In consequence, Spelman claims, she has come to see "the phrase 'as a woman' as the Trojan horse of feminist ethnocentrism" (x, 13).

Spelman argues that its focus on the importance of women as a category led white middle-class feminist theory to position other categories as "additive." She uses Simone de Beauvoir and Nancy Chodorow as examples of additive thinkers who make comparisons between sex or sexism and other categories or oppressions considered as distinct from gender (sex *and* class, sexism *and* racism). Spelman calls this additive analysis "*the ampersand problem*" (1988, 115, emphasis added). Recognizing the conceptual difficulty of managing the interrelationships among various categories, she sees as pivotal the conception of how categories are linked. For example, she indicates that in an additive analysis, sexism would be a burden for Black women, and racism would simply be a "*further* burden." In contrast, she argues, using an intersectional analysis, Angela Davis (1971) and others demonstrate that the combination creates a "*different* burden" (123). The relationships among categories and oppressions are *not* merely "additive" in intersectional thinking: rather, the interrelationships posited by intersectionality change the very nature of the categories and oppressions and in consequence the experience of them.

Gender taken as a single-axis category was the impelling force for feminism; the investment in gender as a "separable" category encouraged dominant feminists to downplay or ignore relevant differences such as race, class, and sexuality. Similarly, unified struggle against racist domination often ignored or even augmented the power of Black men over Black women. Assumptions that gender and race were discrete categories, with consequent "additive" analysis of other categories, were central to both feminism and antiracism prior to intersectionality's intervention. Intersectionality intervened in these debates to insist that social categories did not operate in isolation, but relationally, co-constitutively, simultaneously. The function of shared social amnesia is to conceal the limitations of feminism's problematic conceptions of categories, while attributing those very limitations—fixity, stasis, and additivity, for example—to intersectionality. As a result, feminist critique tends to hinder rather than help intersectionality's retheorizing of entrenched social categories that ground systems of subordination.

The fourth challenge is to reconsider what might be the most productive approaches for feminists with respect to critique and to criticism of theory. Although relentless and effective criticism remains crucial to the advancement of feminist theory and practice, uninterrogated powerblind conventions of feminist argument such as those I analyze in this book can enlist feminists in the work of domination even when they imagine themselves to be engaged in the work of resistance. Transforming the terms of feminist reading and writing requires reconsideration of what feminist critiques *do* and what they are *for*. Arguing that radical criticism is vital in promoting change, Foucault cautions that a transformation that remains within "the same mode of thought" will be merely superficial. He provides a definition of critique that dramatically contrasts with the definitions that implicitly ground powerblind critiques of intersectionality. He declares:

> A critique is not a matter of saying that things are not right as they are. It is a matter of pointing out on what kinds of assumptions, what kinds of familiar, unchallenged, unconsidered modes of thought, the practices that we accept rest. . . . Criticism is a matter of flushing out that thought and trying to change it: to show that things are not as self-evident as one believed, to see that what is accepted as self-evident will no longer be accepted as such. *Practicing criticism is a matter of making facile gestures difficult.* (1988, 154–155, emphasis added)

Critiques of intersectional thinking are replete with "facile gestures," with weakly developed claims that find it self-evident that intersectionality is not right without white feminist correction. These facile gestures undermine the accuracy and rigor of feminist argumentation: they focus on the purported faulty assumptions of intersectionality without properly addressing the structures of power and conditions of subordination that intersectionality attempts to address.

Critiques often deploy powerblind strategies to judge whether intersectionality fits specific definitions of a theory, or the right kind of theory, or a theory that is "good enough" for one thing or another. Ghassan Hage (2016) suggests ways to approach discussions of theory that might help feminists to rethink how they criticize intersectionality. Hage argues that it is not helpful to hold a "fetishistic" attitude toward theory, as a product with intrinsic power, treating it as "a church you adhere to [or] a football team you support"

(222). In fact, critiques of intersectionality tend to "fetishize" the intersectional theory of women of color—treating it as something with excessive power to damage feminist thought—as a church or football team that must be destroyed or taken over by a new owner. Hage argues that overcoming the problems of fetishizing theory requires "a different mode of interaction and a different mode of experience of theory" (224), refusing to assume that a theory must be adopted or rejected as a whole. Rather, he suggests, ask: "What has this theory helped me see, understand or explain that I otherwise would not have seen?" (224). Hage maintains that a "theory is not a generalization but a generative device . . . [that] offers a tool or set of tools. . . . If a theory is a set of tools, one can pick one particular tool from the set without being committed to use the whole set, as long as one understands the ramifications of the particular tool one is using" (221–222).

Hage also argues that an ethics of respect is central to changing one's way of thinking about the theoretical encounter. He encourages people "to think in terms of a labour theory of value of the theoretical works they are reading to learn to be respectful of them as works of labour" (2016, 224). He encourages following the example of scholars whose work reflects "an ethic of critical respect, who even while critical of others respect and value the labour of others and see them as engaged with them in a common pursuit" (225). Hage notes that he finds this ethic more present among women who are feminist scholars, such as Lauren Berlant (2011), Judith Butler (1990), and Marilyn Strathern (1988). Feminist powerblind critiques of intersectionality apparently do not share these values: they seldom demonstrate either an ethic of respect toward the labor of intersectional scholars or the sense that they are engaged in critical disagreement with cognitive equals engaged in a common pursuit. Hage provides a set of practical suggestions that could be of particular benefit to feminist discourses seeking to think through intersectional theorizing with scholars of color. First, he proposes that one should think in terms of not finding a theory useful, rather than in terms of finding a theory wrong: "If you don't like a theory just ignore it. There is no need to scream 'I don't like it' from the rooftops" (222). Hage's second practical suggestion is particularly relevant to transforming powerblind discourses, so frequently built on condemning arguments that have not been well understood or represented. Hage suggests: "If you are reading a well-established thinker and you feel they need to be given a 101-type lecture in 'social causality', 'essentialism', or whatever else, you should think twice and three times before doing so, as there is a high chance you have not understood them and it might be useful to read them again" (225). The productivity of powerblind critiques would be greatly improved by following this suggestion.

The final challenge for feminist argument here requires reflecting on symptomatic moves emanating from the specific difficulties of thought and action in feminism and similar fields with goals that are political as well as conceptual. As Robyn Wiegman explains, feminism proceeds from and promotes desires to change the world (2010). It can be frustrating to hold political aspirations that have not yet been realized. Feminists reject sexist hierarchies yet endure them on a daily basis. The political desires that feminism ignites and stokes produce a necessary dissatisfaction with the status quo. That dissatisfaction, however, can easily be turned on feminism itself and its analytic tools because they have not yet successfully changed the world. What Seth Moglen calls the "torment of hope" (2007, 175 and passim) makes disappointments and defeats hard to endure, generating a *desire for distance* from prevailing paradigms, concepts, and theories that seem tainted with failure. Wiegman argues that, in effect, feminism is constituted at a nexus of desire and failure.

The desire to distance ourselves from that nexus of desire and failure interpellates us—whether we resist or not—as certain kinds of subjects, with consequences for the life we inhabit together as feminists. In search of a new and untainted feminism, Wiegman argues, feminist criticism can too quickly discard still useful concepts and categories, replacing them with "new objects and analytics in the hope of making its investments come true" (83). The powerblind strategies examined in this book use discursive devices framed by the desire to distance: they *produce* a rendition of intersectionality tainted by flaws and failures, justifying the critics' distance, their condemnation of these past analytics, and their promotion of new analytics. They frame intersectionality as the site that has already made feminists' desires not come true. In so doing, powerblind critiques adopt a model of subjectivity that enshrines a desire to distance themselves from the failures of the imperfect present in order to arrive at a more perfect feminist future. This model invites feminists to join the desire for distancing. It also distracts attention from the damage incurred when feminists remain silent or passive as such inadequate and subordinating criticism discredits the field's small supply of tools for radical critique.

PREMISES OF THIS PROJECT

The arguments in this book that feminism has failed to respond honestly and honorably to the ideas advanced by intersectional women of color theorists proceed from some clear premises that are not universally shared in feminist practice. These premises hold that (1) the systematic subordination of people on racial, gender, sexual, and other grounds constitutes an urgent social crisis; (2) analyzing the constitution and simultaneity of social categories is crucial to countering subordination; (3) the intellectual production of feminists of color provides generative ways of thinking about antisubordination; (4) the continuing difficulty of feminist scholars in coming to grips with problems of categorization reflects not the "limitations" of the thinking of feminists of color, but rather the entrenched and constantly reinscribed power of social categories; (5) white feminist scholars may be insufficiently attentive to the racial dynamics of the critiques they mount from a position of racial dominance; (6) insufficient attention to the racial dynamics of white feminist critique may lead conventional argumentative strategies to be used in "powerblind" ways that inadvertently promote racial hierarchy; (7) these powerblind strategies are not evidence of the subjectivity of individual scholars, but evidence of what discursive strategies are authorized within feminism as a discursive arena; (8) because racial hierarchy among women violates feminism's commitment to social justice, feminism needs to transform its terms of reading and writing; (9) transforming the terms of feminist reading and writing to avoid reinscribing racial hierarchy is achievable through a practical set of challenges, tasks, and habits. Provisionally adopting these premises may allow readers to follow my analysis that reveals otherwise occluded moves at the scene of argument, moves that, I argue, have consequences that are disastrous for feminism as a project of social justice.

The very strength of neoliberalism's emphasis on the individual may make readers think that I am blaming individuals or attempting to compete with them myself, that in conventional neoliberal fashion I am offering a new brand to replace their previously entrenched work. On the contrary, I am seeking to step back and see the systematic structural forces and the concrete conventions and practices that poison the well from which we all must drink. People often assume that racist practices emerge primarily from personal racial animus or aversion, that racism requires intentional actions by individuals. Indeed, this kind of racism sadly remains all too present in our society. Yet overt and intentional racism is only the tip of the iceberg, the most visible part of a larger and even more deadly danger lurking beneath the surface. In societies suffused with long histories of racial exclusion and subordination, racist premises and perceptions permeate apparently innocent practices that at first glance appear to have little to do with race. They operate invisibly and institutionally through a series of taken-for-granted procedures and commonsense positions. Inside feminist analyses and arguments, racial hierarchies are reinforced and remade every day, institutionally yet invisibly. They are nurtured and sustained by shared commonsense assumptions about which questions should be asked and answered, about how ideas and evidence are articulated and analyzed, and about how intellectual debts are acknowledged or avoided. Inside feminist arguments, racist outcomes emerge as the unintentional and unexpected by-products of uninterrogated approaches to evidence, analysis, and argument.

The dominant subject position that produces what I call powerblind white feminist critiques of intersectionality should not be thought of as an embodied identity inhabited only by white middle-class, heterosexual women, but a privileged standpoint and structural advantage, a matter of foregrounding dominant interests and deprecating the interests of antisubordination scholars and activists (see Bilge 2013; Frankenberg 1993). Hence when I talk about powerblind white critique I am not necessarily talking about white people but about a conditioned acceptance of certain ideas rather than an embodied identity grounded in color or phenotype. As Sirma Bilge argues, "one does not need to be White to 'whiten' intersectionality" (2013, 413). As a white feminist myself, I am not claiming to be racially innocent or immune to the ways in which embodied whiteness can impede knowledge about racial formation and racial projects.

Yet to work to prevent feminist discourses from wittingly or unwittingly reinscribing racial hierarchy requires white feminists to interrogate what it means to identify and inhabit whiteness as an institution, as a standpoint, and as a set of unearned privileges that must be countered and contested. This is what Moreton-Robinson describes as the "real challenge" for white feminists: "to theorize the relinquishment of power so that feminist practice can contribute to changing the racial order" (2002, 186).

Theorizing the relinquishment of white racial power is difficult in part because we must in the process reflect on what Sara Ahmed calls "how racism operates in language," reflecting on "what we are talking about when we are talking about racism" (2011, 122). For example, much of my argument about racial powerblindness rests on specific textual examples—sometimes examples of general strategies whose authors are not named, other times examples from specific texts whose authors are named. My *claim* is that feminists need to see these examples not as reflecting the subjectivities of individual authors but rather feminists' socially shared metadiscursive regime. But racism offers many ways to avoid coming to grips with the problem I am addressing. Ahmed argues that racism works particularly effectively when it reduces a case about exemplars—about broader social phenomena—to a case about an individual: an accusation of racism. "To make the case into a case *about* an individual is to lose its status as an exemplary" (124), and to shift the discursive terrain to claims about personal credentials in order to counter the purported accusation of racism that has never been made. According to Ahmed:

> These responses fail to respond to the actual critique of [racist discourses] *as they take the form of self-recognition* ("I don't recognize myself in the critique of racism"). . . . To respond to a critique requires not referring to what is said or written back to oneself (self-reference makes the object of a critique into a subject) but engaging more closely with what is being asserted. When self-reference happens too quickly (when someone responds by defending themselves against a critique by hearing it as an attack on their credentials), the opportunity for an engagement is lost. . . . [Reducing the critique to evoking] the figure of "the racist" also means that critiques of racism are heard as personal attacks on reputation. . . . It becomes an injury to whiteness. . . . The charge becomes *about their hurt*. . . . The reduction of racism to an accusation is part of the reproduction of racism. (2011, 122–123, emphasis in original)

This book is written with every faith that dominant white feminists can meet the challenge of theorizing the relinquishment of structures of power that have made invisible their reinscription of racial hierarchy at the scene of argument in critiques of intersectionality. Structures of dominance are the conditions of possibility for antisubordination arguments. Feminists cannot escape all the traps set by the racialized and gendered history of the disciplines, but we can destabilize them, explore their contradictions, and work through them to open up new possibilities. Yet *intending* our arguments to be resistant or oppositional cannot make them so. Discursive effects cannot be known in advance nor assumed to reflect the intentions of those who argue; we cannot know fully or control completely the consequences of our own roles in the circulation of discourses. Rather, as Foucault argues, "We must make allowance for the complex and unstable process whereby discourse can be both an instrument and an effect of power, but also a hindrance, a stumbling block, a point of resistance and a starting point for an opposing strategy" (1980a, 101). The specific arguments we make, their textual form and evidence, the consequences we draw from them, all can be points of resistance or stumbling blocks that trap us into deploying dominant discourses when we think we are resisting them. Yet these discourses are what we have—the sites, the circumstances, and the means—to understand ourselves and change our conditions.

Without looking through a conscious and deliberate antiracist lens, racism will persist as a default position corrupting all social analysis. In this society, racism is not a disruptive or aberrant act or idea but something absorbed from the air we breathe. It is an integral part of a perpetual motion machine that runs on its own momentum. This book does not argue that individual feminists are racists, although some may be. It does not seek to shame or blame individuals for the decisions they have made as authors, editors, readers, and reviewers. Instead it identifies and critiques the shared social languages, citational practices, truth tests, and argumentation strategies that pervade and imperil feminism in order to point the way toward more principled and more productive approaches.

PLAN OF THE BOOK

The first part of the book—Chapters 1, 2, and 3—provides a general structure explaining the premises of the book. Chapter 1 elucidates the project of intersectionality and the counterproject propelled by powerblind white critiques of intersectionality. It establishes the central problem of unexamined conventions of feminist argumentation appearing at the "scene of argument"—socially shared conventions authorized by uninterrogated metadiscursive regimes that establish what rhetorics are acceptable in feminist argumentation. It presents a series of necessary challenges facing feminist argumentation if it is to develop the precise conceptualization needed to advance its goals of social justice. It presents the premises of this project as well as this plan of the book. Chapters 2 and 3 introduce concepts of "category anxiety" and "metaphor anxiety"—misunderstandings of race and language that underpin many powerblind critiques of intersectionality. Chapter 2 explains how confusion about the construction and deployment of social categories—particularly race—leads scholars to distort core concepts of intersectional thinking. Chapter 3 identifies the consequences for critique of fundamental misunderstandings of metaphoricity in discourse. The second part of the book—Chapters 4 through 9—develops the concept of powerblindness and analyzes its specific strategies, tactics, and textual moves as revealed in various critiques of intersectionality. These chapters range widely for their objects of study, traversing a broad range of disciplines, methods, and theories that nonetheless cohere around a predictable set of discursive moves that together produce what I call in Chapter 9 an "Epistemic Machine." In Chapter 10, I identify the cumulative and continuing nature of powerblind discourses and present suggestions about concrete things feminist researchers, readers, authors, and editors can do to counter the conventions of powerblindness and promote more productive and principled engagements with intersectional thinking.

CATEGORY ANXIETY

The idea of the category seems particularly vexing for many authors who mount powerblind feminist critiques of intersectionality. These critiques sometimes appear to resent the enduring centrality of race in Black feminist thought, charging that the women of color making intersectional arguments about race fail to understand that race is a socially constructed fiction, not a biological fact. They accuse race-based work of being race bound, of treating the relative, contingent, and provisional categories of domination as if they are absolute, fixed, and final. None of these charges are true, but category anxiety makes them seem so to many feminists. This lack of clarity about the role of the category in intersectional thinking stems from inadequate sensitivity to the actual social and political processes that produce contemporary categories of gender and race. It proceeds from the false premise that claims about categorization represent endorsement of it rather than tactical engagements with classifications deployed routinely in society as technologies of power.

Scholars trained in feminist, gender, sexuality, or women's studies who become interested in intersectional analysis are often unfamiliar with the enormous existing body of scholarship on the social construction of race. They may be prone to misinterpret the arguments of intersectional scholars whose training includes expertise in race as well as gender. They may find critical arguments about race scholarship made by prominent white feminists to be plausible without realizing that such criticism often misrepresents the actual arguments of intersectional scholars because the critics are ill informed about scholarship on race. These misinterpretations are then repeated confidently across multiple texts through a specific, yet deficient, politics of citation that organizes these claims into something "generally known" about intersectional thinking, even though it is untrue.

For more than two decades, white feminist critiques of intersectionality have paid insufficient attention to the racialized power dynamics permeating their own arguments. Critics have assumed that substantial knowledge about *gender* authorizes them to criticize, co-opt, or dismiss intersectional arguments about *race*. Yet because they have not engaged deeply with the scholarship on race, and because they often demonstrate only superficial engagement with the texts they criticize, they attribute to intersectional scholars of color exactly what these scholars are challenging: dominant commonsense and neoliberal notions about race. Some feminist texts may give the impression that perspicacious white scholars know things about social categories that intersectional scholars of color do not, for example, that social categories are not empirical, but always epistemological, hermeneutic, or interpretive (see Turner 2010). The critics' assumptions have been bolstered in light of their success—the validation they receive from publication and citation within a field dominated by other white feminists whose training also focuses on gender or sexuality rather than race. Reviewers, editors, and readers in their fields of expertise tend to be equally ill informed about scholarship on race. The powerblindness that permeates feminist discussions of categories is so ubiquitous that it cannot be attributed accurately to the shortcomings of individuals but instead must be understood as a product of the entire field of feminist discourse.

Category anxiety inhabits the frequent claim by critics—against all textual evidence—that intersectional scholars of color such as Patricia Hill Collins and Kimberlé Crenshaw treat categories as "static" or "fixed." Some of these critics charge that intersectional thinking focuses on too few categories, that it directs too much attention to gender, race, and class—to categories that are too "traditional," or not to the categories of more interest to the critics. Still other critics accuse intersectionality of producing more categories than scholars can competently comprehend. One frequent but incorrect criticism holds that intersectional analysis cannot serve as a productive tool because it merely reflects dominant categories rather than enabling transcendence of them. Other critics charge that intersectionality fails because the word "intersect" assumes that social categories have been "discrete," "pure," or "pre-existing." In each of these instances, anxiety about categories and inadequate understanding of Critical Race Theory leads the critics to attribute to intersectionality the very conceptions that intersectionality has been created to challenge and contest.

Critics then propose solutions for the putative flaws of intersectional thinking that do not acknowledge but actually simply echo the very arguments that intersectional scholars of color have been raising for decades.

Claims about allegiance to static and fixed conceptions in the intersectional theorizing of scholars of color are generally advanced as simple assertions, made without textual evidence. Such claims are often supported merely by a chain of citations, implying that the claim is generally accepted and that others have properly explained the problem. Yet on examination, these chains of citation prove inaccurate and unreliable. Many of these allegedly supporting citations simply reference previous unsubstantiated dismissals of intersectionality. Other articles and books cited as evidence of fixity do not even discuss the topic at all. The relentless repetition of such poorly supported claims positions them as things that feminists simply "know" about the intersectional theorizing of women of color. White feminist critiques routinely treat as "fact" these claims about the fixed and static nature of intersectionality's categories. As a result, contemporary scholars who wish to use intersectionality often feel defensive and justify its use by asserting that their own conceptions of social categories—which they figure as fluid and flexible—should be distinguished from the putatively deficient static and fixed conceptions attributed to the originating scholars of color. The frequency (and brevity) of this rhetorical gesture reveals that critical authority has been ceded to the racialized and powerblind arguments embedded within the Epistemic Machine of white feminist critique. Scholars hoping to protect their own emerging intersectional scholarship from condemnation feel compelled to reinscribe these false claims about the deficient thinking of women of color by echoing the previous history of unfounded disavowal, dismissal, and distortion. They insist that, unlike intersectionality's originators, their own work recognizes that identities are adapted and changeable rather than set and congealed.

This entrenched pattern of critique frames the texts authored by intersectional scholars of color in peculiar ways. Collins's and Crenshaw's texts provide overwhelming evidence of specific arguments directly contradicting these claims about fixity and stasis, but these arguments are treated as if they were absent. Frequently cited but consistently misrepresented, the original texts that developed intersectionality as a heuristic and conceptual tool become treated as *palimpsests unavailable for deciphering.* The specific arguments made boldly and clearly in the original texts become systematically erased and overwritten by the misrepresentations of white feminist critiques. These arguments are rendered nearly invisible, with only traces of the original peeking through.

The charges about fixed and static categories in intersectional analysis function as freely floating commonplaces. I argue that part of their success stems from their overdetermined congruence with structures of racialized dominance. They frame themselves according to a narrative of progress: the thinking of women of color is described as attached to a primitive rigid notion of categories, and then is replaced by white women's more refined notions. This progress narrative is congruent with commonsense racial hierarchies that valorize the conceptual abilities of white women over the thinking of women of color. It protects the existing racial order by assuming that the political investments of women of color in challenging racial categories undermine rather than strengthen their thinking.

INTERSECTIONALITY AS PROVISIONAL THINKING

Category anxiety leads some critics to charge that intersectional thinking fails to "transcend" dominant racial categories. This claim evades the ways in which intersectional theorizing frames itself as a political as well as an intellectual endeavor. Crenshaw's "Race, Reform, and Retrenchment" (1988)—published a year before her introduction of the term "intersectionality" in "Demarginalizing the Intersection of Race and Sex" (1989)—provides a rationale for the politicized approach she takes in developing intersectionality. In "Race," Crenshaw asserts that U.S. racial politics make it difficult for whites to engage with Black thought. She argues:

> The most significant aspect of Black oppression seems to be what is believed *about* Black Americans, not what Black Americans believe. . . . It matters little whether the coerced group rejects the dominant ideology and can offer a competing conception of the world; if they have been labeled "other" by the dominant ideology, they are not heard. Blacks seem to carry the stigma of "otherness," which effectively precludes their potentially radicalizing influence from penetrating the dominant consciousness. . . . The challenge for Blacks may be to pursue strategies that confront the beliefs held *about* them by whites. For Blacks, such strategies may take the form of reinforcing some aspects of the dominant ideology in attempts to become participants in the dominant discourse rather than outsiders defined, objectified, and reified by that discourse. (1988, 1358–1359, emphasis in original)

The political terrain that Crenshaw maps requires political, metaphorical, and conceptual tools that engage with taken-for-granted dominant discourses in a material world that subordinates aggrieved groups through the use of social categories. Women of color do not have the luxury of acting as if dominant racial categories need not be acknowledged and confronted. To mount arguments countering dominant discourses requires engaging with them, even if only on a temporary basis (see an argument on this point in Carastathis 2016). For this reason, using the tools of subordination for antisubordination purposes always requires a calculus of risks and benefits. Crenshaw argues that unless women of color intersectional thinkers respond, *in part,* to the assumptions of those discourses, their arguments will never be heard, their tools will never be used to shift dominant discourses. She makes this point about the very use of the term "intersectionality":

> I consider intersectionality a provisional concept linking contemporary politics with postmodern theory. In mapping the intersections of race and gender, the concept does engage dominant assumptions that race and gender are essentially separate categories. By tracing the categories to their intersections, I hope to *suggest a methodology that will ultimately disrupt the tendencies to see race and gender as exclusive or separable.* (1991, 1244n9, emphasis added)

Particularly significant here is Crenshaw's point that "to *engage*" dominant assumptions does not mean "to *adopt*" them, but rather that contesting categories requires participating with or becoming involved with them, in order to hold dominant categories *in tension* with postmodern challenges to taken-for-granted categories.

Crenshaw frames intersectionality as an *argumentative* as well as a theoretical tool engaged in *real-world* acts of persuasion, created under conditions of urgency, damage, and loss. Dominant assumptions that identity categories are "exclusive or separable" are the *conditions of possibility* for mounting her counterargument. Crenshaw is *not* claiming that race and gender are discrete and mutually exclusive categories; she is, in fact, insisting they are *not,* but it may be necessary to talk of them in that way temporarily to gain traction for arguments undermining racial regimes that are, as Cedric Robinson points out, "hostile to their own exhibition" (2007, xii). Crenshaw recognizes that there are risks *both* in engaging with *and* in failing to engage with dominant discourses:

> Popular struggles are a reflection of institutionally determined logic and a challenge to that logic. People can only demand change in ways that reflect the logic of the institutions that they are challenging. Demands for change that do not reflect the institutional logic—that is, demands that do not engage and subsequently reinforce the dominant ideology—will probably be ineffective. (1988, 1367)

Intersectional theorizing challenges general public discourses as well as institutions—the law, the government, the academy—deploying dominant assumptions that race and gender are essentially separate categories, often framed in terms of biology and nearly always in terms of hierarchy. Crenshaw argues that for intersectionality to succeed in its challenge it will necessarily require engagement with those assumptions in ways that oppose them but also inescapably reinforce them to some degree. Citing Frances Fox Piven and Richard Cloward (1977), she argues that "reforms necessarily come from an existing repertoire of options" (1988, 1367n139).

THE EXIGENCIES OF THE POLITICS OF CHANGE

Some manifestations of category anxiety seem to assume that political and social change occurs only through positing theories that "transcend" dominant categories. Yet feminist and poststructuralist critiques often revolve around immanent critiques of social contradictions rather than transcendent critiques of entire regimes of knowledge and power. The search for transcendence seems to assume that people can idealistically proclaim the nature of the world they wish to live in by imagining living outside dominant categories and so transform them. In responding to this approach I want to revisit the argument in Chapter 1 about the role of intersectionality as a form of "mid-level" theorizing suitable for what Antonio Gramsci describes as the "war of position" (Gramsci 1971; for further discussion of mid-level theorizing, see Tomlinson and Lipsitz 2013b).

The Gramscian view is that, at all moments, the "common sense" of society is created within a historical bloc, a floating equilibrium or coalition made up of many groups and conversations (1971). The nature of hegemony can make us unwittingly complicit in our own domination. We believe things that are not good for us—*even if we imagine ourselves as oppositional.* Because hegemony has made us what we are, we are not yet the people we would need to be to imagine a new society with different values. This is part of the point Karl Marx is making in *The German Ideology* when he argues that in the act of revolutionary struggle the oppositional class is "ridding itself of all the muck of the ages" in order to "become fitted to found society anew" (1973, 95).

Gramsci contrasts the war of maneuver with the war of position. The war of maneuver replaces one ruling group with another but can keep in place the same common sense. In contrast, the war of position tries to establish new historical blocs to struggle for a new hegemony and a new common sense. The war of position, then, involves *persuasion,* working inside the contradictions of what exists now in the hope of producing something new. In the war of position the persuasive struggle itself is valuable, even within bourgeois institutions. It questions the naturalness of the assumptions of those institutions. It engages people in a process where they learn to see things differently. It throws forth new imaginaries of how things should be. To accomplish that, it needs to contest the diffuse sites where power is learned and legitimated. Governments, academies, and other sites are institutions that have legitimacy for people and that make meaning for them. Oppositional groups have to win over some parts of these institutions and discredit some parts of them, transform other parts, and work on supplanting the existing historical bloc by creating what is likely to be a coalition of opposites (Gramsci 1971). So the revolution itself is a *process* of a war of position to constantly try to shake things up so that new things are possible, without assuming that there is a fixed solution, a once-and-for-all fix for social problems (Hall 1986).

As I indicate in Chapter 1, "mid-level theorizing" attends to concrete struggles over what structures of power and identities are *now* and what they are *capable of becoming,* rather than focusing solely on ideal and abstract schematic formulations about what structures of power and identities should be. Mid-level theorizing can address heterogeneous objects of study across many different sites and temporalities. Racial, sexual, and gender projects are both local and global; different social arenas require different arguments and different forms of theorizing. Mid-level theorizing is rhizomatic—emerging and flourishing in diverse places through different forms that are nonetheless connected organically.

The advantage of the war of position is that it does not presume that we already know now how power works. It is oriented around process, not a product. It positions itself as an immanent critique, rather than posing as a transcendent one. It emanates from convergence and contestation in a promiscuous scene of argument, rather than presenting itself as a declaration of pure radicalism, as some feminist critics of intersectionality seem to desire.

AVOIDING BINARY THINKING

The framing of intersectionality as a force for social change motivates the arguments of intersectional scholars about social construction, fluidity, flexibility, and *both/and* categorization. These conceptions address social relations in an empirical world, countering entrenched relations of gender and racial subordination. Despite feminism's history of commitment to theorizing and enacting social change, white feminist critiques frequently deploy propositions of logic in attempts to undercut what are primarily issues of politics. These critiques challenge conceptions authored by women of color that are grounded in the empirical breadth and variation of race, gender, and other categories. The white feminist critiques often insist that such arguments are not successful unless they adhere to the strictures of logical dichotomies.[1]

Yet grounding political arguments in the structure set by logical dichotomies has already been challenged repeatedly and successfully within feminist thought. In "Gender and Dichotomy" Nancy Jay describes the basic rules of logic by which dichotomies are constructed as principles of order, *not* features of the empirical world (1981, 42). According to Jay:

> The most basic of these [Aristotelian] logical rules are three. They are the Principle of Identity (if anything is A, it is A); the Principle of Contradiction (nothing can be both A and Not A); and the Principle of the Excluded Middle (anything, and everything, must be *either* A or Not A). (42)

Feminist scholars have long been aware of this problematic logic with regard to gender: if anything is male, it is male; nothing can be both male and not male; anything, and everything, must be *either* male or not male. Historically, the U.S. racial order has been constructed by the same dichotomous logic: if anything is white, it is white; nothing can be both white and not white; anything, and everything, must be *either* white or not white. Jay points out that A/Not A dichotomies are social creations not supported by any natural order, so in the empirical world to create and maintain A/Not A dichotomies requires an "enormous amount of social effort . . . sustained, cooperative work . . . and . . . oppression and violence" (49). While feminist scholars have analyzed the efforts and violence underlying the social construction of gender dichotomies, they may be unfamiliar with the extensive scholarship delineating the social efforts and violence required to establish and maintain the dichotomy white/not white as a structure of dominant racial thinking.

At the core of category anxiety in feminist critiques of intersectionality lies a failure to come to grips with intersectional thinking's flexible use of framing of categories, especially the concept of *both/and,* which explicitly rejects the deep-seated binary thinking that is central to both Western thought and white feminism's unease about categories. Binary thinking sets traps because each term conflates differences to create the notion of a contrast between two single unified wholes. The result is to make differences *within* each term invisible. Jacques Derrida (1978) maintains that the relationship of binary categories is *constitutive:* the first privileged term of a binary cannot be defined, exist, or function *without* the secondary, unprivileged term; the second term is indispensable in defining the privileged term.[2] Feminists have much knowledge about the problems of binary thinking but may still draw on binary arguments in their discursive practices. I argue that many white critics of intersectionality attribute binary thinking to intersectional scholars of color, while remaining unaware that the underlying assumptions of their *own critiques* replicate such categorical, binary, *either/or* thinking (see, for example, Chapters 3, 5, 8, and 9).

Attributing simplistic binary thinking to intersectional scholars of color evades the evidence clearly presented by their arguments. Crenshaw, for example, demonstrates how constructions of racial binaries characterize the U.S. racial order. She argues that racist ideology establishes a hierarchical pattern of opposing categories: "Historically, whites represented the dominant antinomy while Blacks came to be seen as separate and subordinate" (1988, 1373). Crenshaw notes that establishing racial binaries can serve as a powerful hegemonic tool: for example, dominant interests benefit from "the creation of a clearly visible 'other,' whose interests are seen as being opposed in every way to the interests of those who identify—by virtue of color and culture—with the dominant class" (1988, 1360). It is not just that the position of the racialized other is disfavored, according to Crenshaw; this framing of the position of the racialized "other" also serves to reinforce *"an illusion of a white community* that cuts across ethnic, gender, and class lines" (1371, emphasis added). *Contra* the critics, Crenshaw is discussing the construction of racial categories that have no possibility of being "discrete" or "pure." The illusory white community is not "discrete" or "pure," but an amalgam of different ethnic, gender, and class groups—as is the disfavored group. The groups—both the illusory white community and the contrasting conspicuous disfavored group—are relational or *co-constitutive*. These categories are not "pre-existing," but constantly reproduced relationally. Applying Derrida's analysis to Crenshaw's argument, whiteness cannot be defined, exist, or function without the disfavored group; the disfavored group is indispensable in defining whiteness. Crenshaw's Derridean analysis (1988) demonstrates this to be her position. When category anxiety manifests itself, scholars miss the subtlety of arguments such as Crenshaw's.

This chapter illustrates and challenges the ways of thinking that legitimate acceptance of powerblind critiques saturated with category anxiety. I first ground contemporary racial categorization and its influence on powerblind critiques of intersectionality through the history of coloniality and its enduring influence in the "colonial matrix of knowledge." I then clarify the grounds for intersectionality's treatment of race by providing an overview of theoretical and empirical approaches to race that intersectionality draws on and blends together. I examine the political and legal history of racial categorization in the United States as a way of resituating intersectionality as strategic political thought with concrete political origins, implications, causes, and consequences. This trajectory emphasizes intersectional thinking's relationship to the politics of social change and its constitutive challenge to binary thinking about categories.

THE COLONIAL MATRIX AS AN INFLUENCE ON CONTEMPORARY RACIAL CATEGORIES

Category anxiety depends in part on inherited and deeply sedimented contemporary structures of knowledge and power that Walter D. Mignolo (2011) calls the "colonial matrix." Understanding the influence of the colonial matrix on contemporary structures of knowledge is important here because intersectional thinking is a decolonial project, attempting to "de-link" from the long colonial history of categorical subordination that works to reproduce the false notion that social hierarchy by category is inevitable and appropriate (see related arguments in Carastathis 2016; Lugones 2007, 2010; also Alcoff 2007b).

The tendency to see intersectional thinking as primitive, underdeveloped, and in need of refinement by white outsiders that characterizes many powerblind feminist critiques of intersectionality reflects foundational practices and principles of European modernity. Mignolo argues that Western knowledge is necessarily and constitutively part of a colonial matrix of power and knowledge that imposes its particular temporality of development on the whole world. The social categories central to modern thought are technologies of management that structure subordination and privilege. Mignolo contends that concepts of linear chronological progress have been central to the rhetorics and logics used for classifying and devaluing non-European peoples. In the sixteenth century, Christian concepts of time were imposed on non-European peoples, with time framed as a linear narrative from Creation to Final Judgment (Mignolo 2011, 162). In the eighteenth century, sacred history was replaced by secular history; concepts of time were key elements in the creation of modernity (163). In the late eighteenth and nineteen centuries, temporal concepts of "progress" and then "development" served to support notions of colonial difference. All these rhetorics rely on conceptions of time as linear, aimed at a "point of arrival" (164).

According to Mignolo, concepts of time were pivotal to the development and modification of colonial practices of hierarchical classification. Coloniality frames time as a category of reckoning that belongs to *culture,* not a category of experiencing that belongs to *nature.* Linear notions of time, progress, and evolution also underpin a crucial distinction between *modernity* and *tradition*—a distinction used to license colonial categorization. Mignolo argues that modernity established its own (European) tradition as part of its self-invention, treating itself as, in essence, the "point of arrival"—the "zero point" of observation. Inventing the traditions of other cultures, modernity then classified the differences imputed to other cultures according to the cultures' temporal proximity to the "point of arrival." The dominant particulars of Europe were proclaimed as universals. Just as Greenwich Mean Time started the nautical and business day in England, European history traced the history of civilization from Greece and Rome to Paris and London. Europe and its colonized others lived in the exact same historical moment, but temporally inflected categories posited Europe as the baseline norm, as fully modern (and fully human), while Asia, Africa, the Caribbean, and Latin America were seen as not yet fully developed. Thus conceptions of time and progress were naturalized as universal criteria for celebrating modernity as the benchmark of human history, and for identifying the timescale of "primitives" according to their proximity to or distance from modernity. Culture and modernity were constructed as dynamic and progressive; nature and tradition—relegated to colonial difference—were constructed as inert and fixed (Mignolo 2011, 173).

The elevation of *either/or* over *both/and* in powerblind feminist critiques of intersectionality also bears traces of the epistemology of modernity. The era of the Enlightenment was also the era of conquest and colonialism, of indigenous dispossession and Afrodiasporic slavery. Dichotomous thinking emerged as a central tool for classification. In Mignolo's argument, those considered human—*humanitas*—manage knowledge production and categories of thought through a process of categorizing cultural difference in order to disqualify those classified as deficient—*anthropos*. He argues that historically

> rational classification meant racial classification. And rational classifications do not derive from "natural reason," but from "human concepts" of natural reason. Who establishes criteria of classification and who classifies? Those who inhabited the epistemic zero point (*humanitas*) and were the architects of global linear thinking. And who are classified without participating in the classification? People who inhabit the *exteriority* (the outside invented in the process of defining the inside) created from the perspective of the zero point of observation (*anthropos*). To manage, and to be in a position to do so, means to be in control of knowledge—to be in the zero point. (Mignolo 2011, 83, emphasis in original)

But positioning as anthropos can be a result of other structural conditions and classifications, not just the racial. Mignolo maintains:

Anthropos doesn't refer literally to the native barbarians . . . but to every instance in which people, institutions, and disciplines where knowledge is managed and controlled, defines humanitas and uses the definition to describe the place they inhabit. Since humanitas is defined through the epistemic privilege of hegemonic knowledge, anthropos was stated as the difference—more specifically, the epistemic colonial difference. In other words, the idea was that humans and humanity were all "human beings" minus the anthropos. (2011, 85)

Mignolo argues that humanitas arrogated the right to classify racial and geographical others, particularly anthropos, who did not have the privilege of self-classifying but were required to live with the consequences. While the methods of classifying and specific classifications change over time, the hierarchical nature of social classification continues to the present. Thus, an unacknowledged investment in Europe's partial perspectives elevated to the status of universals, as well as the overdetermined sedimented history of the relentless hierarchical categorizing of anthropos by humanitas, frame the terms of contemporary thought and debate, and infuse powerblind feminist critiques of intersectionality. Mignolo notes, however, that these harsh realities do not close down our options, our ability to de-link from the colonial matrix, to engage in localized and alternative ways of thinking that go beyond merely accepting or rejecting the terms of the colonial matrix. Intersectional thinking is precisely that kind of option.

Thinking intersectionally serves as one way of "de-linking," in Mignolo's term, from the continuing legacy of this temporal process of colonial categorization. Intersectional thinking challenges the baseline norms of dominant social categorization by drawing on the experiential and epistemological resources of those who *have been defined* to expose the machinations and mendacity of those *who have defined*. In powerblind critiques of intersectionality, category anxiety can encourage attempts to re-impose the management of humanitas over the intellectual constructions of anthropos, insisting that intersectionality adhere to the hierarchical terms of thinking established by the colonial matrix.

THEORETICAL AND EMPIRICAL ANALYSIS OF RACIAL CATEGORIES

Contemporary iterations of feminist intersectionality emerged in tandem with the political and intellectual ferment associated with Critical Race Theory (CRT). As John O. Calmore explains, "Critical Race Theory begins with a recognition that 'race' is not a fixed term. [I]nstead, it is a fluctuating, decentered complex of social meanings that are formed and transformed under the constant pressures of political struggle" (1995, 318). In key articles, Crenshaw emphasizes this decidedly dynamic and fully fluid understanding of social identities. She argues that those "whose agendas include challenging hierarchy and legitimation must not overlook the importance of revealing *the contingency of race*" (1988, 1385, emphasis added). Racial categories that are contingent, that change over time, that are constructed in part by political power and legal decision-making, are not "discrete," "pure," "pre-existing," "static," or "fixed," although a great deal of social effort may go into establishing the impression that they are.

Scholarship on the social and political construction of race in the United States has long framed racial hierarchies—like hierarchies based on gender, class, or sexuality—as ever-adjusting achievements. Robinson (2007) argues that regimes of dominance and subordination propose race as justification for the relations of power. According to Robinson, their stratagem is to frame such distinctions as inherent, natural, and self-evident, rather than grounded, as they are, in specific interests, histories, and mechanisms. Apologists for structures of social relations justify them through claims of naturalism and inevitability. They resist revealing their mechanisms of fabricating distinctions steeped in hierarchy, control, and inequality. Yet these claims to be natural are always coming undone and need to be constantly revised, reaffirmed, and renewed. Thus formations of dominance and subordination coalesce around rhetorical moves, episodes, and patterns of events and arguments that are unstable, unpredictable, precarious, and contingent. As a result, Robinson argues,

> racial regimes are . . . unstable truth systems. . . . [T]hey may "collapse" under the weight of their own artifices, practices, and apparatuses; they may fragment, desiccated by new realities, which discard some fragments wholly while appropriating others into newer regimes. . . . [T]he production of race is chaotic. It is an alchemy of the intentional and the unintended, of known and unimagined fractures of cultural forms, of relations of power and the power of social and cultural relations. (2007, xii)

According to this line of argument, racial regimes are always in a process of modification, amendment, emendation, revision, and reorganization. They have been formed by and steeped in hierarchy and subordination but are presented *as if* they are inherent, natural, and self-evident. Intersectional thinking sees racial and other social categories including gender in ways similar to those delineated by Robinson: not as "static" and "fixed," as those immersed in category anxiety would have it, but as socially and politically constructed and contingent.

Analysis of contemporary notions of race by intersectional scholars emphasizes the dynamism of variation in contemporary discourses about race. They show that categorization is not a simple process. The categories that critical race theorists engage with are rarely their own inventions but rather creations of the relentless streams of negative ascription attached to aggrieved racialized peoples. Ann Morning helpfully argues that in the contemporary United States various discourses about race characterize different groups in disparate ways, with strong distinctions both within and between groups (2011). She indicates that discrete sites (such as the law, the census, and medicine) instantiate and take for granted different notions of race within as well as across sites, often in contradictory ways. I focus here on Morning's discussions of the concepts of race as found through her interviews with college undergraduates and faculty members to demonstrate why intersectional scholars can neither fully evade nor fully embrace existing categories of social identity.

When interviewing college undergraduates, Morning found that students' reasoning about race varies according to whether they are considering race in the abstract (defining race, for example) or whether they are accounting for racial disparities. Students ground their concepts of different races according to the fixed characteristics they attribute to whites; they represent other races with characteristics that are *the opposite* of those attributed to whites. As Morning puts it: "Ideas about race are always ideas about whiteness" (2011, 171). Racial discrimination generally does not enter the picture for students when accounting for racial disparities, for instance, in patterns of low birth weight or success in professional sports. One exception is the 20 percent of students who mentioned the possibility that apparent Black superiority in some sports might be related to recruiters engaging in "reverse discrimination." Thus the only time discrimination is considered relevant to race is when it can be construed as "reverse discrimination" against whites. Significantly, students did not treat differences in the same ways *across* racial groups. Rather, students assumed that

> deep-rooted biological difference separates blacks from all other races, who in turn are distinguished from each other by cultural differences in practices and norms. In short, these students' racial conceptualization is heavily colored by what might be called "black biological exceptionalism." (2011, 144)

For these students, culture assumes different meanings according to whether Black or non-Black groups are under consideration: for non-Black groups, culture is framed as habitual practice or tradition, while for Blacks it is framed in ways similar to biological accounts, as, in effect, "hard-wired." According to Morning, "When it comes to blacks in the United States[,] culture functions like biology" (2011, 170, citing Balibar 1991).

Morning's findings about undergraduates' conceptions of race have considerable relevance for thinking about the politics of feminist intersectionality. Anti-Black categorization will not disappear by pretending it does not exist. All identity categories are constructed, but their effects are not interchangeable. Debates about intersectionality have included both overt and covert arguments proposing that feminist studies or specific disciplines would benefit if intersectional thinking could only be freed from its originating ties to Black women in order to replace Black particularity and parochialism with "general" theories of identity and power. These proposals flow from problematic positions: that feminist studies and other disciplines should feel free to appropriate and manage the intellectual legacy of women of color for the benefit of dominant white scholarship, that the partial views of Black women are somehow *more limited* than the partial views of white women, or that intersectionality's originating focus on Black women is no longer urgent. Morning's findings indicate that none of these is the case. Her work reveals the dubious evasions of politics and power that underlie such arguments. Leaving Black women behind by assuming that because their thinking is race based it must be race bound constitutes a form of collaboration with dominance masquerading as critique.

Moreover, social construction is still a contested claim, even in academic circles. Interviewing faculty members, Morning found that professors in biology, physical anthropology, and cultural anthropology differ in their definitions of racial categories both within and across these disciplines. Their responses tend to fall into one of three categories: essentialist (defining racial difference as a biological phenomenon, though perhaps with imprecise boundaries), antiessentialist (holding that defining race as a biological phenomenon is factually incorrect), and constructivist (defining race as a socially produced phenomenon). Morning notes that antiessentialism and constructivism have some points in common, but their advocates tend to use different rhetorics and assumptions. Of these academic scientists taken together, 39 percent saw race as biological, 27 percent saw it as not biological, 12 percent as "social and not biological," and 22 percent as social (2011, 111). Thus the largest proportion of academic scientists see race as biological, a lesser portion see it as social or "social not biological," while a slightly smaller portion see it as not biological, but without mounting arguments that would situate it as a social construction.

Morning's study suggests that dominant notions of race in the academy are quite varied. She emphasizes that her evidence "soundly refutes the claim that constructivism is the consensus position at which all academics have arrived" (2011, 104). However, not all scholars recognize this to be the case: few biologists and no physical anthropologists predicted that their own various notions would be shared by their colleagues, while scholars who tended to support social constructionist notions of race overwhelmingly (and wrongly) predicted that their perspective was shared by others in academic science. If this kind of overestimation is shared by feminist scholars, it may account for some critics' complaints that the social constructionist view of social categories posited by intersectional scholars merely reflects conventionally dominant notions of racial categories, when in fact it is still a minority and an oppositional stance.

Both Morning and intersectional scholar Dorothy Roberts (1998, 2011, 2012) maintain that biologically essentialist notions of race have not only been revived but also *redeemed* in recent years. Roberts mounts detailed criticism of the burgeoning "reinvention" of race as a biological and genomic category used to authorize research and pharmaceutical and other scientific entrepreneurial ventures (2011). She argues that developments in contemporary genomic science and biotechnology serve to perpetuate notions of race as a "biological reality" rather than a social construction. Scientists search for racial markers transmitted genetically for genetic research and forensic examination. Pharmaceutical companies produce and market drugs said to address racially specific genetic diseases. Because the "color-blind" discourses in law and scholarship that intersectional thinkers seek to engage and transform avoid mention of the political and economic causes of racial stratification, scientifically untenable but socially appealing genetic claims become the default explanations and justifications for race-bound inequalities.

Roberts counters these popular dominant discourses about race. She notes that in recent years the Human Genome Project has demonstrated that race is neither genetic nor scientifically verifiable: 99.9 percent of human genes are identical to the genes of other humans, 98.7 percent are identical to those of chimpanzees, and 90 percent are identical to those of mice. Roberts argues that the 0.1 percent difference in humans is undoubtedly significant, but not in ways that align with popular conceptions of racial difference. Popular conceptions define race according to a few phenotypic features—such as skin color—that are visually salient but relatively insignificant genetically. These features neither map onto the categories of race nor represent the full view of genetic variation among groups. According to Roberts, commonly used racial categories do not correspond to the genetic issues important for pharmacogenomics. She notes that a gene variant that affects the body's ability to metabolize some drugs is not a general feature of "Africans": it is found in 9 percent of Ethiopians, 17 percent of Tanzanians, and 34 percent of Zimbabweans. Similarly, an allele predicting severe reactions to an HIV drug is found in 13.6 percent of the Masai in Kenya, 3.3 percent of the Luhya in Kenya, and 0 percent of the Yoruba in Nigeria (2011, 160). In fact, Roberts argues, people from various parts of Africa differ more from one another genetically than they differ from a person from France.

Roberts maintains that race is politically grounded in conquest, colonialism, and exploitation; its function shifts over time and space to meet sociopolitical imperatives. What bonds American Blacks, she argues, is not their biology but their "distinctive collective experience of creatively resisting racial oppression" (2011, 254), their struggle to improve their "linked fate" (see Dawson 2003). Roberts emphasizes, "Race is not a biological category that is politically charged. It is a political category that has been disguised as a biological one" (2011, 4).

Agreeing with Roberts that biological racial essentialism has been redeemed by its framing within modern medicine and genetic research, Morning argues that biological essentialism is also redeemed politically because doing so exonerates the nation from its responsibility for the continuing existence of racial inequality. Because intersectional arguments seek to deconstruct biological essentialism and hold the nation accountable for continuing racial inequality, they cannot be judged to be mere reflections of dominant social categories. Nor can they be deemed static and fixed. On the contrary, they seek to interrogate and overturn the constant efforts to fix race. They do so within academic, legal, and social contexts that have been structured for centuries by practices of relentless racial classification.

THE LEGAL CONSTRUCTION OF WHITENESS

Intersectionality frames racial categories as sites of social contestation, activated by a series of concrete practices and processes that cannot be evaded or wished away. To engage with racial categorization, then, is not to overemphasize race or to evoke essentialist notions of race, but to confront the causes and consequences of the history of racial categorization entrenched in structures, systems, and discourses. Particularly relevant in understanding this history are analyses of the legal construction of whiteness.

Critical race theorists as well as feminist historians and political scientists have demonstrated that white supremacy in the United States was grounded on the legal reproduction of a dominant white/not white dichotomy, implemented through legislation (laws), litigation (court interpretation of laws), and administration (the actions of officials and bureaucrats). These formal social efforts were furthered by discretionary decisions available to only those deemed racially white. To illustrate the extent of these efforts, I draw on arguments demonstrating how immigration laws regulating who was eligible to become a naturalized citizen (Carbado 2009; Haney López 2006; Lyman 1991) and marriage laws regulating miscegenation (Brattain 2005; Novkov 2002; Pascoe 1991, 1996, 2010) defined and produced the significance of racial categories in the United States, reinscribing white supremacy and racial hierarchy well beyond the mid-twentieth century.

Naturalization Law

Naturalization law is a window into the construction of racial categories in the United States. It illuminates both why intersectional scholars need to use categories structured in dominance, but also why they cannot leave those categories uninterrogated and unchallenged. Feminist scholars from disciplines other than law may think that categories can be overturned or disposed of more easily than can be done in legal analysis and argument. Law sets the rules by which society is organized. For example, critical legal theorist Ian Haney López (2006) demonstrates the enduring salience of past racial categories, even those that have been discredited by scholars and in the law itself. His research also reveals how the contingency of the legal construction of race precludes thinking of race as either static or separable from social action.

Haney López delineates the powerful influence of naturalization law in establishing racial boundaries and, in consequence, racialized material advantage, contributing to nearly two centuries of white supremacy in the United States (see also Carbado 2009; Lyman 1991; Molina 2010). From 1790 to 1952 the U.S. Congress restricted naturalized citizenship to "free white persons."[3] Haney López focuses on a group of cases from 1878 to 1944 in which courts ruled on *whether* and *why* male immigrants who sought naturalization met the requirement of being "white persons"; these fifty-two cases are now known as the "racial prerequisite" cases. According to Haney López, court transcripts revealed confusing and shifting reasons for deciding whether or not a person requesting naturalization should be considered a "white person," among them ancestry, appearance, personal history, perceived character, and imputed "natural" inclination toward Western political principles. Starting from racial physicality, the courts imposed normative meanings for racial categories; they created categories of physical difference at the same time that they created the social significance to be assigned to those categories. As the courts gradually constructed a white race through exclusion of those whose physical features, intellect, and/or appearance were explicitly framed as inferior, previously naturalized citizens could be stripped of their citizenship by subsequent court decisions.

The "racial prerequisite" court cases engaged in a project of racial categorization with both epistemological and normative dimensions. As Devon Carbado argues, the "problem of racial classification is essentially epistemological: how do we come to know what is white and what is yellow, for example, and who gets to define what these words mean?" (2009, 687). Both anthropological definitions of race and "common knowledge" definitions—what the courts called "popular understanding of the term 'white person'" (Haney López 2006, 4)—served to ground decisions in the prerequisite cases. However, Carbado maintains, the distinction between the two types of knowledge should not be overdrawn: seeing the two as dichotomous obscures their interdependence in justifying racial classification (2009). Both science and common knowledge reflect broader social processes: common knowledge helps determine what counts as science, scientific knowledge is socially situated and constructed, common knowledge may be grounded in scientific knowledge. Carbado argues that the legal epistemology of race emerges from the two types of knowledge working together.

Carbado examines the negotiation of scientific and common knowledge in the rhetoric of two prerequisite cases: *Ozawa v. United States* (260 U.S. 178 [1922]) and *United States v. Thind* (261 U.S. 204 [1923]). Both cases reflect a complex negotiation of the two types of knowledge: "*Thind* relies on science even as it purports to repudiate it, and *Ozawa* relies on common knowledge even as it purports to privilege science" (2009, 638). The *Ozawa* court determined that Takao Ozawa—a long-term resident of the United States born in Japan—was not white because he did not meet scientific definitions of whiteness; he could not be classified as Caucasian. The *Thind* court determined that Bhagat Singh Thind—a long-term resident of the United States born in India—could indeed be classified as Caucasian, meeting the scientific definition of whiteness, but could not meet its "popular" or "common knowledge" definition. *Thind* establishes being classifiable as Caucasian as "necessary but not sufficient" for being deemed white (2009, 638).

In an astute and perceptive analysis, Carbado explains how the law helped create the racial categories it purported to find. In the *Thind* and *Ozawa* cases, Carbado explains, the Supreme Court instantiated whiteness as a racial boundary and articulated a set of rules—about phenotypes, science, and common knowledge—that was to govern the policing of this border. "These rules were not in the 'nature' of things. They were socially contingent and, more particularly, the product of judicial agency" (2009, 691). In these cases the court was not engaging in armchair theorizing: it rendered decisions with epistemological, material, and ontological consequences—racial categorizations that produced racialized experiences (2009, 691).

There were immediate material advantages to being categorized as white and therefore eligible for naturalization. Haney López contrasts the treatment of Armenian and Japanese immigrants. Initially the racial classification of both groups was uncertain. Armenians were originally classified as "Asiatics" and therefore ineligible for naturalization; some Japanese had been naturalized as white persons, while others were denied citizenship as nonwhite. In 1909 the court ruled that Armenians were racially white, while Japanese were soon ruled to be nonwhite. State laws also entered the picture in establishing material consequences of racial classification. In California those not eligible for citizenship were also not eligible to purchase agricultural property: having been ruled white and eligible for citizenship, many Armenians purchased agricultural land and became wealthy farmers in Fresno County, a material advantage denied to Japanese immigrants (2006, 91–92; see also Takaki 1989).[4] The differences in wealth that resulted from the racially based legal restrictions could then be used to support claims about the "natural" abilities of whites compared to nonwhites.

One of the most significant consequences of the many legal decisions regarding race and immigration as well as related laws has been to create first, a "physical reality evident in the features of the U.S. citizenry [that] supports the ideological supposition that Whites exist as a race" (Haney López 2006, 13), and, second, the assumption that the United States should be considered a "white" or "European" country. In fact, Haney López argues, the "complexion" of the United States is a legal production based on the tenets of white supremacy. Immigration laws favoring whiteness directly influenced reproductive choices in two ways: controlling who entered the country and regulating marriages between those deemed white and those deemed nonwhite. While changes occurred at various historical moments, immigration quotas generally differed according to racial categories, particularly whether one belonged to a racial category eligible for citizenship (i.e., deemed white). From 1924 to 1952 people who were not eligible for citizenship (i.e., not deemed white) were routinely denied entry to the United States. Legal strictures regarding racialized immigration also worked to shape women's reproductive choices: until 1931 a woman eligible for naturalization could not be naturalized if her husband was not eligible; women could lose their citizenship by marrying men not eligible for citizenship (Haney López 2006, 11). The legal production of the "complexion" of the United States according to the tenets of white supremacy also influenced women's reproductive choices through the promulgation and enforcement of anti-miscegenation law.

Anti-miscegenation Law

Anti-miscegenation laws—laws forbidding marriage and sexual relations across what states established as different "racial" groups—offer another window into the construction of racial categories in the United States. Anxieties about maintaining the social and material advantages of white supremacy fueled the creation and enforcement of anti-miscegenation laws. According to Julie Novkov, "The struggle against miscegenation was at bottom a struggle to establish and maintain whiteness as a separate and impermeable racial category that all observers could easily identify" (2002, 226). In the United States, whiteness was defined in terms of exclusion (Brattain 2005, 643). Defining in terms of exclusion meant that whiteness was defined according to the logical dichotomy of A/Not A: if anything is white, it is white; nothing can be both white and not white; anything, and everything, must be *either* white or not white. Marvin Harris explains the consequences of the white/not white dichotomy:

> In the United States, the mechanism [of racial categorization] employed is the rule of hypo-descent. This descent rule requires Americans to believe that anyone who is known to have had a Negro ancestor is a Negro. We admit nothing in between. . . . "Hypo-descent" means affiliation with the subordinate rather than the superordinate group in order to avoid the ambiguity of intermediate identity. . . . That a half-white should be a Negro rather than a white cannot be explained by rational argument. . . . The rule of hypo-descent is, therefore, an invention which we in the United States have made in order to keep biological facts from intruding on our collective racial fantasies. (M. Harris 1964, 56, quoted in Almaguer and Jung 1998, 5n5)

Attempting to impose the principles of order of the logical dichotomy white/not white on the empirical world required elaborate adjustments about partial ancestry that varied from state to state (in some states as little as one-sixteenth Negro ancestry made one "nonwhite," while other states imposed the infamous "one-drop rule," where one was "nonwhite" if any ancestor might have had Negro "blood") (Brattain 2005; Novkov 2002; Pascoe 2010).

Anti-miscegenation laws were initiated first and abandoned last in the South but were most elaborate in the West; many remained in place through the twentieth century until declared unconstitutional in 1967 (Pascoe 1991). As with the racial prerequisite cases, court records for miscegenation cases demonstrate the difficulty of establishing definitive racial classification out of the ambiguity of complex contingencies of ancestry, appearance, personal history, and imputed character. The racial disposition of property tended to be central to most of the miscegenation cases brought to court before the mid-twentieth century (Pascoe 1991). For example, the state or white relatives made ex post facto attempts to invalidate longstanding marriages after the death of the white husband; they were frequently successful in taking inheritance and property away from the surviving spouse, usually a woman of color (Pascoe 1991). In other cases, white men sought annulments after years of marriage on the grounds that the marriage had been illegal because the woman was not white; an annulment would release the man from the economic obligations that would have accompanied a divorce (Pascoe 1996).

Administration—the actions of officials and bureaucrats—had a significant role in creating the United States as a country with a "naturally white" complexion, as officials responsible for issuing marriage licenses screened candidates for marriage according to imputed racial categories. In some states officials responsible for maintaining vital statistics undertook more thorough investigations of citizens' racial backgrounds to ensure the correct racial background for those the state deemed white (see Brattain 2005 and Pascoe 2010 for the role of officials in establishing racial categories in twentieth-century California, Louisiana, and Virginia).

Legal Reification of Whiteness

The result of the various legal, political, and social mechanisms that these scholars describe is never a "coherent" or "unified" racial group, but something quite otherwise. All racial groups are heterogeneous and unstable. Haney López makes this argument with regard to whiteness:

> Whether one is White . . . depends in part on other elements of identity . . . just as these aspects of identity are given shape and significance by whether or not one is White. . . . Moreover, like . . . other social categories, race is highly contingent, specific to times, places, and situations. . . . Being White is not a monolithic or homogeneous experience, either in terms of race, other social identities, space, or time. Instead, Whiteness is contingent, changeable, partial, inconstant, and ultimately social. . . . Whiteness [is] a complex, falsely homogenizing term. . . . [It is a social] group recognized to possess fluid borders and heterogeneous members . . . [not] a rigidly defined, cogeneric grouping of indistinguishable individuals. It refers to an unstable category which gains its meaning only through social relations and that encompasses a profoundly diverse set of persons. (Haney López 2006, xxi–xxii)

White exceptionalism has created whiteness. But the formulation of whiteness as a racial category—its contingency, variability, mutability, fragmentation, and co-constitutive relation with other social categories—is not exceptional. It is the nature of all racial categories, shaped and reshaped in ways that provide an illusion of stability and homogeneity in the face of an actuality of instability and heterogeneity.[5]

The long history of legal and legal-administrative decisions described by Haney López and other scholars demonstrates the creation of explicitly hierarchical racial categories structured according to the dichotomy of white/ not white. The disfavored side of the dichotomy (not white) could be separated into various other racial categories (also ranked hierarchically), but such differentiation could not challenge the supremacy of whiteness, which was maintained through the reification of whiteness. According to Haney López, the law has served as a powerful force to reify whiteness. He argues:

> Law constructs races through a process of reification. Reification here means more than simply the act of categorization, which arguably reifies the world insofar as it strips subjects of their uniqueness and supplants individuation with abstraction. *The term here refers to the manner in which ideas take on material forms which in turn reinforce the ideas that shape the world. To reify racial categories means to transform them into concrete things, making the categories seem natural, rather than human creations.* In the context of the prerequisite cases, the disparate experiences of Armenian and Japanese immigrants demonstrate how law transforms ideas about race into differences in rights and wealth, which then confirm racial ideas. (91, citing Gabel 1980, emphasis added)

The contemporary notion that the population of the United States is composed of distinct races, then, depends on two closely connected consensual illusions produced in part through the force of law. The first consensual illusion folds together into one group disparate peoples deemed white and contrasts them to groups deemed nonwhite and therefore subordinate and inferior; groups are treated as to some degree monolithic, homogeneous, coherent, and constant over time. The second consensual illusion both denies and emphasizes the real material advantages and disadvantages stemming from the legal reification of these hierarchical categories. In fact, it creates what Cheryl I. Harris calls "Whiteness as Property" through the law's construction of "who is white[,] . . . what benefits accrue to that status[,] . . . and what *legal* entitlements arise from that status" (C. Harris 1993, 1725). Reification turns these advantages for those deemed white into expectations, objective fact, and property. As Harris argues:

In a society structured on racial subordination, white privilege became an expectation and, to apply Margaret Radin's concept, whiteness became the quintessential property for personhood. *The law constructed "whiteness" as an objective fact, although in reality it is an ideological proposition imposed through subordination. This move is the central feature of "reification":* "Its basis is that a relation between people takes on the character of a thing and thus acquires a 'phantom objectivity,' an autonomy that seems so strictly rational and all-embracing as to conceal every trace of its fundamental nature: the relation between people." Whiteness was an "object" over which continued control was—and is—expected. (C. Harris 1993, 1730, citing Radin 1982 and quoting Lukács 1971, 83, emphasis added)

Harris demonstrates a panoply of legal, economic, and psychological privileges for whites made "objective" by legal reification of whiteness. This reification of whiteness written into law and enacted in economic activity also permeates the practices of scholarship, including white feminist critiques of intersectionality.

RESITUATING INTERSECTIONALITY AS STRATEGIC POLITICAL THOUGHT

Category anxiety in powerblind white feminist critiques of intersectionality is especially pronounced among scholars trained in disciplines dedicated to producing typologies and classifications. For very different reasons, sociology and philosophy seek to clear up the ambiguities of a disorganized world though the use of ordering terms and narratives. Yet the logic of "A/Not A" and the binary thinking of *either/or* rather than *both/and* guide scholarly investigation and argument across the disciplines. Grounded in the politics of antisubordination, decoloniality, and social change, committed to immanent rather than transcendent critique, and dedicated to a Gramscian war of position, the categories of intersectional thinking understandably lead to anxiety among those seeking abstract and once-and-for-all solutions to contingent and political social problems. Yet rather than seeking to discipline intersectional thinking, to smooth off its rough edges, and to loot its assets, feminists could instead choose to engage in humble, friendly, and respectful engagement with the ways of knowing and ways of being that have emerged from the freedom dreams of oppressed people. Intersectional thinking has utility and value inside the reward structures of this society, but ultimately its true worth lies in its capacity to serve as an antisubordination, decolonial practice that leads to new ways of knowing and new ways of being.

METAPHOR ANXIETY

The metaphorical conceptions that infuse intersectional theorizing seem to pose an enormous problem for critics mounting powerblind feminist critiques of intersectionality. In Chapter 2, I argued that category anxiety authorizes critics to treat their own deployment of dominant racial hierarchies as "objective" tools fully authorized to criticize the intersectional thinking of women of color, while remaining ignorant of the knowledge about racial categorization that underpins intersectional thinking. In Chapter 3, I argue that metaphor anxiety authorizes critics to treat their own limited and "literalist" notions of language as fully sanctioned "objective" tools fully authorized to disparage the terms that women of color proposed to consider multiplicity, while remaining oblivious to metaphoricity as a social and discursive practice that grounds the metaphors of intersectional analysis.

Despite the widespread adoption and manifest utility of the metaphors of "intersection" and "intersectionality," critics frequently lose sight of their roles as conceptual frames, arguing that they should be jettisoned on the basis of a "literal" rather than metaphorical analysis. Often they object that the terms do not convey sufficiently the full complexity of social relations and social identities, as if that could be achieved by any term. Critics have proposed a seemingly endless list of other terms to replace intersectionality. Surprisingly, however, their proposals remain at the highest levels of abstraction, as though assertion is equivalent to argumentation. Critics do not demonstrate that the terms they nominate to replace intersectionality can do the work that intersectionality does, can link racial justice to gender justice, can reveal how single-axis approaches preserve domination and subordination, can advance flexible and dynamic situated struggles with power by insisting on examining structures of power and identities in terms of *both/and* rather than *either/or*. On the plane of politics, these moves to dislodge the term intersectionality disavow feminism's responsibility to confront racism's ruinous effects. They are products of the anxieties instigated by the disturbance of race and the enduring specter of the historical moment when white feminism perceived itself to have lost control of feminism. On the epistemological plane, however, the weak grounds for dismissing the metaphor of intersectionality and the production of replacement metaphors as Platonic ideals rather than usable tools for social justice reveal a fundamental misunderstanding of all metaphors and of metaphoricity itself as a discursive practice.

Metaphors used routinely throughout the social sciences and the humanities are generally treated as interpretive tools. They are deployed as frameworks or heuristics to guide theory and research. They are often analyzed and contested. Yet treatment of the metaphor of intersectionality is distinctly different from treatment of other metaphors that permeate scholarship across the disciplines, such as stratification, assimilation, and alienation. In powerblind critiques, the metaphor of intersectionality is often treated as specious or defective. These critiques invariably rest on decontextualized analyses that display little cognizance of the complexity of social identities and power or even of the nature of metaphor itself. Whether because of the disturbance of race, the challenges of moving concepts across the disciplines, or revanchist desires to place white women back at the center of feminism, relentlessly faulty criticisms of metaphor and metaphorical thinking constitute core moves, mechanisms, and masks in the misrepresentations of intersectionality. As with category anxiety, these powerblind moves evade the tactical engagement with social power that intersectionality provides. They also evade their own engagement with and possession of social power: powerblind critics treat *their* criticisms as routine, abstract, and virtually apolitical, as if working to denigrate and abrogate metaphors proposed by women of color as tools for antisubordination is without racialized political consequences in scholarship or activism. This is not the case.

Powerblind critiques often misconstrue the nature, function, and context of metaphor. Metaphors such as "intersection" succeed as interpretive and analytic tools because they use terms drawn from well-known and often concrete arenas of activity to apprehend and theorize concepts that are complex, abstract, difficult, and poorly understood. Metaphors have a specific status as figures of language: in this case, for example, the metaphor of intersectionality *invites* thinking about the simultaneous and co-constitutive nature of categories *as if* they were operating at traffic intersections. Context is crucial to interpreting the meaning of metaphors, in both general and specific contexts (see Kövecses 2015, for example).[1] The metaphor's immediate textual context (for example, in a complex argument about the social and legal construction of race and gender for audiences in sociology and legal studies) is essential to understanding its meaning. Its meaning is shaped by its role in an arena of discourse about the limitations and material effects of the way social categories have been framed previously in social life. Its meaning is also marked by its emergence in the historical contexts of feminist and antiracist social struggle. The context used to interpret the metaphor must also reflect how its meaning is shaped by its ongoing life and trajectory within feminist antiracist studies and activism.[2]

A METAPHOR ABOUT A CIRCULATING NETWORK OF IDENTITY-RELATED EFFECTS

Kimberlé Crenshaw provides her most striking and generative image for the metaphor of intersectionality in "Demarginalizing the Intersection of Race and Sex" (1989). The context of Crenshaw's argument is crucial to interpreting the meaning of the metaphor she proposes. Crenshaw argues that legal doctrine, feminist theory, and antiracist politics have all tended to rely on categorizing people *as if* the categories such as race and gender were conceptually distinct, pure, durable, and nonoverlapping. She maintains that such single-axis assumptions about categories are conceptually limited and politically damaging. Analyzing several court cases, she explains that civil rights law denies Black women legal remedies because it fails to acknowledge their multiply situated identities. The core model of civil rights law allows them to claim discrimination only as women *or* as Black persons, but not in their specificity as Black women. Thus Crenshaw draws on the particular experiences of Black women in these legal cases to identify the contours of broader social processes and practices.[3] Black women do not experience discrimination as a simple and singular event, but rather as part of the ways in which patterns of power converge. Crenshaw's metaphor of "intersections" serves as a direct challenge to single-axis approaches that treat categories as distinct and nonoverlapping. It encourages thinking in terms of fluid, flexible, and multidimensional categories as a way of struggling against subordination.

Crenshaw deploys the "intersections" metaphor specifically to illustrate the complications of civil rights law. Black women plaintiffs arguing that they were discriminated against were not held to have a valid case if Black men as a group or white women as a group were not discriminated against. Their specific situation is obscured by treating them as *only* raced or *only* gendered. According to Crenshaw, the courts held that the law did not apply to a "compound class" such as Black women; therefore, as long as Black men or white women were not discriminated against, no discrimination could be found against Black women, and therefore there is no legal remedy for such discrimination.

Crenshaw introduces the intersectional metaphor when she argues:

> The point is that Black women can experience discrimination in any number of ways and that the contradiction arises from our assumptions that their claims of exclusion must be unidirectional. Consider an analogy to traffic in an intersection, coming and going in all four directions. Discrimination, like traffic through an intersection, may flow in one direction, and it may flow in another. If an accident happens in an intersection, it can be caused by cars traveling from any number of directions and, sometimes, from all of them. Similarly, if a Black woman is harmed because she is in the intersection, her injury could result from sex discrimination or race discrimination. (1989, 149)

Not recognizing Black woman's location in the intersection could lead to mishandling any traffic accidents. According to Crenshaw:

> Judicial decisions which premise intersectional relief on a showing that Black women are specifically recognized as a class are analogous to a doctor's decision at the scene of an accident to treat an accident victim only if the injury is recognized by medical insurance. Similarly, providing legal relief only when Black women show that their claims are based on race or on sex is analogous to calling an ambulance for the victim only after the driver responsible for the injuries is identified. . . . [In complex cases] the tendency seems to be that no driver is held responsible, no treatment is administered, and the involved parties simply get back in their cars and zoom away. (1989, 149)

This is not a metaphor of a "fixed" or "static" location as some critics claim. Myra Marx Ferree, for example, argues that she shares "the critical view of intersectionality as a static list of structural locations," so she will "adopt a more dynamic and institutional understanding of intersectionality" (2009, 87). (There are 219 citations to this article in Google Scholar as of May 10, 2018.)

Crenshaw's image is both spatial and temporal: it describes a *circulation network of identity-related effects*. Crenshaw's intersection metaphor demonstrates the power of structural discrimination underlying what appear to be singular identity-related claims. The metaphor does not group people by category at particular intersections (i.e., a particular corner for "Blacks" and "women"), and there is not the slightest suggestion in the metaphor or elsewhere in Crenshaw's arguments that social categories or their consequences are fixed and static, or that categories such as "Black women" have a singular or unchanging meaning. The metaphor suggests that *different kinds of discrimination* are always changing, always on the move, "flowing" through the streets like "traffic" or "cars," flowing in one direction and then another, experienced in "any number of ways" at different street crossings or intersections. Crenshaw's metaphor is actually a metaphor about the nature and consequences of *intersecting discriminations* supported by structures of power as they operate in heterogeneous spaces to impact people with differing trajectories in different ways. Crenshaw implies that courts treat differently three kinds of accidents caused by discriminatory actions or "drivers" moving along the street. Given appropriate evidence, the courts might assume that a vehicle hitting a Black man is propelled by racial discrimination and a vehicle hitting a white woman, by gender discrimination. In both cases the courts might propose the proper remedy—sending for the proper (race or gender) ambulance. It is the third kind of accident that concerns Crenshaw here: given the courts' definition of the compound status of the Black woman, she could be hit by a vehicle propelled by racial discrimination, or by gender discrimination, or by both. If the specific driver cannot be identified (or if it is a compound driver), then no ambulance is called, no remedy is proposed, no one is held responsible. The courts in effect *produce* the Black woman as a category of person whose specific trajectory can be interrupted with impunity.

From the courts' single-axis perspective, gender discrimination is posed as an issue facing white women, and race discrimination as an issue facing Black men. Yet making gains for an aggregate category of "Blacks" composed of only Black men or an aggregate category of "women" composed of only white women will not directly help Black women. The result is that the particular compound grievances of Black women, including both racism and sexism, will not be addressed, on the grounds that "sex and race claims cannot be combined because Congress did not intend to protect compound classes" (Crenshaw 1989, 142n12).

Crenshaw notes that white males who bring claims of reverse discrimination have, in fact, *the same compound status* as Black females, but in such cases the problem of compound classes is simply not acknowledged by the courts. She argues that "no case has been discovered in which a court denied a white male's attempt to bring a reverse discrimination suit on similar grounds [compound status]" (1989, 142n12). Crenshaw maintains "that Black women's claims automatically raise the question of compound discrimination and white males' 'reverse discrimination' cases do not suggests that the notion of compoundedness is somehow contingent upon an implicit norm that is not neutral but is white male" (1989, 142n12).

Crenshaw contends that legal practice operates by evaluating the claims of plaintiffs in terms of their distance from the norm of white males. Moderate distance from this norm occurs in the case of white women (whites who are not male) and Black men (men who are not white). In contrast, Black women are two steps removed from the norm: not whites (male *or* female), Black (but not male). Because the privileging of the white male is not acknowledged, gender and race work together only to explicitly disadvantage other plaintiffs (1989, 151).

According to Crenshaw, the courts expect Black women to show that their claims are "the same" as the claims of Black men or the claims of white women. They can be injured as women or as Blacks, but not specifically as Black women. Guided by the single-axis assumptions of civil rights law, the courts conclude that Black women are too "different" to represent all Black people or all women. Yet they judge them to be sufficiently the "same" as Black men or white women to be the beneficiaries of decisions that address only racism or only sexism. In a pattern emblematic of the social confusion generally engendered by sameness and difference, Black women are judged particular when they make universal demands, but rendered universal when they try to raise particular claims. Crenshaw argues that the courts' treatment of these plaintiffs flowed from the plaintiffs' intersectional experiences as Blacks *and* as women. Even more important, she attributes this injury to a *constitutive* rather than incidental inadequacy in the way that civil rights laws frame the sameness/difference problem. In addition, she notes the harm done by the tactical acceptance of the single-axis approach by feminist and antiracist activists.

THE SOCIALITY, SPATIALITY, AND TEMPORALITY OF INTERSECTIONS

A peculiarity of many critiques of the metaphor of intersectionality is their undertheorized view of traffic intersections. Crenshaw's intersection contains sociality, spatiality, and temporality. However, critiques often empty out the intersection in order to criticize it in terms congruent with inherited structures of dominance. A metaphor about dynamic axes of discrimination is thus misrepresented as a metaphor about static identities—and then criticized for the stasis that the critics themselves have imposed. Sometimes the issue of traffic circulation is entirely suppressed, with assertions that the metaphor consists simply of geometrical lines (see Chapter 5). In these misrepresentations, the focus on discriminatory practices drops out and the metaphor is read as an assertion of "static" place and identity, simply a crossing of two single-axis categorizations, a classification "bin" that contains Black women, for example. This is a dramatically inaccurate and thoroughly insupportable misreading of a metaphor that emphasizes a network of constantly changing and circulatory discriminatory effects that "Black women can experience in any number of ways." Black women are not always at the same location and subject to the same effects. Intersectionality is thus emphatically not "additive" in Elizabeth V. Spelman's terms (1988, 123, as discussed in Chapter 1): the courts' treatment does not create "a *further* burden" because the plaintiffs are both "women and Black"; it is a "*different* burden" because they are Black women. In fact, the courts' treatment produces and reproduces the category of Black women as those inhabiting a category that is illegible to the law. Powerblind critics who characterize intersectionality as static or additive are, in fact, translating the metaphor back into hegemony, suppressing its focus on power, subordination, and the nature of the streets as places where discriminatory flows circulate. Such critics reframe the metaphor to conform to hegemony's focus on naturalizing categories along a single axis, interpreting intersectionality as if Crenshaw's *only* point was to cross two single-axis categories to make visible gender and race.

When critics empty out the intersection of Crenshaw's metaphor to find it "fixed," they often lose sight of its extensive sociality. Rather than an empty space, the intersection is full of people engaged in various social relations, including vehicles and their drivers, injured people, doctors, ambulances. The people are heterogeneous, with different histories, trajectories, and intentions. It is particularly surprising that this vibrant and dynamic aspect of the metaphor is so frequently overlooked, given the social contestation at its center. The metaphor focuses attention on the public nature of actions that are framed socially as random private gestures, as individual acts of private violence. The trajectory of the injured person is interrupted, but this does not interrupt the circulating discriminatory vehicles, or if so, only briefly. The drivers may stop briefly, but if the cases are complex, drivers are not held responsible, "and the involved parties just get back to their cars and zoom away" (1989, 149). The intersection is a civic site of sociality where all sorts of people interact with one another.

The claim that the metaphor is "static" *because* it is spatial draws on a long and defective tradition of dichotomous thinking closely associated with radical distinctions between genders, with rendering time as dynamic and masculine, and with rendering space as lacking, static, and feminine (Jay 1981; Doreen Massey 1993). Rather than positioning space as static, Crenshaw's metaphor is congruent with much more flexible understandings well known to cultural geographers. In *For Space* (2008), for example, Doreen Massey articulates three propositions for understanding the nature of space that are relevant to Crenshaw's metaphor. Massey proposes the following:

> *First,* that we recognize space as the product of interrelations; as constituted through interactions . . . [and *s]econd,* that we understand space as the sphere of the possibility of the existence of multiplicity in the sense of contemporaneous plurality; as the sphere in which distinct trajectories coexist; as the sphere therefore of coexisting heterogeneity. Without space, no multiplicity; without multiplicity, no space. If space is indeed the product of interrelations, then it must be predicated upon the existence of plurality. Multiplicity and space as co-constitutive. *Third,* that we recognize space as always under construction. Precisely because space on this reading is a product of relations-between, relations that are necessarily embedded material practices that need to be carried out, it is always in the process of being made. It is never finished, never closed. Perhaps we could imagine space as a simultaneity of stories-so-far. (2008, 9, emphasis in original)

Crenshaw's metaphor demonstrates an understanding of space congruent with Massey's propositions: distinct trajectories of coexisting heterogeneity, dependent on a plurality of interrelations that must be negotiated—often in conflict. The trajectories of the circulating network of effects may be interrupted, but as the cars zoom away, the circulation continues. That is part of the temporality of the metaphor.

Consistent with Massey's arguments, Sarah Sharma analyzes the temporality of a "scramble crossing" intersection outside Shibuya Station in Tokyo in her book *In the Meantime: Temporality and Cultural Politics* (2014). In a scramble crossing, traffic enters the intersection from four or more directions, but all the vehicles are stopped at the same time, allowing people to move through the intersection in every direction, including diagonally. The intersection is not merely a surface but is three-dimensional, surrounded by buildings reflecting screens of constantly changing advertisements. According to Sharma, "Thousands of people move through the intersection at any one time. . . . The crossing at Shibuya pulses with an intensity incomparable to any other city street in the world" (2014, 1). Sharma argues that there are "multiple interdependent and relational temporalities tangled together at Shibuya"; the "crossing is shared by masses of people whose convergence is not random but temporally ordered," who therefore come to inhabit and experience time differently (4). Sharma's temporal analysis facilitates examining "power relations as they play out in time" (4), tracing how different political and economic contexts influence the patterns of who crosses the street at different times, their activities and trajectories. She argues that "the temporal operates as a form of social power and a type of social difference" (9). The temporal flows of people and vehicles through the intersection appear richly chaotic yet demonstrate systematic social and economic inequalities.

According to Massey's and Sharma's lines of argument, space and time are socially constructed, and, concomitantly, the social is spatially and temporally constructed (Doreen Massey 1993; Sharma 2014). Rather than being "static," Massey maintains, the spatial form of the social has causal effects (Doreen Massey 1993). Crenshaw's metaphor frames the ambiguous and abstract nature of multidimensionality in terms of a more accessible, concrete image from the material world. But while concrete, the image is not a simple one. Traffic intersections are not flat two-dimensional lines: socially they are inhabited; spatially they are three-dimensional; with temporality they are four-dimensional.

An intersection can be democratic and unpredictable, full of mixing and multiplicity, constantly changing. To block an intersection limits multiplicity and can impede democracy. In fact, preventing multiplicity and mixing in intersections has been used historically in the United States as a mechanism to generate racial inequality. In the 1940s and 1950s racialized "opportunity hoarding" was structured into the federal government's loan programs for buying and repairing homes, as whites restricted access to scarce resources (Douglas Massey 2007). Federal Housing Administration (FHA) loans were channeled to all-white areas; even white areas adjoining Black neighborhoods were rated ineligible for FHA loans. In consequence, all-white neighborhoods adjacent to Black or mixed-race neighborhoods sought to block off intersections and create structural barriers to separate neighborhoods. In Yonkers, New York, and adjacent areas of Westchester County (*Brick by Brick . . . A Civil Rights Story* 2007), in Detroit, Michigan (*Race, the Power of an Illusion* 2003), and in Ferguson, Missouri (C. Gordon 2008), walls were built to block intersections, to separate white areas from Black neighborhoods, preventing Blacks from entering the through streets and intersections of white areas. Ferguson, Missouri, at the time an all-white suburb, designed many of its streets to come to a dead end before entering the adjacent Black municipality of Kinloch (C. Gordon 2008). The city then blocked the remaining through streets to eliminate connecting roads and intersections. As a result, Blacks living in Kinloch and employed in Ferguson could not walk or drive through directly but had to follow a circuitous route to get in. This pattern persists today in Southeast Ferguson, where an arrangement of roads and sidewalks requires people walking to downtown to jaywalk. Consequently, the police frequently cite and fine them for "manner of walking in roadway." Blocking through streets and intersections served as a tool of white supremacy. It advanced the identity of whiteness as a racial cartel. It benefited white home owners while devaluing Black homes, serving as a subsidy for segregation and a reward for racism.

Some critics of intersectional analysis recognize that the intersection metaphor does not refer to geometric figures "intersecting" but involves roads. They change the term to label it a "crossroads" metaphor. Crenshaw seldom uses the term "crossroads" (although see Crenshaw 1992, 2003). It is not clear what is intended by the scholars who reframe the intersections metaphor in terms of a "crossroads," since replacing "intersection" with "crossroads" shifts the meaning of the metaphor. It could be read as simplifying it. Yet reducing an intersection to a two-road "crossing," rather than "a place where two or more roads meet," encourages misreading the metaphor as simply the meeting place of two single-axis categories. A more fortuitous but seldom mentioned complication of the substitute metaphor could reflect the role of the "crossroads" as a sacred concept in Afrodiasporic traditions, the place of the trickster (see Lipsitz 1994; Thompson 1984). The Afrodiasporic notion of "crossroads" draws attention to choice: without a crossroads there is only one direction to go, no choice. With a crossroads come choices, possibilities of different ways to go. With a crossroads comes the possibility of sideways movements and sideways gazes. Rather than simply responding to the power above, or looking anxiously to those below, one can look to the sides to imagine the solidarity of equals. Yet these multiple and equally dynamic implications of the crossroads do not appear in the critiques of intersectionality that condemn the metaphor for its purported stasis.

METAPHOR AS A PRACTICE OF THINKING

Another peculiarity of many critiques of the metaphor of intersectionality is their undertheorized view of the role of metaphor as a practice of thinking. Metaphors open up thought across the disciplines. Anthropologists describe cultures as "texts" and "dialogues"; sociologists liken social hierarchies to "layered configurations" and "stratifications" of rocks and minerals; Marxists consider the relationships between ideas and material conditions through metaphors of the dynamics that connect the "base" of a building to its "superstructure"; political theorists of modernization deploy biological models of development rooted in references to "birth," "blight," "decay," and "death." The history of the disciplines is replete with metaphors used as productive tools for conceptualization, interpretation, and analysis (see Barnes 1992; R. Brown 1977; Hallyn 2000; Keller 1996; Leary 1994, 1995; McCloskey 1995; Shapiro 1985–1986; Silber 1995; Sternberg 1990).

The rich scholarship on conceptual metaphor in philosophy, linguistics, and cognitive science as well as disciplines such as sociology and political science helps us see that intersectional thinking has become important for antiracist feminism *because* of its metaphorical qualities, not in spite of them. Those disciplines frame conceptual metaphors such as intersectionality not as flat descriptions vulnerable to "literal" analysis but as tools to "think with." For them, conceptual metaphors are generative exactly because they are not reducible to homogenous, discrete, and atomized entities. Conceptual metaphors bridge boundaries connecting different arenas of thinking. Because each metaphor highlights some aspect of the difficult concept and overlooks others, metaphors are often used in concert with other metaphors. In linguistics and cognitive sciences, metaphors are seen as provisional, not comprehensive; a lens, not a label; an option, not a vise. The "movement" of the word from one domain to another creates *new meanings* that may resonate in both domains, so that the word *no longer means* what it once did. Scholars in linguistics and cognitive science do not isolate the meaning of metaphor in the *word itself* but consider its meaning in its *contexts of use* (see Gibbs 2008; Goatly 2011; Holyoak and Thagard 1996; Johnson 1990; Kittay 1987; Kövecses 2015; Lakoff and Johnson 1980; Ortony 1996; Semino 2008).

Metaphor as a social force works in a world of persuasion and contradiction. Useful metaphors are felt to provide creative insight to generate thought, particularly when approaching intractable problems. Critics sometimes demand that the "intersections" metaphor should be a full representation of all subjectivities and social relations rather than a tool for exposing occluded structures of subordination. But to expect metaphors to account for all the important facets of a problem is to assume it can be a perfect map. But there are no perfect metaphors or perfect maps. As Jorge Luis Borges says in a well-known short story aptly titled "The Exactitude of Science" (1999), a perfect map would have to be the size of the whole kingdom and, therefore, no longer a map.

It is social, political, and argumentative contexts, not the "internal properties" of a metaphor, that may lead to different—even unexpected—interpretations and consequences. Different social contexts can lead to metaphors *enabling* understanding, but they can also *inhibit* it. Under concrete circumstances at the scene of argument, the same things that make metaphors productive may contain hidden implications that are decoded in particular ways by knowing subjects. This is particularly evident in examples of metaphors in political history.

For example, in the nineteenth-century United States, the Populist Movement challenged the moral and political legitimacy of bankers by comparing them to the money changers whom Jesus drove from the Temple. This metaphor struck a resonant chord with farmers and helped win them over to the Populist cause. But there also was an alternative interpretation: the Bible's message could also mean that believers would get in the next world all that they did not obtain in this one, so that questions of justice should be left to God (Palmer 1980). The same frame of reference that made the metaphor *meaningful* to religious believers also served to *disempower* its effects, promoting political passivity. Similarly, in the early twentieth-century United States, Italian American syndicalists challenged the class exploitation of workers by framing it as an intolerable slight to their manhood. The metaphor of emasculation rendered the class injury concrete. The syndicalists offered participation in radical violence as a means of recuperating that diminished masculinity, an appeal that helped the movement gain adherents among the ranks of working-class men. But when thousands of women went on strike in the textile mills of Lawrence, Massachusetts; Lowell, Massachusetts; and Paterson, New Jersey, in the years before World War I, the anarchist invocation of manly virtue *inhibited* rather than *enabled* mass support for their program (Topp 2001). The fact that metaphors do not close down thinking but their meaning responds to social conditions is part of the social and political life of all metaphors: many can open up new ways of thinking; many can be coopted by hegemonic logics. This requires attention to what intersectionality does in practice, not what it implies abstractly.

The context of the emergence of the metaphor of intersectionality and its adoption across scholarly fields transforms it into a "term of art": a word or phrase that comes to have a specialized meaning within a particular field or profession. Its meaning is shaped by its role in feminist antiracist argument, theory, and method. Its metaphoricity, its contexts, and its circumstances of origin influence its meaning. Therefore the metaphor of intersectionality is not a word whose meaning and usage can be ascertained by reference to ordinary language. Yet one of the most common powerblind strategies to derogate the meaning of the metaphor for feminist argument is to ignore both the nature of metaphor and the significance of context for determining its meaning: to take "intersection" *not as a metaphor, not as part of an argument,* and *not as part of a set of discursive practices countering long-standing ways of framing categories for purposes of subordination.* Instead, the word is wrenched out of context and taken as a single word in isolation. The word floats free from any meaning other than that imputed to it by the critic, but is treated as ineluctably bound and destroyed by the scolding critic's strictures (see examples in Chapters 5, 6, and 9).

This commonplace strategy for criticizing intersectionality "encapsulates" the metaphor. It treats it abstractly and philosophically but not analytically and politically. Powerblind critics using this strategy radically decontextualize intersectionality from the social and discursive contexts of its origins. They deny the metaphorical nature of the term, treating it "literally," asserting that it is constrained by a definitive meaning that exists independently of the discursive practices and contexts that worked to establish the metaphor as a tool against subordination. This powerblind move serves the interests of power. As Charles L. Briggs and his colleagues have argued, "Decontextualization and recontextualization play a crucial role in infusing texts with power" (Briggs 1993, 408, citing, for example, Bauman and Briggs 1990; Briggs and Bauman 1992). A term with a rich life as a tool for racial and gender justice becomes grist for abstract musings about the limits of language in capturing the full complexity of personal identity and social reality.

What makes such strategies powerblind? After all, generalizing about conceptions and criticizing terminology are scholarly commonplaces; academic arguments almost always involve generalizing about concepts and manipulating parts of other people's analyses—selecting, extracting, quoting, paraphrasing, reframing. But powerblind feminist critiques of intersectionality display a pattern of framing the metaphor in ways that make invisible their own methods of constructing their particular view. They erase the actors and the agency that produced the metaphor. Frequently they ignore and even misidentify the context of the original arguments they cite to justify and explain the term. They aggregate together all women of color, failing to identify the specific arguments made by different intersectional scholars of color. They place intersectionality back in the past, especially in the late 1980s and early 1990s, and in the process fail to address contemporary arguments about the metaphor by intersectional scholars of color (see Chapters 5, 6, and 9). They refuse to use all available resources of language and argument to interpret how the metaphor of intersection captures particular texts and experiences.

The effect of these strategies is to extract the metaphor of intersectionality from its rich context and social life and repackage it as an *object*—a single *word* whose definition and characteristics may be freely redefined for purposes of critique. Such discursive practices work by "reifying" the metaphor of intersectionality as an object rather than situating it, as all metaphors actually are, as a product "of socially, politically, and historically constituted processes of discourse production and reception" (Briggs 1993, 420).[4] This reifying disguises the scholarly moves that have "repackaged" the metaphor for criticism. Some critiques even make the metaphor into a monster—charging that the metaphor of the intersection bears primary responsibility for frustrating feminism's aims, ideals, and intellectual and social mission—or into a figure of seduction, claiming that feminists should be protected from its temptations leading to poor scholarship.

Reifying the metaphor of intersectionality leads to arguments about which word would be the perfect word. This decontextualizes the metaphor and authorizes feminist critiques to treat issues of politics as if they were propositions of logic: as if the politics of antisubordination could or should be conducted according to abstract rules about meaning divorced from their determinate social and discursive contexts. Most metaphors have many potential entailments, but not all possible entailments will be in play in every context. Discursive contexts determine which potentially relevant entailments are in play in an instance of language use. It is not useful to treat as propositions of logic what are significantly issues of politics (see Chapters 5, 6, and 9).

In their zeal to disparage the metaphor of intersection or invent replacement metaphors, powerblind critics fail to see the reasons for intersectionality's widespread adoption and embrace. The term "intersectionality" is significant here *only* as part of intellectual and political debate about categorization and subordination. It is deployed in public and scholarly arguments that have both intellectual and political consequences taking place in a "real world" where intersectional theorists of color do *not* assume that categories can be "pure," but where dominant discourses frame categories that way. Steven L. Winter (2001) helpfully argues that analogies and metaphors are persuasive not when people judge them to be "sound," but when people find them congruent with or helpful in understanding their world. According to Winter, analogies (or metaphors) are more likely to be persuasive when conventional concepts have become exhausted: "The analogy or metaphor with the best chance of adoption is the one that opens up the most useful possibilities"; when changing social circumstances vitiate categories still widely used, the analogy or metaphor "that accommodates the new realities by extending or otherwise changing prior conceptions is likely to succeed" (249). It is exactly the ability of the metaphor of intersectionality to extend prior conceptions and to open up useful possibilities that has made it persuasive. Winter argues that analogies or metaphors that are "sound" but too unconventional will fail to be persuasive, as will those that conflict "with highly conventional or deeply entrenched concepts or categories" (250). Crenshaw proposed the intersections metaphor as a provisional but politically necessary tool for extending prior conceptions and accommodating new realities.

METAPHOR AS ACADEMIC PRACTICE: INTERSECTIONALITY VERSUS STRATIFICATION IN SOCIOLOGY

In academic argument, disciplinary-specific contexts encourage interpretive practices that may serve to expand or truncate the significance of metaphorical thinking. But practices also respond to social factors—such as the continuing disturbance of race—leading to particularly turbulent interpretive practices. Feminist social scientists and those who cite them are particularly prominent among those who argue that the metaphor of intersectionality emerged from "geometry" and is therefore ineluctably fixed and static. To radically decontextualize the metaphor of intersection but then recontextualize it in powerblind ways allows critics to present for critique not an accurate reflection of the metaphor but a facsimile, a simulacrum—a rhetorical foil or "fantasy opponent."

Powerblind strategies deployed in white feminist critiques often radically decontextualize the metaphor of the intersection, particularly in order to argue that the metaphor is fundamentally flawed by its "origins" in geometry. The disturbance of race is fully in play here. The nature of metaphoricity is ignored in favor of a kind of "literalism" about the dangers of "geometric thinking" and the threat of its power to shut down thought. The critique of geometry functions here as Crenshaw claims the concept of color blindness does: as a rhetorical prophylactic more prized for what it prevents—that is, engagement with racialization—than for what it produces.

As I illustrate more fully in Chapter 5, feminist sociologists Candace West and Sarah Fenstermaker (1995) and anthropologist Kath Weston (1996a) criticize the use of "geometric" metaphors that they purport to see as central to conceptions of intersectionality, without defining "geometry." They treat geometry as a vise that holds and squeezes thought, making it immovable and inflexible. Their approach stands in direct contrast with the persuasive, enormous, and unrefuted body of scholarship on metaphor as a social force (see, as only one example, Lakoff and Johnson 1980). These texts frame the meaning of metaphor as absolute, ineluctably bound to the *word itself.* In this view, geometry is not something to think with, but *neither is metaphor.*

What work does this reductive framing of the metaphor of intersectionality accomplish at the scene of argument? Extracting words from their contexts allows the critics to treat intersectional thinking as permanently wedged into an uninterrogated conception of geometry that is radically reductive and stereotypical. It authorizes the critics to frame the women of color feminists who created intersectionality as merely previous and apparently less perspicacious users of the metaphor—as dupes, dopes, or disciplinarians. Yet *these are all problems of the critique, not of the metaphor.* Radically decontextualized critiques of the metaphor of intersectionality, therefore, serve as discursive technologies of power structured in dominance.

The significance of the attack on intersectionality because of its purported inability to escape geometry's ability to "close down" thinking becomes evident when comparing the treatment of the metaphor of "intersectionality" with sociology's treatment of another potentially static, "scientifically based" metaphor used to discuss social hierarchy and inequality: "stratification."

Douglas S. Massey explains the geological basis for the metaphor of "stratification" in *Categorically Unequal: The American Stratification System:*

> The term "stratification" comes from the Latin *stratum,* which in the geological sense refers to an identifiable layer of sediment or material in the ground. Over time, changing environmental conditions produce identifiable layers within the earth's crust, known as strata, which are distinctive in composition and can be associated temporally with different geological eras. In an analogous manner, societies may be conceptualized as having social strata, different layers that are distinctive in composition and characterized by more or less access to material, symbolic, and emotional resources. (2007, 1–2)

A generative metaphor productively emphasizes some aspects of its target, but not all, so a metaphor's use needs to be balanced with an awareness of where it may mislead or what it may neglect. For example, when thinking of society in terms of stratification, people in different groups interact with one another, and even change places in social hierarchies, which Peter Saunders claims is not the case with geological strata. In *Social Class and Stratification,* Saunders contends that the stratification metaphor does not represent well the occasional movement of individuals between strata: "The notion of individual bits of granite or limestone or whatever moving up and down within the earth's crust is absurd, yet most human societies have enabled some degree of individual movement between strata" (1989, 3). Saunders continues: "The idea of a system of stratification composed of *solid and immutable layers of different composition* seems highly misleading when applied to the analysis of most contemporary human societies" (4). Saunders uses the term "stratification" in his title and throughout his text to generate and organize thinking, even though his view of geology is limited—inaccurate and stereotypical. In fact, geological strata are composed of many different types of material, some soft, some porous, some hard, most susceptible to change. In this sense, his argument resembles many critiques of the metaphor of intersectionality, which try to limit its possibilities by referring to exaggerations or stereotypes of what they consider its originating matrix of "geometry."

John Scott, in *Stratification and Power,* argues that critics (such as Ralf Dahrendorf) who claim that the metaphor of stratification does not properly reflect group formation and conflict are mistaken because they are adopting a simplistic rather than a sophisticated understanding of the nature of geology.

> Geological formations are certainly not akin to the simple, unidimensional structures of inequality that critics of the metaphor im-

ply. They are complex structures that are characterized by fissures, faults, folds and intrusions, and that involve complex metamorphic processes. Strata do not simply lie on top of one another in neat layers like a jam sandwich. They are compressed and distorted into complex shapes that can be understood only through painstaking research and with an analytical imagination that is able to reconstruct the processes through which they have been formed. Indeed, it is precisely the *complexity* of geological formations that makes the metaphor of social stratification so appropriate. It is, of course, essential to use the concept in a way that grasps the specific features of the social world, but the model of stratification itself, properly understood, is a powerful tool of sociological analysis. (1996, 191–192)

Scott's explanation of the nature of geological movement among strata assumes that eliminating a potentially useful metaphor on the basis of simplistic or inaccurate understanding of its field of origin would not be of benefit to sociological inquiry. This seems to be the position of many scholars working on social stratification: although he makes stereotypic and exaggerated claims about the immutability of strata, Saunders nonetheless adopts "stratification" for the title and subject matter of his book, as does Scott. The use of "stratification" is commonplace in sociological analysis; scholars usually deploy the metaphor in a matter-of-fact manner without discussing differences between geological and social stratifications (see, for example, R. Collins 2000; Douglas Massey 2007). Though it has been subject to debate, its usefulness for sociological analysis has led "stratification" to become a "term of art," with a specialized meaning for that discipline.

The manner in which "stratification" is used in sociology is in distinct contrast to many feminist sociologists' use of intersectionality, introduced ubiquitously with a flurry of disparagement and disclaimers about its allegedly fixed and static origins in geometrical thinking or in the allegedly problematic and simplistic thinking of Black American feminists. For many feminists, "intersectionality" has already become a "term of art," but critiques of intersectionality repeatedly try to remove it from its specific meaning in feminist antiracist scholarship to reduce it to geometrical or mechanistic single-axis thinking, or—as I discuss in Chapter 9—disparage its use by claiming it is a "buzzword."

REFRESHING NOTIONS OF CATEGORICAL RELATIONS

In Chapter 2, I argue that resistance to interrogating and deconstructing dominant categories is particularly evident in the work of critics who charge that

intersectional thinking inevitably fails epistemologically and ontologically because categories can "intersect" only if they are presumed to have been "discrete," "pure," or "pre-existing." Metaphors such as hybridity and *mestizaje* have
been criticized on similar grounds. The charge of categorical purity rests on a
platonic ideal that is directly contradicted by the histories, social structures, and
political actions linked to intersectional thinking—features seldom acknowledged by such critics. It is not intersectional scholars who assume social categories are "pure," using social categories that frame categories that way. Rather,
critics deploy discursive technologies of power to resist intersectional thinking
by arguing that intersectionality cannot help but treat social categories as if
they are immutable. I am going to follow the logic of this line of argument
about metaphors and categories even though the people who raise it generally
do not develop their positions in detail, in order to contest problematic ways of
construing metaphors of multidimensionality.

Purifying, Hybridity, and Mediation

I draw on the work of Richard Bauman and Charles L. Briggs (2003) in
their treatment of the metaphor of hybridity to explore how intersectionality
illuminates heterogeneous social categories such as race and gender.[5] These
theorists are concerned with the *cyclical nature* of rhetorics of purity and
hybridity and the function of mediation in bringing "hybrid" forms together
to form new forms that at that point might be considered "pure." Their use
of the metaphor of "hybridity" would appear vulnerable to some of the same
criticisms as "intersectionality"—especially that using the term implies that
the original categories are "pure." Bauman and Briggs suggest that the situation is not so simple. They argue:

> When applied to epistemological constructions or to cultural forms
> more generally, of course, hybridity is a metaphor, which carries with
> it from taxonomic biology the notion that the hybrid "offspring" is a
> heterogeneous mixture of relevant constituent elements contributed by
> the homogeneous (pure) "parent" forms. *To be sure, classificatory purity
> is itself an epistemological construction, and every "pure" form can be
> conceived as hybrid by some measure or other.* (2003, 5, emphasis added)

Key here is an emphasis on the *constructed nature* of classifications of *both*
classificatory purity and hybridity; this argument is a strong counter to the
taken-for-granted notion that there are originals of any kind that are pure "by
nature." The fact that specific criteria must be used to establish what counts

as "pure" or "hybrid" demonstrates the problem often found in critiques of intersectionality: the assumption that any gender or racial category is "pure." Bauman and Briggs continue:

> That is just the point: it is not the ontological status of supposedly "pure" forms that interests us here, but rather the epistemological *work* of purification, and the concomitant vulnerability of pure, bounded constructions to hybridizing relationships. (2003, 5, emphasis in original)

Distinguishing epistemological from ontological purity draws attention to the constructed nature of categories, boundaries, and objects, and the work—the human labor of thought and language—accomplished to create both "purification" and "hybridity" (particularly useful in understanding the work of classification is Bowker and Star 1999). Bauman and Briggs draw attention to the important role of mediation in performing the cycle of hybridity:

> Mediation is a structural relationship, the synthetic bringing together of two elements (terms, categories, etc.) in such a way as to create a symbolic or conventional relationship between them that is *irreducible to two independent dyads*. A hybrid is thus a mediating form, but we use the term mediation to foreground the role of mediating terms in bringing "pure" elements—the categorical products of purifying practices—into relational conjunction. (2003, 5, emphasis added)

Powerblind critiques that condemn the metaphor of intersectionality on the basis that it presupposes separate pre-existing categories such as gender or race simply ignore the processes of human conceptual labor working to separate them, while at the same time refusing to acknowledge other available conceptual tools, such as mediation, that can enable intersectionality to think otherwise. Mediation can be seen as an interpretive tool designed to illuminate and manipulate otherwise occluded realities, not a process designed to distinguish the pure from the impure. Construction of what counts as pure, impure, or hybrid is both political and cyclical.

Purity, Impurity, and Separation

Like Briggs and Bauman, María Lugones (1994) helpfully deconstructs how metaphorical relationships can structure social categories. Many critiques of intersectionality assume that dynamics of purity, impurity, and separation always foster the continuing power of dominant categories and dominant discourses. Lugones argues otherwise. Exploring *mestizaje,* she questions the notion that one must ever be anchored in one place, suggesting a more fluid movement from one position to another. She contends that "those who separate may do so not in allegiance to but in defiance of the dominant intention" (458). Those who separate, who explore purity and impurity, may do so to demonstrate the impossibility of dominant categorizations. Lugones draws on two separation metaphors: the process of separating an egg and the separation that occurs when mayonnaise curdles. Lugones explains her process of separating an egg:

> I will *separate* an egg. I crack the egg and I now slide the white onto one half of the shell and I place the egg white in a bowl. I repeat the operation till I have separated all of the egg white from the yolk. Si la operación no ha sido exitosa, entonces queda un poquito de yema en la clara. If the operation has not been successful, a bit of the yolk stains the white. . . . So I must try to lift all the yolk from the white with a spoon, a process that is tedious and hardly ever entirely successful. The intention is to separate, first cleanly and then, in case of failure, a bit messily, the white from the yolk, to split the egg into two parts as cleanly as one can. This is an exercise in purity. . . . I want to investigate the politics of purity and how they bear on the politics of separation. (1994, 458, emphasis in original)

Was the egg the "whole" and were the separated parts "pure"? Are processes of separation always the creation of purity? Compare her metaphor of curdling mayonnaise:

> I am making mayonnaise. I place the yolk in a bowl, add a few drops of water, stir, and then add oil drop by drop, very slowly, as I continue stirring. If I add too much oil at once, the mixture se separa, it separates. . . . Mayonnaise is an oil-in-water emulsion. As all emulsions, it is unstable. When an emulsion curdles, the ingredients become separate from each other. . . . [R]ather, they coalesce toward oil or toward water[;] most of the water becomes separate from most of the oil—it is instead, a matter of different degrees of coalescence. The same with mayonnaise; when it separates, you are left with yolky oil and oily yolk. (Lugones 1994, 459)

Is the emulsion the "whole" and are the curdled parts "impure"? What is the significance of "pure" and "impure"?

Lugones indicates that for her to use the term "separate" is a form of cultural *mestizaje*:

> When I think of mestizaje, I think both of separation as curdling, an exercise in impurity, and of separation as splitting, an exercise in purity. I think of the attempt at control exercised by those who possess both power and the categorical eye and who attempt to split everything impure, breaking it down into pure elements . . . for the purposes of control. Control over creativity. And I think of something in the middle of either/or, something impure, something or someone mestizo, as both separated, curdled, and resisting in its curdled state. Mestizaje defies control through simultaneously asserting the impure, curdled multiple state and rejecting fragmentation into pure parts. In this play of assertion and rejection, the mestiza is unclassifiable, unmanageable. She has no pure parts to be "had," controlled. (1994, 460).

In her metaphors and her arguments, Lugones does not concede power to those who want to control categories but holds that purity, impurity, and separation reveal the impossibility of the control desired by those with power. This reveals that the notion of purity is ultimately a fiction. Lugones's metaphors, like other metaphors of multidimensionality, insist on resistance and change, on the capacious nature of multiplicity, on impurity at the center of the fictions that are constantly revised, reaffirmed, and renewed to reestablish dominant categories that can be presented as pure.

Lugones provides a good example of metaphors compatible with intersectionality that enrich the concept and augment its utility. She also provides an independent and resistant argumentative stance that could serve as a useful model for many critiques of the intersections metaphor—critiques that use the fictional purity of social categories to condemn intersectionality. Lugones shows that scholars can analyze purity, impurity, and separation "not in allegiance to but in defiance of the dominant intention" (1994, 458).

The analytic metaphors of Bauman and Briggs and of Lugones refresh and enrich multidimensional intersectional metaphors, extending their breadth and depth. Because metaphors are constructed in specific social contexts, different metaphors for multidimensionality work under different social conditions (see, for example, the arguments of Charles R. Hale [1999]).[6]

RESTRICTING NOTIONS OF CATEGORICAL RELATIONS

In contrast to the lively and dynamic metaphors discussed by Bauman and Briggs and by Lugones, critiques of intersectionality often cite or propose metaphors that are in effect "competitive." Critics often offer alternative terms or metaphors as "replacements" or "refinements" of the intersections metaphor or other multidimensional metaphors. These "competitive" metaphors, however, often display theoretical premises that differ dramatically from the premises of intersectionality. Critics offering "competitive" metaphors seldom bring the implicit theoretical and political differences to the fore. Because substantive underlying theoretical differences are suppressed, critics may claim that the competitive metaphor could replace or "refine" multidimensional or intersectional metaphors when, in fact, their theoretical frames are incongruent (see further discussion of competitive metaphors in Chapters 5 and 9).

Mechthild Bereswill and Anke Neuber (2011), for example, offer a competitive metaphor that appears to offer nothing useful conceptually while draining the original metaphor of intersection of its richness and value. They build their metaphor from a picture of a cluster of Mikado or Pick-Up Sticks that appears on a flyer for a German conference on intersectionality (Lewis 2009), as well as on the cover of an edited collection of conference papers emerging from the conference, in which Bereswill and Neuber's article appears (Lutz, Herrera Vivar, and Supik 2011). They suggest that there is "a connection between a game of skill and concentration such as Mikado and the complexity associated with the intersection and overlapping of various axes of difference and of associated constellations of inequality" (2011, 69).[7] It is not immediately evident how a game with separate, distinct pieces—which crisscross one another but never meld—would seem anything other than overlapping single-axis categories that one must dislodge without moving any other single-axis category—a political goal that would not meet conceptions of intersectionality as a tool for antisubordination. Early on, the critics suggest the game leads to "the provocative idea of society as a randomly thrown conglomerate which starts to wobble if the necessary steady hand is lacking" (2011, 69). Such an image both ignores the historical development of gender, race, and other social categories in favor of the notion of "randomness" but also presents a deeply conservative image suggesting the need for top-down control of society by sociologists or other leaders—a theoretical position quite different from that of intersectional analysis.

Rather than offering a Mikado-based analysis of intersectional theory, Bereswill and Neuber emphasize through the game a structural theoretical approach that expresses their specific concern with gender as a "universal master category." This approach is antithetical to the thinking of intersectionality. The sticks are layered upon one another but in themselves are wholly separate; they fail to provide co-constitutive, mutual influence in the construction of different categories—an important theoretical tenet of intersectional thinking. The critics devote considerable attention to the role and rank of the single most powerful, valuable, and apparently desirable stick: they note that in Mikado "the highest-value stick has a special master status and is the most prized trophy" (2011, 69). Reflecting on their research on marginalized masculinity, the critics claim, "Masculinity would be the most sought-after stick that falls out of the middle of the bundle, and which everyone wants to get hold of without disturbing the arrangement. Masculinity is thus the master category that structures the game and subordinates the other sticks" (77). Developing this notion, the critics argue, "The master stick, the Mikado, would be hegemonic masculinity, the sought-after ideal. When we look more closely, though, we see that the master stick is not . . . the central point of reference for the game as a whole, but at most a desirable trophy which both men and women want to get hold of" (78). This last point should be an assumption politically disturbing for feminists—that feminists' real goal is to take on the ideal of hegemonic masculinity for themselves. According to this description, power in the game is gendered male, with less power measured from the distance of each stick from the "master stick" seen as the most desirable trophy. Rather than "refining" metaphors of intersectionality, this metaphor seems to demonstrate exactly the situation that intersectionality challenges: power centered on the male and lack of power being measured by the stick's scoring distance from the power of the male.

Enriching Competitive Metaphors

Bereswill and Neuber's move to proffer substitute or elaborating competitive metaphors is a symptomatic move evidenced in many critiques of intersectional thinking (see examples in Chapters 5 and 9). Substitute metaphors are frequently mentioned in ways that shield them from examination, as when Nancy A. Naples reports a graduate student finding Crenshaw's metaphor of the traffic intersection "[too] simple and too one dimensional," proposing instead a visual metaphor of a multidimensional star (2009, 572–573). The problem of such proffered substitutions is *not* that they engage in critical examination of multidimensional metaphors, *not* that they might recommend different, more successful metaphors; the problem is that such suggestions give the appearance of analytic contestation without the substance. The new metaphors are permitted to indulge in any number of variations, while powerblind critiques suppress the many variations and flexibilities that have been proposed by women of color. The suggested metaphors do not present adequate and full comparison with existing intersectional metaphors; they rely on limited understanding of the role of metaphor in language, and they act as though they can replace the metaphor of intersectionality without altering its role in antisubordination arguments.

Intersectional metaphors are part of an elaborate structure of theory and research—that is what makes them "terms of art." Whether compatible or competitive, metaphors seeking to challenge multidimensional metaphors should work to demonstrate how they can account for the full range of benefits currently offered by intersectional metaphors. Yet metaphor anxiety prevents powerblind critics from recognizing that their purported refinements and replacements for intersectionality are simply ways to evade its racial justice imperatives.

LEGITIMATING POWERBLINDNESS

At the scene of argument the conventions of disciplinary research and writing teach people to pursue and propose color-blind solutions to color-bound problems, suppressing the contemporary presence of the racial hierarchies discussed in Chapter 2. In critiques of intersectionality, power-blindness is often linked with color blindness. The Countering Colorblindness across the Disciplines Project that I have been part of for nearly a decade defines colorblindness as "an institutional practice that reproduces its own appeal by limiting the means by which counter-information is legitimately produced" (Crenshaw, Harris, et al. 2018). Color blindness is not a social theory, a moral imperative, or a route to racial equity but rather a way to hide, excuse, justify, and protect the unfair gains and unjust enrichments of centuries of expressly racist practices and policies. Color blindness pervades feminist critiques of intersectionality through repeated attempts to wrest intersectionality from its origins in, and its continuing commitments to struggles against, racist suppression and subordination. These moves need not be based in racial aversion or animus; they emanate as well from an unstated but deeply rooted commitment to a willed blindness to power that pervades neoliberal culture and politics. It is not simply that the critics neglect intersectionality's antiracist origins and intentions but that they advance arguments that seek to make intersectionality safe for power. The reward structures of neoliberal institutions cultivate experts who are unwilling or unable to identify power or to challenge it. Deeply political problems are translated into matters in need of greater technical or administrative expertise. Collective public problems become rendered as private and personal concerns. Pretending that asymmetrical power does not exist constitutes the core condition of bourgeois respectability within the neoliberal framework. Inside the audit cultures of academic institutions, inside the economy of prestige and attention online and in print, and inside competitions for fellowships and grants from philanthropic institutions rewards flow freely to power-aversive formulations.

People who proclaim proudly to be color-blind in a society suffused with racist oppression and exploitation are not so much evading color as evading acknowledgment of power. The discursive move to color blindness functions to place off-limits and beyond the pale of legitimate discussion a crucial axis of identity and power, encouraging powerblind discourses. Intersectional thinkers would never contend that color must always be at the center of analysis and argument; they do insist, however, on always placing power at the center of analysis and argument. One key purpose of intersectional thinking is to discern in any given social and historical situation *which differences make a difference.* By evading racism, marginalizing it, or relegating it to the historical past, feminists are not just embracing color blindness; they are associating themselves with a powerblindness that is fundamentally fatal to feminism's entire project.

Unacknowledged structures of power infuse color blindness. Color blindness proceeds from an uninterrogated baseline norm that imagines a world where racism does not exist until an isolated and aberrant event or individual injects it into social life. For intersectional thinkers Indigenous dispossession, slavery, and colonialism have been foundational forces in the making of the modern world. The academic disciplines that emerged in the eras of conquest and colonization to help rationalize and legitimize European world dominance are saturated with racist presumptions and assumptions. Their *either/or* rather than *both/and* perspectives have long served to legitimate the domination of men over women, rich over poor, white over nonwhite, straight over not straight. Training in the disciplines instructs people *not to see* the social subordinations that they can witness every day with their own eyes, if those eyes are open. This state of powerblindness is to be expected. In Cedric Robinson's deft formulation, social systems deploy race as justifications for relations of power that "are unrelentingly hostile to their exhibition" (2007, xii). Claims of naturalism and inevitability are mere contrivances grounded in specific interests, histories, and "mechanisms of assembly." As "unstable truth systems," Robinson argues, racial regimes are always in a process of modification, amendment, emendation, revision, and reorganization. Color-blind and powerblind discourses—discourses posing as unaware of their own racial power—are part of this system of continuing modification.

This chapter analyzes feminist texts that do not directly evoke color-blind discourses but deploy color blindness and powerblindness as part of a textual structuring of racial dominance that demonstrates a hidden allegiance to what Eduardo Bonilla-Silva and Tukufu Zuberi (2008) call "white logic and white methods." I examine two texts concerned with intersectional theorizing. Both texts appropriate intersectional theorizing by devaluing the intellectual labor of women of color, enveloping their works in an unmarked "feminism." Both texts are examples of what I call "neoliberal asset-stripping," attempts to delegitimate the intersectional thinking of women of color in order to appropriate the valuable conceptions of intersectionality for management by an unmarked—but white—feminism. They are blind to not only the social and historical workings of racist power but also the racialized power that scholars wield in the tactics they deploy at the scene of argument. These tactics contain uninterrogated ideological allegiances. As Jochen Walter and Jan Helmig explain:

> Discourses do not simply depict or reproduce the world, but instead *constitute* and *construct* reality in a selective and contingent manner. They have a *productive character* which means that discourses are practices which are systematically *producing* the very objects that they apparently describe. (2008, 121, citing Foucault 1972, emphasis in original)

INCLUSION IS A ONE-WAY STREET

Before turning to analyze examples of powerblind color-blind discourses, I want to situate them in Walter D. Mignolo's arguments about coloniality introduced in Chapter 2. Mignolo explains that contemporary Western knowledge is necessarily and constitutively a *colonial matrix* of power and knowledge (2011). This matrix was established by Europe treating its dominant particulars as universals, as the baseline norm that defines the fully human. Europe framed its culture and modernity as dynamic and progressive. Other parts of the world were seen as not yet fully developed, embedded in nature and tradition, passive and static, defined by the terms of colonial difference (Mignolo 2011, 173). In consequence, those considered fully human—*humanitas*—are charged with managing knowledge production and establishing the categories of thought. Those classified as not fully human, as more connected to nature than to history, as *anthropos*, are deemed rationally and ontologically deficient. Mignolo argues that the racialized power produced and perpetuated by this process does not stem from the conscious intentions and actions of culpable individual scholars but rather emerges as part and parcel of a framework for managing all of Western civilization and its institutions of knowledge production. Its managerial logic does not exclude anthropos—for our purposes, all racialized, gendered, and sexualized others—from academic knowledge production, but it controls the unequal terms by which anthropos can be admitted and participate. Everyone is included, but not everyone has the right to include. As Mignolo emphasizes:

> Inclusion is a one-way street and not a reciprocal right. In a world governed by the colonial matrix of power, he who includes and she who is welcomed to be included stand in codified power relations. The locus of enunciation from which inclusion is established is always a locus holding the control of knowledge and the power of decision across gender and racial lines, across political orientations and economic regulations. (2011, xv)

In these settings, then, whites manage not only the categories of thought and the terms of debate but also the conditions by which people of color are permitted to participate in systems of knowledge production. According to Mignolo, the logic of the colonial matrix is not a vestigial remnant of history but continues to shape all the knowledge practices of Western civilization. Adopting its precepts is not voluntary or conscious. He argues: "It is a managerial logic that by now has gone beyond the actors who have created and managed it—and in a sense, it is the colonial matrix that has managed the actors and all of us" (2011, 16).

Because feminist studies presents itself as concerned with social justice and attracts scholars who think of themselves as progressive, one might expect not to find there common scholarly logics based on the colonial matrix or logics claiming color-blind "neutrality." But at the level of argumentation, research design, and execution, retentions of disciplinary frameworks and interdisciplinary inventions are replete with masks, moves, and mechanisms steeped in color-blind logics. There is a tendency to resort to the "interdisciplinary evasion"—assuming that declaring feminist studies interdisciplinary means that the problems of the disciplines go away. But because disciplinary allegiances and perspectives remain, scholars may badly mishandle arguments and strategies characterizing other disciplines.

Even academic disciplines that claim to produce knowledge explicitly for transformative social change, such as feminist studies, can be seen to use strategies of disciplinary authority to limit and control the terms of inclusion of racialized subjects. Clare Hemmings (2011) argues that feminist studies' reframing of its own past is not innocent but structured in dominance, reinforcing racial, sexual, and even gendered power. Hemmings provides strong evidence that narratives of feminist history are constructed in repeated and patterned ways motivated by the positions scholars occupy or wish to occupy (13). The result is the creation of a closed feminist past that incessantly frames new achievements as transcending and eradicating old problems. Black women and lesbians are not included for their influence on feminist scholarship and histories but as marginal figures, emerging and disappearing to fit the dominant story of white feminist history. Hemmings argues that "problematic configurations of race and sexuality are key rather than tangential to how feminist progress narratives operate. . . . Erasure of a complex past is a necessary condition of their positivity" (57). Such narratives position the critiques provided by Black feminists and other women of color, lesbians, and poststructuralists as having performed an important service—but *in the past*. In these histories, concepts of difference are seen as serving as *catalysts* for feminist discussion that quickly became unnecessary because feminism presented itself as quickly "incorporating" difference. Dominant white feminists stand in "codified power relations" to the racialized feminists and others they welcomed—welcomed not as cognitive equals but as evidence of the capaciousness of feminist studies.

Feminist studies declares itself an interdisciplinary field of inquiry, but it is composed of subgroups of scholars who also share allegiance to the disciplines of their training and practice—in the case of the white scholars I analyze here, forms of sociology. Sociology has been a managerial discipline since its inception in race relations theory, where scholars chose to focus on "race relations" rather than racial subordination (Steinberg 2007). It is also what Foucault might call a "hegemony-seeking" discipline (1980c, 85). According to Linda Martín Alcoff, Foucault contrasted "subjugated knowledges"—here the intersectional thinking of women of color—with "hegemony-seeking knowledges," arguing that

> subjugated or local knowledges always tend to do less violence to the local particulars and are also less likely to impose hierarchical structures of credibility based on universal claims about the proper procedures of justification that foreclose the contributions of many unconventional or lower-status knowers. (Alcoff 2007b, 80)

Exactly because they see themselves as on the side of social justice, feminists may fail to see how their own practices of reading and writing serve as discursive technologies of power, framed in terms of the colonial matrix of knowledge and allegiances to specific hegemony-seeking disciplines. Under such circumstances, specific discursive strategies can serve as potent tools of dominance, infusing reading and writing situations with strategies of racial subordination that go unremarked because they are authorized by tradition and convention.

BLIND TO (SOME) COLOR, BLIND TO (SOME) POWER

As I argue in Chapter 1, since its inception in the nineteenth century the intersectional thinking of women of color has frequently been ignored by white feminists (see, for example, May 2015, and also Bambara 1970; Giddings 1984; Guy-Sheftall 1995) but gained traction in the 1970s and 1980s. Intersectional thinking vigorously argues that categories such as gender, race, and class are not stable and discrete but, rather, variable and changing constellations that are *interrelated, co-constitutive,* and *simultaneous.* By the late 1980s and 1990s these arguments insisting on the heterogeneity of social difference created a dramatically successful intervention in feminist studies.

This moment provoked a shock and sense of loss for many white feminists: they were forced to abandon illusions of the wholeness and homogeneity of the category "woman," its primacy as a social category, and the centrality of white women as representatives of feminism. I argue in Chapter 1 that significant traces of this moment of loss remain, that this intervention is still being resisted at the scene of argument through the specific claims and rhetorics of scholarly texts. White feminist critiques of intersectionality are replete with arguments and citations seeking to discredit and delegitimate the intersectional thinking of scholars of color in order to appropriate intersectional thinking for a general, unmarked, white feminism (see Bilge 2013, 2014; see also Chapters 7 and 8). Strategies of powerblind color blindness contribute to this goal.

While including arguments about and by gendered and racialized subjects, feminist studies, like many other disciplines, systematically forecloses inquiries into the nature of its *own* historical reliance on deployments of racial power and hierarchy, its *own* privileging of color-blind solutions to color-bound problems. Color-blind tactics pretend to overlook, and thereby make invisible, white racial dominance. If one is blind to color, one is also blind to power. One of the privileges of racial color blindness is to ignore one's own power when speaking as humanitas, as the one who classifies, who benefits from strategies of color blindness that rely on, yet disavow, the presumed superiority of humanitas over the racialized position of anthropos, those who have been classified and are to be managed.

The construction of humanitas and anthropos was a thoroughly gendered enterprise: it was European male elites who developed systems of classification to justify the subordination of others through various categories—geographical, racial, gendered. In this historical tradition, European women were not positioned as humanitas. Given this history of power in social relations, the position of contemporary professional white women dominant in feminist studies appears anomalous. They are no doubt subject to subordination, but not to the degree or in the ways that colonized and racialized people continue to be. In the discipline of feminist studies, they are in the position to welcome racialized others, yet still hold "the control of knowledge and the power of decision across gender and racial lines" (Mignolo 2011, xv). To hold the "control of knowledge" authorizes dominant white feminists to decide the nature and value of any intellectual contributions by racialized subjects. This process comes into sharp relief through the history of intersectional and multidimensional analysis: the intellectual production of women of color, it has successfully challenged and altered disciplinary thinking, making it a central site for examining the problems of color-blind discourses in feminist studies. When adopting a color-blind stance, dominant white feminist critiques assume they can transmogrify theoretical and conceptual history and appropriate this intellectual production. The textual strategies to accomplish this both deploy and deny white racial power. As a result, the subject position of the white feminist tends to be unmarked within its own discourse, but all too visible to those it seeks to manage.

Color-blinding rhetorics erase racial specificity, encourage white authors and readers to feel that they are not white but neutral and color-blind, appropriate intersectional theorizing for the subject position of the "unmarked" white woman, and hide the stripping of intellectual assets from women of color. I argue that such color-blinding rhetoric appears at the scene of argument in the introduction of Leslie McCall's "The Complexity of Intersectionality" (2005), one of the most widely cited feminist critiques of intersectionality (with nearly 4,500 citations in Google Scholar as of May 10, 2018), providing an illustrative example of a broader process. The article begins:

> Since critics first alleged that feminism claimed to speak universally for all women, feminist researchers have been acutely aware of the limitations of gender as a single analytical category. In fact, feminists are perhaps alone in the academy in the extent to which they have embraced intersectionality—the relationships among multiple dimensions and modalities of social relations and subject formations—as itself a central category of analysis. *One could even say that intersectionality is the most important theoretical contribution that women's studies, in conjunction with related fields, has made so far.* (2005, 1771, emphasis added)

Despite intersectionality being a result of the theorizing of women of color, *race does not appear here.* In praising intersectionality in her introduction, the critic erases the racial specificity of the scholars who developed intersectional theorizing. Rather, in a remarkable move of appropriation, she declares intersectionality a product of "women's studies" ("in conjunction with related fields"). The passage alludes to disciplinary differences ("in conjunction with related fields"), while treating racial difference as invisible. This "color-blinding" rhetoric is a move of neoliberal "asset-stripping," transferring the intellectual assets of intersectionality to an apparently raceless color-blind feminism.

In a footnote, the critic credits several intersectional scholars, noting:

> As for the origins of the term itself, it was probably first highlighted by Kimberlé Crenshaw (1989, 1991). Many other key texts introduced the conceptual framework and offered similar terms: see [A.] Davis 1981; Moraga 1983; [B.] Smith 1983a; hooks 1984; Moraga and Anzaldúa 1984; Glenn 1985; Anzaldúa 1987, 1990; King 1988; Mohanty 1988; Spelman 1988; Sandoval 1991. (2005, 1771n1)

McCall simply erases the racial specificity of the cited scholars. Nothing in the passage signals to readers that the scholars cited in the footnote nearly all identify as women of color: five as Black, three Latina, and one each Japanese American, South Asian, and white. This colorblindness is not innocent in the argument of the text. The passage elides racial difference in order to claim the knowledge production of women of color as a legacy of *feminism* and creates *feminism* as a singular site for intersectional analyses by eliding the intersectional work of ethnic, queer, racial, and American studies. The result is to claim intersectionality to speak through only gender—to historicize intersectionality "nonintersectionally."

Color-blinding rhetorical strategies appear in both the passage and the footnote, congruent with what Hemmings argues to be a systematic treatment of women of color in feminist histories (2011). I note five strategies in McCall's text that serve to devalue the theoretical and analytical arguments of women of color and to relegate them to the historical past. First, the footnote of this article published in 2005 limits the contributions of those who introduced intersectional theorizing to the decade 1981–1991.[1] With the exception of Evelyn Nakano Glenn, the text does not cite more recent work done by the intersectional scholars it lists. The intellectual production of these scholars of color is encapsulated in the past. Second, the text itself begins with a tendentious color-blinding feminist origin story: "*Since critics **first** alleged that feminism claimed to speak universally for all women, feminist researchers* have been acutely aware of the limitations of gender as a single analytical category" (McCall 2005, 1771, emphasis added). This narrative implies that the response of "feminist researchers" to "critics" was immediate, thereby erasing conflicts of race and power from a contentious disciplinary history. As Judith Butler points out, in the 1980s, "the feminist 'we' rightly came under attack by women of color who claimed that the 'we' was invariably white, and that that 'we' that was meant to solidify the movement was the very source of a painful factionalization" (1995, 49). Nothing in the passage signals to readers that the scholars relegated to the footnote were prominent among the critics objecting to the suppression of racial difference in feminism. Third, while the term a "range of disciplines" is mentioned, the specific training of the cited scholars is not, as if the scholars' training in law, philosophy, or political science serves simply to enable contributions to the development of feminist sociological theory.

Fourth, the footnote deprecates the intellectual labor of these scholars of color, reducing their theorizing and analysis primarily to *words,* to the apparently lucky identification of one or more "catchy" terms, rather than the sustained development of an analytic strategy. Crenshaw "highlighted" the term, and others contributed other "similar terms": according to this formulation, no one actually conceived or theorized the framework of intersectionality. Fifth, in erasing the race of the scholars it notes, the footnote also erases the influence of the *politics of antiracism* to the development of intersectional thinking—its role as a tool for analyzing and countering subordination. The women on McCall's list are not just feminists who incidentally are also (primarily) women of color. They are all feminists who see gender justice as inextricably linked to racial justice. The scholarly work of most, if not all, those cited emerged from experience with organized social action groups and social movements countering racism. Examples include Angela Davis's continuing commitment to organized efforts for social justice (see 2005), Barbara Smith's participation in the Combahee River Collective (1983b), and Kimberlé Crenshaw's involvement in organized action at Harvard Law School leading to the development of Critical Race Theory (see Crenshaw, Gotanda, et al. 1995; Crenshaw 2011c). Chela Sandoval notes that the form of "oppositional consciousness" she advocates "was enacted during the 1968–90 period by a particular and eccentric cohort of U.S. feminists of color who were active across diverse social movements" (2000, 44). The result of suppressing the significance of the cited scholars' race, disciplinary training, and activities to promote racial justice is a powerblinding color-blinding rhetoric that systematically diminishes and trivializes the conceptual labor of women of color, contributing to the appropriation of their intellectual assets according to the "hegemony-seeking" logics characterizing the discipline of sociology. These rhetorical strategies at the scene of argument display a hidden allegiance to color blindness: they rewrite the history of a traumatic historical moment by folding intersectional critics into a feminism "writ large," eliminating the motivating force of racism in the development of intersectional thinking. They also make visible a revanchist desire to regain territory, to restore white racial centrality in the discipline of feminist studies.

THE SOCIAL CONSTRUCTION OF STRAW BODIES

Critiques of intersectionality tend to reinscribe *whiteness* as if it were *color blindness.* As I indicate in Chapter 1, structurally, white commentary on and critiques of intersectionality are inevitably racializing discourses: the original intersectional theorizing is a production of women of color, yet critiques are generally written by white women who rely on the subject position of the "neutral" or "unmarked" white woman. This "unmarked" subject position of the white woman treats herself as color-blind to the interdisciplinary and disciplinary expertise about race of those whose positions she critiques. Given the historically sedimented logic of the colonial matrix, it is not surprising to find that color-blind critiques may frame the concepts proposed by women of color as fixed and inert, cognitively deficient, embedded in tradition and in nature.

In such circumstances, some critiques represent themselves as color-blind and powerblind through the use of the *representation* form of the *straw person fallacy* (see Talisse and Aikin 2006). In the representation form of the straw person fallacy, (1) critics misattribute and misrepresent the arguments of their target and (2) they suppress and ignore their target's other relevant arguments. Critics quote their target's words out of context, for example, misrepresenting the target's actual claim, or oversimplify the claims, then attack the oversimplification. The critics covertly replace the target's precise argument with false but superficially similar claims that they discredit. This discrediting is "knocking down a straw person." To be persuasive, a straw person argument requires an audience that is ignorant or uninformed about the original argument. This tends to be precisely the case when white-dominated audiences primarily interested in gender encounter multidimensional analyses of gender and race. An illustrative example of the representation form of the straw person argument is found in the widely cited article "Doing Difference" by Candace West and Sarah Fenstermaker in *Gender and Society* (1995) (there are nearly 2,000 citations in Google Scholar to this journal article, and some 870 to its reprints as of May 10, 2018). The example I examine here purports to critique an argument made by Patricia Hill Collins.

In *Black Feminist Thought* (1991), Patricia Hill Collins makes a series of detailed and sensitive arguments countering notions of biological determinism and developing conceptions of social construction. She argues that "while expressions of gender and race are both socially constructed, they are not constructed in the same way" (1991, 28), so the struggles of different groups "to articulate self-defined standpoints represent similar yet distinct processes" (27). Collins maintains:

> While race and gender are both socially constructed categories, constructions of gender rest on clearer biological criteria than do constructions of race. Classifying African-Americans into specious racial categories is considerably more difficult than noting the clear biological differences distinguishing females from males (Patterson 1982). (1991, 27)

Collins is not claiming that gender is based on biology but that processes for articulating self-defined standpoints in groups differ because socially constructed methods of gender classification rely on notions of a clear biological binary. Such a binary is continually reinscribed, for instance, when parents of children born hermaphroditic are required to choose whether the child should be "classified" male or female (Dreger 1998). Collins's citation of Harvard sociologist Orlando Patterson's *Slavery and Social Death* (1982) clarifies the point she is making about variation in socially constructed methods of identifying gender and race. Patterson argues that slavery is characterized by a *generalized condition of dishonor* conveyed by visible marks of servitude, but in the Americas it was *not color but rather hair type,* that served as the badge of slavery. This was the case because skin color in both whites and Blacks varied more widely than most assume, in part because of geographical origin and also because of racial mixing. According to Patterson, "Hair type rapidly became the real symbolic badge of slavery, although like many powerful symbols it was disguised, in this case by the linguistic device of using the term 'black'" (1982, 61). Collins draws on Patterson's arguments about the roles of hair texture and skin color in creating and legitimating social death for Afrodiasporic people to illustrate how the myth of biological difference as destiny in relation to gender has been even easier to sustain than the parallel myth about race.

West and Fenstermaker ignore both the proximate and larger context of Collins's comment to allege that by mentioning the widely shared social perception that women are marked by biological difference, Collins herself is embracing biological essentialism. Their zeal to catch a woman of color making what they allege to be an error that feminists have long criticized about out-of-date theories of "sex differences" and "sex roles"—and thus to render Collins rationally and ontologically deficient—leads them to make a claim that directly contradicts Collins's careful arguments about social construction. West and Fenstermaker highlight Collins's alleged "mistake" by adding emphasis to Collins's own words:

> While race and gender are both socially constructed categories, constructions of gender *rest on clearer biological criteria* than do constructions of race. Classifying African-Americans into specious racial categories is considerably more difficult than noting the *clear biological differences* distinguishing females from males. . . . Women do share common experiences, but the experiences are not generally the same type as those affecting racial and ethnic groups. (1995, 16, quoting Collins 1991, 27, emphasis added by the critics)

The critics go on to argue:

> Of course Collins is correct in her claim that women differ considerably from one another. . . . The problem, however, is that what unites them as women are the "clear biological criteria distinguishing females from males." Here, Collins reverts to treating gender as a matter of sex differences (i.e., as ultimately traceable to factors inherent to each sex), in spite of her contention that it is socially constructed. Gender becomes conflated with sex, as race might speciously be made equivalent to color. (1995, 16)

West and Fenstermaker treat Collins's echo of socially constructed notions of biological binaries as if it were a theory proposed by Collins about the nature of gender. But Collins is not reporting what she theorizes about the nature of gender; she is discussing how gender and race are constructed in society. This kind of misreading is not uncommon among students and scholars carelessly encountering discussions of social construction.

Part of the powerblind strategy is to ignore sentences on the same and next page that would demonstrate to readers that the critics' interpretation of Collins is false. Collins indicates that "expressions of gender and race are both socially constructed" (1991, 28), and notes that "women do share common experiences" (1991, 27, the latter quoted in West and Fenstermaker, 1995, 16). "Expressions" and "experiences" are *not* biological criteria inherent to each sex. In addition, focused on denigrating Collins's claims about gender, the critics tend to neglect her claims about race, failing to include the citation to Patterson or to explain Patterson's argument, which would clarify the contrast Collins is making. The critics are being casual about something important. While discrediting Collins for allegedly making a feminist error, the critics miss the moral and political challenge offered by scholarship that contends with the afterlife of slavery and social death.

West and Fenstermaker's use of the representation form of the straw man fallacy is embedded in sedimented social constructions of race that link Black women to bodies and biology, and that judge their thinking as "behind the times" and self-contradictory. The critics' rhetoric reaffirms racial hierarchy.

VENTRILOQUIZING STRAW WOMEN OF COLOR

White privilege entails the ability and the propensity to criticize the intellectual production of women of color without acknowledging the power of one's own racial identity or one's own role in structures of racial subordination. White privilege allows commonplaces about concerns with race to accompany rhetorical devices that reinforce racial hierarchy. White privilege authorizes the freedom to choose when one points to the racial identities of scholars of color and when one ignores them. White privilege allows critics to racialize nonwhites without racializing whites (Moreton-Robinson 2000, 344).[2] White privilege assumes that in the segregated academies and journals where feminist scholars do their work the preponderance of readers will be white and will know little about scholarship on race, so that "authoritative" claims by white scholars about what racialized scholars say and think will appear plausible to these readers.

Deploying revanchist moves to regain white centrality in feminism while addressing audiences unfamiliar with the scholarship of women of color makes a second form of the straw person fallacy particularly significant in analyzing color-blind and powerblind discourses. Robert Talisse and Scott Aikin term this the *selection* form of the fallacy (2006). In the selection form, critics misrepresent a "generic" position by selecting a fictitious, imprecise, naïve, uninformed, or inept position of the view they wish to be seen as refuting, while implying that they are taking up and successfully refuting the best arguments.

I turn again to West and Fenstermaker's "Doing Difference" (1995), which provides many examples of the selection form of the straw person fallacy. The article as a whole promotes ethnomethodology to redress what the critics allege to be a lack of unity and quality of various metaphors and methods for multidimensional theorizing that appear in an introductory survey anthology.[3] The vast number of citations to West and Fenstermaker's article and its reprints indicates that apparently the critics have been successful in conveying the impression to audiences unfamiliar with racial studies that they have effectively refuted the best arguments about intersectionality and created a significantly more sophisticated notion of multidimensionality. Although arguments about the simultaneous experiencing of gender, race, and class had been commonplace in scholarship by women of color for several decades, the text ultimately presents itself as discovering this simultaneity and has been widely cited in that regard.

In this discourse situation, the critics "ventriloquize" arguments of racialized others that they falsely present as "typical" generic positions. In colorblind and powerblind discourses, the act of false refutation may well be less significant than the rhetorical device of broadcasting weak arguments *as if they were the best arguments*—disseminating caricatures of what Black scholars think or what women of color would say. Selecting weak arguments for refutation—including arguments already refuted by the very texts by intersectional scholars cited in the article—gives the impression that arguments by and about race and intersectional thinking by women of color are generally unintelligent and can be easily quashed and surpassed by white scholars.

Talisse and Aikin argue that the selection form of the straw person fallacy *depends on* and *perpetuates* the ignorance of its audience (2006). Like the representation form, the selection form succeeds when audiences are unfamiliar with the specific arguments of racialized scholars and fail to explore them further. Audiences have no reason not to be satisfied with the information they receive from "authoritative" sources whose articles appear in highly ranked, peer-reviewed scholarly journals. Audiences assume that critics are vetted to ensure that they counter the strongest arguments available. When only weak arguments are presented, audiences unfamiliar with scholarship on race assume that there are no stronger arguments available. Talisse and Aikin argue that the selection form of the fallacy "is vicious because it is posited on a misrepresentation of the variety and relative quality of one's opposition. . . . When it succeeds, it convinces one's audience not only of the correctness of one's view, but also of the absence of reasoned and intelligent opposition to it" (2006, 347, 351). According to Talisse and Aikin, correcting the selection form of the fallacy requires audiences to come to understand the larger discourses that critics purport to be representing accurately. Particularly when critics use rhetorical devices to appear to be "even-handed" or "friendly" to these positions, the selection form of the straw person fallacy can serve to reestablish in a new and especially strong context the notion that women of color are cognitively inferior.

I focus here on a series of questions posed in "Doing Difference" that assume that the "theoretical implications" of intersectionality require or logically lead to a desire to count, hierarchize, or calculate relationships among categories. The critics' line of argument engages with the introduction to Margaret Andersen and Patricia Hill Collins's anthology (1992a). West and Fenstermaker's questions are embedded in the rhetoric of the first-person plural ("we"), presenting a false scene of "collaborative thinking" that serves to camouflage the degree to which the critics' argument relies on both representation and selection forms of the straw person fallacy. Used this way, the first-person plural—used previously to fold together white feminists and women of color—initially presents as plausible and jointly held what is actually a *false* position, a position actually held by *neither* the critics *nor* the intersectional scholars they cite.

Two important argumentative problems are entwined in this and following passages: one involving the accurate attribution of claims, the other involving the correct definition of "theoretical implications." The form of misattribution in this text silently replaces the best scholarly arguments about intersectional analysis with general political positions of the type found in political commentary and blogs. The shortcut of substituting general positions for the specific positions of scholars presents "what women of color must be thinking" as less flexible, farseeing, and complex than what the white scholars authoring the article are thinking. Evidence that would refute such a position—such as passages in the critics' cited primary source texts on intersectional thinking (for example, Andersen and Collins 1992a; P. Collins 1991) that demonstrate more care and complex thinking than the critics— are interpreted simplistically or simply not acknowledged. In consequence, theoretical development of scholarly ideas in feminist studies is truncated because critics are refuting "straw positions" rather than the *actual* positions of those they criticize, reinforcing the notion that white critics can easily dismiss the limited thinking of scholars of color.

In "Doing Difference," two general questions are presented without grounding as if they were "theoretical implications" specific to theorizing through the metaphor of the "intersection": (1) Will people "count" and "rank" number and "quantity" of oppressions? (2) Will people assume that groups will "bond" if both have the same number of categories of oppression? First, these are *questions,* not "implications." Second, they are *not* "implications" of the metaphor of "intersection."[4] They are not suggested, tied to, or implied by the term "intersection." They do not demonstrate a possible *result* or *consequence* or *entailment* or *implication* of thinking *intersectionally.* They are, rather, simply fabricated political and intellectual questions that might emerge in *any* discussion of multiple oppressions. In fact, thinking "intersectionally"—in terms of *both/and* rather than *either/or*—as intersectional feminists of color have done, works precisely to loosen the traction of such questions.

The critics advance their claims through a pattern of specific moves. They gesture toward a comment or quotation apparently by a racialized scholar, pose a question as if it emerged in the comment or in consequence of it, provide a naïve or unsophisticated answer to the question they have posed as if the answer represents the commonly held position of these raced scholars, and then finally reveal as faulty the fictitious unsophisticated answer they have supplied to the fictitious unsophisticated question they have fabricated. The critics then "solidify" their correction of the fictitious misreading by pulling the words of another racialized scholar out of context to imply that she is supporting their criticism.

For example, in one case, West and Fenstermaker appear to echo Andersen and Collins, who have argued that multiple oppressions interrelate in life experiences. West and Fenstermaker ask:

> What conclusions shall we draw from comparisons between persons who are said to suffer oppression "at the intersection" of all three systems and those who suffer in the nexus of only two? *Presumably, we will conclude* that the latter are "less oppressed" than the former (assuming that each categorical identity set *amasses a specific quantity of oppression*). (1995, 13, emphasis added)

The first-person plural ("Presumably, *we* will conclude") falsely presents a position held *neither* by the critics *nor* by the intersectional scholars they cite. However, since many concerned with both gender and racial oppression are women of color, readers might well assume it would be the position of a "generic" woman of color. The critics are not claiming *for themselves* what "presumably, we will conclude," because they immediately cite as authoritative a counterargument against this presumption. The implication is that the word "intersection" *compels* the "generic" woman of color to count the "specific quantity of oppression" in a category, *compels* comparisons and the ranking of oppressions, and these activities must be curbed. *None of this is the case.* Such a position is explicitly countered in Collins's *Black Feminist Thought* (1991)—also cited by the critics—which provides much more complex refutations than the critics and their selected straw persons.[5] If the intersectional scholars the critics cite did not make these arguments, who did? Why is that position voiced as if it might be found in contemporary arguments by intersectional scholars? In fact, why is it presented as a contemporary position needing refutation when such positions have long been criticized? In fact, the critics demonstrate they know the long history refuting such positions when they cite the authority of decades-old articles by racialized scholars.

For example, when considering the question of "calculation of oppressions," West and Fenstermaker rebut the naïve apparently "generic" position, or what is implied to be the position of Andersen and Collins (1992a), by turning to the words of Cherríe Moraga (1981). They argue: "Moraga warns, however, that 'the danger lies in ranking the oppressions. *The danger lies in failing to acknowledge the specificity of the oppression*'" (West and Fenstermaker 1995, 13, quoting Moraga 1981, 29, emphasis in original of Moraga).

The critics here display the familiar diorama wherein dominant whites present people of color as disciplining one another for the benefit of whites, here "staged" for ill-informed white readers. Andersen and Collins are fully aware of Moraga's argument: Moraga's 1981 article was reprinted in the first section of Andersen and Collins's anthology (1992b), a few pages after the preface that the West and Fenstermaker quote.[6] Furthermore, Moraga made this point about facets of her own identity in a specific context; the claim should not be taken out of context and presented as a universal rule closing down future argumentative options. The decontextualized "rule" that the critics attribute to Moraga is deployed here to foreclose future political and analytic choices. Such rhetorical foreclosures serve to delegitimize the important question of *which differences make a difference,* a question of great significance at the intersections of race and gender.

The rhetorical structure framing the other "troubling theoretical implication" of "intersection" is almost identical. The questions constructed by the critics echo a phrase about "simultaneous and intersecting *systems of relationship and meaning*" that the critics have previously quoted (West and Fenstermaker 1995, 12, quoting Andersen and Collins 1992a, xiii, emphasis added). The critics speculate that thinking through the metaphor of "intersection" has a "theoretical implication" that might lead to concluding that disparate groups with different but the *same number* of oppressions are eager to "bond." Once again calculation based on number rather than substance of oppression is treated as central to intersectionality when it is not. The critics ask:

> What conclusions shall we draw from potential comparisons between persons who experience oppression on the basis of their race and class (e.g., working-class men of color) and those who are oppressed on the basis of their gender and class (e.g., white working-class women)? Would the "intersection of two systems of meaning in each case be sufficient to predict common bonds among them?" Clearly not, says June Jordan: "When these factors of race, class and gender absolutely collapse is whenever you try to use them as *automatic concepts of connection*." (West and Fenstermaker 1995, 12–13, quoting Jordan 1985, 46, emphasis added here)

This point-counter-point is a fascinating construction. It presents two rather inept questions of limited theoretical and political interest rather than the strongest positions of intersectional scholars (for example, positions found in the critics' cited sources, including Andersen and Collins 1992a and P. Collins 1991). The critics provide no argument explaining why they should treat as their original contribution a refutation that appears in much more sophisticated form in the very texts they cite. The first question about quantity of oppression is not attributed. The second question—"Would the 'intersection of two systems of meaning in each case be sufficient to predict common bonds among them?'" (12–13)—is structured with quotation marks, but no source is cited; an online search finds it only in "Doing Difference" and its reprints. The question appears to be a fictional ventriloquized construction designed to implicate Andersen and Collins 1992a by repeating some of their words previously quoted ("intersecting," "systems of meaning"). As fictional constructs, the questions reinscribe the polarities of power inherent to the positions of humanitas and anthropos.

Having insinuated that the compulsion to calculate implicates the "generic" woman of color and intersectional scholars such as Andersen and Collins, the critics provide correction not in their own voices but *once again* in the voice of a woman of color. The passage manages this move by treating June Jordan as if she were involved in the same conversation, when she is not. The text frames Jordan's comment as a refutation of the question vaguely attributed to Andersen and Collins or some generic woman of color by inserting a connecting phrase, "Clearly not, says June Jordan"—as if Jordan is responding specifically to the question posed. At the scene of argument, juxtaposing the three elements—the fictional "quoted" question, the fictional connecting phrase that implies Jordan is responding to that question, and the quotation from Jordan—all work to frame Jordan as the critics' Black woman ally. But Jordan was never asked this question and is not answering it. Jordan's essay is a sustained meditation on the complexity of local and global relations among people of the same and different classes, races, and genders. In fact, Andersen and Collins are fully aware of Jordan's argument: Jordan's 1985 essay was reprinted in the first section of Andersen and Collins's anthology (1992a), only a few pages after the preface that the critics quote.[7] Once again, "correction" to Andersen and Collins is staged for naïve white audiences. Producing Jordan to counter fictional simplistic propositions treats her as a puppet being ventriloquized. The rhetorical structure of "false quotation" and "false rebuttal" serves to present as relevant not intersectional scholars' strongest arguments but arguments already refuted in the texts cited by the critics.

Like the European colonial administrators in Africa who ceded limited power to traditional leaders to rule over others, and like the settler colonialist troops in the U.S. West who recruited unassimilated but nonhostile Native Americans to work as "friendlies," the white feminist critics seek to secure their dominance yet hide their racial privilege by using the words of women of color (taken out of context) to undermine the legitimacy of other women of color. Yet unlike the European colonial administrators in Africa or the settler colonialist troops in the U.S. West, they do not even interact with the people they use as proxies. Instead, they conjure them into existence as imaginary friends of white feminism whose words are used in false ways to delegitimate positions of other women of color.

As I have demonstrated, techniques of color-blind and powerblind rhetorics in feminist critiques of intersectional analysis include incorporation, appropriation, erasure, ventriloquizing, arguing with straw persons, and adopting imaginary allies. These ways of positioning intersectional scholars appear plausible to largely white feminist audiences because they are congruent with dominant notions that racialized people are unsophisticated and simple thinkers—that "we" have theories suitable for them but "they" do not have theories adequate for us (see Lugones and Spelman 1983). These argumentative problems do not stem from feminist scholars' *intentions* but from their unacknowledged use of conventional rhetorics and arguments that are imbued with uninterrogated white racial privilege. Further, white privilege infuses and authorizes the metadiscursive regimes that frame how feminist scholars approve these critiques—vetting, editing, publishing, anthologizing, and citing as authoritative—according to what they perceive to be the shared, "color-blind" standards of feminist scholarship. Interrogating feminist metadiscursive regimes would encourage resisting the resort to straw person fallacies and easy misrepresentations that often seem plausible because they align with histories and epistemological structures of racial dominance. These moves are grounded in modernity's longstanding distinction between humanitas and anthropos, between the definers and the defined, between the subjects of knowledge and its objects. The color-blind standards that permeate feminist scholarship suggest that dominant white knowledge about gendered racial arguments is sufficient for mounting adequate critiques of intersectionality. It is not.

NEOLIBERAL ASSET-STRIPPING

Color-blind and powerblind rhetorics are used in feminist studies to erase racial specificity, to make white authors and readers feel that they are color-blind, to proclaim white innocence, to devalue the research of women of color, to hoard academic resources (honors, awards, and recognition) for white scholars who purport to supersede the work of women of color, and—significantly—to disguise the neoliberal stripping of intellectual assets from women of color. I argue here and elsewhere (Tomlinson and Lipsitz 2013a, 2013b) that hegemonic neoliberal cultural conceptions serve as a pedagogy for those inside and outside of the academy.[8]

Central to many critiques of intersectionality is the logic of asset-stripping. In one of his last publications before his untimely death, Clyde Woods (2010a) mounts a powerful explanation and critique of the asset-stripping accomplished in post-Katrina New Orleans by a neoliberal regime devoted to the rapid and systematic stripping of public assets created by the Black working class in the city. Woods explains that public housing dwellings—desperately needed because of widespread tolerance for systemic residential segregation that violates the 1968 Fair Housing Act—were torn down, their inhabitants made homeless in order to make room for state-subsidized but privately owned residential developments designed to encourage white suburban residents to move to the city. Jobs in industry, construction, and service industries—which had been open to Blacks only through collective social movement struggles—disappeared as a result of state subsidies for automation, importation of lower-wage immigrant labor, and rampant employment discrimination. A public school system that provided jobs to seven thousand Black employees—as a result of decades of battles for desegregation—was dissolved and replaced by a privatized system of charter schools that fired all of the teachers with union contracts, and placed the schools under state rather than local control.

Woods explains that those governing New Orleans presented the destruction and expropriation of public assets by private individuals not as theft but "as a form of progress that should be celebrated" (2010a, 343). According to their argument, Black spaces are devalued, so making those places "less Black" increases their value. This perverse logic uses the success of segregation as justification for continuing it. Neoliberal insistence that government's job is to serve capital at all costs valorizes open evasion of legal protections for city residents; enforcing these protections would interfere with the ability of capital to extract the maximum profit from the opportunities funneled to it. Neoliberal strategies to replace all public spaces with profit centers glorify the replacement of public education with charter schools exactly because they serve to *extract* profit from the people of New Orleans. Neoliberal efforts to "manage" New Orleans are premised on a commitment to only the goals of capital, ignoring and distancing groups that have more particular kinds of commitments and knowledge. One example is the commitments to and knowledge of the lives and needs of those in the community, found in the working-class Black women mobilized by Shana Griffin through the Women's Health and Justice Initiative (see Woods's [2010b] interview with Griffin in "The Politics" and also Luft 2010).

Key to asset-stripping are not only the unfair gains and unjust rewards taken by others but also the resulting losses to each and every one of us. Asset-stripping occludes and guarantees distance from the critiques and activism of the most sophisticated theorists of raced and gendered capitalism—that is, the people and communities who are direct witnesses to racial and sexual violence, labor market segmentation, social stratification, economic exploitation, and the reduction of humans to profit-making instruments. There is a high price paid by *all of us* for the dire lack of democracy in our society. Neoliberal assertions that all problems are best served by individualism "all the way down" are not "innocent" ways of solving problems but practices saturated by blood, theft, and power.

Woods argues that the asset-stripping of New Orleans is another moment in a long history of creating "social-spatial enclosures" (2010a, 348) in which (often racialized) populations create wealth not for their own benefit but for extraction and use by others. He argues that the boundaries of these enclosures are defended in a variety of ways, but not least through "a representational system that provides intellectual justification for, and naturalizes, this form of social conflict" (348). He argues, "Increasingly, asset-stripping has been examined as a key pillar of neoliberalism" (349).

I argue that intersectional theorizing is treated by many "color-blind" critics as a potentially valuable "profit center," but one that—like the Black spaces in New Orleans—is devalued by its origins in the thought of Black feminists. Subsuming the intellectual legacy of the feminism of women of color into a "unified," nonraced feminism removes intersectional thinking from the sphere of its creators and its important work as a tool in antisubordination struggles. The result is to extract from Black women the intellectual and cultural capital they created through the uniquely generative analytic possibilities of the concept of intersectionality for the benefit of others who feel themselves more deserving. *We all lose from their asset-stripping.*

THE VISE OF GEOMETRY

In Chapter 1, I argue that powerblind discourses disparaging intersectionality provide an enduring and visible manifestation of the moment in the mid-1990s when white women perceived that they were losing control of feminism. As the universal category of "woman" around which the field initially cohered became complicated by women of color critiques that exposed the uneven dynamics of social difference (see Hemmings 2011), a white feminist revanchism turned consistently to a small set of discursive moves at the scene of argument in an attempt to reclaim white women's centrality in feminism. These moves pervade feminist scholarship to this day. They continue to frame the field as they are relentlessly reproduced through quotation, citation, and replication. This chapter identifies and analyzes strategies and moves that function to reinforce white women's symbolic domination of the field.

I demonstrate these dynamics in this chapter through analysis of two separate but related powerblind critiques from the mid-1990s—"Doing Difference" by Candace West and Sarah Fenstermaker (1995) and "Me, Myself, and I" by Kath Weston (1996a). Both critiques resolutely protect racial hierarchy by reinscribing the dominance of white women in feminism. Both use powerblind strategies to construct a distinction and distance between themselves—privileged white feminist knowers—and those designated as their objects of criticism: women of color feminists. Both texts arrogate to themselves authority for the proper interpretation of theories, categories, and metaphors produced by women of color, dismissing the originators as rationally and ontologically deficient. As I mentioned in Chapter 3, both texts devote much attention to decontextualized discussions of the metaphor of intersectionality itself, disparaging it for its alleged "geometric origins." This focus on geometry, I argue, is a placeholder for gestures serving other ends, particularly to empower and authorize versions of feminism that evade structural power.

Both texts present arguments that are structured in dominance. They evidence no self-reflexive awareness of the problems that might emerge from the assumption that white critics are fully competent to dismiss the language, embodied experience, and analytic heuristics proposed by women of color. They do not acknowledge the asymmetry that results from treating their own criteria for evaluating terms and ideas as transparent and self-evident, as not requiring justification, while overlooking the criteria and justifications used by intersectional scholars. The critics subject the language of intersectional scholars to scrutiny using standards that they do not apply to their own language and claims. The arguments made in these texts are *not accurate*: they are suffused with radical decontextualization, misrepresentation, and misattribution, all of which are central moves in discourses of dominance. The arguments are *not dialogic*: they fail to acknowledge and respond precisely to what intersectional scholars have argued. On occasion, they even present intersectional scholars' positions as their own discoveries. The critics' arguments and textual strategies resonate with the techniques central to what Sirma Bilge sums up as the project to "whiten intersectionality": to engage in "genealogical and disciplinary whitening and the erasure of race through denial, reductionism and disassociation" (2014, 176).

Both critiques rely on what I call "rhetorics of rejection and replacement."[1] They reject intersectionality and propose to replace it with their own preferred research method: ethnomethodology in the case of West and Fenstermaker, narrative analysis in the case of Weston. The arguments made by West and Fenstermaker—and their warm reception by subsequent feminist scholars—produce a story that identifies intersectionality in feminist scholarship as successful when shaped as the production of white women. The arguments made by Weston celebrate the infinite difference of the individual at the expense of analyses that explain how difference is structured in dominance. Both texts could have made arguments in favor of the critics' preferred methods without mentioning intersectionality at all, yet the critics and those who approvingly cite and quote them seem less concerned with what their arguments *produce* than what they *prevent*: a feminism that embraces women of color critique and advances its social justice mission on the basis of it.

Significantly, both texts demonstrate egregious errors of attribution and citation. West and Fenstermaker create straw positions and then attribute them to intersectional thinkers. They pass off as their own invention the concept of simultaneity and caution against ranking oppressions, arguments that had long been articulated by intersectional theorists of color. West and Fenstermaker not only fail to acknowledge that the positions they present as new had long been commonplace in intersectional writing; they actually present their gloss on these ideas as a corrective to intersectionality's purported flaws. Weston provides no citations to verify the accuracy of her vigorous critical claims about the nature of intersectionality. These texts emerged at a particular point in time, but they exert continuing effects on the field through a politically inflected politics of citation. The positions articulated by West and Fenstermaker and Weston have been reiterated repeatedly in feminist scholarship, generally without criticism. The constant repetition and reinscription of these powerblind discourses frames the centrality of white feminism in intersectional thinking as taken-for-granted, with inevitable political impact.

DOING DOMINATION BY DOING DIFFERENCE

In "Doing Difference," West and Fenstermaker (1995) argue that understanding the multidimensional relations of gender, race, and class can be best achieved through the procedures of ethnomethodology (see Collins et al. 1995; Marshall 1998a; Mehan and Wood 1983).[2] (As I indicated when discussing it in Chapter 4, there are nearly 2,000 citations in Google Scholar to this journal article, and some 870 to its reprints as of May 10, 2018.) The authors propose widespread adoption of ethnomethodology in order to counter what they consider to be feminists' tendency to frame multidimensionality through inadequate mathematical metaphors such as "addition" and geometrical metaphors such as "intersectional" and "interlocking."[3] Despite what I would call the terms' strong "family resemblance" (Wittgenstein 1953), the critics represent the metaphors as "confusingly" disparate.[4] The critics recommend that feminists turn to ethnomethodology for its ability to reveal the "actual mechanisms that produce social inequality" (West and Fenstermaker 1995, 13). However, they do not employ the method they recommend in this article because to do so would undercut the powerblindness that pervades the piece. Approaching the topic of intersectionality through ethnomethodology would require the authors to cede authority to those they wish to criticize, to examine how women of color use the conceptions of intersectionality that they have constructed to make sense of their social world and daily lives. The methods of ethnomethodology would require that the meaning of terms such as intersectionality would then be ascertained in reference to other words and contexts, rather than through the decontextualized claims that West and Fenstermaker adopt.

West and Fenstermaker present a critique of mathematical and geometrical metaphors for multidimensionality in a way that seems oddly blind to gender as well as to racial dynamics. They argue that gender stereotypes portray mathematics as "unfeminine." According to their argument:

> Few persons think of math as a particularly *feminine* pursuit. *Girls are not supposed to be good at it and women are not supposed to enjoy it.* It is interesting, then, that *we who do feminist scholarship* have relied so heavily on mathematical metaphors to describe the relationships among gender, race, and class. (1995, 8, emphasis added)

It is a bit puzzling to find two feminist scholars setting up their argument through reference to demeaning gendered stereotypes as if they were valid reasons for curtailing women's thinking. Their position is particularly puzzling given the contemporaneous criticism of such sexist stereotypes and as well as the critics' own overwhelming evidence that women *have* used mathematical language for scholarly purposes.[5] The text does not subsequently repudiate its use of this criterion nor signal that its repetition of sexist stereotypes is meant to be a joke; it has not been treated as a humorous comment by subsequent scholars.[6] This opening gesture in the text creates a shared gendered subject position gesturing toward female phobic affect about mathematics and geometry.[7] Given the absence of a definition or explanation of geometry elsewhere in the article, this introduction of the pressure of sexist stereotypes appears to be the critics' only justification for declaring geometry off-limits to feminists *by fiat.*

The authors go on to state:

> Some of us have drawn on basic arithmetic, adding, subtracting, and dividing what we know about race and class to what we *already know* about gender. Some have relied on multiplication, seeming to *calculate the effects* of the whole from the combination of different parts. And others have employed geometry, drawing on images of interlocking or intersecting planes and axes. (West and Fenstermaker 1995, 8, emphasis added)

The critics here are constructing a false equivalence between "mathematical" metaphors and the "geometric" metaphors that superseded them, obscuring what should be a sharp distinction: "additive" metaphors were generally used by white feminists to "add" race or sexuality to what they "already knew" about their primary category of gender subordination; "multiplicative" metaphors were generally used by women of color or others to emphasize experiences with multiple categories of subordination. Both types of "mathematical" metaphors were superseded by "geometric" metaphors as a result of persuasive arguments, primarily by women of color feminists, that gender, race, class, and other categories worked together simultaneously (for example, P. Collins 1991; Crenshaw 1989, 1991; Glenn 1985, 2002; Lowe 1991, 1996; Rodríguez 2003; Sandoval 1991, 2000). Previous critiques of additive metaphors—such as that of Elizabeth V. Spelman (1988)—argue that the problem of additive metaphors is one of *conception:* additive metaphors misconceive the interrelationship of the constitutive categories. In contrast, West and Fenstermaker present the problem of additive and multiplicative metaphors as one of *calculation,* in effect asserting that the goal of feminist scholars of multidimensionality is to measure and rank and calculate the effects of various proportions and types of gender, race, and class. So tenacious is their picture of calculating scholars that they assume—against available evidence cited in their own text—that a desire to calculate oppressions compels intersectional thinkers to count and rank both the number and quantity of oppressions. That this argument is "staged" for white scholars is evident because the charge is clearly refuted by the very texts that the critics use as primary sources on geometric metaphors (Andersen and Collins 1992a; P. Collins 1991), which *explicitly reject* models of calculation. Despite this, West and Fenstermaker foster the notion, now widespread in critiques of intersectionality and apparently accepted as "true" by many feminist scholars, that intersectional scholars relied on geometry and as a result framed categories as "fixed" and "static" (calculable): *exactly the opposite* of the position of their sources. (Arguments countering other variations on this dynamic are found in Carbado 2013 and May 2014, 2015; see also Hancock 2016).

West and Fenstermaker simply ignore arguments that refute their position, arguments that were previously published and evident in their reference list, including P. Collins 1991, a text they cite and quote. For example, the compulsion to count that West and Fenstermaker deride assumes interchangeability, yet according to Collins (1991), "adhering to a both/and conceptual stance does not mean that race, class, and gender oppression are interchangeable" (226). Collins argues that attention should be focused on how variables *interconnect,* how each system needs the others in order to function as "part of one overarching structure of domination" (222). She continues, commenting that "Embracing a both/and conceptual stance moves us from additive, separate systems approaches to oppression and toward what I now see as the more fundamental issue of the social relations of domination" (226). Collins points out, "By embracing a paradigm of race, class, and gender as interlocking systems of oppression, Black feminist thought reconceptualizes the social relations of domination and resistance. . . . Assuming that each system needs the others in order to function creates a distinct theoretical stance that stimulates the rethinking of basic social science concepts" (222). Thus a text that West and

Fenstermaker cite as deficient and position themselves as "correcting" already contains the very critique they make of it, a critique that they present as their own invention.

Intersection

In a critique saturated with metaphor anxiety, West and Fenstermaker adopt the powerblind strategy of decontextualizing and reifying the metaphor of intersectionality. They treat the term "intersection" as bound to geometric entailments that they frame as literal rather than metaphorical. Opening their critique of the term "intersection," West and Fenstermaker argue: "Geometrical metaphors further complicate things, *since we still need to know* where those planes and axes go after they cross the intersection (if they are parallel planes and axes, they will never intersect at all)" (9, emphasis added). Why would scholars "still need to know" this? There is no evidence that the critics intend this baseless claim to be a witty little joke or that subsequent readers have interpreted it as such. Yet the claim dismisses a hermeneutic device designed to illuminate the deployment of power in concrete social and historical situations because it does not account for all the features of a perfect map of an imaginary physical universe.

This is a more complicated argumentative move than it may seem. The claim treats the "geometric" metaphor *not as a metaphor* but as a literal use of language that can be discredited unless it accounts for all things geometrical, providing a full global spatial map of an imaginary "geometric" world: intersections and nonintersections, tracing edges and lines everywhere. How far must intersectional analysts trace those lines beyond the intersection—to the edge of the city, the nation-state, the globe, the universe? Why would a metaphor focused on intersecting axes or planes fail because not all potential axes intersect? Why should scholars of gender, race, and class abandon their focus on significant social power to extrapolate lines, planes, and spaces that are not of theoretical interest? Why should feminist antiracist scholars need to become geometers when their actual goal is to deploy metaphors that can provide insight into social relations and structures of power?

Do *all* scholarly fields—or only feminism—require that those who use geometric metaphors become geometers, that those who use geological metaphors (stratification, say) become geologists? Do sociologists eschew the use of "stratification" because the metaphor of geological stratification does not perfectly map onto social hierarchies? Are all metaphors that have been used in sociology "tested" for their literal entailments? If so, why is this not evident in the many discussions of metaphor in the social sciences (such as R. Brown 1977)? Or is this rule specific to feminist studies? How would feminist scholarship benefit from such a rule? Where is it taught? Or is it to be used simply as a tool for suppressing and silencing nonwhite feminist analyses? If this is simply a de-authorizing gesture, a "secret rule" created ad hoc to discredit intersectional theorizing, what are the consequences for feminist studies of allowing scholars to enact subordination by promulgating idiosyncratic standards that are repeatedly cited as authoritative? What are the consequences for feminist studies of failing to interrogate its powerblind discursive practices that legitimate such manifestly inappropriate criteria of evaluation in order to discredit the theorizing of women of color?

Interlocking

West and Fenstermaker's reliance on powerblind critique also leads them astray as they complete their rejection of the metaphor of "intersecting" by championing a variant of the metaphor of "interlocking." Their argument is already in a state of crisis because it has neglected to define geometry; it has neglected to explain why geometry should not serve as a source of metaphors about social life; and, to this point, it has failed to provide adequate evidence that geometric metaphors are deficient. Rather than abandon or modify the critique of geometric metaphors, however, the text (without explanation or justification) unaccountably turns to use several geometric metaphors for its *own* purposes, quarantining them from critique by framing them as something *other than* geometrical.

For example, the critics claim they do not approve of the metaphor of "interlocking" generally, but indicate that thinking about the term inspires them to offer a new metaphor that they present as their own invention: "interlocking rings."

> The image of interlocking rings comes to mind, linked in such a way that the motion of any one of them is constrained by the others. Certainly, this image is *more dynamic* than those conveyed by *additive, multiplicative, or geometric models:* we can see where the rings are joined (and where they are not), as well as how the movement of any one of them would be restricted by the others, but note that this image still depicts the rings as separate parts. (West and Fenstermaker 1995, 13, emphasis added)

The text's proposed metaphor demonstrates all the problems of extracting metaphors and terms from arguments in the process of *rejection and replacement.* Words are not microcosms of research enterprises: an image considered "dynamic," for example, is not a guarantee of "dynamic" thinking. Nor does a metaphor or word taken out of context suggest how scholars would actually use it. Ethnomethodologists, of all people, should know this, since indexicality is central to ethnomethodology (see Mehan and Wood 1983). Indexicality emphasizes that the meaning of an expression is tied to a particular context. The crucial questions should be: How would the metaphor be to think with? What does it enable? What does it reveal or hide? What does it convey, how, and for what purpose? As is so often the case, West and Fenstermaker's *rhetorics of rejection and replacement* do not explain the consequences of their proposed replacement for intersectionality: what results is more like *reject and fantasize.*

Proffering "interlocking rings" as if the image overcomes the vise of geometry demonstrates the crisis in the text's critique. This crisis emerges in part because the authors have built their arguments on undefined, vaguely implied stereotypes of exercises in elementary school textbooks that they project as making geometric metaphors "static." This is both inaccurate and deeply anti-intellectual. The reiteration of this position through the text's subsequent citation and its mention in literature reviews of intersectionality reveals that this assumption is not an individual problem but rather a failure at the heart of feminist discursive practice—a willingness to shut down inquiry based on stereotype rather than argument. Yet an understanding of geometry that goes beyond elementary-school textbook exercises would have saved this critique from collapse and strengthened its ability to contribute to, rather than undermine, critical feminist inquiry. Geometry is simply a branch of mathematics that deals with points, lines, angles, circles, spheres, surfaces, topological spaces, and solids. It is a human construction emerging from and connected to historical, cultural, social, and political contexts. It offers a myriad of productive ways of thinking that could be helpful for understanding social life (for particularly fascinating and generative takes on this, see the video *Not Knot* 1991; Taimina 2009; and Wertheim 2006).[8]

In praising their own image of "interlocking rings" as superior to intersectional thinking, West and Fenstermaker frame the image of interlocking rings as outside and beyond the vise of geometry and claim specifically that the rings are "more dynamic than [the images] conveyed by additive, multiplicative, or geometric models" (1995, 13, emphasis added). However, rather than being beyond or outside the vise of geometry, this model of interlocking rings is, in fact, a rather famous geometric model called a "Borromean ring" (Wertheim 2006).[9] The name of the three-ringed link stems from its addition to the crest of the Italian family of Borromeo in the fourteenth century. But the figure has a long symbolic history in Western and non-Western cultures, including its recent use by Jacques Lacan (Wertheim 2006). This history implies that, depending on one's analytic goals, geometric metaphors can indeed be good to think with. At the scene of argument, to frame Borromean rings as "more dynamic" than "additive, multiplicative, or geometric models" is to attempt to insulate the critics' own *geometric* image from the critique of the vise of geometry by claiming it is "*non-geometric.*" This gesture demonstrates that West and Fenstermaker's critique of the vise of geometry has already collapsed.

Venn Diagrams

While West and Fenstermaker praise the dynamism of the Borromean rings, they recognize that the image cannot be translated easily into an accessible tool for generating research on the multidimensionality of gender, race, and class. Desiring to develop such a tool, they attempt to "flatten" the three dimensions of the "dynamic" Borromean rings into two dimensions, producing a Venn diagram. The critics eventually treat Venn diagrams as being able to escape the vise of geometry, but it is difficult to see how this could be the case. Venn diagrams use geometric forms (usually overlapping circles) to show collections of mathematical elements (sets) and what those elements have in common. These familiar pedagogical analytic diagrams are both mathematical (using set theory) and geometric (using the geometric object of closed curves or circles). In Venn diagrams, the "background" screen is called the "universe"; the area where all of the circles *combine* is called the "union"; the area where the circles *overlap* is called the "*intersection.*" Thus any use of a Venn diagram is actually *an intersectional analysis* illustrated through geometric figures.

"Doing Difference" presents two different Venn diagrams, the first apparently clamped in the vise of geometry, and the second apparently not. This differential framing of the two diagrams turns out to have profound implications for political goals specific to the text and for the authors' agenda for feminist scholarship. The first Venn diagram presented in the text declares the universe of concern to be "oppressed people." The circles within the "universe" of "oppressed people" then represent sets of people categorized as oppressed in different ways—by gender, by race, by class—with the overlap of the circles revealing the relationships among the sets of oppressed people (1995, 14, fig. 1). The critics comment on the first diagram: "This [diagram] allows us to situate women and men of all races and classes within the areas covered by the circles, *save for white middle- and upper-class men, who fall outside them*" (1995, 13, emphasis added).

Something is allegedly wrong with the first diagram (but whatever is wrong can apparently be solved in constructing the second diagram). In the first Venn diagram, "white middle- and upper-class men" appear to "belong nowhere"; they do not have a defining circle, so the critics just tuck them randomly into the "background" screen. This is not a "geometric" problem or a conceptual problem inherent to analyzing oppression, but a problem of the critics' *incorrect execution of the diagram*. According to the rules for constructing Venn diagrams, if the universe of concern is oppressed people, then the groups of people represented in the circles *must include only oppressed people*. Those who are not defined as "oppressed people" do not belong in the diagram at all.

The critics imply that the problem of the first Venn diagram is an issue of geometry, but it is not. It is an issue of skill or competence in diagram construction. But it also appears to be an issue of politics: West and Fenstermaker's second diagram solves what appears to be a political problem presented by the first, for the critics' solution to the problem of the Venn diagram is to change the entire subject of the analysis—the "universe"—from "oppressed people" to "experience." They suggest: "However, what if we conceive of the whole as 'experience' and of the rings as gender, race, and class?" (1995, 13).

To solve the flaw that the critics claim to have identified in the first diagram, the second Venn diagram makes no alteration in its geometric form.[10] It simply establishes a different "universe" that will account for all people, both oppressed and privileged. The circles within this universe then, represent sets of people categorized according to different forms of experience ("gender," "race," "class"); the area where different circles overlap reveals the relationships among the sets of people classified by gender, race, and class. In the second diagram, the *entire population* falls in the overlapping area. *No one is "left out."* The critics here are substituting a map of experience for a map of the effects of power. A reasonable inference (made by one citer)[11] is that "the problem" with the first diagram is that it fails to account for *all people*, by "leaving out" "white middle- and upper-class men."

West and Fenstermaker's move to shift the universe of the diagram from "oppression" to "experience" is a symptomatic move to shift and make "universal"—and in the process weaken—a frame established to reveal oppression. This move has significant political implications. It clarifies that thinking in terms of oppressed people leaves one caught in the vise of geometry, while de-linking from oppression allows a claim for theoretical and political universality. The critics appear unaware of arguments suggesting that "experience" is insufficiently attentive to structures of power, as is foregrounding "difference": Patricia Hill Collins argues that this is "a difference that didn't make any difference at all" (Collins et al. 1995, 493, quoting Hall 1992, 23).[12]

Appropriating the Discovery of Simultaneity

Having constructed the second Venn diagram so that the entire population of all people falls in the overlapping area, West and Fenstermaker construct a dramatically powerblind claim that has proved pivotal for the text's politics of citation and is particularly revealing about how feminist discursive practices reinscribe racial inclusion and exclusion. The authors claim:

> Here, *we face an illuminating possibility* and leave arithmetic behind: no person can *experience gender* without *simultaneously* experiencing race and class. As Andersen and Collins put it, "While race, class and gender can be seen as different axes of social structure, *individual persons experience them simultaneously.*" (1995, 13, emphasis added, quoting Andersen and Collins 1992a, xxi)

What do the critics mean when they claim, "Here, *we* face an illuminating possibility"? The Venn diagram was constructed by a method that made its results a foregone conclusion, so in that sense, nothing is "illuminated." A generous reading would be that "we" in this sentence specifically means the critics themselves, expressing pleasure at having finished their diagram. The claim that "no person can experience gender without simultaneously experiencing race and class"—and all of the permutations of simultaneous multidimensionality—is by no means a new "discovery" made by the critics; careful reading of the sentence reveals that it uses a quotation from Margaret L. Andersen and Patricia Hill Collins's text (1992a) to substantiate the critics' "discovery."

West and Fenstermaker undertake a prodigious rhetorical task across two pages: first admitting that previous work has theorized simultaneity, then admitting that such work might be useful, then denigrating that work in order to declare a "newer better" simultaneity as their own discovery (12–13). The critics begin by quoting a brief phrase from Andersen and Collins about "simultaneous and intersecting systems of relationship and meaning" (12, quoting from 1992a, xiii). They grant that thinking in terms of "simultaneous and intersecting systems of relationship and meaning" might be useful if one thinks oppression occurs "only" through "categories," but they claim that it is untenable if one "conceives of the basis of oppression as more than membership in a category" (12). The critics do not explain what they mean by such a conception of oppression, nor do they offer any evidence that Andersen and Collins or other intersectional scholars of color have claimed that all oppression is limited to membership in a category. Instead, the critics immediately lapse into assuming that these conceptions of simultaneity promote the same compulsion to calculate that they have already attributed to additive models, ridiculing them accordingly. West and Fenstermaker conclude this sequence of moves by announcing their own "discovery" of simultaneity.

These rhetorical strategies are suffused with powerblindness. The powerblind white critics, speaking to a largely white audience unfamiliar with critical scholarship on race, conceal from their audience the long history of political and scholarly conceptions of simultaneity produced by women of color. West and Fenstermaker fail to reveal to their audience passages from the very intersectional scholars they cite that would demonstrate that their own argument merely repeats rather than discovers simultaneity. For example, the full sentence from which the critics drew the quotation of "simultaneous and intersecting systems of relationship and meaning" demonstrates that simultaneity is already fully discussed by Andersen and Collins, who argue: "Once we understand that race, class, and gender are simultaneous and intersecting systems of meaning, we come to see the different ways that other categories of experience intersect in society" (1992a, xiii).

The critics also cite Collins's *Black Feminist Thought* (1991) without informing their audience of Collins's extensive discussions of simultaneity there, such as this:

> Viewing the world through *a both/and conceptual lens of the simultaneity of race, class, and gender oppression* and of the need for a humanist vision of community creates new possibilities for an empowering Afrocentric feminist knowledge. Many Black feminist intellectuals have long thought about the world in this way because this is the way we experience the world. (P. Collins 1991, 221–222, emphasis added)

Nor do West and Fenstermaker inform their audience that most of the intersectional scholars of color cited in their reference list have *already* argued that simultaneous co-constitutive categories are in play,[13] such as Aída Hurtado, who asserts: "White feminist theory has yet to integrate the facts that for women of Color, race, class, and gender subordination are experienced simultaneously" (1989, 839). Simultaneity has been central to the theorizing of Black feminist scholars and other women of color not just for decades, but for centuries. How can the simultaneity of categories in experience emerge in "Doing Difference" as "an illuminating possibility" when it already, for many years, had been a firmly established position presented in numerous arguments by scholars who were women of color? Because powerblind discourses allow the critics to hide this history of conceptual thought generated by women of color.

"Doing Difference" has been widely cited as announcing *the authors' own original discovery of simultaneity,* replacing the "static conceptions" and "fixed notions of categories" said to be proposed by previous intersectional scholars.[14] This politics of citation requires some explanation, since the quotation of Andersen and Collins, presented as support for the critics' "illumination," in fact precedes the critics' argument and establishes the theoretical basis for their claim. Since scholars of color working on the intersection of race, gender, and class would find nothing "illuminating" about West and Fenstermaker's reiteration of very old news, it would appear that the "illuminating credit for discovery" is aimed at uninformed white scholars—and has been very successful as a strategy of racial subordination and appropriation. Subsequent citers portray as the discovery of West and Fenstermaker what is actually a position developed previously by numerous scholars of color. West and Fenstermaker further reveal their agenda of appropriation and asset-stripping by casual and inaccurate denigration of the work of previous scholars of multidimensionality, whom they fold into a racially unmarked yet markedly inept feminist sociology:

> It is this simultaneity that has *eluded our theoretical treatments* and is so difficult to build into *our empirical descriptions*. . . . Capturing it *compels us* to focus on the actual mechanisms that produce social inequality. How do forms of inequality, *which we now see are more than the periodic collision of categories,* operate together? How do we see that all social exchanges, regardless of the participants or the outcome, are simultaneously "gendered," "raced," and "classed"? (1995, 13, emphasis added)

The critics' stirring rhetoric encourages the impression that it is they who have discovered simultaneity, as if those who discussed simultaneity previously actually did not see categories as intermeshed but merely "periodically colliding" (similar dynamics of misrepresentation in other critiques are analyzed by Bilge 2013, 2014; Cho 2013; May 2014, 2015). The critics present themselves as authoritative judges about what has been lacking and what their own new discovery will enable. Despite evidence in the text itself that the critics are building on previous work by scholars of color, for many ill-informed white audiences their condemnation of the vise of geometry serves to establish the inadequacy of the theorizing of women of color and reposition the "discovery" that categories operate simultaneously as the intellectual work of white feminists. This is a powerblind discourse of dominance subordinating the intellectual labor of women of color and appropriating it for white feminists. María Lugones and Elizabeth V. Spelman identified some important aspects of this dynamic in their aptly titled article, "Have We Got a Theory for You!" (1983). The actions of West and Fenstermaker suggest a similar but dynamic new claim: "Have we got your theory for ourselves!"

RENDER US INDIVIDUALS

In *Render Me, Gender Me: Lesbians Talk Sex, Class, Color, Nation, Studmuffins
. . .* (1996b), Kath Weston indicates that she wishes to "complicate contemporary discussions of gender" (2) based on narratives obtained in the late 1980s in the San Francisco Bay Area from forty women who identified as lesbian. Desiring to be accessible to a variety of readers, Weston eschews footnotes and other scholarly apparatuses, though she does include a bibliography.[15] Weston could have explicitly acknowledged that hers is actually an intersectional analysis (focusing on lesbian sexuality and sociality, but including considerations of race, class, and other categories). Instead, Weston seeks inclusion and legitimation for LGBT experiences and perspectives by an unnecessary and counterproductive argumentative gesture that excludes and delegitimates intersectionality. She establishes the "independence" of her own intersectional analysis and seeks to protect the dominance of white feminism by treating the theoretical tools of women of color as a rhetorical foil, a "fantasy opponent." (See Chapter 8 for a more recent use of a similar strategy.)

Geometric Rigidity

Like West and Fenstermaker, Weston deploys powerblind arguments condemning the vise of geometry to distort intersectionality, in her case in a chapter aptly titled "Me, Myself, and I" (1996a [which was reprinted in Taylor et al. 2011]). (There are some seventy citations in Google Scholar to Weston's book, and nineteen to the chapter reprinted in Taylor et al. 2011, as of May 10, 2018.) Weston condemns intersectional thinking as imposing a rigid geometric regulatory force, limiting the flexibility that she desires for herself and for her narrative protagonists. Her argument forcefully refutes *not* actual concepts of intersectionality but rather simplistic images of a regulative intersectionality bound to stereotypes of elementary-school textbook exercises in "geometry." Weston argues that "the intersections model portrays all axes as equivalent, all lines coming together, all of the time" (126). She goes on to scoff that "identities do not simply meet at some mythical point of intersection" (142) and claims that an intersection implies a "geometric point where all identities meet" as well as "preassembled axes of race or class, each defined in isolation and coming together after the fact" (145). Weston has fabricated a rigid model of intersectionality that can be dismissed because it cannot cope with even the most minimal adjustments of "real life"; if there are complications, "so much for a nice neat meeting point of all those lines" (126).

This decontextualized "intersectionality" is radically removed from the originating conceptions of intersectionality and bears not the slightest resemblance to the arguments of intersectional scholars listed in Weston's bibliogra-phy.[16] For these scholars the creation and recreation of categories are socially constructed (therefore by definition *not* "fixed" or "regulated," but socially and historically contingent and in a constant process of change).

The regulatory rules of the vise of geometry—clamping down and pre-cluding recognition of individuals and their complexities—are fantasies with powerful effects at the scene of argument and echoed in the politics of cita-tion (see Taylor 2011). Intersectionality, with its imputed vise of geometry, is framed as limiting the critic's freedom of method and her subjects' freedom of complex expression. Weston recruits her readers into seeing intersectionality as a threat to their own freedom, repressing their own bodies. She addresses readers directly in the second person ("you") in arguing, "Think . . . back to geometry class, when an intersection named the point where two or more lines meet. . . . [T]his time the drawing isn't done on graph paper. *This time your body occupies the point where all those lines meet*" (Weston 1996a, 125–126, emphasis added). Weston here exploits as real and necessary what Foucault has argued to be a false rebellion that is structured in dominance (1980a); it presumes that the individual needs to be "free" (rather than acknowledging that currents run through individuals). Foucault argues that individuals' de-sire to free themselves from *repression that is actually mythical* is one of the most powerful culturally structured motivations for subjects in the West. Through the vise of geometry, Weston constructs intersectionality as a figure of such re-pression. Given intersectionality's origins in the theorizing of women of color, this discursive move participates in a long history of discourses in which white people present assertions of subjectivity by nonwhite people as oppressive and dictatorial (see Glass 2012; Haney López 2014; Harper 2012; Peterson 1998).

Like West and Fenstermaker, contra the arguments of intersectional schol-ars such as Patricia Hill Collins (1991) and Kimberlé Crenshaw (1989, 1991), Weston sees the vise of geometry as compelling calculation, creating obsession with conscious measurement of degrees of identity:

> Can you say that you are more queer than Cubana, more middle-class than lapsed Catholic, more woman than American, more Latina than light-skinned? Who's to say which is most important? . . . Can inter-sections explain the gut-wrenching feeling that ushers in conflicts of identity? What happens when people do not formulate every axis *as* an identity? (1996a, 126)

Weston argues as if intersectional theorizing fails as an analytic tool if she can find people who claim to ignore their intersectional influences, to deny or not attend to various axes of identity, to be unconscious of controlling their identities. This is not the case. (See Chapter 7 for a critique of this position.) Weston's argument relies on "commonsense" notions that unique individuals are fully cognizant of how they are situated, a drastically oversimplified conception of how individuals construct images of themselves in social relations. The validity or efficacy of an intersectional lens does not rely on the assumption that people are *conscious* of all their thoughts and feelings, positions of power, and axes of identity, or that they can fully "map" their identities and negotiations of social relations. Structures of power are often unknown to individuals or unacknowledged by them, "prompted by social positioning that fosters significant epistemic differences among diverse groups" (Dotson 2011, 248). As a challenge to intersectionality, Weston's rhetorical questions and criticisms are nonsensical.

At-Risk or Can-Do Subjects

Weston does not quote or even cite intersectional scholars to support her claim that the vise of geometry forecloses intersectional thinking. She does, however, make dramatically revealing use of Crenshaw's metaphor of multidimensional flows of traffic through intersections (1989), discussed in Chapter 3. Crenshaw's metaphor includes cars representing discriminations traveling from many directions, accidents treated as illegible and unresolvable, in an effort to capture the dilemmas created when discrimination specific to Black women (on both race and sex) goes unacknowledged by the courts. Crenshaw uses the metaphor to illustrate an impasse where the structural power of law undermines the efficacy and agency of Black women. Crenshaw does not frame these women as responsible for their injuries or exceptionally vulnerable to injury, but, rather, exceptionally vulnerable to having their injuries overlooked, responses delayed, and no one held accountable, because of structures of social power.

In a remarkable move that appears blind to its extraordinary deployment of racialized power, Weston mocks the metaphor and its depiction of the deleterious effects of structural power. Without citing Crenshaw or mentioning Crenshaw's original metaphor, Weston uses the terms of the metaphor— cars, driving, traffic—to distinguish her protagonists strikingly from those of Crenshaw. Weston draws on metaphors of cars and driving in a witty series of riffs on her interview protagonists' skills as *drivers*. These protagonists do not get themselves run over by other drivers: no; they successfully drive those cars to negotiate the roads of life. According to Weston:

> None of the women in this chapter was inclined to sit at an intersection of identities with the engine idling, waiting for the light to change. Any one of them could run figure-eights around the parking

cones marked, "Who are you?" "Who am I?" and "Who are we?" . . . Some of their identities put them in the driver's seat. Some relegated them to the trunk. . . . [T]hese multiple aspects of gender force people to negotiate constantly. (1996a, 144)

Despite a few disclaimers, the argument tends to emphasize the agency of the protagonists. Weston's protagonists are *active,* resembling what Anita Harris calls "can-do girls": young women constructed as "ideal late modern subject[s]," "self-making, resilient, and flexible," and held up as an attainable norm for all young women (2004, 6). Weston's mocking reflection of Crenshaw's metaphor implicitly disparages Crenshaw's individuals: Apparently *they are* women "inclined to sit at an intersection of identities with the engine idling, waiting for the light to change"; rather than doing figure-eights, they get hit by other people's cars. In contrast to Weston's drivers, Crenshaw's individuals are implicitly framed by Weston as individually at fault, passive, allowing themselves to be victimized; in Harris's terms, these would be failed subjects, "at-risk girls," victims of their own poor choices (2004, 6). The notion that women of color are passive victims, failed subjects, or "at-risk girls" is in every way congruent with hegemonic structures of racial dominance. From this point of view, people who *have problems* are seen as *being the problem* (see Ferguson 2013; Kaplan 1997; Nadasen 2009; Roberts 1998; R. Williams 2004). Weston's powerblind strategies reduce a metaphor used to interrogate racialized structural power to a rhetorical foil designed to amplify Weston's praise for the agency of her protagonists, "self-grounded human actors."

Focusing on individuals' agency in negotiating their identities results here in a tension between the role of social structures—obstacles that Weston recognizes "littering the roadway . . . constrained by inequality or historical circumstance . . . [and even] forced" (1996a, 146)—and the agency of the individual to "choose" different identities, different roads, different driving strategies. Continuing the metaphor of protagonist-as-driver, Weston notes that some individuals are forced to "shift gears."

A person doesn't shift gears all the time unless she has to weave her way in and out of categories already littering the roadway. Yes, she can make the choice to jam that transmission into third or fourth. But she's in trouble if she thinks she can freewheel it around the corners. Most choices about identity are constrained by inequality or historical circumstance. And more than a few are forced. (146)

As this comment demonstrates, Weston acknowledges social constraints, but having positioned intersectionality as a foil—as if it *represents* confining structures rather than *challenging* them—she tends to frame social structures through an individualized lens. She focuses on how social experiences and social relations are inflected by racism and sexism but offers no analysis of social structures and social power or how to combat them.

Celebrating Individualism

The protagonists of "Me, Myself, and I" are represented as "coming alive" by *knowing themselves,* by being fulfilled individual subjects, as if that ideal itself is not structured in dominance. This position promotes an endless identitarian politics of the self and stokes desires for a personalized "designer identity," free from ascription, free from a linked fate with anyone else. As a result, the social world will always disappoint because it does not provide automatic and immediate recognition of the full complexity of the protagonist. For example, one protagonist in the chapter, Eriko, explains:

> I think it's different being Japanese, I really do. In some ways you attract the worst kind. I have had one woman who I met at a bar in LA [Los Angeles]. We danced, and she bought me a beer, and we were talking, and she said how she really loved Japanese girls. I wanted to pour the beer over her head. I said, "Oh, you do? Well, you should find one. I hope you do a good job of it. Good-bye." I just don't want to attract the kind of people who say, "Oh, I want a Japanese girl." That, to me, is very offensive, in a way that I want to kill them. (Quoted in Weston 1996a, 127)

Here an individual lens is used to eclipse structural power. "Racism" appears as a failure to acknowledge the infinite complexity of the individual, as when someone who meets the protagonist in a bar is seen as "fetishizing" her identity, failing to know the "real" person in all her complexity. Protagonists' stories are all about *them*—how hard life is, how people treat them, how they treat people.

Weston frames the vividness, the "coming alive" of personal storytelling as surpassing any benefits of intersectional analysis because it escapes the repression of the vise of geometry. Just as West and Fenstermaker sought to replace "intersectionality" with the phrase "doing difference," Weston seeks to replace it with the term "renditions" (deployed only lightly in her own text and seldom used by other scholars). She suggests:

> Could it be that stories do a better job than geometric models of conveying how race, class, gender, sexuality and the like come alive? Em-

bedded in stories are particular renditions of gender that are already raced and classed, renditions that show people in action, chasing down the curve balls that identity throws their way. . . . Maybe "renditions" is a better term than "intersections" [because it] implies no geometric point. (125–126, 145)

Weston's claim treats "renditions" and "intersectionality" as encompassing the same arena of meaning, so that adopting the term "renditions" would replace use of the term "intersectionality." This is not the case. The term "rendition" does a certain job for Weston; it frames her narratives as something more important than individual stories—performance, interpretation, or expression.

Weston implies that "intersectionality" cannot escape the vise of geometry, yet treats her own term "renditions" as isolated from its full range of connotations—such as the distressing illegalities of "extraordinary rendition." Further, nothing makes the term immune from the kind of taunting Weston applies to "intersectionality." We can ask the same questions of "renditions" that Weston asks of "intersectionality": Can renditions explain how structural power influences your life when you are not even aware of it? Can renditions explain your structural connections with people you have never met and thought of? Can renditions explain how you deploy power in ways that you do not acknowledge and are not aware of? "Renditions" cannot do these things, because one term cannot capture all the kinds of analyses necessary for antiracist, antihomophobic, antisexist feminist inquiry.

The Individual or the Phobic Relation to the Social Aggregate

Weston's argument is also powerblind because it does not interrogate its own investment in celebration of the humanist subject that it promotes at the expense of an accurate depiction of intersectional analyses. Weston positions her protagonists as vivid narrators of lives full of agency, negotiation, and complexity. Intersectionality, Weston alleges, cannot account for their infinite diversity. But highlighting the individual agency of the protagonists of these narratives is not ideologically innocent. The architecture of narratives of individual lives is overdetermined, frequently smuggling in the return of the humanist conception of an autonomous self. Focusing on what individual subjects are doing and feeling constructs them as "subjects who know." Conceptions of intersectionality are thus constructed in explicit opposition to— and in inferior relation to—lauding the individual as a source of uniqueness, infinite difference, and change.

Celebrating the individual's resistance to and successful negotiation of social forces has a long ideological history explicitly linked to narration. Nancy

Armstrong argues that the British novel formulated a new kind of subject—
"the individual":

> To produce an individual, novels had to think as if there already
> were one, that such an individual was not only the narrating subject
> and source of writing but also the object of narration and referent of
> writing. To produce an individual, it was also necessary to invalidate
> competing notions of the subject—often proposed by other novels—
> as idiosyncratic, less than fully human, fantastic, or dangerous. The
> result was a cultural category and a bundle of rhetorical figures that
> were extremely fragile and always on the defensive yet notably flexible
> and ever ready to adapt to new cultural-historical conditions. (2005, 3)

Armstrong argues that establishing the modern subject required discrediting alternative conceptions of subjectivity *in phobic terms.* The individual
reestablishes itself *as an individual* "in opposition to an engulfing otherness,
or mass, that obliterate[s] individuality" (25). In Armstrong's argument, investment in the self-governing individual is based exactly on projected fear of
its own loss. This argument that the hegemonic modern subject constitutes
itself in opposition to "phobic representations of the human aggregate" (25)
offers insight into the difficulties of attribution, affect, and anxiety characterizing critiques of intersectionality. Despite its contemporary hegemony,
Armstrong argues, the individual is still positioned as vulnerable, required
constantly to reconstitute itself against phobic threats of encroachment. For
Weston, the engulfing otherness against which the innocent subject emerges
is not homophobia, misogyny, racialized capitalism, or sexual violence, but
intersectionality's prominence and the vise of geometry she attributes to it.

The Western cultural imaginary reflects a long ideological history of pro-
jecting racialized subjects as a mass, a mob, or an aggregate (see Armstrong
1990; Lezra 2014; McKittrick 2015; Mignolo 2011; Moreton-Robinson 2015).
Thus to valorize the individual is simultaneously to devalue others: those positioned as not capable of being individuals, framed through affect-laden images
of fear, anxiety, apprehension, and aversion. Within the cultural imaginary,
"individuals" are in constant need of differentiating and distancing themselves
from the aggregate. Intersectionality, as a disposition and heuristic tool, serves
to expose sedimented and occluded structures of subordination that position
racialized subjects as less-than-human, as an undifferentiated mass. Weston
tends to frame the "intersectional" as a repressive force for obliterating individuality, a threat to the self-governing individual negotiating her own destiny,
failing to negotiate carefully potential participation in this phobic cultural
imaginary.

If anxiety about the loss of selfhood is the engine of individualism, then framing intersectional thinking in terms of the intrusive demand of the aggregate is also laden with anxiety. Claims that individual narration should be elevated over other forms of social analysis, that early intersectional scholars thought in terms of only "fixed" and "static" categories, that metaphors are imprisoned by their site of origin, but that racially dominant feminist scholars easily advance beyond these problems to think flexibly and fluidly—all serve to proclaim the white scholar as free from the constraints of social categories, while consigning racialized scholars and their thoughts to the undifferentiated aggregate.

These moves rest on unacknowledged and problematic liberal conceptions of categorization as inherently negative (for a critique of this position, see Crenshaw 1991, 1242). If one assumes that some or all identity categories are inherently oppressive, one might also assume that focusing on and celebrating individuals can "empty" categories of social and structural significance, thereby freeing individuals from the constraints of categorization. In contrast, intersectionality's insistence on examining the workings of social categorization as structures of power may raise anxiety in its reminder that individuals are not and will never be free of categorization. Fearing that categories are fixed, predetermined, and inescapable, one might anxiously attribute such a position to those who use a structural lens like intersectionality, positioning their thinking as rigid and unable to account for complexity and lived experience. But it is not intersectionality's recognition of social categories and critique of subordination that are "fixed." It is, rather, sexism, racism, and racial hierarchy that are relentlessly re-fixing themselves (see Crenshaw 1988; Hall 1986; Hall et al. 2013; Robinson 2007).

ENACTING RACIAL DOMINANCE AT THE SCENE OF ARGUMENT

Both critiques examined here make vigorous use of the vise of geometry as a rhetorical foil in distorting intersectionality: They reject intersectional analysis as a geometrical clamp on feminist thought and replace it with fictions of transparent "actual mechanisms," analytic flexibility, and celebration of individual stories. These powerblind critiques are actually engaged in enacting racial dominance. Both critiques create false entailments of the metaphors of geometry to justify dismantling intersectional analysis in favor of their own type of inquiry. Both critiques emphasize their own analyses' ability to show *relations of power* but ignore their inability to examine *structures of power*. Both critiques demonstrate reliance on treating their objects of analysis as transparent—the "actual mechanisms" of inequality in the case of West and

Fenstermaker and narratives in the case of Weston. Both critiques remain grounded in epistemological liberalism, resisting radical critique. So it is not just acknowledgment of race that the critics resist; it is also intersectionality's epistemological and political radicalism.

It could have been otherwise. Rather than using rhetorics of rejection and replacement to elevate their preferred methods at the expense of the conceptions of racialized scholars, the critics could have demonstrated how their preferred methods might contribute to intersectionality's ability to critique subordination. The critics could have eschewed competition for accompaniment, working with intersectional scholars of color and theorizing with them to counter subordination. Instead, the critics distanced themselves from antisubordination projects by depoliticizing white feminism's relations to struggles against subordination: West and Fenstermaker by seeking to replace analysis of oppression with analysis of "difference," Weston by celebrating individualism. These moves segregate the interests of white feminists from the interests of feminists of color, who do not have the luxury of ignoring structural power. I have argued that this symbolic violence against conceptions of intersectionality and the scholars of color who have produced them—these attempts to invalidate the rich and complex knowledge of scholars of color—reflect the enduring legacy of a time of crisis in white feminism when intersectional theorizing challenged the primacy of gender as an analytic category and ethical grounding of feminist arguments. In the face of the possibility that other oppressions might assume equality or even precedence over gender, or that white feminists might have to acknowledge fully their privileged racial identities, both critiques demonstrate willingness to condemn the theorizing of feminist scholars of color as under the thrall of the vise of geometry. But, in doing so, they sacrifice notions of oppression that so galvanized feminisms of the past in order to privilege their own theorizing as "general theories" of "difference" and "individualism." The result is a contemporary feminist discourse about intersectionality that relies on powerblind strategies that reinscribe racial dominance.

INTERSECTIONALITY TELEPHONE AND
THE CANYON OF ECHOES

Powerblind feminist critiques often proceed through a particular politics of scholarly citation. Decisions at the scene of argument about quotation, citation, and reviews of the previous literature reinforce white women's symbolic domination of the field by distorting knowledge claims about intersectionality. Citational practices shape matters of visibility, agency, and accountability. Sara Ahmed, identifying the importance of visibility, argues that citation is a screening device that foregrounds some scholars while relegating others to the background (https://feministkilljoys.com/2013/09/11/making-feminist-points/). Vivian M. May connects citational practices to the issue of agency (2014, 2015). May contends that widespread practices of citation in regard to intersectionality misrepresent intersectional thinking by shifting credit for intellectual agency from women of color to white women. In carelessly written literature reviews, powerblind citational practices advance inaccurate claims about the limitations of intersectionality—its alleged inadequacy for thinking about "experience" or "narrative," for example. In these instances, no efforts are made to cite the large body of writings on experience and narrative actually produced by scholars of color. In addition, powerblind citational practices encourage negative claims to be *augmented, oversimplified, exacerbated,* and *intensified.* For example, Nina Lykke cites a study that, she claims, argues that intersectionality proves "much too crude and too static as a tool" (2010, 73). In fact, the study does not describe intersectionality as "crude," though it does criticize it in more moderate ways. Lykke's claim misrepresents its source, intensifies the criticism of intersectionality, and displaces responsibility for inflated negative claims. Such powerblind citational practices allow critics to distance themselves from their reinscription of racial hierarchy at the scene of argument. These problems of citation are not small matters. They stand at the center of problems of feminist responsibility that have important ramifications for the work of social justice. May notes that "Angela Davis has issued a call to reconceive citation as a practice of mutual recognition and accountability, not authorization via erasure" (A. Davis 2009, cited in May 2014, 104). Reformulating the problematic racial politics of feminist citation along these lines is part of the task of transforming feminist practices of reading and writing.

This chapter reveals how powerblind practices of citation give seemingly casual and prosaic moves at the scene of argument an afterlife that extends far beyond their original moment of iteration and publication. I first consider the arguments in a well-known essay by Wendy Brown, "The Impossibility of Women's Studies" (1997, 2005, 2008), as well as related arguments in her *States of Injury* (1995). I demonstrate that Brown's arguments cannot justify their frequent contemporary citation as an authoritative critique of intersectionality. I subsequently move to consider the arguments of Nira Yuval-Davis in "Intersectionality and Feminist Politics" (2006b). I demonstrate that Yuval-Davis creates a dramatically misleading reference to Crenshaw's intersectional metaphors; I then trace some of the problems created through citational echoes of Yuval-Davis's misrepresentation. I argue that the citational practices that inappropriately elevate Brown and Yuval-Davis as authorities whose work can be used to dismiss the intersectional thinking of scholars of color are not isolated cases but symptomatic of two key mechanisms to circulate powerblind discourses, mechanisms that I call "Intersectionality Telephone" and the "Canyon of Echoes."

WHAT CAN BROWN DO FOR YOU?

A striking pattern of powerblind citational politics with respect to critiques of intersectionality emerges in reference to Wendy Brown's "The Impossibility of Women's Studies" (1997, 2005, 2008). (There are nearly 1,200 citations in Google Scholar to the journal article and the volumes in which it is reprinted as of May 10, 2018.) Brown's main thesis is evident in her title: she argues that women's studies faces inevitable failure as a field of inquiry because it focuses on a single social category, that its major achievements already lie in its past, that its research should focus on subject formation and power ("how to come to terms with the problem of the powers involved in the construction of subjects" [1997, 86]), and that its teaching activities could be subsumed in other departments. The text and its challenge to women's studies was widely read and cited around the turn of the millennium (see criticism of Brown's arguments about women's studies in Wiegman [1999–2000, 2005]). Ultimately, it appears, the major arguments of "The Impossibility of Women's Studies" did not gain traction: women's, gender, sexuality, and feminist studies in the academy remain as departments and programs, research in the field addresses a range of topics rather than focusing centrally on the powers of subject formation. Brown's text is seldom cited now as an authority to criticize the limitations of the gendered identity politics of women's studies.

However, a sustained history of citation has positioned Brown's text as an authority for criticism of intersectionality—as fatally grounded in racial identity politics or simplistic and inadequate in other ways—based on Brown's scathing and perhaps ill-considered broad-scale attack on conceptions of multidimensionality. Many who cite Brown's text as authoritative appear unconcerned with her text's primary arguments condemning women's studies as an identity politics and oblivious to the text's manifest failings as a critique of multidimensional thinking by feminist intersectional scholars of color. I demonstrate here the problems of citing Brown in contemporary arguments as an authoritative source of critique about intersectionality.

It is particularly important to note that Brown's argument is grounded in her proclamation that the primary task of women's studies is to develop an understanding of the powers of subject formation. Brown establishes this goal at the center of women's studies by fiat, not by consensus or even persuasion. Her own conceptual values are foregrounded, subordinating the conceptions, goals, paradigms, and politics of scholars focusing on other goals. Yet most who cite Brown's authority to criticize intersectionality do not demonstrate awareness of her criterion for judgment, the differing goals of many intersectional analyses, or the fact that their own work does not contribute an understanding of the powers of subject formation and should therefore garner disapproval from Brown.

Contributing to understanding the powers of subject formation is, then, the explicit criterion by which Brown judges multidimensional theorizing, largely ignoring or denigrating other goals. Her critique of multidimensional thinking by women of color—casual, limited, dismissive—accuses them of simplistic thinking and failure to adopt Foucauldian conceptions of power. Brown does not acknowledge that multidimensionality can be used for a variety of political and intellectual purposes inside and outside the academy. She does not acknowledge how multidimensional scholars of color began to theorize the interrelationship of dominant social categories framed as discrete in dominant discourses, assuming, impatiently, that they reflect dominant categories. She systematically decontextualizes words and phrases in order to denigrate them wholesale. For example, she provides a decontextualized list of some ten different terms for multidimensionality that emerged in the arguments of women of color primarily in the 1980s. She does not cite the scholarly sources for these terms or provide their definitions, contexts, and uses, nor does she explain fully what specific problems are incurred by their use. While she cites a few very brief phrases from three intersectional scholars, her argument rests on treating as evidence of intersectional scholarship what appear to be unattributed comments of the type one hears from undergraduate and graduate students.[1] Brown may no longer stand behind her formulations in these polemical arguments, but through citation they have developed a life of their own that transcends her past or present intentions.[2] While the article is not about intersectionality, nor does it mount a robust critique of it, it nonetheless operates as license to criticize intersectionality.

Since Brown assumes that understanding the powers of subject formation is the primary task of women's studies, she is particularly concerned with what she presents as inappropriate discussion of subject formation on the part of scholars of color. She treats brief phrases as if they were failed attempts to theorize the powers of subject formation, when the scholars' goals are quite different. For example, at one point Brown states—as if she were responding to the misguided claims of multidimensional scholars—that "powers of subject formation are not separable in the subject itself" (1997, 86). She argues:

> These powers neither constitute links in a chain nor overlapping spheres of oppression; they are not "intersectional" in their formation (Crenshaw); they are not *simply* degrees of privilege (Hurtado); and they *cannot be reduced* to being "inside or outside, or more or less proximate to, dominant power formations" (Hill Collins). (86, emphasis added)

It is unclear to whom Brown refers as suggesting that the powers of subject formation "constitute links in a chain" (a web search of the phrase produces only Brown's article, its reprints, and its citations); it is also unclear who might have framed the powers of subject formation as "overlapping spheres of oppression" (the phrase appears to be used for different purposes but not to discuss the powers of subject formation). Delaying discussion of Brown's assertions about Crenshaw to Chapter 9, I turn here to Brown's assertions about the work of Aída Hurtado and Patricia Hill Collins, which reveal major problems of misrepresentation.

According to the structure of Brown's sentence, she has found Hurtado to argue that the powers of subject formation are "simply degrees of privilege," while Collins has allegedly argued that these powers can be reduced to being "inside or outside, or more or less proximate to, dominant power formations." The use of "simply" and "can be reduced to" modifies Brown's claim to emphasize her judgment that the scholars' arguments are simplistic: in Hurtado's case, unable to or refusing to see these powers as anything other than degrees of privilege, and in Collins's case, unable to produce a complex characterization or denying that one is needed. Unfortunately, Brown misrepresents Hurtado's position. Social psychologist Hurtado makes an argument not about subject formation, but about the relational nature of subordination and privilege (1989; developed further in 1996). Hurtado is specifically concerned with the varied strategies by which differently raced women negotiate their relations to white men. This would appear to be an argument about types of privilege, not degrees of privilege. Since Hurtado is not arguing about the powers of subject formation, nor about "degrees of privilege," she could not be said to argue that such powers are "simply" degrees of privilege, as Brown asserts.

The case of Collins turns out to be a bit more complex. According to Brown, in *Black Feminist Thought* Collins states that the powers of subject formation can be reduced to being "inside or outside, or more or less proximate to, dominant power formations" (1991 [Brown's typographical error states 1981]). But tracking down this quotation proves difficult. The first version of "The Impossibility of Women's Studies," published in *differences* (1997) offers no page number; the slightly revised version published in Brown's *Edgework* retains the erroneous publication date, adding "quotation, 42" (2005, 152). In my copy of *Black Feminist Thought* (1991), page 42 is blank; the phrase does not appear elsewhere in the book. Online searches produce the language attributed to Collins in only Brown's text or others quoting Brown's text. While Collins is well known for her metaphors using spatiality, and her metaphor of "the outsider within" (1986) has been generative, it would be hard to characterize accurately her flexible use of such metaphors as "reductive," and it would be worthwhile to know the grounds for Brown's claim.

Because Brown discusses Collins in *States of Injury* (1995), I examine it for an explanation of her criticism of Collins. (There are almost 3,400 citations in Google Scholar to *States of Injury* as of May 10, 2018.) While *States of Injury* includes no such quotation, Brown does comment there several times on *Black Feminist Thought*.

Brown's treatment of *Black Feminist Thought* in *States of Injury* demonstrates explicitly argumentative strategies that are also present in "The Impossibility of Women's Studies" but disguised by the minimal method of attribution and citation that characterizes "The Impossibility." Notably, Brown consistently fails to acknowledge the specific arguments made by Collins and the women of color that Brown cites. The most systematic argumentative strategy that Brown uses in responding to women of color is to present boldly as her own fresh counterarguments what are actually repetitions of the arguments of the scholars of color she is criticizing. For example, with respect to Collins, in *States of Injury*:

1. *Brown lists objections* to earlier standpoint theories and casually folds Collins into them *without acknowledging* that *Collins* has already articulated *exactly the same objections,* including criticism of the positivist consequences of Marxist efforts to position oppressed groups as having access to the one "true" interpretation of reality (see W. Brown 1995, 41–48).

In contrast to the position Brown attributes to her, Collins's previous argument refuting claims of access to "true" interpretations holds that

earlier versions of standpoint theories, themselves rooted in a Marxist positivism, essentially reversed positivist science's assumptions concerning whose truth would prevail. These approaches suggest that the oppressed allegedly have a clearer view of the "truth" than their oppressors because they lack the blinders created by the dominant group's ideology. But this version of standpoint theory basically duplicates the positivist belief in one "true" interpretation of reality, and, like positivist science, comes with its own set of problems. (P. Collins 1991, 235)[3]

2. *Brown maintains that* what she has positioned as "naïve" standpoint theories, including the theories of Collins, can move beyond their limitations using the arguments of Donna J. Haraway's "Situated Knowledges" (1988). *She does not acknowledge* that Collins has already adopted Haraway's stance (see W. Brown 1995, 51).

In contrast to Brown's claims, Collins has previously clearly declared her use of Haraway's position:

Even though I use standpoint epistemologies as an organizing concept in this volume, they remain controversial. . . . Haraway's (1988) reformulation of standpoint epistemologies approximates my use here. (P. Collins 1991, 39n1)[4]

3. *Brown does not acknowledge* the complexity of Collins's arguments about Black women drawing on shared cultural practices. Brown therefore positions Collins's use of Black women's experiences as a naïve essentialist positioning of experience and instructs Collins instead to recognize that "experience" is "thoroughly constructed,

historically and culturally varied, and interpreted without end" (see W. Brown 1995, 41).

Yet Brown is misrepresenting Collin's argument. Throughout *Black Feminist Thought* Collins emphasizes the constructed, changing, historically and culturally varied experience of Black women as well as other social groups (1991).

4. *Brown uses Collins's failure to ground her text in the language of poststructuralism* to claim that Collins is unaware of poststructuralist understandings of power and knowledge, that she does not recognize that all knowledges are "imposed and created rather than discovered" and that all truths are "power-suffused, struggle-produced" (1995, 47–48).

Yet Collins repeatedly demonstrates that her arguments are grounded in such assumptions. In *Black Feminist Thought* Collins specifically refers to Foucault's concept of subjugated knowledges, an argument about ways of knowing concerned with "the historical knowledge of struggles" (Foucault 1980c, 83). Collins argues that, according to Foucault,

> subjugated knowledges are thus those blocs of historical knowledge which were present but disguised, [namely], a whole set of knowledges that have been disqualified as inadequate to their task or insufficiently elaborated: naive knowledges, located low down on the hierarchy, beneath the required level of cognition or scientificity. . . . [Subjugated knowledge is] a particular, local, regional knowledge, a differential knowledge incapable of unanimity and which owes its force only to the harshness with which it is opposed by everything surrounding it. (P. Collins 1991, 18n3, quoting Foucault 1980c, 82)

5. *Brown undermines Collins's position* by "speculating" about what Collins "really" thinks, *positioning her as untrustworthy, perhaps not veracious.* Comparing Collins's arguments to those of standpoint theorist Nancy Hartsock (1983), Brown notes that Collins "does not claim the same tight connection between privileged perspective and privileged access to the good" and has "affirmed as an alternative . . . epistemology rooted in black women's lived experience, not as The Standpoint for knowing The Truth" (1995, 47n41). But Brown nonetheless expresses suspicion about whether one can rely on what Collins "really" thinks. Brown goes on to claim:

Nevertheless, one senses that practices [that Collins] examines as dialogue and emotional expressiveness in knowledge production are being *implicitly valorized as both true and superior* ways of knowing, *not merely forwarded* as black women's way of knowing. (1995, 47n41, emphasis added)

Brown makes no effort to explain why she "suspects" Collins of being "unduly" enthusiastic about the ways of knowing she discusses, or why these practices might be acceptable for consideration only if they were offered on a limited basis, "forwarded" as a kind of self-report about Black women, as if Collins should agree that she can only offer a subordinate kind of thinking.

6. *Brown accuses* standpoint theorists, including Collins, of developing a social epistemology with norms that can serve "exclusionary and regulatory functions" (1995, 48). She argues:

African American women who do not identify with Patricia Hill Collins's account of black women's ways of knowing, *are once again excluded from the Party of Humanism*—this time in a feminist variant. (1995, 48, emphasis added)

Contra Brown's claim, Collins has articulated a remarkably capacious social epistemology not limited to Black women that proposes ways of developing better answers for social problems by bringing together people from multiple groups, each recognizing their own partial perspectives and situated knowledges. Rather than developing exclusionary or "universal" norms, Collins proposes political norms and "truths" developed by discussions of many different groups, each recognizing "its own truth as partial, [so] its knowledge is unfinished. . . . Partiality and not universality is the condition of being heard" (1991, 236).[5] Brown does not acknowledge Collins's emphasis on multiple positions and inclusion. Brown instead criticizes Collins's position as if it were a standpoint theory based on biology or claims of privileged positions, rather than properly representing the specificities of Collins's arguments or her distinctions among ways of knowing.

Part of the peculiarity of Brown's claim here stems from her counterfactual but characteristic assumption that Collins is *concerned with* and *of concern to* only Black women; that Black women can enter the public sphere only through the epistemologies of other Black women; that because Collins is Black and has developed a social epistemology that she claims is based on Black women's experiences, Collins would maintain it to be the *only one* available for Black women. In consequence of this misconception, Brown argues that an African American woman who does not "identify with" Collins's account would be virtually excluded from the public sphere. Brown's gesture would appear to be a troubling response to the assertion of Black subjectivity: to claim that Collins has the remarkable power to rule out any Black woman with a differing position from "the Party of Humanism"—as if everyone had been included up to that moment. Collins's arguments about a Black feminism broadly conceived—one that unmasks and seeks to remedy previous exclusions—are reconfigured by Brown into a powerful force for exclusion. In a remarkably disingenuous gesture, considering the condemnation of the thinking of women of color that characterizes "The Impossibility of Women's Studies," Brown positions herself as rescuing the unfortunate African American women subject to Collins's alleged exclusion.

To recapitulate: Brown names only three scholars of color in "The Impossibility"—Crenshaw, Hurtado, and Collins. In the case of all three, Brown's claims are not reliable. Hurtado has not argued about "the powers involved in the construction of subjects," much less that they are "simply degrees of privilege." Collins has not argued that those powers are reduced to being "inside or outside, or more or less proximate to, dominant power formations." Instead, Collins is working to develop practices of dialogic knowledge production that go beyond her own racialized identity to incorporate multiple ways of knowing, including not only the partial perspectives of Black women but also those of men and women in other social groups. Brown is also inaccurate in her claims about Crenshaw, as I argue in Chapter 9.

The inaccurate and illegitimate strategies that Brown uses in *States of Injury* duplicate similar strategies in "The Impossibility of Women's Studies." In "The Impossibility," Brown treats as equally significant evidence (1) various anonymous verbal comments about individuals' own multidimensionality that appear to be overheard from unidentified students' discussions or constructed ad hoc as "examples" and (2) *decontextualized* lists of terms for multidimensionality used by scholars of color. In the essay, Brown tucks brief dismissive comments about multidimensional terms into paragraphs full of claims about the nature of power, identities, and subject formation, and particularly the alleged failure of multidimensional scholars to recognize the value of Foucauldian conceptions of power. The architecture of her argument treats these surrounding claims about power, identities, and subject formation as if they were powerful counterarguments demonstrating the weakness of the terms women of color use to theorize the convergence of different kinds of identities or subject positions. However, the positions that Brown promotes are *not refutations of* the flexible and insightful claims about power already articulated by the scholars she dismisses; her claims about power are often *congruent with* their arguments.

For example, Brown sets an explicit agenda for feminist scholarship that she implies is beyond the reach of scholars of color:

> We need a combination of, on the one hand, analyses of subject-producing power accounted through careful histories, psychoanalysis, political economy and cultural, political and legal discourse analysis, and, on the other, genealogies of particular modalities of subjection that presume neither coherence in the formation of particular kinds of subjects nor equivalence between different formations . . . a historiography that emphasizes instead contingent developments, formations that may be at odds with or convergent with each other, and trajectories of power that vary in weight for different kinds of subjects. (W. Brown 1997, 94)

Brown's agenda is for a field, not an individual, yet it is remarkably close to a complex political, psychoanalytic, Foucauldian genealogy of Asian American citizenship and multidimensional subject formation that was already evident in the work of Lisa Lowe (1991, 1996). Brown derisively mentions Lowe's terms "multiplicity" and "hybridity" without citing her, yet the existence of Lowe's work flatly refutes Brown's claims that feminist scholars of color think simplistically about power and subject formation without reference to Foucauldian theories of power. Because so many of the contemporary critiques of intersectionality that cite "The Impossibility" in order to belittle intersectionality appear completely unaware of the inaccuracy of Brown's claims, I attend here to the specifics of Lowe's argument.

Providing precisely the kind of analysis that Brown claims does not exist in women of color feminism—an analysis "of subject-producing power accounted through careful histories" and "a historiography that emphasizes instead contingent developments"—Lowe proposes that "Rather than considering 'Asian American identity' as a fixed, established 'given,' perhaps we can consider instead 'Asian American cultural practices' that produce identity" (1996, 64). Lowe explains that Asian American identity is the product of contingent developments, arguing that "the processes that produce such identity are never complete and are always constituted in relation to historical and material differences" (1996, 64). Without providing evidence or citations, Brown scolds women of color feminists tout court for failing to consider "formations that may be at odds with or convergent with each other, and trajectories of power that vary in weight for different kinds of subjects"

(1997, 94). Yet this is precisely what Lowe does in analyzing Asian American identity, quoting Stuart Hall's argument that cultural identity

> is a matter of "becoming" as well as of "being." It belongs to the future as much as to the past. It is not something which already exists, transcending place, time, history and culture. Cultural identities come from somewhere, have histories. But, like everything which is historical, they undergo constant transformation. Far from being eternally fixed in some essentialized past, they are subject to the continuous "play" of history, culture and power. (1996, 64, quoting Hall 1990, 225)

Lowe goes on to argue that the essence of Asian American cultural critique is the insistence that group formation encompasses "a spectrum of positions" that include both assertions of uniform fixed traits and "challenges to the notion of singularity and conceptions of *race* as the material *locus* of differences, intersections, and incommensurabilities" (1996, 64).

Brown contends that women of color feminism finds it impossible to attend to genealogies of particular modalities of subjection that presume neither coherence in the formation of particular kinds of subjects nor equivalence between different formations. Yet Lowe states explicitly that Asian American critique

> not only accounts for the critical inheritance of cultural definitions and traditions but also accounts for the *racial formation* that is produced in the negotiations between the state's regulation of racial groups and those groups' active contestation and construction of racial meanings. In other words, these latter efforts suggest that the making of Asian American culture may be a much less stable process than unmediated vertical transmission of culture from one generation to another. The making of Asian American culture includes practices that are partly inherited, partly modified, as well as partly invented. (1996, 64–65)

Brown ignores the ways that the clarity and complexity of Lowe's arguments contribute to what Brown has declared to be the proper agenda for feminist studies, quoted above. The terms that Lowe defines are among those in the decontextualized list of terms for multidimensionality proposed by women of color that Brown dismisses wholesale: "multiplicity," "intersections," "crossroads," "borderlands," "hybridity," and "fracturing" (1997, 94). Brown argues:

> To conclude this excursus into the question of subject production, as feminism has for many become irreversibly connected to the project

of multicultural, postcolonial, and queer analysis, terms such as "multiplicity," "intersections," "crossroads," "borderlands," "hybridity," and "fracturing" have emerged to acknowledge—without *fully* explaining or theorizing—the complex workings of power that converge at the site of identity. (94, emphasis added)

The structure of Brown's passage suggests that it is "multicultural, postcolonial, and queer analysis" that has failed to achieve the goal of "*fully* explaining or theorizing . . . the complex workings of power that converge at the site of identity." Brown earlier made clear that feminist theory as a whole has failed to explain "the complex workings of power that converge on the site of identity," but at this point she shifts responsibility for full explanation to academic arguments that had been circulating for slightly more than a decade. Brown's method of decontextualized dismissal authorizes similar strategies in contemporary critiques where intersectional terms are treated in isolation, extracted from context: the use of such terms in academic arguments is radically misrepresented.

For example, Lowe emphasizes the terms "hybridity" and "multiplicity" listed by Brown, as well as "heterogeneity," not listed. She also uses the term "intersection." She defines terms in ways that demonstrate their contribution toward thinking through "the complex workings of power that converge at the site of identity." The complexity of Lowe's definition situated in the larger argumentative context repudiates Brown's casual dismissal. Lowe argues that she deploys the terms "heterogeneity," "hybridity," and "multiplicity" not as rhetorical or literary devices but rather as part of an effort to name the material conditions that define Asian American life. In an argument that completely fulfills Brown's call for attention to "the complex workings of power," Lowe posits that heterogeneity names "the existence of differences and differential relationships within a bounded category—that is, among Asian Americans, there are differences of Asian national origin, of generational relation to immigrant exclusion laws, of class backgrounds in Asia and economic conditions within the United States, and of gender" (1996, 67). Delineating the importance of hybridity as an analytic tool, Lowe explains that it represents "the formation of cultural objects and practices that are produced by the histories of uneven and unsynthetic power relations. . . . [The term] marks the history of survival within relationships of unequal power and domination" (67). Turning to multiplicity, Lowe argues that it designates "the ways in which subjects located within social relations are determined by several different axes of power, are multiply determined by the contradictions of capitalism, patriarchy, and race relations, with, as Hall explains, particular contradictions surfacing in relation to the material conditions of a specific historical moment" (67, referring to Hall 1985).

In her condemnation of the terminology and positions on power of "multicultural, postcolonial, and queer analysis," Brown folds together a variety of different arguments and treats them as virtually the same. She valorizes poststructural positions on power and assumes that an alleged failure to draw on Foucauldian or poststructuralist conceptions of power condemns multidimensional arguments. Yet Brown fails to recognize those projects that explicitly do draw on Foucault, such as those of Lowe and Collins. Brown appears to be evoking Foucault's work in strikingly inappropriate ways in order to dismiss the thinking of women of color. Foucault was interested in the "insurrection of subjugated knowledges" in order to develop a historical understanding of struggles that could be used tactically in the present (Foucault 1980c, 83). Rather than insisting that knowledges be judged by the degree to which they met the standards of a "unitary body of theory," he was interested in "entertain[ing] the claims to attention of local, discontinuous, disqualified, illegitimate knowledges" (83), the kind of knowledges that could be said to emerged from the lived experiences of women of color. There is no evidence that Foucault would demand that subjugated knowledges be treated as valuable only if they emerged in the form of Foucauldian notions expressed in Foucauldian terms. In fact, his comments in "Two Lectures" urge critics attempting to disqualify knowledges to interrogate their own purposes in ways that bear enormous relevance to Brown's argument: "What types of knowledge do you want to disqualify[?] . . . Which speaking, discoursing subjects—which subjects of experience and knowledge—do you then want to 'diminish'[?] . . . Which theoretical political *avant garde* do you want to enthrone in order to isolate it from all the discontinuous forms of knowledge that circulate about it?" (85). In rejecting the subjugated knowledges of women of color, Brown is expressly involved in a project such as Foucault warns against. It would seem that Brown's purposes are not entirely Foucauldian: she moves to shut down or discipline subjugated knowledges, to "enthrone" poststructuralist discourse, and to "diminish" the feminist scholars of color theorizing multidimensionality.

Yet in the citational practices of contemporary critiques of intersectionality, negative claims like those made by Brown have a long and extensive life, marshaled without acknowledging how positions impelling the original criticism actually undermine the validity of their contemporary citation as authorities "against intersectionality." For example, Brown's main argument is that women's studies is impossible—a criticism that is totally ignored by the many feminist scholars who use her authority to criticize intersectional thinking. Brown sets the goal of women's studies as studying the powers of subject formation and criticizes multidimensional scholars for not contributing as she would wish to those goals—yet she is cited as an authoritative critic of multidimensionality by scholars who *themselves* are not studying the powers of the formation of the subject and should, therefore, not receive Brown's approval. Brown establishes Foucauldian conceptions of power as the central requirement of both feminist and multidimensional analysis—yet she is cited as an authoritative critic by scholars who do not *themselves* adopt a Foucauldian analytic. Brown condemns what may be artificial examples or students' comments about their identities and ten different scholarly terms for multidimensionality in decontextualized lists (finding *none* useful)—yet those citing her frame her criticism as specifically focused on "intersectionality," a word mentioned only three times in the 1997 article (once in praise). Brown's critique wrongly frames multidimensional analysis as promoting racialized identity politics that were actually being challenged by multidimensional scholars. Those citing Brown sometimes report that she objects to "identity politics"—by which they mean assertions of subjectivity by women of color—even though Brown's primary criticism is that it is women's studies that is "impossible" because *feminism* is an "identity politics." Brown's powerblind arguments and their inappropriate circulation in contemporary critiques of intersectionality demonstrate how white feminist critiques of intersectionality use casual and inaccurate arguments and citations to reinforce racial hierarchies.

THROUGH YUVAL-DAVIS'S EYES

My second example of powerblind citational practices focuses on arguments initiated in Nira Yuval-Davis's (2006b) "Intersectionality and Feminist Politics" (with more than 1,800 citations in Google Scholar as of May 10, 2018) and circulated through a specific politics of citation. In her article, Yuval-Davis expresses concern about the treatment of concepts of intersectionality in reports organized in preparation for the World Conference against Racism (WCAR), held in Durban, South Africa, in August–September 2001. Intersectionality was an important concept for the 2001 WCAR. The 2001 conference was the first to include "related intolerances," including the ways that racism intersects with other subordinations; at previous UN-sponsored conferences, gender subordination and racism were often treated as if they were separate, mutually exclusive, and incommensurable concerns (Chan-Tiberghien 2004; Falcón 2016). Preparation for the conference involved numerous preliminary meetings among a wide range of diverse local, national, and international groups developing position statements and other arguments seeking to shift prevailing worldwide public discourses about multiple and compound discrimination. One of these preliminary meetings was the Expert Meeting on Gender and Racial Discrimination in Zagreb in 2000, at which law professor Kimberlé Crenshaw—critical race theorist and intersectionality scholar—served as a consultant and provided a background paper (2000). Crenshaw subsequently presented a related paper at WCAR (2001).

In "Intersectionality and Feminist Politics," Yuval-Davis expresses concern about three reports that she indicates "came out of" the Expert Meeting at Zagreb. She claims that "the analytic attempts to explain intersectionality in the reports that came out of this meeting are confusing" (2006b, 196), apparently because the discussions of intersectionality in each report differ from one another and, she argues, some appear to confuse "identities" and "structures." Yuval-Davis here does not explain how the diffuse, collaborative, and also independent nature of group authorship involved in creating position papers related to WCAR might lead different reports to have different arguments and agendas.

To criticize the reports for their differences seems to assume that independent groups sending delegates to the Zagreb meeting are required to speak in one voice about intersectional thinking and discrimination, as if they represented one author and argument. This is not the case. The "authorship" involved in producing preparatory statements, position papers, and presentations for conferences such as WCAR is collaborative within specific groups but also diffuse and independent across groups. In effect, authority in the preparatory meetings and WCAR is shared across stakeholders, who are entitled to hold differing opinions about how racial and gender discrimination should be defined, conceived, and countered.

My concern here is to follow the citational threads emanating from a moment in Yuval-Davis's text immediately following her claim that the three documents that "came out of this [Zagreb] meeting" are "confusing." There Yuval-Davis argues:

The imagery of crossroads and traffic as developed by Crenshaw (2001) [*sic*] occupies a central space.

> Intersectionality is what occurs when a woman from a minority group . . . tries to navigate the main crossing in the city. . . . The main highway is 'racism road.' One cross street can be Colonialism, then Patriarchy Street. . . . She has to deal not only with one form of oppression but with all forms, those named as road signs, which link together to make a double, a triple, multiple, a many layered blanket of oppression. (Yuval-Davis 2006b, 196)

This block text that Yuval-Davis attributes to Crenshaw (2001) does not come from that or any other academic source written by Crenshaw. Yuval-Davis dismisses the text she inaccurately attributes to Crenshaw as "additive" but does not discuss it further. The placement of the block text in her argument implies that it contributes to the "confusion" she finds in the three documents. This kind of casual dismissal is frequent in critiques of intersectionality, disciplining readers to know *what* to say is wrong with the concept, but not *why*. (See further discussion of the problems of this kind of casual argument in Chapter 7.) Perhaps the claim that the metaphor is "additive" rests on the phrase about multiple "layers" of oppression, yet perhaps not: Yuval-Davis treats her own history of "additive" arguments—about "layers" of citizenship, for example (2007)—as if she is immune from the same kind of casual dismissal.

This moment in Yuval-Davis's argument is a nexus or node in a network of errors, confusions, and misrepresentations. While metaphors of traffic flowing through intersections are found in Crenshaw's publications (for example, 1989, discussed in Chapter 3), the material in the block text quoted by Yuval-Davis is found in *none* of Crenshaw's publications. Crenshaw's paper for the Expert Meeting at Zagreb—"The Intersection of Race and Gender Discrimination" (2000)—and her paper presented at WCAR—"The Intersectionality of Race and Gender Discrimination" (2001)—both include traffic metaphors, but those metaphors are not similar at all to the block text. There is no imagery of "crossroads" or traffic at all in the other two source documents that Yuval-Davis cites (Australian Human Rights and Equal Opportunity Commission 2001; Center for Women's Global Leadership 2001). It is simply inaccurate to claim that the metaphor presented in the block text occupies "a central space" in the documents that Yuval-Davis examines, since it appears *in none of them*.

Yuval-Davis's construction of the sentence introducing and laying out the block text mimics the manner by which scholars would signal that the block text is a direct quotation—in this case, she appears to claim, from "Crenshaw (2001)." Numerous scholars have interpreted Yuval-Davis's construction in exactly that way, as asserting that the block text is a direct quotation from Crenshaw (for example, Aydemir 2009, 2012; Bailey 2009, 2011; K. Davis 2008; Dhamoon 2011;[6] Fish 2008; Garry 2012; Jibrin and Salem 2015; Lalander 2016; Marchetti 2014; Truscan and Bourke-Martignoni 2016; Tuider 2014; Vakulenko 2012; Vives 2010). Yet the block text is *not* a quotation from Crenshaw (2001) or, for that matter, from any of Crenshaw's scholarly publications. The conventional structure is so compelling that few have noticed the endnote following the block text, revealing that the source is not Crenshaw (2001) but a summary report on WCAR provided by human rights activist

Indira Patel in the United Kingdom. Patel did attend the Zagreb Expert Meeting, but her report that Yuval-Davis is quoting refers not to the Zagreb meeting but to WCAR, as Yuval-Davis's endnote indicates: "Report of the WCAR meeting as presented by Indira Patel to a day seminar in London organized by WILPF UK [The Women's International League for Peace and Freedom], November 2001" (2006b, 206n3). Yuval-Davis (2006b) does not include Patel in her list of references, though others have specifically cited Patel as the source of this version of the metaphor (see Asylum Aid 2002, 11, citing Patel 2002). What Yuval-Davis does include in the list of references is an *inaccurate reference source* for "Crenshaw (2001)," the ostensible source of the block text. The wording by Yuval-Davis (2006b) insinuates that the metaphor is found in Crenshaw's formal scholarship. It is not.

Yuval-Davis further misidentifies what she claims to be the source of the block text: Crenshaw (2001). She identifies the source in her reference list as "'Mapping the Margins: Intersectionality, Identity Politics and Violence against Women of Color,' paper presented at the World Conference against Racism; at www.hsph.harvard.edu/grhf/WofC/feminisms/crenshaw.html" (Yuval-Davis 2006b, 207). This citation is inaccurate. Crenshaw's curriculum vitae lists her presentation at WCAR as "The Intersectionality of Race and Gender Discrimination" (2001). "Mapping the Margins" is an article published in the *Stanford Law Review* ten years earlier (1991) and subsequently reprinted several times (for example, 1994, 1995a, 1995b). The website Yuval-Davis lists as the source is not a site concerned with WCAR. It is hosted by the Harvard School of Public Health (hsph), in the section for the Global Reproductive Health Forum (grhf), and the Woman of Color Web (WofC). In any case, "Mapping the Margins" does not develop *any* traffic metaphors for intersectionality. Yuval-Davis's misattribution of material from Crenshaw here is not unique but proves to be systematic.[7]

To summarize: the block text framed by Yuval-Davis as a direct quotation from Crenshaw—and taken as such by numerous scholars who cite Yuval-Davis 2006b—appears to be Patel's individually inflected paraphrase of a comment made by Crenshaw in an informal workshop for a broad audience of participants from many countries for the gender caucus at WCAR.[8] Reports of the details vary, though the workshop appears to have included an introduction to a traffic metaphor, some concrete examples of street names, and likely mention of a many-layered blanket of oppression. The various reports created by delegates and brought back to their own social activist groups—like Patel's—do not attempt to quote Crenshaw, but summarize and revise her comments, adapting them to suit each group's particular interests. This becomes evident, for example, as different reports provide different names for the examples of thoroughfares with dangerous traffic. According to the report by the Australian National Committee on Refugee Women (ANCORW):

> The main highway is 'Racism Road.' One cross street might be Colonisation Causeway, then Patriarchy Street, Religion Road, Slavery Street, Culture Cul de Sac, Trafficking Way, Forced Migration Road, Indigenous Exploitation Highway, Globalization Street, Caste Road—we could go on naming the town. (2002, 25–26)

According to the report by Asia Pacific Forum on Women, Law and Development (APWLD), the streets are

> Racism Road, Patriarchy Parade, Sexism Street, Colonization Crescent, Religious Persecution Road, Indigenous Dispossession Highway, Class Street, Caste Street, and so on. . . . To use this model as an analytic tool, each of the "Road Names" must be unpacked to explore the origin of the oppression, and the impact of these on women across a range of situations. (2003, 18)

The locally inflected "uptake" of the metaphor is evidence of its ability to offer a strategic point of entry for activism and practical action; this is true even though people from different nations have different definitions of intersectionality (see Falcón 2016). The developing and refining of the traffic metaphor was further carried on in the aftermath of WCAR, in reports to and by human rights groups involved in WCAR, sometimes mentioning that their metaphor was "developed by" Crenshaw, other times not mentioning Crenshaw at all. That metaphor is no longer "Crenshaw's" in an academic sense.

Adapted by different participants for different audiences, the metaphor becomes part of a repertoire of collective action, perhaps similar to what Charles Tilly likens to improvisational jazz, wherein composers provide an initial line which is taken up by those who improvise in their own ways, in interaction with one another (1983, 463, cited in Tarrow 2013). At WCAR intersectionality was both generative and contentious language. Sidney Tarrow points out that changes in contentious language are "dialogic" (2013, 12, citing Bakhtin 1981).

Yuval-Davis indicates that she sees in the preparations for WCAR and particularly in the block text a disturbing similarity to the Black "identity politics" that she criticized long ago (2006b, citing Anthias and Yuval-Davis 1983). While it would be valuable for Yuval-Davis to develop her argument, to explain fully what specifically about preparations for WCAR and the material she presents in the block text evoke past concerns with identity politics, she does not do so. Perhaps it is the notion of multiple layers of oppression that Yuval-Davis links to previous arguments, since Floya Anthias and Yuval-Davis (1983) chastise Black British women for thinking they are multiply oppressed because they do so "mechanically." Without irony, Anthias and Yuval-Davis (1983) celebrate in contrast the more flexible issues that they find when analyzing communities like their own which are "ethnic" rather than "racial." When Yuval-Davis (2006b) evokes her previous condemnation of Black identity politics as disturbingly present in the discourse preliminary to WCAR, she shows no signs of acknowledging the enormous changes in the understanding of identity politics between 1983 and 2006, of feminist and antiracist recognition that some of the most powerful forms of identity politics are those of white people (see, for example, Ahmed 2004, 2012; Blee 2003; Bonilla-Silva 2001; Feagin 2001; Frankenberg 1993; Gallagher, 1999; Haney López 2006; Lipsitz 1998; McKinney, 2004; C. Mills 1997; Roediger 1991). These are the forms of identity politics that should be of great concern to feminists, rather than resurrecting white critiques of the historical rhetoric of Black identity politics and implying that intersectional thinking promotes those politics.

I HEARD IT THROUGH THE GRAPEVINE

Yuval-Davis models the reductive, reified, decontextualized representation of complex arguments that often characterizes critiques of intersectionality. She assumes, without attempting to defend the notion, that a brief passage can pinpoint Crenshaw's thinking so precisely that it is unnecessary to acknowledge Crenshaw's many complex arguments about fluidity, flexibility, contingency, and *both/and* thinking. That Yuval-Davis provides no defense for her procedure reveals its function as a move of dominant discourse, a discursive technology of power. Ignoring the responsibility to justify specific argumentative moves demonstrates the role of dominant discourses, according to Richard Terdiman (1985). Terdiman argues that

> the inherent tendency of a dominant discourse is to "go without saying." . . . [T]he dominant is the discourse which, being everywhere, comes from nowhere: to it is granted the structural privilege of appearing to be unaware of the very question of its own legitimacy. Bourdieu calls this self-assured divorce from consciousness of its own contingency "genesis amnesia." (1985, 61, citing Bourdieu 1977, 79)

Yuval-Davis does not justify her procedure and appears unaware that the question of its legitimacy reveals its function as a discourse of dominance. Robert Stam argues that "language and power intersect wherever the question of language becomes involved in asymmetrical power relationships" (1988, 123). Yuval-Davis creates asymmetrical power relationships at the scene of argument not only by providing false claims about Crenshaw's traffic metaphors but also by treating an instance of a metaphor as if it could stand in for the entirety and full complexity of Crenshaw's many arguments about intersectionality. Powerblind citational practices echo Yuval-Davis's discourse of dominance, assuming that denigrating the words of the block text is adequate grounds to dismiss virtually all that Crenshaw has argued about intersectional thinking.

It is evident that Yuval-Davis (2006b) is an unreliable source about Crenshaw's arguments and metaphors. Scholars who rely on unreliable sources unwittingly enter what I call the "Canyon of Echoes," in which they create their own unreliable arguments. Most scholars who repeat Yuval-Davis's block text follow the signals of her textual structure, attribute the text to Crenshaw, and treat it as a quotation from Crenshaw's published work. In fact, many who quote Yuval-Davis's formulation or cite her argument appear confused, treating the block text as if it were the *only* traffic metaphor created by Crenshaw. They often reify the material isolated in Yuval-Davis's block text in ways that are common in powerblind treatment of Crenshaw's original traffic metaphor: critics wrest the metaphor out of context and treat it as neatly encapsulating *everything* Crenshaw has argued about intersectionality, so that dismissal can be a simple, efficient process. Some scholars referring to Yuval-Davis's block text do not criticize it; others declare (incorrectly) that the material in the block text has been thoroughly criticized in the past; others use the material in the block text as a basis for attributing simplistic thinking to Black American feminist intersectional scholars.

Sabrina Marchetti (2014), for example, relies on Yuval-Davis's (2006b) block text. (There are fifteen citations to Marchetti's book in Google Scholar as of May 10, 2018.) Marchetti states:

> Initially, in 1989, the US scholar Kimberly [*sic*] Crenshaw suggested the *following image of the black woman at a crossroads,* saying:
>
>> Intersectionality is what occurs when a woman from a minority group . . . tries to navigate the main crossing in the city. . . . The main highway is "Racism Road." One cross street can be Colonialism, then Patriarchy Street. . . . She has to deal not only with one form of oppression but with all forms, those

named as road signs, which link together to make a double, a triple, multiple, a many layered blanket of oppression. (Marchetti 2014, 22, quoting the block text incorrectly attributed to Crenshaw in Yuval-Davis 2006b, emphasis added)

Marchetti here continues Yuval-Davis's pattern of multiple errors. She relies on the block text of Yuval-Davis, but rather than attributing it to "Mapping," as Yuval-Davis wrongly does, Marchetti adds an error of her own by wrongly attributing the block text to an unidentified publication from 1989. Since Crenshaw's "Demarginalizing" was published in 1989 and included a traffic metaphor, Marchetti appears to attribute the block text to it and assumes that Crenshaw has produced only one traffic metaphor. (Crenshaw's more complex traffic metaphor of "Demarginalizing" [1989] is discussed in Chapters 3 and 9.)

Furthering the notion that Black women can and do speak for only Black women (also reflected in Wendy Brown's texts [1997, 2005, 2008]), Marchetti introduces the block text by describing it as Crenshaw's image of "the black woman at a crossroads," despite the fact that the actual block text— quoted immediately following Marchetti's remark—describes the protagonist not as a Black woman but as "a woman from a minority group." Marchetti is so satisfied with the view from Yuval-Davis's eyes that she appears not to refer to any of Crenshaw's actual publications to assess the arguments she is criticizing. Marchetti does not cite Crenshaw's publications in her argument; she even misspells Crenshaw's first name. Marchetti goes on to comment on the block text:

Later on, in Europe, scholars *preferred* images such as that of the "kaleidoscope" (Botman, Jouwe and Wekker 2001), or that of "intersecting boundaries" (Anthias and Yuval-Davis 1983) in order to go beyond Crenshaw's simpler model of the multiple oppressions, which had already received much criticism in the US ([K.] Davis 2008). Today, intersectionality is seen as a powerful tool for the analysis of inequalities and differences, as a way to talk about multiple identities and Foucaultian power dynamics, rather than oppression (ibid.) (Marchetti 2014, 22, emphasis added)

Perhaps because Marchetti views Crenshaw through the eyes of Yuval-Davis, she is not aware that Crenshaw (1989) does not offer a "simpler model of multiple oppressions" (nor, in fact, does Kathy Davis [2008] report that she does). Crenshaw (1989) does not use the term "multiple oppression." Rather, Crenshaw developed there a *different traffic metaphor* as part of developing a complex theoretical argument about the politics of *both/and,* sameness/difference, embedded in complex discussions of civil rights law and sharing multiple points of connection with the positions of many poststructuralists. While there are certainly some political benefits in using terms such as "multiple oppressions," and the term has been used by other Black feminist scholars, Crenshaw has seldom done so (though see its use in the title of an article for the general public in 2003). Rather, Crenshaw has argued repeatedly and systematically for complex intersectional models of power and identity. Marchetti continues by relying on a trope endemic to European critiques of intersectionality: American Black feminists are simplistic in their thinking and their concern for "oppression," while Europeans have improved the concept of intersectionality with superior thinking (for example, implying that because they have read Foucault they know better than to think in terms of "oppression"). (See discussions of the complexities of European reception of intersectionality in Bilge 2013, 2014; Lewis 2009, 2013; and Chapters 7 and 8.)

Marchetti also indulges in a problematic trope shared across the Atlantic: the assumption that the use of any race- or ethnicity-related term or metaphor other than "intersectionality" represents a studied criticism or invalidation of the term "intersectional." This logical leap increases the scope of what can be presented as negative criticism of intersectionality. The argument is often expressed, as it is by Marchetti, as a case of "preference," with little or no explanation provided justifying the significance of the "preference." Marchetti's citation of the work of Maayke Botman, Nancy Jouwe, and Gloria Wekker (2001)—who used the image of a "kaleidoscope" in a title—cannot serve as evidence that these authors have repudiated the term "intersectionality." For example, in Wekker's most recent book, *White Innocence: Paradoxes of Colonialism and Race* (2016), Wekker indicates that she is deeply invested in intersectional thinking; in the book she frequently uses the terms "intersection," "intersectional," and "intersectionality." Further, Anthias and Yuval-Davis (1983) were not in a position to "prefer" "intersecting boundaries" to "intersectionality" because the latter term was not in use when their article was published in 1983: the article in which Crenshaw presented her formulation of the term was published six years later, in 1989. Note that Marchetti herself uses the term "intersectionality," and it also appears in the title of Yuval-Davis's article under discussion here—"Intersectionality and Feminist Politics" (2006b)—obviating Marchetti's entire line of argument denigrating or repudiating the term.

Anastasia Vakulenko (2012) also relies on Yuval-Davis's block text. (There are four citations in Google Scholar to Vakulenko's chapter and thirty-four to the anthology in which the chapter appears as of May 10, 2018.) Vakulenko asserts that Crenshaw's metaphor to explain intersectionality is that of the crossroads:

> Intersectionality is what occurs when a woman from a minority group . . . tries to navigate the main crossing in the city. . . . The main highway is 'racism road.' One cross street can be Colonialism, then Patriarchy Street. . . . She has to deal not only with one form of oppression but with all forms, those named as road signs, which link together to make a double, a triple, multiple, a many layered blanket of oppression. (Vakulenko 2012, 207, inaccurately citing source of block text as Crenshaw, "Mapping the Margins" Harvard School of Public Health, http://www.wcsap.org/Events/Workshop07/mapping-margins.pdf at 9 December 2008)

Vakulenko's citation of the source of the block text, like that of Yuval-Davis, is structured to imply that it appears in a published scholarly text, "Mapping the Margins" (http://www.wcsap.org/Events/Workshop07/mapping-margins.pdf at 9 December 2008). However, Vakulenko's citation of the source is also inaccurate. The site "wcsap" is provided by the Washington Coalition of Sexual Assault Programs, which has affiliations with the Harvard School of Public Health. The citation appears to be for an event that used "Mapping the Margins" as a source for discussion. However, "Mapping the Margins" does not contain the block text presented by Yuval-Davis (2006b) or any traffic metaphor.

Vakulenko goes on to interpret the block text to criticize intersectionality. She argues:

> *Accordingly, an individual is treated as a composite of (discrete) identity elements* such as gender, race. . . . This is problematic precisely because it seems to defeat the very point of intersectionality—that one strand of identity (gender) cannot exist in isolation from others. (2012, 207, emphasis added)

While the block text is not from one of Crenshaw's published articles but apparently Patel's paraphrase of an informal presentation by Crenshaw at the gender caucus at WCAR, it has become fodder for powerblind criticism. Vakulenko misinterprets the text in part by relying on widely used powerblind citations of scholarly authority. She assumes that the names of streets represent *identity categories,* concluding that Crenshaw is isolating gender from other categories. This assumption is faulty.

The street names mentioned in the block text are not identity categories but specifically *discriminations*: racism, colonialism, and patriarchy. Both *grammatically* and *substantively* these are not the same as *elements of identity.*[9] For example, racism tends to categorize people consequentially according to imputed elements of racial identity; patriarchy tends to attribute qualities and allocate power according to imputed elements of gender identities. Because the streets are not names of identity categories, the street that is relevant for Vakulenko would not be named "Gender," an *identity category,* but "Sexism," a *discrimination* that often targets others according to their imputed gender identity. The fact that gender is an element of identity does not make it *all* that gender is.

As is true of many critics of intersectionality, Vakulenko confuses a claim about structural sources of discrimination and discriminatory experiences with an encapsulated conception of "identities." But the metaphor is not about identities. The block text, as a traffic metaphor, describes dominant structures and patterns of discrimination or oppression. These discriminations or oppressions are labeled, but intersectional scholars do not argue that they operate discretely; they are often created by structures of power and people who conflate and combine them, so that they link together. The fact that various kinds of discrimination have different names (i.e., the road names), and that the minority woman's trajectory may be interrupted by the traffic on more than one road makes various discriminations *an aspect of her experiences and their structural influences, not an element of her identity.*

These misreadings may occur because for so many white feminists it is the identity of "the minority woman" and her expression of subjectivity that is particularly salient, rather than the structures of power that influence her experiences. Perhaps that salience encourages the slippage from the block text's claims of *discriminations* and *potential experience* to Vakulenko's and others' redefinition of them as claims of *identity.* There are relationships between identities and experiences, but these are complex and variable. To see race and gender as triggers for discriminations is to treat them as inherent to individuals rather than systematic attributions ascribed to individuals according to dominant structures of power. The terms "gender" and "race" are better thought of not as single categories but as processes or clustered fictions, reified by the force of law and sedimented histories. It may be helpful to think of gender in the terms that Cheryl Harris used when discussing the reification of whiteness (see Chapter 2). Like race, gender is "a relation between people [that] takes on the character of a thing and thus acquires a 'phantom objectivity,' an autonomy that seems so strictly rational and all-embracing as to conceal every trace of its fundamental nature: the relation between people" (Lukács 1971, 83, quoted in C. Harris 1993, 1730).

It is a logical error to conflate the existence of discriminations or oppressions with elements of identity, as if people did not have political agency and resistance of many kinds. The attributions of dominant structures of power do not encompass or control the identity and agency of subordinated peoples. As related by Oneida poet Roberta Hill Whiteman:

> *You have helped me to understand*
> *their fear of the dark*
> *is not my identity.*
> (WHITEMAN 1996, 91)

As Cedric J. Robinson argues, "We are not the subjects or the subject formations of the capitalist world-system. It is simply one condition of our being" (1996, 122).

Vakulenko, like Yuval-Davis and others, misunderstands the polysemic and flexible nature of metaphor and its multiple meanings—reading metaphor through a hegemonic lens as limited to mapping one territory, rather than understanding the role of metaphor in offering a series of snapshots and differing points of view to clarify various aspects of theory for social activists. Neither Patel and the other reporters from WCAR nor Crenshaw argues that identity elements begin discretely; Vakulenko's argument is undermined by her apparently unwitting reliance on an entire set of powerblind white feminist critiques of intersectionality, without acknowledging that their claims are radically underargued—providing little evidence that intersectional scholars actually hold the positions claimed (she draws on, for example, Brown 1997 [see criticism earlier in Chapter 6 and also Chapter 9], McCall 2005, 1771n5 [see criticism of the note in Chapter 9], Prins 2006 [see criticism in Chapter 8], Yuval-Davis 2006b [see criticism earlier in Chapter 6 and also in Chapter 8.)

TWO KEY MECHANISMS OF POWERBLIND FEMINISM

In this chapter, I demonstrate that contemporary scholars often establish citational authority on faulty, uninterrogated arguments such as those of Brown (1997) and Yuval-Davis (2006b) and carry them forward into the present without reexamination. The specific contexts and problems of these arguments are obscured, closed off, or "black-boxed" by their successful history of circulation as authoritative citations. They are often *cited* but not *scrutinized.* Such citational practices operate as a conservative force, so that contemporary critical discussion of intersectionality ultimately congeals around powerblind strategies deployed in the past to reinforce white women's symbolic domination of feminist studies. I also demonstrate the peculiarly casual grounding of negative claims about intersectionality that are taken up and repeatedly cited across contemporary texts. The claims of white critics—however erroneous—are treated as so persuasive as to obviate the necessity of double-checking their claims by referring to the actual arguments of intersectional scholars of color.

These citational practices are so widespread as to demonstrate that they are fully authorized by feminist scholarship's shared metadiscursive regimes. Such citational practices rest on two key mechanisms of powerblind feminism: Intersectionality Telephone and the Canyon of Echoes. These mechanisms of discursive dominance authorize a shared discourse of casual and perfunctory commentary about intersectionality among readers and authors of powerblind white critiques.

Intersectionality Telephone treats citation and commentary about intersectionality according to rules similar to the childhood game that those in the United States call "Telephone." In Telephone, the first player originates a phrase and whispers it to the next person down a line of players: participants successively whisper what they believe they have heard to the next player, until finally the last listener announces to the entire group the statement that he or she may have heard. In the game of Telephone errors typically accumulate in the retellings; the statement announced by the last player differs significantly, and often amusingly, from the one uttered by the first. Some players also deliberately change what they pass on in order to guarantee an altered message by the end of it. The "entertainment" of the childhood game of Telephone is the difference between the original statement and the final representation of it. I argue, however, that there is little entertainment provided by evaluating the tools for feminist and antiracist analysis according to the standards of fidelity provided by Intersectionality Telephone. Advancing critiques that amplify their mishearing and misrepresenting of the original claims of intersectional scholars with each paraphrase, reiterating inaccurate earlier work until what is said and heard at the end bears precious little relationship to what was said at the start, Intersectionality Telephone treats the important political and intellectual tools of feminism as "fodder" for confusion and chaotic communication.

Readers who are not knowledgeable about what intersectional scholars of color have *actually* argued might find it difficult to detect the widespread use of Intersectionality Telephone, since it is essentially a disinformation campaign at the expense of intersectional scholars of color, depending on complex knots of misstatement, insinuation, false comparisons, and other strategies. For example, in her much-cited critique of intersectionality, Kathy Davis claims "Controversies have emerged about whether intersectionality should be conceptualized as a crossroad (Crenshaw 1991), as 'axes' of difference (Yuval-Davis 2006b), or as dynamic processes (Staunæs 2003)" (Davis 2008, 68). It is not evident from Davis's description that the word "crossroad" never appears in Crenshaw 1991—casting some doubt on Davis's claim that the article argued that intersectionality should be conceptualized as a crossroad. (See Chapter 3 for distinctions between the metaphors of "intersection" and "crossroad.") It is also not evident from Davis's description that Yuval-Davis's use of "axes" (2006b) appeared eighteen years after Crenshaw (1989) had interrogated the problems of "single-axis" categorization in the law. Finally, Davis does not acknowledge that Dorthe Staunæs's use of "dynamic process" (2003) appeared twelve years after Crenshaw (1991) used the term at least seven times to discuss intersectionality (for example, "the dynamics of structural intersectionality" [1245], "recognizing the failure to consider intersectional dynamics" [1251], "the intraracial dynamics of race and gender subordination" [1281]). The result of Intersectionality Telephone is by no means random: it works systematically to reduce the status of the intellectual legacy of the women of color who developed intersectionality.

Intersectionality Telephone is not unusual, but rather a preferred method of inviting readers to find deficient the intersectional arguments of women of color. For example, as I mentioned earlier, Yuval-Davis criticizes the crossroad metaphor that she incorrectly attributes to Crenshaw, remarking simply that it is "additive" (2006b, 197). Davis (2008) claims that Yuval-Davis (2006b) provides a "critique of the 'crossroad' metaphor." According to Davis, Yuval-Davis "implies that once a road is taken, all other roads become irrelevant, at least for the time being" (K. Davis 2008, 81n15, citing Yuval-Davis 2006b). I find no such criticism in Yuval-Davis's article. In fact, such a criticism would appear to be an erroneous interpretation not only of intersectional theorizing, but of the metaphor found in the block text, which appears to state the opposite: "A woman from a minority group . . . has to deal *not only with one form of oppression but with all forms*" (Yuval-Davis 2006b, 196, block text presented as if a quotation from Crenshaw). Further, it is part of experiences of subject formation that at particular moments, single identities, experiences, or structures of power may be salient. It is impossible to encompass all identities, experiences, or structures of power at all times. In any case, such a criticism is not relevant to this image. There is no mention of the woman taking a particular road, since she is negotiating a "crossing," or intersection, not heading down a single road. I found no statement either asserting or implying such a criticism in Yuval-Davis (2006b).

This would appear to be but one of many false citations found in powerblind white critiques of intersectionality, creating a chain of negative commentary through powerblind citations without legitimate grounding. These and other violations of responsible citational practices pervade powerblind critiques of intersectionality, creating a Canyon of Echoes full of inaccurate discussion of intersectionality and the scholars of color who produced it. Vivian M. May (2014, 2015) notes that many critiques repeatedly cited as evidence of intersectionality's failings in fact approach intersectionality "nonintersectionally," using the very strategies of *either/or* thinking that intersectionality challenges (2014, 102). Framing intersectionality in narrow and inaccurate ways, critics then propose to repair the concept by applying what they claim to be their own insights without acknowledging—perhaps without even knowing—that what they present as their own arguments are already central aspects of intersectional thinking (103). Contradictory and inaccurate claims are made—intersectionality is static, intersectionality attends to only identities, intersectionality looks at only structures of power, intersectionality ignores contexts—all by failing to research adequately the conceptions developed by intersectional scholars of color (103). Broad claims about weaknesses in the conception of intersectionality as a whole are made with reference to few or no intersectional scholars and without grounding or proof in specific arguments. Critics often do not evaluate and screen the claims of the texts of other white critics that they cite. So while critics bolster their scholarly authority through long chains of citations, these chains treat as equally valid what are often antithetical and irreconcilable arguments. The result of these citational practices is to create uncertainty and confusion about the nature of intersectionality and to imply that this confusion stems from the inadequate thinking of women of color, rather than the poor scholarship and uninterrogated assumptions of white feminist critiques.

In the Canyon of Echoes, scholars citing other scholars of similar mind-set create an inaccurate and inexcusably distorted view of women of color feminism. In the Canyon of Echoes, negative claims about arguments are repeated without proof they are true as long as they seem plausible, entertaining, or satisfying to the immediate participants in the debate. The Canyon of Echoes is a busy, noisy place that all of us work in, that we think of as familiar and natural, and that we regularly fail to criticize. Presenting itself as a place of analysis, it reverberates with bits and residues, *echoes not claims,* disconnected from originating speakers and arguments, bounced forward and back as fragments, resonant as whispers, gossip, innuendo, insinuation, repeating claims caught from air as if they were faithful to the original. Rather than providing accurate information about what a scholar's claim *actually is,* the Canyon abounds with claims of "seems like, might be, must be, surely is, comes close to, similar to, resembles, brings to mind, passes for, shows the signs of, conveys the impression of, has the features of, could pass for, suggests, strikes one as being." As it stands, the Canyon provides what any scholar and her cohort deem a "good enough" approximation. The "good enough" approximation serves as the foundation to judge the claim, to find that it "insinuates, implies, insists, compels, reinscribes, replicates, fails to escape, endorses, reduces, means 'something'" and, in fact, does so "necessarily, simply, only, merely, exclusively." There is apparently no time or reason to reread originals or related arguments by women of color, so critical comments circulate like rumors on the grapevine. As one might expect, the echoing, mimicking, and mirroring of original arguments in the Canyon of Echoes accumulates errors and misrepresentations.

Controversial claims about feminism and race are often situated deep in the Canyon of Echoes, so that all the examples I have offered are not particular to individual authors; they are *symptomatic.* Life in the Canyon of Echoes authorizes and naturalizes denigrating and dismissing the claims of intersectional scholars of color without acknowledging the purpose, the precision, and the context of originating arguments. In a practice remarkable for a purportedly interdisciplinary field, critics often focus so closely on their own disciplinary concerns that they lose sight of *other people's* disciplines, interests, and needs. In the Canyon of Echoes, critics frequently treat *any object of analysis* as if the only proper criteria for judgment are those authorized by their own discipline. To assume that one can serve as arbiter of the standards of all disciplines seems something of an act of hubris. Worse, dwelling in the Canyon of Echoes invites us to substitute hearsay and careless citation for the precise, rigorous development of concepts and tools. The prevalence of techniques grounded in Intersectionality Telephone and the Canyon of Echoes reveals the preeminence of a shared feminist metadiscursive regime that satisfies the presumptions of white racial dominance, yet works fatally to undermine the generativity and social responsibility of feminist knowledge production.

THE INVISIBLE WHITE WOMAN

I have argued that powerblind strategies pervade feminist discourses in part because the past is still present in the contemporary reception of intersectionality. Their discursive strategies suggest that for many critics intersectionality looms as a symbolic marker of a moment when white women perceived their central place in feminism to be threatened, when they were forced to account in feminist analysis for the heterogeneity of social difference and for the contributions of women of color in forging a feminism capable of reckoning with the pervasive presence of racism. The generative moment of rupture that marked a new beginning for women of color feminists and their allies stands for others as a symbol of the trauma of lost power and diminished centrality, provoking powerful articulations of longing and loss.

As a result, that moment of generative rupture is still being resisted at the scene of feminist argument through specific rhetorics and claims in contemporary scholarly texts suffused with unacknowledged desires to reject race, to recover lost territory, and even to retaliate. Rather than committing themselves to honoring, extending, and augmenting the extraordinary advances in feminist analysis made possible by intersectionality and related concepts, contemporary feminist critiques of intersectionality are filled with efforts to contain, control, co-opt, delegitimate, and appropriate it at the scene of argument. A cluster of powerblind rhetorical devices and conventions of argument that I call "managing intersectionality" works relentlessly, particularly in the arena of European academic feminism, to reinscribe the white middle-class heterosexual woman as the dominant subject position of feminist politics.

The practice of managing intersectionality is political, but it does not proceed politically. It is ideological, but it does not proceed ideologically. It is epistemological, but it does not proceed epistemologically. Instead, it works surreptitiously through rhetorics, moves, tropes, and mechanisms at the scene of argument. In the arena of European feminism (caught, according to Maria Carbin and Sara Edenheim [2013], between the "ghost of Black feminism" and the "ghost of poststructuralism"), managing intersectionality is a discursive practice infused by anxiety about what Cengiz Barskanmaz (2010) calls the "fetish" of intersectionality. While sharing some characteristics with American critiques of intersectionality (see Alexander-Floyd 2012; May 2014, 2015; see also Chapters 6 and 8), European critiques tend to use both racial and geographical difference to argue for the superiority of (white) European thinking over the parochial thinking of Black American feminists. All distinctions—however ungrounded, inaccurate, tendentious—are treated as grist for the partisan mill through hierarchical binary claims in these critiques. They allege that Black feminists thought of only three categories, while Europeans can think of many categories; that Black feminists posited categories as "fixed" and "static," while Europeans know they are "fluid"; that Black feminists focused on only "oppression," while Europeans know identities are "positioned"; that Black feminists conceived of intersectionality as a "metaphor" bound by "experience," while Europeans transformed it into a "theory" with a "methodology"; that Black feminists were enmeshed in "identity politics" (racialized subjects challenging their racialization), while Europeans are "free of race" and thus capable of creating an intersectionality "fit for universality" (see, for example, Carbin and Edenheim 2013; Lutz, Herrera Vivar, and Supik 2011; Prins 2006; Yuval-Davis 2006b). Kimberlé Crenshaw addressed these and related problematic arguments specific to the European arena in her "Postscript" to a German conference that disingenuously titled itself "Celebrating Intersectionality?" (2011b). With one exception, the essays resulting from the conference did not respond to her arguments (see Lutz, Herrera Vivar, and Supik 2011).

Structurally, managing intersectionality is inevitably a racializing discourse because the originating intersectionality is a production of women of color, and because the European critiques of intersectionality tend to rely on the subject position of the invisible white woman. While often claiming "race" as a category inapplicable to Europe, these critiques of intersectionality at the same time reinscribe racial dominance at the scene of argument through incessant moves to re-racialize, encapsulate, and distance themselves from "the ghost of Black feminism" (see congruent criticism by Barskanmaz 2010; Bilge 2013, 2014; Erel et al. 2011; Petzen 2012; see also May 2014, 2015; and Chapter 8). As Walter D. Mignolo argues (2011), whiteness manages not only the categories of thought and the terms of debate but also the conditions by which people of color are permitted to participate in systems of knowledge production. As a result, the subject position of the white woman tends to be unmarked within its own discourse, but all too visible to those it seeks to manage (see, with regard to European feminist discourses, Ahmed 2012; Bilge 2013, 2014; Erel et al. 2011; Lewis 2009, 2013; Petzen 2012).

The practice of managing intersectionality by recognizing yet encapsulating and ultimately rejecting it as a racial production renders *invisible* the white feminist manager. The dominant subject position of the white (middle-class, heterosexual) woman is not the embodied identity of the individual but a privileged standpoint and structural advantage, a matter of foregrounding dominant interests and deprecating the interests of antisubordination scholars and activists (as Sirma Bilge argues, "One does not need to be white to whiten intersectionality" [2013, 413]). Following Sara Ahmed, we could consider it an "institutional position" (2012). Particularly in European feminist discourse, the term "identity politics" appears to be used to characterize mainly the claims of women of color as racialism and essentialism or to advance stereotypes about their imputed role in U.S. racial politics in the last decades of the twentieth century. Such discussions do not acknowledge feminism itself as an identity politics. The result is to reinstate the managerial subject position of the invisible white woman as the uninterrogated norm for conceptual and political feminist theorizing. The discursive moves of managing intersectionality are framed within a feminist imaginary that suppresses acknowledgment of feminism as an identity politics in order to appropriate from women of color the intellectual assets and the academic prestige of intersectionality and to distance its origins in radical and racial critique.

Managing intersectionality is evidenced at the scene of argument when European feminist critiques of intersectionality repeatedly turn to Judith Butler's interrogation of concepts such as "categories," "identity," or "the subject" as justification for countering or closing down the validity of all claims about difference except those discursively administered by the invisible white woman. Specific passages from Butler's *Gender Trouble* (1990) are deployed frequently as justifications for these critics' claims. In *Gender Trouble* Butler interrogates the category of "woman," arguing that, rather than being a stable subject that we can take for granted as a "natural" category, it is a "phantasmatic construction," one that appears unified only through exclusions that it fails to acknowledge. Butler argues that feminist presuppositions about the need to posit the unity of "woman" lead feminists to paper over the exclusions built into creation of such a unified category. She urges feminists to see the radical instability of the category not as a "cause for despair" but as the condition of new possibility (1990, 142).

Here and elsewhere, Butler counters the notion that there must be a universal basis for feminism—a stable, unified female subject—and that the prior existence of this subject is necessary to ground feminist politics. She argues that identity categories (such as "woman" or "queer" or "race") are "performative"; they are "political effects" created *in* politics, not *prior* to politics (see Hall 1996; Lloyd 2005; Mirón and Inda 2000; Rodríguez 2003). Butler argues that identities do not express what one is but what one does. She is questioning the exclusionary nature of the very act of categorization. She argues that invocation of a unified identity immediately produces resistance "within the very constituency that is supposed to be *unified* by the articulation of its common element" (1995, 49). This is the moment when Butler argues that, in the 1980s, "the feminist 'we' rightly came under attack by women of color who claimed that the 'we' was invariably white, and that the 'we' that was meant to solidify the movement was the very source of a painful factionalization" (49). Butler's challenge in *Gender Trouble* targets a hegemonic political fantasy of unified white heterosexual feminism, *not* the multiple identities discussed by feminists of color. In fact, Butler's work is in many ways aligned with the critique that women of color feminists have been making for nearly three decades, yet she is often cited as if her work delegitimates their arguments. The use of Butler's scholarship as a club to be used against women of color feminism often revolves around a specific iteration: the repeated invocation of a passage in *Gender Trouble* (1990) that I call the "Case of the Et Cetera."

THE CASE OF THE ET CETERA

The Case of the Et Cetera appears in the concluding chapter of *Gender Trouble.* At this point in the book, Butler is drawing together her arguments about the problems of framing agency in political action if one assumes there must be a prior stable autonomous subject, "a doer behind the deed." In the passage in question, Butler argues:

Theories of feminist identity that elaborate predicates of color, sexuality, ethnicity, class and able-bodiedness invariably close with an embarrassed "etc." at the end of the list. Through this horizontal trajectory of adjectives, these positions strive to encompass a situated subject, but invariably fail to be complete. This failure, however, is instructive: *what political impetus is to be derived from the exasperated "etc." that so often occurs at the end of such lines?* This is a sign of exhaustion as well as of the illimitable process of signification itself. It is the *supplément,* the excess that necessarily accompanies any effort to posit identity once and for all. This illimitable *et cetera,* however, *offers itself as a new departure for feminist political theorizing.* (Butler 1990, 143, emphasis added)

In this chapter of *Gender Trouble,* and throughout her work, Butler is arguing that *all* categories are inescapably exclusionary and constitutively incomplete. She contends that the nature of language is one of the reasons that this is so. She is not arguing that too many annoying and illegitimate differences are being asserted, but rather that talking about and negotiating identities are discursive acts that can never be closed. Her reference to the *supplément* makes this clear: any effort to posit identity once and for all is bound to fail because there will *always* be an *excess* that cannot be accounted for. Further, in that excess, that illimitability, theorists might find new ways of thinking. The textual context of the Case of the Et Cetera demonstrates that Butler is not critical of, but in fact sympathetic toward, those who must conclude with what is termed the "embarrassed etc." or the "exasperated etc." They—and everyone—are in that "embarrassing" and "exasperating" situation because, in current conditions, acknowledging the political significance of ever-shifting discursive construction of identities frequently makes sense, yet cannot be complete.

Contemporary European critiques of intersectionality, however, present the Case of the Et Cetera as destroying claims of difference. To do so, they misrepresent Butler's arguments. They treat her comments as destroying the legitimacy of arguments about "predicated identities" while eliding the concomitant argument that *all* identities are predicated, that the invisible white middle-class heterosexual woman is "unpredicated" only because dominant structures of subordination render her predication "invisible" or "unmarked." They tend to ignore Butler's claim—made twice in the passage—that recognition of the illimitability offers new possibilities for feminist theorizing.

I examine here seven occasions where the Case of the Et Cetera is evoked in critiques of intersectionality, six located in the European arena and one repeating the claims of a European argument. These instances of the Case of the Et Cetera are used for several related purposes: to portray Butler as having already in the past demonstrated the illegitimacy of arguments about intersectional difference (creating a "ghost" of Black feminism); to express a kind of "category anxiety" that finds intersectionality flawed because it lacks a recipe to manage the full complexity of social categories in the world; to frame Butler as not really feminist or now irrelevant to feminism (creating a "ghost" of poststructuralism), so that scholars can disregard her cautions about categorizing in order to *manage intersectionality*; and—in a move that is not actually contradictory—to use Butler as a figure in a peculiar and particularly European call for a "broader genealogy of intersectionality" that identifies any number of white feminist scholars as previously "unacknowledged" intersectional scholars (see Bilge 2013, 2014). This last move, in particular, evidences a desperate white revanchism suffused with an unacknowledged desire to retaliate and recover lost territory by ejecting antiracism from feminism. This is a kind of neoliberal asset-stripping: appropriating a particular intellectual product of women of color feminists who used their situated knowledge as the basis for a more fully theorized understanding of universality and presenting it as the triumphant creation of a racially unmarked (but white) feminism. All of these moves, particularly the last, fall under what Bilge calls the "whitening" of intersectionality, a specific "depoliticization" that Bilge argues is taking place in European feminist circles (Bilge 2013, 2014; see also Barskanmaz 2010; Erel et al. 2011; May 2014, 2015; Petzen 2012; see also Chapters 4 and 8 on neoliberal asset-stripping).

FORMULAIC HISTORIES

Through the practice of managing intersectionality Butler's words are cited and represented again and again as claiming the opposite of what she actually argues. For example, presenting a formulaic history of intersectionality, Gudrun-Axeli Knapp (2005) draws on the Case of the Et Cetera in a way that reverses Butler's argument. (There are some 330 citations in Google Scholar to the journal article as of May 10, 2018.) Knapp claims:

> Debates on "differences" among women climaxed in the late 1980s and early 1990s *in a clash between* identitarian articulations of "differences" and radical questionings of the epistemological and political foundations of feminism, ambivalently labelled "postfeminist" theory. In this respect Judith Butler's (1990) *Gender Trouble: Feminism and the Subversion of Identity* marks a peak of this development *by radically subverting all "theories of feminist identity that elaborate predicates of color, sexuality, ethnicity, class, and able-bodiedness* [and] invariably close with an embarrassed 'etc.,' at the end of the list." (Knapp 2005, 254, quoting Butler 1990, 143, emphasis added)

Knapp represents Butler's argument as its opposite by inaccurately representing the specific historical debate, by misleadingly labeling the parties of the debate, by ignoring a significant party, and by misrepresenting the relation of the passage she quotes to the whole of Butler's argument. Knapp sets the stage for her misrepresentation of Butler's argument by oversimplifying her historical scene as the moment of a "clash" between "identitarian articulations of 'differences' and radical questionings of the epistemological and political foundations of feminism" (254). At the scene of argument, Knapp has simply made *invisible* a significant third party, the actual target of Butler's critique: a long-standing dominant group invested in the maintenance of a unified (white) feminist identity that has "agreed" to overlook difference, a group wishing to foreclose interrogation of that identity, to legislate in advance its existence as the sine qua non of feminist politics (see Lloyd 2005).

While the term "identitarian" addresses a complex debate and simplifies it beyond recognition, if it must be used, it would be reasonable also to call those who demand unquestioned maintenance of a unified feminist identity "identitarians" (or, perhaps more specifically, "white middle-class heterosexual unifying feminist identitarians"). But, in a move characteristic of many critiques of intersectionality, Knapp misleadingly labels as "identitarians" only people who insist that "difference" is an important site of social power, often lesbians or racialized women. Using the label "identitarians" in this way replicates hegemonic structures of power. Claims by nondominant groups that power infuses the construction of "identity" become marked and labeled, while claims about "identity" by dominant groups become invisible. Feminism is presented as something other than what these critiques demonstrate it to be: a deeply "identitarian" politics. Butler's critique of a unified subject of feminism—in many ways congruent with the claims of feminists of color—is presented as if it countered and closed down the validity of any identity claims made specifically and only by Black feminists, other women of color, and lesbian theorists. If Black feminist claims about identity have been defeated, then, such subjects have no claims to the intellectual resources they have developed, making those resources available for new depoliticized white neoliberal management.

Finally, Knapp misrepresents the role of the Case of Et Cetera in Butler's argument. Butler's challenge is to the inherent problems of categories and to feminism relying on "woman" as a unified identity. One of Butler's arguments is exactly that *all* identities are "predicated" and have "modalities"— that feminist identities are not all the same and one could never iterate all the possible differences they might have: "If one 'is' a woman, that is surely not all one is; the term fails to be exhaustive" (1990, 3). But in Knapp's presentation, the Case of the Et Cetera serves as "evidence" for the opposite argument: Butler's critique becomes directed specifically and only to theories of feminist identity "modified"—in effect, to the theories proposed by women of color, including intersectionality theorists. Knapp is simply incorrect: Butler did not "radically subvert" all "theories of feminist identity" modified or predicated; she "radically subverted" all theories of feminist identity *unified*.

Even the arguments of Stephanie A. Shields (2008), a North American who has done important and supportive work on intersectionality, are undermined by an unfortunate echoing of Knapp's narrative, relying on Knapp's

structuring of the historical moment and the significance of the Case of the
Et Cetera (as is true of Randi Gressgård 2008).[1] (There are nearly one thousand citations in Google Scholar to the journal article as of May 10, 2018.)
Because Shields is building on Knapp's argument, she falls into many of the
same traps, including creating the kind of formulaic history that infuses so
many critiques of intersectionality. Shields echoes Knapp in arguing:

> Knapp (2005) asserts that the rapidity with which ideas of intersec-
> tionality gained purchase was "the political and moral need for femi-
> nism to be inclusive in order to be able to keep up its own foundational
> premises" (p. 253). At the same time, the impulse toward inclusivity
> was challenged by the "postfeminist" controversies of the late 1980s
> and early 1990s[,] which either threatened to fragment feminism in a
> re-radicalized identity politics or reject the meaningfulness of identity
> categories (Knapp 2005). Butler's (1990) *Gender Trouble,* for example,
> posed a challenge to "theories of feminist identity that elaborate predi-
> cates" (p. 143). Indeed, Butler and others critique the very notion of
> "woman" as a stable category. (Shields 2008, 303)

Because she follows Knapp's pattern, Shields comes to use the Case of the
Et Cetera to argue inaccurately that Butler criticized specifically "predicated"
feminist identities (though acknowledging that Butler criticized the category
of "woman"). Following Knapp's narrative, Shields uses the Case of the Et
Cetera as an example of controversial arguments of the time that "threatened
. . . to reject the meaningfulness of identity categories" (303). In fact, Butler
does *not* "reject the meaningfulness of identity categories" but, more precisely,
"calls them into question" or "interrogates them." She does not deny their
political meaning but seeks to dislodge them so they can be re-thought. For
example, she finds the category "woman" politically meaningful and a rich
site for generative thinking (Butler 1995, 49–50).[2] But if it were in fact the
case that Butler had argued that identity categories are meaningless, why
should she be a resource for condemning only "predicated" feminist identities, rather than all feminist identities?

This is the kind of formulaic progressive narrative that Clare Hemmings
argues to be characteristic of feminist histories (2011). The "story" of these
histories begins with an idealized, ahistorical vision of pre-1980s feminism:
a unified (apparently nonclassed, nonraced, nonsexual) feminism that could
be said to have "foundational premises" such as "inclusiveness." According to
the story, intersectionality did not gain purchase because of its theoretical and
analytic power for conceptualizing difference, power, and subordination but
because the unified dominant feminism wanted to see itself as "inclusive." But

one might ask why a feminism that deeply desired to be inclusive insisted that political action required women to maintain a unified identity, and so fiercely opposed arguments about racial, sexual, and epistemological differences as "fragmenting" and challenging the existence of "feminism" (see Lloyd 2005). There is no room in this idealized story for the recalcitrance of dominant white women in acknowledging difference as part of feminism, as revealed, for example, in Donna Haraway's claim that "white women, including socialist feminists, discovered (*that is, were forced kicking and screaming to notice*) the non-innocence of the category 'woman'" (1991, 157, emphasis added).

Part of what makes such histories "formulaic" is that the racialized "identity politics" of this prelapsarian dominant feminism—the managerial role of the invisible white woman who defines "inclusion" on her terms—is uninterrogated, while the claims of feminists of color, queer feminists, and poststructural feminists are positioned as Otherness, their presence threatening to "fragment" feminism. The use of "postfeminist" carries particular weight in the narrative: the label "postfeminist" seems to situate women of color and Butler as radically "Other," beyond or outside of feminism (see Hemmings 2011). Yet women of color feminists and feminist poststructuralists such as Butler situate themselves *as* feminists. Their arguments could be considered "postfeminist" only if "feminism" is predicated on the subject position of the invisible white woman. An "impulse toward inclusivity" would not appear very robust if it frames as "fragmenting" and "Other" all feminisms that do not take up the subject position of the invisible white woman. These feminist histories suppress the dominance of the subject position of the invisible white woman in order to frame her as innocent within structures of racial subordination (see Flax 1991).

THE CLASH IN THE PAST

These examples of managing intersectionality demonstrate a peculiar and problematic misrepresentation of Butler (and other poststructural thinkers) as having already in the past defeated the arguments of those asserting the importance of difference, particularly the claims of feminists of color who developed concepts of intersectionality as part of an analysis of the workings of power. Yet in this argumentative structure, once Butler serves this purpose of defeating women of color and ejecting their concerns from feminism, her cautions about categorizing are quickly discarded. Sometimes Butler is herself positioned as also already defeated, segregated from feminism, or consigned to the past on the basis of her allegedly reductive criticisms about categories. Butler's actual vigorous arguments about sexuality and difference disappear from the scene of argument, as do the forceful counterarguments that white

heterosexual feminists made against her in the belief that recognizing difference would destroy the unity of feminism.

The effect of these disappearances is to create an inaccurate historical "diorama," a moment in the past when a miniature figure of Butler—stripped
of her own arguments articulating "difference"—defeats miniature "identitarians"—composed of nothing but their articulations of racial or sexual
"difference." The complex conjuncture of arguments about language, difference, and categorizations is reduced to a miniature three-dimensional battle
scene, in which poststructuralist and "identitarian" figures "fight it out," as
though no other feminists were present at the scene of debate. Poststructuralists and identitarians are puppets manipulated by the invisible white woman.
The diorama is an encapsulation of the past that leaves the present open
for management by the "unpredicated" feminist. These rhetorics repeatedly
situate Butler as the figure who defeated the political and intellectual claims
of Black feminists, the person who deconstructed "identities" and thereby
undermined Black feminists' intersectional theorizing with its insistence that
race and other categories of ascribed identities were infused with power. This
argumentative device situates feminist debates about difference firmly in the
past, obscuring ongoing discourses about race and sexual difference. It serves
to authorize the appropriation of a recreated intersectionality, free from attention to structural power, that can now be "improved" and utilized without
the burden of reckoning with race or, to some degree, heterosexism.

Thus the key to understanding what might otherwise seem a central
argumentative contradiction lies in recognizing the specificity of this use of
Butler and how it serves to salve the wounds of the trauma of lost centrality among white feminists. It suppresses and manages claims about power
and antisubordination that are not aligned with neoliberalism's framing of
difference as individual. The historical specificity of Butler's challenge—deconstructing a universal, unified, stable feminist identity grounded in the
experiences of white (middle-class heterosexual) women—is erased.

This positioning of Butler therefore creates a particular rhetorical effect:
if Butler can be positioned as having transcended and defeated the arguments
of feminists of color in the past, then she is the one who can be held responsible for making them anachronistic. Using their false framing of Butler as
"alibi," contemporary white scholars can then position themselves as innocent
of ungenerous behavior toward scholars of color at the moment they undercut
intersectionality's authority as a method of analyzing the structural dominance enacted through sexism, racism, and homophobia. These critics repress
radical challenges and recuperate them for hegemony, not least by promoting
the repeated *disappearance* at the scene of argument of the actual target of
criticism by Butler and others who articulate the importance of difference:

the unifying white middle-class heterosexual feminist. I argue that her invisibility at the scene of argument demonstrates exactly her tenacity in protecting and preserving the central role of the "unpredicated" feminist subject.

THEORY ANXIETY

Alice Ludvig (2006) uses the Case of the Et Cetera to posit *failings in theories of intersectionality* that compound the problems of category anxiety discussed in Chapter 2. (There are more than 230 citations in Google Scholar to the journal article as of May 10, 2018.) Quoting the Case of the Et Cetera, Ludvig argues that Butler's list of infinite differences "becomes the Achilles heel of intersectional approaches" (2006, 247):

> The *weaknesses of intersectionality* become more obvious when trying to apply it to empirical analysis: its implications for empirical analysis are, on the one hand, a seemingly insurmountable complexity and, on the other hand, a *fixed* notion of differences. This is because the list of differences is endless or even seemingly indefinite. It is impossible to take into account *all* of the differences that are significant at any given moment. . . . This is *precisely the problem of intersectionality*: the axes of differences *cannot be isolated and desegregated.* (2006, 246, emphasis added)

Ludvig goes on to argue:

> The endlessness of differences seems to be a weak point in intersectional theory. The approach starts to get blurred with questions that are often avoided in published work: *Who* defines *when, where, which,* and *why* particular differences are given recognition while others are not? (2006, 247, emphasis in original)

Positioning illimitability as demonstrating "weakness" in intersectional theories rests on four arguments: that the full complexity of illimitability cannot be captured completely by empirical analysis; that illimitability—despite being limitless, boundless—somehow requires differences that are "fixed"; that axes cannot be isolated and desegregated; and that decisions must be made about what categories to include in empirical analyses. This kind of complaint appears to be both geographically and disciplinarily specific, endemic to European critiques of intersectionality by social scientists. It presents a logical problem based on a misunderstanding of the nature of the social sciences, blaming a theory for the complexities and challenges of research in the world.

Ludvig is not completely wrong: intersectional theory triggers a rich set of heuristics with possibilities that can never be fully realized in analysis; the complications of the world will always exceed any empirical analyses; and theories function not as recipe books but as frameworks, as general maps, not sets of instructions, so that many decisions must be made at the scene of analysis. But Ludvig's argument is wrong in assuming that research could be otherwise, that it is a failing of intersectional theory, specifically, that it has not been fully packaged to remove the need to make any decisions about analysis. This critique ignores the mid-level nature of intersectional theorizing (discussed in Chapters 1 and 2) at the same time it works to contain, control, and co-opt intersectionality.

Ludvig, like many European critics, faults intersectionality as if it were a unitary, corporatized enterprise that has failed to provide an irrefutable set of instructions for all possible research endeavors. In fact, a number of scholars have worked to establish methodologies for qualitative and quantitative intersectional analysis, including analysis of large data sets (see, for example, Bowleg 2008, 2012; Hancock 2013; Harnois 2013). But all research enterprises require scholars to debate questions of "*who* defines *when, where, which,* and *why* particular differences are given recognition while others are not." These debates reflect the *agency* and *intellectual activity* required of all scholars. Ludvig herself makes such choices in a perfectly reasonable application of intersectionality. Yet in the discursive economy of critiques of intersectionality, the demand for agency on the part of analysts is treated as a "theoretical failure" that justifies demands that intersectionality be either jettisoned or "repaired." The discursive arena becomes preoccupied *not* with developing intersectional analyses but with managing intersectionality.

DISLODGING BUTLER

Nira Yuval-Davis cites the Case of the Et Cetera and comments on it in almost identical passages in three different texts (2006a, 200–201; 2006b, 202–203; 2011, 159–160). (There are nearly 2,800 citations in Google Scholar for the three texts that repeat three virtually identical paragraphs: 808 to Yuval-Davis 2006a, nearly 1,840 citations to Yuval-Davis 2006b, and 64 citations to Yuval-Davis 2011, as of May 10, 2018.) Quoting Butler on the "exhaustion" created by "the illimitable process of signification itself," Yuval-Davis rejects Butler's argument that illimitability is a characteristic feature of all language use. In a remarkable move—one that she claims in one article (2006a) is authorized by Gudrun-Axeli Knapp (1999) and in two others (2006b, 2011) by Knapp (1999) and Nancy Fraser (1997)—Yuval-Davis evacuates Butler's comment on the nature of language: she claims that the illimitability of language concerns *only* assertions of identity politics. Yuval-Davis argues:

> *Do we have to be concerned that the list is limitless?* Judith Butler (1990) *mocks* the "etc." that often appears at the end of lists of social divisions mentioned by feminists (e.g.[,] at the beginning of this article) and sees it as an embarrassed admission of a "sign of exhaustion as well as of the illimitable process of signification itself" (Butler 1990, 143). As Fraser (1997) and Knapp (1999) *make clear, such a critique is valid only within the discourse of identity politics* where there is a correspondence between positionings and social groupings. This is the way additive/fragmentation models of social divisions operate. (Yuval-Davis 2006b, 202, emphasis added)

According to this passage, Butler's claim that all language is limitless is simply not true and therefore bad. Seeing language as limitless is a feature of only identity politics, of additive/fragmentation models, which are bad. Butler is thus linked to "unsophisticated" thinkers, which is bad. This is not an argument but a series of assertions that are "sticky," in Ahmed's terms, involving a transfer of negative affect through repetition (2004, 91). Ahmed argues that stickiness operates through the very performativity of language that has dropped out of the discussions of Butler in critiques of intersectionality: discourses "produce effects through their reiteration" (see Ahmed 2004; Butler 1993). Within the discursive arena of critiques of intersectionality, the reiterated term "identity politics" sticks to the position of Black American feminists but not to the managerial identity of the invisible (white) woman. Similarly, the vague and disputed term "additive/fragmentation models" sticks to "unsophisticated thinkers." Yuval-Davis's is one of many critiques that rely less on argument than on reiteration of "sticky terms" to de-authorize and discredit previous arguments about intersectionality.

Yuval-Davis's passage demonstrates how discursive practices create a totalitarian, closed field of argument in many critiques of intersectionality. For example, a limited and familiar range of texts is used for reference so that white feminist critiques of intersectionality constantly echo one another, as in the Canyon of Echoes (see Chapter 6). Many claims authorized by this limited set of cited texts are radically truncated and underargued, so that both arguments and criticisms become "black-boxed," their inner components hidden, not available for inspection. Such black-boxing requires readers to rely solely on Yuval-Davis's authority as an evaluator of their arguments (she argues that the critics "make clear" the limitations of Butler's claim, and "find rightly" that Butler's claim can be "reductionist"). Black-boxing in this way also allows citations to serve as "false authorities." For example, Fraser (1997) does not make the specific claim attributed to her (that the illimitability of language is valid only within a reductive view of social categories); Knapp (1999) does not assess the "validity" of illimitability and makes no claim about it being "valid only within" the discourse of identity politics. Thus black-boxing allows scholars to modify significantly the claims of those they cite without acknowledging this modification to their readers.

In a move characteristic of citation practices in many critiques of intersectionality, Yuval-Davis bolsters her dismissive claims by failing to disclose that the authorities she cites so confidently have been subject to much critical commentary. For example, Yuval-Davis treats as irrelevant Fraser's much-criticized politics of argument, with its insensitivity to Butler's actual claims. A review of Fraser's own arguments reveals that she serves as a quintessential example of the managerial subject position of the invisible white woman. Fraser translates Butler's arguments back into hegemony, then refutes their translated form.[3] While Fraser positions herself as able to properly adjudicate claims for recognition, she has been criticized for treating culture as static and failing to account for the production of new political subjects (Pfeifle 2012), for viewing identity politics as "essentially politically pernicious" in ways that are not supported by empirical evidence, for holding a mistaken conception of culture and identity that assumes that identities are "dispensable" because they are "invented" rather than "real," and for overlooking the ways that her framework for redistribution actually requires identity politics (Alcoff 2007a). In addition, it is quite possible that Fraser would not "approve" of Yuval-Davis's arguments any more than Butler's, undermining her significance as an authority for Yuval-Davis's claims. This treatment of authorities as unmoored, floating free of argumentative contexts, and free from nuanced criticism by scholars who cite them, is a practice endemic to white critiques of intersectionality: litanies of criticisms—including contradictory criticisms—are taken out of context and repeated, without explication of their grounds, scope, and evidence. The result is to float any complaint as potentially valid to condemn a generalized "intersectionality," a practice that contributes to contradiction and stasis in critiques of intersectionality.

Kathy Davis (2008) deploys the Case of the Et Cetera in arguing that Butler is essentially irrelevant to feminist theorizing about categories (in consequence allowing those managing intersectionality to set aside Butler's cautions in order to reinscribe hegemonic ways of thinking about categories). (There are more than 1,750 citations in Google Scholar for the journal article, which has also been reprinted, as of May 10, 2018.) Davis claims that poststructuralists such as Butler are not concerned with women or their lives but merely with theoretical or philosophical issues such as "essentialism." She argues that their real intent is simply to eliminate *all* categorical thinking. Davis argues:

> For many poststructuralist feminists, the essentialism of gender was the main problem. Their concern was less with how gender is shaped by other categories of difference in the social and material realities of women's lives than with finding ways to abandon categorical thinking altogether. (2008, 73)

As evidence of the poststructuralists' desire to "abandon categories" Davis provides a trim version of the Case of the Et Cetera in a note: "A case in point is Judith Butler's (1989) well-known critique of the 'embarrassed "etc."' which ends the list of predicates (gender, race, ethnicity, class, sexuality, able-bodiedness) that 'strive to encompass a situated subject, but invariably fail to be complete'" (81n12, quoting the 1989 edition of Butler 1990, 143).

Davis here makes three interrelated claims: that poststructuralists were not particularly interested in how "gender is shaped by other categories of difference in the social and material realities of women's lives," that poststructuralists were looking for ways to "abandon categorical thinking altogether," and that the Case of the Et Cetera is an example of Butler "abandoning categorical thinking altogether." None of these claims is true. Such tired tropes denigrating Butler's arguments have been refuted many times (see, for example, Kapur's incisive 2001 reply to Nussbaum 1999). Butler is explicitly concerned with how sexuality shapes gender and vice versa (1990, 1993), and deeply concerned for the social and material consequences of lives rendered unintelligible by conventional social categories. Further, Butler does not seek to abandon categorical thinking. Rather, she questions categories to free them for "rethinking," as is reiterated throughout her work (for example, 1995).[4] Butler seeks to release categories from their taken-for-granted sedimentation, to examine how they always operate in a matrix of power and create inclusion by exclusion (similar to the concerns of Crenshaw 1989). The Case of the Et Cetera, appearing in a text devoted to reconsidering the relation between gender and sexuality, is an argument to rethink categories and demand constant reflection on the instability and necessarily incomplete nature of all categories. It is *not* evidence of an attempt to "find . . . ways to abandon categorical thinking altogether." Rather than wishing to "abandon categories," Butler emphasizes *contingent* categorization of identities, "strategic provisionality," using terms conditionally while at the same time politically challenging their usefulness (see Butler et al. 1992). This is exactly the kind of thinking about categories implicit to intersectional thinking and often overlooked by power-blind critiques.

Davis, like so many social science critics of intersectionality, frames her argument by constructing typologies through ruthless categorization of scholars, conceptions, theories, and arguments in often inaccurate and tendentious formulaic histories that treat related theories as incommensurable opposites. Given the field's interest in the nature of social categories, it is surprising that there is so little debate about the validity of the various typologies grounding their arguments. The categorizing of scholarly concepts that enables these moves is treated as transparent when it should be subject to vigorous interrogation for its clearly interested deployments of power, motives, and oversimplifications. For example, categorizing different types of feminist scholars working in the 1980s and early 1990s, Davis treats poststructuralism and intersectionality almost as mutually exclusive, conflicting, and racially homogeneous "camps." Despite disclaimers, the impression is of sophisticated white theorizing opposing the experiential arguments of women of color. This typology is radically distorted, not least by ignoring the many scholars of color whose theorizing about race is informed by poststructuralist premises, such as Crenshaw (1989, 1991), Hall (1996), Lowe (1991, 1996), Rodríguez (2003), and Sandoval (1991, 2000). The result of Davis's formulaic typologies is to treat as incommensurable opposites what are actually related theories. Chela Sandoval, for example, argues that poststructural theories are decolonizing in nature, that "Judith Butler's theorization of 'performativity' . . . transcode[s] and extend[s] the bases and principles of 1968–90 U.S. third world feminist praxis" (2000, 64). Suryia Nayak's (2015) recent book puts the thinking of Audre Lorde in conversation with poststructural theorists, including Butler. In effect, poststructuralists and the women of color developing intersectionality as a tool against subordination tend to agree that in these times there are urgent and pressing political and intellectual needs to question, challenge, and reposition uninterrogated, sedimented notions of language, discourse, and identity. Yet the conventions deployed at the scene of argument in the white feminist critiques analyzed here present intersectionality and poststructuralism as if they were in relations of competition, not cooperation or congruence.

Davis uses Butler to manage intersectionality in ways congruent with Hemmings's (2011) analysis of the systematic positioning of Butler in feminist histories. She treats Butler as one of the poststructuralists who in the past powerfully discredited the arguments of women of color, yet positions her as ultimately outside of feminism and therefore as being of no significance whatsoever for the critic's own contemporary management of intersectionality and its social categories.

"WHITENING INTERSECTIONALITY"

Nina Lykke evokes the Case of the Et Cetera in her chapter titled "Theorizing Intersectionalities: Genealogies and Blindspots" (2010). (There are more than five hundred citations in Google Scholar to the book as of May 10, 2018.) Lykke argues:

> Based on a poststructuralist understanding of signification as an unending process of displacements, Judith Butler argues, for example, for openendedness in the understanding of intersectional processes of subject formation. *Nevertheless,* she also suggests that the *"etc." signals an "embarrassed" and too easy way out* (Butler 1990, 143), perhaps indicating that intersectional analysis of identities, seen from her point of view, is caught up in a dilemma between a wish for completeness and the necessity of recognizing the unending sliding of meanings. (2010, 83, emphasis added)

Lykke here ventriloquizes Butler with specific effect. Butler uses the Case of the Et Cetera to assert illimitability while recognizing the political as well as analytic desire for specificity (one is embarrassed at the difficulty of being properly respectful of politically significant categories). In contrast, Lykke frames Butler as a moralist and the Case of the Et Cetera as chastisement: acknowledging the illimitable complexity of identities is a "too easy way out" (out of what it is not quite clear). Such a claim was never made by Butler and is in contrast to her method of argumentation (as is true of Yuval-Davis's characterization of Butler as "mocking"). It is Lykke who is concerned about others taking a "too easy way out." By implicating Butler here, Lykke takes a scholar noted for resolutely eschewing a "legislative" role and turns her into a nanny.

Lykke also evokes the Case of the Et Cetera in "Intersectional Analysis: Black Box or Useful Feminist Thinking Technology?" (2011). (There are some 88 citations in Google Scholar to the chapter and more than 250 citations to the book in which it appears as of May 10, 2018.) Lykke argues:

> The listing of intersecting categorisations . . . *can be rhetorically seductive* and *generate a push towards making intersectionality an explanation in itself. . . .* Judith Butler articulates the dilemmas related to the *seductive lining up* of categorisations as the "embarrassed" etc. clause. (2011, 210, 210n4, emphasis added)

Lykke here once again suggests a legislative role for Butler that does not accord with Butler's actual claims. Butler notes that those who use the "etc."

are "embarrassed" and "exasperated" by its inadequacy, not "seduced" by it. Lykke also links Butler to the claim that articulating categories "can generate a push towards making intersectionality an explanation in itself," a chastisement unrelated to Butler's arguments. Who has argued that intersectionality is "an explanation in itself"? An explanation for what? For what purpose? This kind of imprecise chastisement, frequently found in European critiques of intersectionality, contributes to their confusion, contradiction, and stasis.

Lykke's use of the Case of the Et Cetera also participates in European efforts to "broaden the genealogy of intersectionality" by identifying any number of white feminist scholars as previous and "unacknowledged" intersectional scholars. According to Bilge, this discursive move disassociates intersectionality from its origins in concerns for racial justice in order to claim that "feminists have theorized intersectionality from many perspectives, that it was 'in the air,' in the *inner* effervescence of feminism or gender studies" (Bilge 2014, 91; see also Bilge 2013). The purpose of such an argument is to claim the valuable tool of intersectionality as the creation of white women: if "intersectionality" was "in the air" all along, then the work of many white theorists must be "always already intersectional." Bilge notes that this discursive move is one of the significant strategies used to "whiten intersectionality" (2013, 2014). It is also a remarkably unmistakable form of neoliberal asset-stripping designed to diminish and then appropriate the intellectual legacy of Black feminists and other feminists of color.

INTERROGATING FEMINIST METADISCURSIVE REGIMES

The Case of the Et Cetera functions to contain "difference" at the scene of argument, in part through reiterating linear, progressive formulaic arguments that reinscribe taken-for-granted categories and racial hierarchies (see Barkley-Brown 1992; Hemmings 2011). Rather than an unbridgeable competition fixed in the history of feminist theories, there is considerable congruence between the arguments of Butler (who articulates the need for recognizing difference) and women of color (who also articulate the need for recognizing difference). Yet powerblind discourses deployed through seemingly neutral conventions of argument misrepresent the thinking of both Butler and intersectional scholars of color. If Butler can be framed as in the past having been powerful enough to defeat women of color, but no longer relevant, and the "theory of intersectionality" can be framed as suffering from the inadequate experiential argumentation of unsophisticated women of color, intersectionality can be treated as a valuable but flawed analytic tool that can be "rescued" for invisible white (middle-class heterosexual) management.

Managing intersectionality is not only an exercise in racial conservatism; it is also a technology of *disciplinary* conservatism, a practice whereby scholars attempt to rein in the radical implications of intersectional epistemologies to make the concept safe for empiricist social science or humanist ideals saturated with liberal and neoliberal values. These powerblind moves are structured in dominance and operate as discursive technologies of power. They serve to defuse radical challenges to the centrality of the unified subject of feminism—the white middle-class heterosexual woman.

The Case of the Et Cetera and other strategies of managing intersectionality reveal the urgency of interrogating feminist scholarship at the scene of argument. Although relentless and effective criticism remains crucial to the advancement of feminist theory and practice, uninterrogated assumptions and conventions of argument can give feminism the impression that it has advanced knowledge without actually doing so. My goal is to encourage what Mignolo calls "a relentless analytic effort to understand, in order to overcome" (2011, 10) powerblind discursive practices of management and control at the scene of feminist argument. To investigate textual cartographies—to acknowledge and revise received metadiscursive regimes and deployments of discursive technologies of power—requires feminist theory to transform the terms of reading and writing (Tomlinson 2010).

COLONIZING INTERSECTIONALITY

The discursive construction of the invisible white woman in feminist argument that I discuss in Chapter 7 reflects the ongoing resonance and reverberation of the political challenges and epistemological critiques raised by women of color feminists during the 1980s and 1990s. Intersectional thinking played—and continues to play—a central role in that conflict, not simply because most of its generative originators were not white but because, as I explain in Chapter 2, intersectional thinking is a decolonial project, a fundamental challenge to the foundational premises and practices of the systems of modern knowledge that emerged in the West in the era of conquest, colonization, Indigenous dispossession, slavery, and contract labor. I argue in Chapter 7 that it is not only the managerial white woman that becomes invisible in the attacks on intersectionality, but also other structures of dominance, including the colonial matrix of power and knowledge on which the conventions of disciplinary research rely. The invisibility of the white woman in feminist discourse reflects the binary distinction that situates white scholars as *humanitas*—as the people who define and inhabit modernity, who place the rest of the world in categories, and who assume the right to determine the nature and pace of inclusion for those marked as Other, while relegating people of color to the status of *anthropos*—as the people who are known but not knowers, who can be the objects of knowledge but not its subjects. The reception of intersectional thinking in Europe is particularly instructive in this respect because it reveals the ways in which the thinking about racial categories in Europe remains tied to traces of colonial thinking that are unwilling to die.

Intersectionality has served as a valuable resource in the European arena of discourse among scholars seeking to develop tools for multidimensional analysis of social identities.[1] Many European scholars understandably seek to create an intersectional analysis that is specific to European contexts.[2] I examine in this chapter several cases in which European social scientists and philosophers dealing with the feminist concept of intersectionality deploy rhetorics of racial hierarchy, perhaps inadvertently, that depict a vast gulf between what they present as their own perspicacious thinking and the collectivized and caricatured thinking that they attribute to intersectionality's originating Black feminist scholars in the United States. I argue that these argumentative devices map closely to structures of thinking described by Albert Memmi (1991) in his analysis of colonial racism. I demonstrate how these European critiques of intersectionality impose a frame on U.S. Black feminists and their constituencies by "depersonalizing" and "collectivizing" them through what Memmi calls "the mark of the plural" (85). I argue that the binary hierarchical rhetoric of these powerblind feminist critiques positions U.S. Black feminists in ways that fit Memmi's three components of the thinking of colonial racism. The unacknowledged expressions of racial privilege that characterize these critiques demonstrate the importance of transforming the terms of feminist reading and writing so that feminist scholars take responsibility for the ways that their discourses function as technologies of power.

European scholars writing about intersectional theorizing must negotiate a complex discursive terrain. They recognize and often freely acknowledge the origins of intersectionality in the thinking of U.S. Black women, yet their allegiance to Europe's prevailing color-blind evasions of race and racisms constricts their recognition of intersectionality's potential to counter subordination. Aversion to racial recognition is inscribed in the European Union's Race Equality Directive (2000), officially establishing what Richard Bauman and Charles L. Briggs (2003) would call a "metadiscursive regime" to manage discussion of race in the public sphere. These denials lie at the heart of what David Theo Goldberg calls contemporary "racial europeanization" (2006). Goldberg argues that racial europeanization is part of a European self-conception emerging from the continent's response to its history, especially the Holocaust.[3] Racial europeanization is purportedly based on a desire to see that race no longer exists as a category in Europe. However, these strictures do not eliminate race as a category of being in the world: race continues to shape European social relations and social life.[4] Yet race and racisms are denied and displaced, silenced yet assumed—"buried but alive" (Goldberg 2006, 334). Europe's colonial legacy is also suppressed and silenced, sealed off from its centrality to the development of contemporary European society: colonialism took place "elsewhere" and therefore is not really "of Europe." The argument becomes: "Race is a problem everywhere but Europe" (Goldberg 2006, 341). Goldberg argues that racisms rendered invisible are no less toxic: racial problems and racisms meld with other categorizations (class, culture, ethnicity, immigration, religion); the role of structural power is elided and irruptions of disparagement and hatred toward those of color are treated as merely "personal," or result from the Others' nature or inability to assimilate to European life.

Particularly important for my analysis here are the discursive problems that result from these conditions of denial, conditions that eliminate the possibility for ethical consideration of racisms. According to Goldberg: "There can be no response if the terms of recognition and response are unavailable. There is no possibility of saying the deleterious effects of racial application are even ethically wrong because there is nothing there by which to recognize the phenomena purportedly at issue" (2006, 339). Goldberg warns that suppressing discourses about racisms in turn suppresses the availability of conceptual tools that allow people to recognize, analyze, and debate what might count as structural racisms and how racial differences can be negotiated effectively. Suppressed also are the tools to examine the dominant discourses and narratives that crystallize identities, that frame races and cultures as totalities that are closed and unchanging (Balibar 2009). Goldberg and others argue that the frameworks of scholarly disciplines tend to reinforce these discourses rather than call them into question (see Grosfoguel and Mielants 2006). Goldberg's discussion of racial europeanization offers an explanatory frame for my analysis.

Academic discourses about intersectional analysis by contemporary white European feminist social scientists and philosophers constitute a specific discursive arena pervaded by shared assumptions, arguments, and rhetorics about nation, gender, and race that are demonstrated at the scene of argument. I argue that this particular discursive arena demonstrates a general failure to interrogate racial europeanization. Scholars desiring to demonstrate compliance with European self-conceptions of exceptionalism assume their own ability to transcend the sedimented problems of racisms. This is particularly noticeable when they must deal with concepts of structural racism, as when they undertake to establish European-inflected intersectionality by freeing it from what they perceive as the "race-bound" frames of U.S. scholars of color.[5] Yet because their discourses fail to interrogate structures of regional European racisms, because they cooperate with the denial of Europe's colonial history and its evasions of race, many scholars are left without tools for sophisticated discussions of race and racisms. Metadiscursive management of racial europeanization is particularly evident in these discursive techniques. As Gail Lewis argues, the disavowal of race at the heart of academic discussions of intersectional thinking conducted by many white European feminist scholars leads to mechanisms of displacement and denial in their relations with European feminists of color. Lewis argues:

> My argument is twofold. First, even while elite and popular discourses across Europe are saturated with processes of racialization, there is a disavowal of the relevance and toxicity of the social relations of race as a pan-European phenomenon, with a corresponding displacement of its relevance to a series of "elsewheres." Second, this process of unconscious and unwitting disavowal and displacement enters into feminist discourse and infrastructure, helping to pattern the experiences and social relations among feminists differentially constituted as raced subjects. (2013, 870)

My argument is that similar moves of exclusion and management are evident at the scene of argument in critiques of intersectionality in the European arena.

If "race" is only "elsewhere," then European scholars of color are not authorized to speak about race (so racialized scholars may be "imported" from elsewhere to speak at conferences). European feminists of color are expected to accede to the regime of racial europeanization: acknowledgment of the dominance of whiteness is erased, because whiteness is not considered a race. As a result, "those who cannot avoid knowing that they are raced subjects" are not authorized to contribute their knowledge of the race and racisms that remain in European social life (Lewis 2013, 883). The people who know the least about structures of European racism as they must be lived—white Europeans—are assumed to know the most and also be innocent, neutral, and unmarked by race. Those who know the most, on the other hand—Europeans of color—find their testimony dismissed and themselves deemed to be self-interested, biased, and bound by embodied identity. The consequences of this insistence on denial and erasure—of deploying rather than interrogating racial europeanization—significantly hobbles many white European feminist scholars' efforts to invent an improved European intersectionality premised on dismissing race as an analytic category. To *extract race* from intersectionality does not make race or racism disappear; in fact, it *requires speaking of race.* Yet those grounded in an uninterrogated racial europeanization ignore the discursive tools that intersectionality has made available, returning instead to default discourses that reinscribe racial hierarchy, that frame race as biological and raced subjects as inferior. As Lewis (2009) relates about critics at one European conference on intersectionality, participants tended to treat race as a "real" biological difference rather than an ideological category, with apparent consequence for their positioning of the claims of racialized scholars. According to Lewis, debates on whether intersectionality was a theory or "only" a heuristic device sometimes seemed to presuppose that "anything that emerged from within the structural experience of marginalized women (in this case African American and other US women of colour) was always already incapable of being understood as theory, always only a category describing experience" (207). My analysis here supports Lewis's arguments about this problematic framing of race and demonstrates evidence of it at the scene of argument where European intersectionality is constructed through discourses evocative of colonial racism.

SPOILED SUBJECTS AND THE MARK OF THE PLURAL

In *The Colonizer and the Colonized* (1991), Memmi provides a number of revealing insights about structures of thinking that characterize the colonizer's attitude in relation to the colonized. While I do not argue that the critics I analyze think of the North American women of color whose work they critique as "colonized" people, nor do I imagine U.S. women of color to be innocent of complicity with their own nation's sordid history of colonialism, I do argue that their geographical, national, and racial perceptions lead European feminist critics to adopt *discursive frames* and *rhetorical strategies* in many ways congruent with the "colonial" structures of thinking that Memmi describes. For example, Memmi argues that the colonizer creates a "myth" of the colonized, "depersonalizing" the colonized as never singular and individual but always already "plural." Memmi argues:

> Another sign of the colonized's depersonalization is what one might call the mark of the plural. The colonized is never characterized in an individual manner; he is entitled only to drown in an anonymous collectivity ("They are this." "They are all the same."). . . . He will say, "You can't count on them." It is not just a grammatical expression. . . . [T]hat life in a specific sense does not interest him. (Memmi 1991, 85)

The mark of the plural depersonalizes the colonized and makes them one, "collective"; it authorizes the extension of a claim based on one person to all the members of a group. In the arguments I examine here, women of color who are U.S. intersectional scholars or the people they discuss become conflated: they are not treated as individual subjects, one stands for all, any can be substituted for another. In effect, they are treated as "spoiled subjects." Their actual arguments or the racialized and gendered lives they consider are "in a specific sense" not of interest to the critic.

Inadvertently drawing on a long history of dominant discourses assuming, emphasizing, and creating the criminality of colonized people and people of color, critics may overlook the specificity of arguments about race in intersectional analyses. For example, Mechthild Bereswill and Anke Neuber have argued that Crenshaw's "Demarginalizing the Intersection of Race and Sex" (1989) introduced the concept of intersectionality to address the excessive criminality of "Black underclass women." (There are some thirty-five citations in Google Scholar to the chapter as of May 10, 2018.) These critics assert:

> At the beginning of the 1990s, black underclass women were appearing in court to face criminal charges much more frequently than white women. In 1991 Crenshaw published a text with the programmatic title "Mapping the Margins", which drew attention to the connection between marginalization and gender. This is very important, not only in the context of societal constructions of criminality. (2011, 71)

Symptomatic here is the linkage of "Black women" to the terms "underclass" and "criminal." Yet there are *no* "Black underclass criminal women" in Crenshaw's discussions. Crenshaw's "Mapping the Margins" (1991) provides resources to rethink the problem of male violence against women of color. Crenshaw argues that policies and programs need rethinking partly because intersections of race, gender, and class have historically led these male crimes to be framed in ways that prove detrimental to women of color. The women of color at issue are *not criminals* but women seeking shelter or redress from the courts in the face of what they allege to be their criminal rape and battery by men who are not limited to either racialized or "underclass" status. Crenshaw's "Demarginalizing the Intersection of Race and Sex" (1989)— also reprinted as part of the same conference proceedings as Bereswill and Neuber (2011)—explicates and provides solutions to the problems of a single-axis framework in *antidiscrimination law*. The Black women at issue are *not criminals* but *working-class plaintiffs* asking courts for redress in the face of what they allege to be the illegal discrimination of large corporations. To conflate "Black women" with "criminal underclass" is to use the mark of the plural. The result perpetuates the deployment of nationalized, gendered, and racialized power. The argument appeared in an edited collection on intersectionality based on a German conference (Lutz, Herrera Vivar, and Supik 2011). Crenshaw's "Demarginalizing" was much discussed at the conference and reprinted in the book; the conference and the book include many discussions of Crenshaw's work, including "Demarginalizing" and "Mapping the Margins." That these critics' mischaracterizations remain in the final version indicates that for them, for the editors of the collection, and for the press and its reviewers, Crenshaw's arguments "in a specific sense" do not interest them.

Memmi's insights help explain why a critic might inhabit a discursive position that treats racialized women in the United States as "spoiled subjects" whose "life in a specific sense does not interest" the critic. From this point of view, conceptions of intersectionality developed by U.S. feminist scholars of color cannot be anything other than limited because the racialized subjects available for their consideration are spoiled. For example, Baukje Prins argues that the subjects of U.S. intersectional analyses are all racialized subjects "positioned on the fringes of society, for whom mechanisms of social power have indeed become reified . . . 'extreme' cases in which power works in a near totalitarian way" (2006, 282). (There are more than three hundred citations in Google Scholar to the journal article as of May 10, 2018.) Prins indicates that the specifics of these subjects and the scholarship concerning them do not interest her: it all "*boils down* to the complexity of *ever more layers* of oppression and domination . . . a *singular* picture . . . *predictable plots* of one party dominating the other" (282, emphasis added).

In opposition to the phantasm of intersectionality she has created, Prins argues that "general" models of identity must be based on "ordinary" people, neither "elite" nor part of "an underclass of social dropouts," people who "neither cause nor represent significant social problems" (282). Prins proposes her own Dutch and Moluccan high school classmates as proper subjects for this "general" model and sets out to interview them to elicit narratives of "origins." Feminists should question the value of a "general" model of identity that simply excludes from consideration people that someone else has decided "cause or represent" social problems. Setting that issue aside, I argue that ample evidence demonstrates that the "model" subjects that Prins proposes are *not* free of social problems and, therefore, do *not* meet her own criteria for grounding a "general" model of identity.

A significant portion of Prins's classmates are racialized subjects, "Moluccans," descended from families that immigrated to her rural area of the Netherlands from the Dutch East Indies. Her text reveals a history of violent political protest by Moluccans that she sets aside, arguing rather patronizingly that ultimately it proved "beneficial" in helping Moluccans and Dutch learn to live together more harmoniously.[6] The text fails to acknowledge the existing contemporary political climate that regularly produces hostile arguments blaming "social problems" on immigrants of color and multiculturalism that the critic subsequently discusses elsewhere (Prins and Saharso 2008). Prins treats her own claims about what kinds of people are proper grounds for "general" models of identity as immaterial through the contradictory evidence she provides on the racially differential life outcomes of her classmates.[7] She also undermines these claims through the evidence of social problems in the narratives she quotes.[8]

The mark of the plural is evidenced by Prins's simplistic and inaccurate representation of the lives of the U.S. women of color that she dismisses and her apparent lack of interest in their analyses of the social relations of power that influence their lives—as well as the lives of her own Dutch and Moluccan classmates. The "extreme" nonnormativity *not* of "actual" U.S. women of color discussed by intersectional scholars but of *her own stereotypes* leads Prins to find such women unfit subjects for developing "general" models of identity. Here Prins adopts and articulates as her own exactly the position that Crenshaw set out to counter in developing the concept of intersectionality in the first place: that because structures of power have *succeeded* in framing Black women as racialized and marginalized, they are treated as unfit for universality.

To ensure that the tools of intersectionality become fit for universality, critics argue that intersectionality must be rethought if it is to attend properly to the complexities of individual subjectivities (Prins 2006; Staunæs 2003) and is not a "theme exclusively related to ethnic (racialized) minorities or women" (Staunæs 2003, 102). (There are nearly four hundred citations in Google Scholar to Staunæs 2003 as of May 10, 2018.) Such claims are not inherently illegitimate, but they are illegitimate when grounded in reinscription of colonizing discourses. For example, Memmi's insight that the colonized are framed as never singular or individual reemerges when critics treat as collective rather than individually specific the varied arguments of racialized scholars: U.S. women of color conducting intersectional analyses may be treated as if one stands for all, as if any can be substituted for another. Critics inhabit such a position when they make speculative claims about the thinking of people who are unidentified, conflated, and treated as if their arguments are the same.

For example, in examining the arguments of U.S. intersectional scholars of color, Dorthe Staunæs fails to acknowledge specific arguments and rests her case on claims about "tendencies" and "assumptions" that she has inferred from a distinctly small number of old texts. For example, she argues that in the work of U.S. intersectional scholars of color, she "traces" "a *tendency* to understand subjects as *determined* by social systems . . . with oppression . . . *forced* by structural systems" (Staunæs 2003, 103, emphasis added). Staunæs attributes this tendency first to Patricia Hill Collins (1998), then claims that it is displayed by a mass of people she does not identify: people in the "practical, political arena (for example, in nongovernmental organizations,) as well as in the theoretical field dominated by standpoint feminism and critical race theory" (2003, 103). For all these people, she argues, "there *seems to be a tendency* toward *fixing categories and identities* and using the concepts in certain *ideologically informed* ways" (103, emphasis added). "The *fixing of categories* can be a useful strategy," she indicates, "if you work in and against a system built upon the privileges and rights of *certain fixed identities and categories* and where 'the natural' and 'the given' can be converted into political activities" (103, emphasis added).

Yet, Staunæs argues, this way of dealing with identities simply is not good enough for thinking about the "complexity and changing nature of lived experience" because of its "underlying assumptions of *determination, clear demarcations* and *fixed substance*" (103, emphasis added). The "American" concept of intersectionality, she argues broadly, "does not include a consideration of how these categories work and intersect in the lived experiences of concrete subjects" (101). Once again, a critic argues that the static, racialized nature of U.S. conceptions of intersectionality would be detrimental to her research, in this case in considering the lives of the schoolchildren she wishes to study, Danish and Turkish immigrant seventh-graders. Rather than simply emphasizing that Staunæs is inaccurate in this representation of the thinking of racialized U.S. feminists studying intersectionality (see Chapter 4 on Collins's standpoint theory and Chapter 2 on Critical Race Theory), I draw attention to her dependence on a rhetoric of the mark of the plural; she fails to characterize individuals in the mass of social activists and scholars she combines and condemns: "The colonized . . . is entitled only to drown in an anonymous collectivity ('They are this.' 'They are all the same.')" (Memmi 1991, 85).

Treating racialized scholars collectively—as if *one* stands for *all,* as if *any* can be substituted for *another*—derails the resulting arguments and, therefore, derails feminists' ability to think carefully about social identities. For example, Staunæs claims that intersectional analysis as it is framed by Black standpoint feminism and Critical Race Theory in the United States focuses on

> the positioning of Black women as "the outsider within" in a system built upon the mainstream, white, male patriarchy and racialized oppression (Collins 1998). It is a structural system that favours wealthy, heterosexual, white, male, Christian, young and slim people. In relation to them, everyone else becomes the Other, the illegitimate, the abnormal and the inappropriate. It is, as the prominent African-American feminist Patricia Hill Collins puts it, "the matrix of domina-

tion" (Collins 1998): a coherent system of different oppression systems, which victimizes the non-wealthy, non-heterosexual, non-white, non-male, non-Christian and those who are not slim and not young. Collins's "catalogue" might be relevant in many cases, but not in all. What about exceptions? What about moves, ruptures, paradoxes? (2003, 102–103)

This argument demonstrates the mark of the plural by folding together several different arguments, presenting them as Collins's when they are not, misrepresenting them, and failing to respond to the actual complex arguments of the article by Collins that the critic cites.

I examine in turn four examples from the passage that I have quoted in order to illustrate how particular argumentative moves can be seen as reflections of Memmi's concept of the mark of the plural. The first example is Staunæs's reference to "Collins's 'catalogue'": What the critic describes as "Collins's 'catalogue,'" and emphasizes by repeating in two different forms (i.e., "wealthy" then "non-wealthy"), is, in fact, not an argument made by Collins. It is a paraphrase of a passage from Audre Lorde's "Age, Race, Class and Sex: Women Redefining Difference" (1980), a speech written by a different Black woman eighteen years earlier. In the passage involved, Lorde is encouraging women to challenge the damaging Western tendency to frame differences in terms of hierarchical binaries. Lorde argues:

> Somewhere, on the edge of consciousness, there is what I call a *mythical* norm, which each one of us within our hearts knows "that is not me." In america, this norm is usually defined as white, thin, male, young, heterosexual, Christian, and financially secure. It is with this mythical norm that the trappings of power reside within this society. Those of us who stand outside that power often identify one way in which we are different, and we assume that to be the primary cause of all oppression, forgetting other distortions around difference, some of which we ourselves may be practicing. (1980, n.p.)

While Collins often quotes Lorde, she does not quote what Staunæs calls "Collins's 'catalogue'" in Collins 1998 or, for that matter, in other works by Collins (1991, 2000a) that the critic does not cite.

The second example is Staunæs's sentence "In relation to them, everyone else becomes the Other, the illegitimate, the abnormal and the inappropriate." Because Collins 1998 is the only source cited in that paragraph, Staunæs implies that this formulation represents or is closely congruent with arguments made there. This is not the case. The critic's sentence conflates quite different relations of subordination and representation as if they were essentially equivalent, which is not the method of thinking about oppressions represented in Collins 1998 or, for that matter, Collins 1991, 2000a.

The third example is Staunæs's failure to properly define and distinguish "structural system" versus "mythical norm" versus "matrix of domination": she treats different ways of talking about social structures as if they were equivalent. This conflation is a crucial problem for her as well as other European critics of intersectionality deploying the mark of the plural, a problem that contributes to their inability to explain accurately the arguments about culture and structures of power that they vigorously disparage.

The fourth example comes in Staunæs's questions: "What about exceptions? What about moves, ruptures, paradoxes?" This cri de coeur is the crux of her critique. She asks:

> Are people at a subject level mere bearers of these master identities? Are they all in "category uniforms"? How do we account for exceptions and subversions? How can we take into account changes and ruptures and grasp the subversions of power, position and categories that sometimes actually do become possible? (2003, 103)

These frustrated questions also raise a different set of questions for consideration. For example, does Staunæs notice that in her use of the mark of the plural she has treated the U.S. feminist intersectional scholars of color she criticizes as if *they* are in "category uniforms," as "mere bearers of . . . master identities" that are specifically intersections of nation, gender, and race? Why does she assume that attention to structures of power straps U.S. intersectional scholars of color into what I would call a "subordination straitjacket"? Why does she assume that Collins and other North American intersectional feminist scholars of color have not thought about ruptures and exceptions and subversions of power? Although women of color feminists have been discussing resistance, multiple positioning, and other kinds of intersectional moves for at least thirty-five years—including in the very texts that Staunæs cites,[9] Staunæs assumes that no evidence from an extensive review of the arguments of women of color is necessary, that she can represent the whole of that work adequately and accurately delineate its shortcomings on the basis of citing and misrepresenting three or four articles published between eight and twenty-five years previously. To make sweeping condemnations of an entire group of nationalized and racialized intersectional theorists on the basis of careless representation of three or four publications and the "assumptions" and "tendencies" of an undifferentiated mass of unnamed people is evidence of the unacknowledged workings of the mark of the plural.

CREATING A GULF BETWEEN THE COLONIZER
AND THE COLONIZED

Memmi provides further insight into the ways in which arguments about race and intersectionality that depend on geographical binaries may, in fact, rely on colonizing discourses. Memmi argues that specific patterned structures of thinking characterize colonial racism:

> Colonial racism is built from three major components: one, the gulf between the culture of the colonialist and the colonized. . . . To search for differences in features between two peoples is not in itself a racist's characteristic, but it has a definitive function and takes on a particular meaning in a racist context. The colonialist stresses those things that keep him separate, rather than emphasizing that which might contribute to the foundation of a joint community. In those differences, the colonized is always degraded and the colonialist finds justification for rejecting his subjects. (1991, 71)

Making distinctions is central to the work of academics, but the analogy I draw to "the gulf between the culture of the colonialist and the colonized" refers to conceiving differences between two geographically separated and differently raced groups of scholars as binary and hierarchical, the position of one group "fixed" to always justify rejection.

Prins constructs a set of dramatic dichotomies that contrast in relentlessly binary and inaccurate terms what she terms "British" and "American" intersectionalities (2006). In a strikingly powerblind strategy, she creates a privileged superior, sophisticated, flexible, theoretical, forward-thinking "constructionist" British intersectional analysis and uses it to justify rejecting its inferior, simplistic, static, inflexible, limited "systemic" American polar opposite. Prins uses the binaries she constructs to justify the individualist lens she adopts for her analysis of the life narratives of her Dutch high school classmates: she seeks to abrogate the authority of intersectional projects that use a structural lens concerned with power in order to celebrate her own project of narration and its vision of idealized human agency. However, since analysis of people's life narratives is a common method of research, an argument devalorizing U.S. intersectional thinking is unnecessary to justify it and must, therefore, be working to satisfy different argumentative goals. In this case, the creation of such a power-laden geographical binary functions as a dramatic example of colonizing discourse that animates Prins's later discussion of her classmates. Memmi reminds us of what motivates such hierarchy when embedded in a context of nationalized, racialized, gendered subjects: "The colonized is always degraded and the colonialist finds justification for rejecting his subjects" (1991, 71). As Memmi's argument would suggest, Prins favors by every criterion the positions she attributes to the European "colonizer" and rejects all she attributes to the American "colonized."

Theorists have long argued that the very structure of binary arguments is problematic (see also Chapter 2). Binaries paper over internal differences to create two distinct groups, to "fix" their positions in order to create dichotomies, then to arrange the dichotomies hierarchically (see Cixous 1980; Derrida 1978; Lorde 1984). Derrida (1978) argues that the first, privileged term of the binary requires for its existence the hierarchical contrast to the second, unprivileged term. The privileged term is valued specifically because it is *not* the degraded term. These problems of binary thinking infuse Prins's arguments. Initially she frames both types of intersectionality as holding "anti-essentialist" views of identity (2006, 281) and as sharing the notion that categories are flexible, contingent, and relational: "Categories like gender, ethnicity and class *co-construct* each other, and they do so *in myriad ways, dependent on social, historical and symbolic factors*" (279, emphasis added).

Prins then embarks, however, on developing binary distinctions that contradict her own claim. Just as Derrida argues to be the case in the formulation of binaries, she establishes British "constructionist" intersectionality in terms of what *it is not*—the faults that it escapes—which I demonstrate in the quotations below through added emphasis. Prins argues that British "constructionist" intersectionality draws on Foucault and Gramsci to see both identity and power as "relational and dynamic" (279–280), with possibilities for modifying relations among elements (280). It assumes that subjects are the source of their own thinking and acting, *not merely* "subjected to" or subordinated to a sovereign power or anonymous system (280). It assumes markers of identity are *not merely* exclusive and limiting (280) but "made and contingent" (281), providing narrative and enabling resources (280). It does *not* assume that identities are "ideological distortions of a suppressed and authentic experience" (281). It does *not* see identities as understood by a "naming," or a "list of characteristics" which indicate the "what" of a person, but instead as "narration," which indicates the "who" of a person (281).

American "systemic" intersectionality, Prins argues, is characterized by the binary opposite of each of these positions. She claims that it barely draws on Foucault and not at all on Gramsci, rendering it unable to see power as "relational and dynamic" (280). It has a "static" view of the meaning of the category of race (280), sees racism as a "single system in which Whites dominate Blacks" (280). It ignores the ways that non-Blacks—the "Irish people, Jews, or refugees from the Third World"—are negatively racialized (280). It foregrounds system or structure, assumes that subjects are "primarily constituted by systems of domination and marginalization," and assumes subjects are "passive bearers" of the meanings of social categories (280). For Prins, American "systemic" intersectionality sees identities as "predominantly . . . matters of categorization and naming" (280–281). It holds the meaning of identities to be determined by racism, classism, and sexism (281) and assumes these to be "static and rigid systems of domination" (281). It does not "discard the concept of agency" (280), but tends to ignore the subject's agency (281), perhaps because it is "predominantly" concerned with revealing the "unilateral" power of social representations (280). "Systemic" intersectionality holds assumptions of "theories of ideology" (281), assuming that identities are made and contingent (281) but that they are "made by the powers-that-be" and "as such false" (281).

Prins grounds her critical claims about "systemic" American intersectionality primarily on four texts—eight to fifteen years old—of Crenshaw (1991), Collins (1991, 1998), and Matsuda (1991), none of which makes the kinds of argument that she condemns. Contra Prins's claims, these scholars do draw on Gramsci and Foucault.[10] None sees racism as experienced by only Blacks.[11] None ignores the possibilities of social and political change. None treats power and categories as static and unilateral. Crenshaw, for example, considers neither categories nor their effects to be rigid and static. Rather, Crenshaw argues:

> This is not to deny that the process of categorization is itself an exercise of power, but the story is *much more complicated and nuanced than that.* First, the process of categorizing—or, in identity terms, naming—is *not unilateral.* Subordinated people *can and do participate, sometimes even subverting* the naming process in empowering ways. One need only think about the historical subversion of the category "Black" or the current transformation of "queer" to understand that categorization is not a one-way street. Clearly, there is unequal power, but there is nonetheless *some degree of agency that people can and do exert* in the politics of naming. And it is important to note that *identity continues to be a site of resistance* for members of different subordinated groups. (1991, 1297, emphasis added)

This argument—despite appearing in one of the four texts that Prins uses to characterize and condemn the thinking of American intersectional scholars of color—does not fit the binary categories that she deploys: Crenshaw does *not* assume a static view of the meaning of race; she does *not* see racism as a single system with Whites dominating Blacks; she does *not* assume that subjects are passive bearers of the meanings of social categories;

she does *not* assume that racism and the like are static and rigid systems of domination; she does *not* ignore subjects' potential for agency; she does *not* see subjects' identities as false constructions of "the powers-that-be"; she does *not* aim to reveal the unilateral power of social representations; in fact, she does *not* think social representations *are* unilateral; she does *not* assume identities are ideological distortions of a suppressed and authentic experience. The evidence of Crenshaw's actual argument stands in refutation of the critic's condemnation through falsely binary claims. The evidence demonstrates that relying on powerblind discourses has enabled Prins to construct a dramatic but deeply inaccurate characterization of the way U.S. intersectional scholars of color examine categories, identities, social structures, and power.

"FIXING" THE "ESSENTIAL" NATURE
OF THE COLONIZED

Memmi argues that after constructing the colonizer as superior and the colonized as inferior, the discourses of colonial racism establish "these supposed differences as standards of absolute fact" (1991, 71). According to Memmi:

> Perhaps the most important thing is that once the behavioral feature, or historical or geographical factor which characterizes the colonialist and contrasts him with the colonizer, has been isolated, this gap must be kept from being filled. *The colonialist removes the factor from history, time, and therefore possible evolution.* What is actually a sociological point becomes labeled as being biological or, preferably, metaphysical. It is *attached to the colonized's basic nature.* (1991, 71, emphasis added)

Memmi's argument here explains some features of the treatment of North American intersectional theorizing in these arguments that might otherwise seem strikingly peculiar: for example, the repeated willingness to accept as factual evidence about the present claims based on texts that have been removed from history, temporality, and contingency. Texts that are ten, twenty, even thirty years old are treated as if they were contemporary to one another and to the critic. These texts are conflated, solidified, reified, encapsulated, their differing conditions of production and reception ignored. Rather than serving as evidence about the historical conditions of their utterance, or about their differing textual construction as literary talks, sociological theory, or law review articles, these texts are taken to warrant claims about the collective, undifferentiated, indistinguishable, programmatic, nontheoretical, rigid, and static thinking of their authors. More recent articles by those authors or other U.S. intersectional scholars of color are often not mentioned at all. This extraordinary treatment of early articles on intersectional thinking written by U.S. scholars of color would appear to violate scholarly norms that scholars situate their arguments in *contemporary* debate. Significantly, this kind of violation is selective: critics do not position the work of their white and European colleagues in the same way; they treat such colleagues as participating in present circumstances and changing debates, so that it is necessary and even productive to cite their more recent arguments. Where those colleagues are concerned, the intersectionality of any year cannot stand in for the intersectionality of any other year. In contrast, the thinking about intersectionality of U.S. scholars of color is positioned as timeless and unchanging.

Memmi's argument that colonizing discourses frame sociological points as inherent to the basic nature of the colonized clarifies another peculiarity of the colonizing rhetorics I examine: their resistance to any revision or challenge based on actual textual evidence of the texts in question. Claims about scholars' positions are made to float free from the actual (contradicting) evidence of their texts. Critics construct as the position of U.S. intersectional scholars of color a monolithic "master argument" wherein all social relations, categories, and identities are "rigid," "static," "fixed," and "clearly demarcated." Negative comments promoting the story of this "master argument" are frequent in critiques and reviews of intersectional thinking circulating in the European arena. In contrast, powerblind critiques seldom criticize other powerblind critiques.[12] Powerblindness is promoted though citational practices that protect the faulty arguments of white scholars from criticism in order to form a united front critical of the work of scholars of color.

The story of this master argument appears impervious to evidence: for example, it does not entail accurate readings of the actual texts of the U.S. intersectional women of color that the critics cite or of those they ignore—texts replete with a plethora of arguments about resistance, rupture, fluidity, flexibility. When specific texts are cited, they are framed in deeply inaccurate terms in order to protect and secure the master argument. Historical, disciplinary, and contingent differences and disagreements among U.S. intersectional scholars of color are ignored. Memmi's insights explain why this pattern of discursive practice has not been called into question. The colonialist already knows what someone arguing about racial categories must have been thinking. Limited constructions are therefore treated as inherent characteristics of the colonized. They are attached to the colonized's basic nature. Within the frame established by unacknowledged reliance on colonizing discourses, to treat the arguments about intersectionality of North American feminist scholars of color in a different way becomes, essentially, unthinkable.

EXPLOITING CLAIMED DIFFERENCES
FOR THE BENEFIT OF THE COLONIZER

Memmi argues that colonial racism exploits the claimed differences between colonizer and colonized "for the benefit of the colonialist" (1991, 71). The powerblind discourses I examine reveal attempts to establish a valuable "purified" intersectionality, quarantined from its exposure to race. Establishing the Black feminist scholars who originated intersectional theorizing as "unworthy"—parochial, "race-bound," incapable of "theorizing"—justifies extracting from them the valuable tool of intersectionality. Such justification also reinforces the self-conceptions of racial europeanization and its construction of its own innocence with regard to its colonial histories and contemporary racisms. Some European feminists may feel that they can win a hearing for themselves through the disavowal of connections to Black women. Groups seeking recognition and respect often perform normativity in front of those who dominate them by disavowing their connections to the even more despised nonnormative members of their own group; seeking respect, they perform respectability (Shah 2001). In this context, European feminists may seek to remedy their subordinated status as women by reassuring men—and themselves—of their status as whites. Ultimately such argumentative moves strengthen the kinds of thinking responsible for sexism and restrict the tools available to counter subordination.

The discursive arena of European academic discourses about intersectional analysis is not uniform, but it does offer an interconnected set of mutually supporting claims about the proper role of intersectionality in Europe that is framed within and limited by the terms of racial europeanization. As a result some scholars in that arena deploy structures of argument that fail to give due attention to the imbrication of race, nation, and power in the representations of intersectional thinking they wish to disparage, the scholars they target, and their own arguments. The powerblind discursive devices I examine here evoke histories of racial hierarchy and colonialism, treating the intersectionality of U.S. Black women as a site to colonize and control. Under such circumstances, critics' claims have effects beyond their intentions. They treat ideas from elsewhere as unwelcome until shaped for assimilation. Doing so echoes the treatment of people framed as from elsewhere as requiring assimilation to become welcome in a shared social space. These powerblind critiques unwittingly reenact at the scene of argument the exact exclusions that national exceptionalisms and xenophobia perform in European social life.

9

AFFECT AND
THE EPISTEMIC MACHINE

This book argues that the moment when the challenge of intersectional thinking gained traction—from the late 1970s to the early 1990s—was infinitely generative for women of color feminism, for feminist studies, and for social theory more generally. Yet as I have argued in earlier chapters, that moment also marked a perception of a traumatic loss of power for white women within feminism, a loss linked to the disturbance of race that has never been fully absorbed or acknowledged. Instead, I contend, it pervades the present primarily covertly but sometimes even overtly at the scene of argument through the widespread use of powerblind discursive strategies that work together to produce an "Epistemic Machine"—*a discursive machine for invalidating knowledge.* The Epistemic Machine of powerblind feminist critique grinds up the arguments and metaphors of intersectionality, discredits its creators, dismisses its intellectual productivity, and frees it for appropriation. An Epistemic Machine is created not by individual scholars but by a significant number of interlocutors who work in implicit concert at the scene of argument by deploying similar conventional strategies to criticize similar imaginary intersectionalities. The widespread use and acceptance of the workings of the Epistemic Machine demonstrate its shared social role as part of the metadiscursive regime of feminist scholarship; shutting down the machine requires a transformation in the terms of feminist reading and writing.

The Epistemic Machine is generated in part by discursive affect. While these discursive affects have been implicit in many of the strategies discussed in previous chapters, in this chapter I make explicit some of the discursive affects that infuse many arguments participating in the Epistemic Machine: ambivalence, anxiety, competitiveness, patronizing condescension, discursive superiority, disavowal, bewilderment, and shame, for example. I conclude the chapter with an argument for turning off the Epistemic Machine.

AMBIVALENCE AND THE PROBLEM OF DISCIPLINARITY

Discursive ambivalence in white critiques of intersectionality is not innocent but a strategy to deploy powerblindness from a position of apparent innocence. An affect of ambivalence is the psychic armor of the strong, who can afford to be ambivalent because they do not face the struggles of subordinated groups. Inhabiting ambivalence is plausible for people with dominant power; the costs of ambivalence for people without power, however, are high. They are forced by urgency to struggle and reach conclusions that matter.

Discursive ambivalence can serve politically useful purposes for white feminist critiques by acknowledging but not actually responding to the challenge presented by intersectionality. Ambivalence can disguise the use of symbolic dominance to control the incursion of the conceptions of women of color into white-dominated fields. As Briggs argues, "Symbolic domination involves controlling the production of authority and value and inducing others to struggle for position and resources within a system designed to favor those in power" (2007, 338, citing Bourdieu and Wacquant 1992).[1] In this context, symbolic domination is established when critics representing specific—even parochial—disciplinary structures such as those of sociology act as if they are singular sources of authority and value, subordinating the goals, expertise, and interests of those seeking to use intersectionality in law and other disciplines. An apparently ambivalent debate about whether intersectionality meets specifically disciplinary strictures can silently restrict the field of evaluation without interrogating disciplinary traditions and acknowledging intersectionality's interdisciplinary role.

The symbolic dominance created by powerblind discourses of ambivalence in white critiques of intersectionality is demonstrated in "Intersectionality as Buzzword: A Sociology of Science Perspective on What Makes a Feminist Theory Successful" by Kathy Davis (2008). (There are more than 1,750 citations in Google Scholar for the journal article, which has also been reprinted, as of May 10, 2018.) Kathy Davis purports to examine intersectionality through the lens of the sociology of science, drawing on an analysis of the nature of classical social theories provided by Murray S. Davis in two articles: "'That's Classic!' The Phenomenology and Rhetoric of Successful Social Theories" (1986) and "That's Interesting!" (1971). "'That's Classic!'" focuses on features that led to the "success" of single-authored social theories now considered "classic," primarily the theories of Marx, Durkheim, Weber, Simmel, and Freud. Drawing on Murray Davis's schema, Kathy Davis explains:

> I explore the features of intersectionality that account for its success: its focus on a pervasive and fundamental concern in feminist theory, its provision of novelty, its appeal to the generalists as well as the specialists in the discipline, and its inherent ambiguity and open-endedness that beg for further critique and elaboration. (2008, 69–70)

While Kathy Davis echoes Murray Davis's use of the term "ambiguity," she transforms it from a positive to a negative trait. The most common meaning of "ambiguity" or "ambiguous" is "admitting more than one interpretation or explanation" (OED).[2] Both Kathy Davis and Murray Davis use "ambiguity" or "ambiguous" (eight or nine times each), but with quite different emotional valences. Ambiguity used in a *positive* sense is central to Murray Davis's argument. He indicates that "social theories whose concepts are only 'loosely coupled' are subject to alternative organizations. . . . Ambiguity in social science is not [an] embarrassment. . . . [R]ather it is *crucial* to the social theorist's appeal" (1986, 295–296, emphasis added). Further, he argues, "their essential equivocality and open-endedness make the sociological classics more like those in the humanities than like those in the natural sciences" (297). He quotes Frank Kermode on the distinguishing features of humanities classics, which include

> an openness to accommodation which keeps them alive under varying [interpretations]. . . . The survival of the classic must . . . depend on its possession of a surplus of signifiers . . . , for [it] must always signify more than is needed by any one interpreter or any one generation of interpreters. (Kermode 1983, 44, 133, 138, 140, quoted in M. Davis 1986, 297–298)

In a key argument, Murray Davis states that relating classic social theories to the humanities serves to clarify the values that have led to the success of these social theories. He writes: *"Regarding the sociological classics as humanistic rather than scientific texts permits us to see the value of what we would otherwise see as a defect"* (M. Davis 1986, 297–298, emphasis added). Thus Murray Davis emphasizes the positive qualities of ambiguity for social theories considered classic, the importance of their close resemblance to classics in the humanities, and the need to see their ambiguity as rich and generative rather than problematic. Faithful interpretation of Murray Davis's argument would position intersectionality's openness positively, as a central reason for intersectionality's success.

Kathy Davis, however, instead positions intersectionality's ambiguity ambivalently and even negatively. While she reports accurately Murray Davis's claim that successful social theories are ambiguous and incomplete, she ignores his emphasis on their resemblance to classics in the humanities and creates a strain of *negative affect* about ambiguity that runs throughout her article. She uses nouns and modifiers not in Murray Davis's text to create negative connotations, for example, to claim that successful theories are "inherently *hazy* and *mystifyingly* open-ended" (2008, 69, emphasis added). "Hazy" means "lacking intellectual distinctness"; "mystifyingly" means "so as to cause mystification, inexplicably." Neither term is consistent with Murray Davis's argument because they present ambiguity and open-endedness in a negative rather than positive light. This is true of a series of other terms also absent from Murray Davis's pieces and inconsistent with his arguments but used by Kathy Davis to describe intersectionality as well as "classic" social theories: "vague," meaning "lacking in definiteness or precision"; "fuzzy," meaning "confused, imprecisely defined"; "indeterminate," meaning "wanting in precision, not clear"; and "imperfect," meaning "not perfect, unfinished, deficient."

Negative affect entirely inconsistent with Murray Davis's argument is intensified by Kathy Davis's use of the word "chimerical" to describe intersectionality. She states: "I raise the question of whether embracing such a *chimerical* and—some would argue—scientifically unsound concept should be only a reason for celebration or also a reason for *some alarm*" (2008, 70, emphasis added).[3] A "chimera" is a fabled grotesque monster, formed from the parts of various animals. In ordinary modern use it is an "unreal creature of the imagination, a mere wild fancy; an unfounded conception." "Chimerical" means "of the nature of a chimera; vainly or fantastically conceived, imaginary, fanciful, visionary." Questioning whether the existence of intersectionality provides cause for "alarm," Kathy Davis frames a significant theoretical resource proposed by women of color as a grotesque monster created of incongruent parts, a wild fancy. Her evocation of the term "chimerical" for the intellectual production of women of color raises a familiar racist trope connecting Blackness to monstrosity (on transfigurations of monstrous Blackness, see Lezra 2014).

Kathy Davis is particularly equivocal—perhaps even negative—about attention to difference in feminist theory and the prominence of the term "intersectionality." At one point she comments, "Race/class/gender became the new *mantra* within women's studies" (2008, 73, emphasis added). Later she adds, with regard to intersectionality:

On the one hand, it has all the makings of a *buzzword,* which can easily capture the interests of the generalists. It appears frequently in the titles of articles in feminist journals on any number of subjects, providing a *catchy* and convenient way of expressing the author's normative commitments. (75, emphasis added)[4]

Kathy Davis is not the first to use the term "mantra"—"a constantly or monotonously repeated phrase or sentence"—to describe systematic attention to salient axes of subordination: conservative political speech often has used the term "mantra" to imply that concern for subordination through race, class, and gender is meaningless "groupthink." In fact, "mantra," "buzzword," "catchy" are all terms used to denigrate political language used by feminists, antiracists, and progressive scholars. The use of the term "buzzword" is particularly significant in Kathy Davis's article, emphasized in the title—"Intersectionality *as Buzzword*" (2008, 67, emphasis added)—as well as repeated in the passage quoted above. The use of "buzzword" is an openly emphatic political claim that one of the most important intellectual productions of women of color is merely "a term used more to impress than to inform" or "a catchword or expression currently fashionable." To label intersectionality a "buzzword" is a political act of revanchism, an attempt to devalorize successful theories of women of color in order to restore the theories of white women to the center of feminist theory.[5] As a powerblind strategy to denigrate intersectionality it has been enormously successful, repeated in many texts that do not even cite its source in Davis 2008. The article's word choice reinforces the superficiality it purports to critique.

Part of the article's projection of ambivalence is its claim that conceptions of difference are currently so central to feminist studies that anyone who does not write about difference will not be published:

> Feminist journals are likely to reject articles that have not given sufficient attention to "race," class, and heteronormativity, along with gender. At this particular juncture in gender studies, any scholar who neglects difference runs the risk of having her work viewed as theoretically misguided, politically irrelevant, or simply *fantastical.* (Davis 2008, 68, emphasis added)

Kathy Davis, who has been one of the editors of the *European Journal of Woman's Studies,* would appear to be a reliable source for information about patterns of publication. Yet her warning is presented in exaggeratedly dramatic terms. She is claiming that to neglect difference would lead not only to an article's being rejected for publication but also to a scholar's work being seen as "fantastical": "bizarre, grotesque; conceived, made, or carried out without adherence to truth or reality." The implication is that people who do not write about difference are a threatened group. The terms "fantastic" and "grotesque" are endemic in the colonial matrix to describe confrontations with the Other and the Other's perceived oppressive expressions of subjectivity (see Glass 2012; Haney López 2014; Harper 2012; Peterson 1998). Here the "demand" to account for difference becomes a phobic projection—white feminist scholars are forced to account for Others, and threatened with the possibility that whiteness will be viewed as the same kind of marked category that Blackness has been and continues to be in the colonial matrix.

Kathy Davis's text also displays ambivalence about which of two stances it should take toward its subject matter: first, that of a commonsense "epistemology" of sociology—a "theory of knowledge and understanding, esp. with regard to its methods, validity, and scope"; and second, that of the "sociology of science." The difference between the two stances is significant, as Howard S. Becker argues:

> Epistemology has been a . . . negative discipline, mostly devoted to saying what you shouldn't do if you want your activity to merit the title of science, and to keeping unworthy pretenders from successfully appropriating it. The sociology of science . . . gives up trying to decide what should and shouldn't count as science, and tells what people who claim to be doing science do. (1996, 54–55, quoted in Bowker and Star 2000, 150)

Kathy Davis claims that her argument is based on the sociology of science, particularly in its evoking Murray Davis's sociology of science framework emphasizing the benefits of ambiguity, and in her article's subtitle—"A Sociology of Science Perspective on What Makes a Feminist Theory Successful."

Yet despite her use of Murray Davis's analysis grounded in the sociology of science, Kathy Davis alternates between praising intersectionality and belittling it from the position of commonsense epistemology. Her text provides numerous comments about intersectionality failing to meet commonsense criteria for good theories, frequent citations and repetitions of previous criticisms of intersectionality, and comments about what intersectionality "needs." These arguments are not congruent with the stance of the sociology of science. Rather they inhabit the authority of a traditional commonsense epistemology of sociology in order to assert that intersectionality has failed to meet its strictures. She comments, "Intersectionality may not fit the sociological common sense concerning 'good theory' as coherent, comprehensive, and sound" (2008, 78), without acknowledging that such standards as "coherence" are *political* as well as *scientific*. She makes backhanded attacks on intersectionality by manipulating the claims of Murray Davis: "As [Murray] Davis has shown, the most successful theories are often not the best ones in the sense of being coherent or capable of providing *encompassing or irrefutable explanations of social life*" (78, emphasis added). Murray Davis and other sociologists of science do not assume that social theories could meet a standard of producing "irrefutable explanations of social life." Social theories relevant to feminist studies generally provide ways of discerning patterns in social life, not finding "law-like generalizations," or "irrefutable explanations of social life."

Kathy Davis's ambivalence toward fully adopting the stance of the sociology of science that she purports to deploy may be due in part to her commitment to the citation, repetition, and promotion of previous white feminist critiques of intersectionality, critiques thoroughly undermined by Murray Davis's arguments, but completely congruent with commonsense epistemology of sociology. She repeats Murray Davis's claims about the benefits of ambiguity and open-endedness while at the same time echoing the complaints of previous feminist sociologists who insist that intersectionality needs to be clearly defined, tightened down, controlled, made "universal"—exactly the *opposite* of Murray Davis's argument for what makes a successful theory. For example, she repeats Mieke Verloo's argument that intersectionality "would be greatly improved with a more clear-cut and *universally applicable* definition" (78, citing Verloo 2006, emphasis added) and Leslie McCall's claim that intersectionality would be better with "more *stringent* methodological guidelines concerning where, how, and to what end it could—or should—be used in feminist inquiry" (78, citing McCall 2005, emphasis added). Thus, despite her claims to approach intersectionality through the lens of the sociology of science, Kathy Davis appears to support these epistemological strictures fully, commenting, "In order to achieve its full potential, intersectionality is in need of a definition, a set of clearly demarcated parameters, and a methodology which would eliminate any confusion among researchers concerning how, where, and when it should be applied" (2008, 78). The penchant for repeating rather than critically re-evaluating previous criticisms of intersectionality in the light of Murray Davis's sociology of science rests on what appears to be a long-standing general practice among critiques of intersectionality: they seldom criticize *one another's* arguments—no matter how incongruous—but rather form a kind of community that centers on complaining about intersectionality instead of engaging in the work to practice and strengthen it.

The sociology of science that guides Murray Davis's arguments directly counters Kathy Davis's notions about how to "clean up" intersectionality. In a passage not cited by Kathy Davis, Murray Davis argues:

Actually, the "Mediocre" in the social sciences . . . can be defined as those who take the text-book rules of scientific procedures too literally and too exclusively . . . [who] fail to take into account the assumption-ground of their audience. . . . Theory construction, in other words, should not be treated as an independent logical or empirical enterprise separate from, and unrelated to, what the audience already "knows" about a given body of data. (1971, 328, 337)

Murray Davis argues that traditional commonsense epistemological rules of sociology are not characteristic of theories that are either "interesting" (1971) or "classic" (1986). He holds that commonsense strictures should be questioned.[6] His argument suggests that "classical" theories cannot be tamed in such mechanical ways, because other researchers would—*quite rightly*—contest the various proposed definitions, guidelines, parameters, and methodologies, thereby continuing the unruly development of the theory rather than resolving its ambiguities.

Kathy Davis's text is even ambivalent about the nature of theory, whether intersectionality can properly be considered a theory, and the consequences of such a decision. Murray Davis's framework is focused specifically on the analysis of social theories. Kathy Davis's subtitle indicates that she will be analyzing a theory ("What Makes a Feminist Theory Successful"). She begins her article by calling intersectionality a theory—and even a good theory (for example, 2008, 67, 69). Although she provides no definition of "theory," she then cites several critics' opinions leading her to suggest that intersectionality *may not be a theory at all*. She remarks that she is "leaving aside the issue of whether intersectionality can be treated as a full-fledged 'theory'" (69). A "full-fledged" theory would have the fullest set of credentials or qualifying characteristics, or, metaphorically, feathers large enough for flight. She assumes that it is worthwhile to suggest that intersectionality does not meet the definition of a sociological theory without the need to examine what that definition might be. There is an arbitrary claim here that does not do justice to the actual role of theory in sociological thought, which provides varied definitions of the term "theory," several of which appear applicable to intersectionality (see Marshall 1998b).[7] The consequences of Kathy Davis's equivocal stance on intersectionality's "status" as a theory are explicitly political, serving to establish the scholars of color who developed intersectionality as "unworthy pretenders" who cannot "theorize" and whose work cannot merit the title of "science."

Even more significant in the context of the field of interdisciplinary feminist scholarship is Kathy Davis's silent reduction of "feminist theory" to "sociological theory." Intersectionality is the production of *many authors* of different disciplines, backgrounds, and concerns. In effect, intersectionality is *a quintessential example of a collective feminist theory*. This being the case, critics could turn their attention to productively developing new strategies for feminists to properly evaluate and develop collective theories, rather than chastising such theories for not meeting criteria inappropriate even for classic single-author theories. Sara Ahmed provides arguments about the political nature of naming theory and feminist theory that are particularly helpful in demonstrating the limitations of Kathy Davis's framework. Ahmed argues that theorizing "involves a set of techniques for moving beyond local sites of resistance, and indeed, of linking the local to other locals, or broader social processes" (2000, 99), which is part of the role of intersectional theorizing. Ahmed also maintains that "part of the work that is done by 'feminist theory' may be, then, *the posing of a critical challenge to the criteria that operate within the academy about what constitutes theory per se*" (99, emphasis in original). Ahmed also cites Teresa De Lauretis to argue that "feminist work becomes recognizably theoretical when it begins to dispute . . . the very categories of analysis that have been used by other feminisms" (1988, 101), certainly the role of intersectionality.

Thinking of feminist theorizing along with Ahmed and de Lauretis offers insight into the powerblind strategy that Kathy Davis adopts to subordinate all interdisciplinary feminist theorizing to the strictures of a commonsense epistemology of the single discipline of sociology. She simply ignores intersectionality's emergence as a challenge or tool to dispute "the very categories of analysis used by other feminisms" and "*the criteria that operate within the academy about what constitutes theory per se*." To call on tenets of sociological theory—however ill-defined—to denigrate intersectionality and declare it "scientifically unsound," not a "full-fledged" theory, or not a "good" theory evades necessary debates about how intersectionality challenges the grounds of sociology and treats it as properly subject to sociology's disciplinary domination. Davis does not treat her strategy of disciplinary control as requiring justification or even explanation, thus revealing it as a move of dominant discourse (see Terdiman 1985 and Chapter 6). In effect, she treats her representation of the interests of sociology as superordinate to the goals and interests of all other feminist academic fields.

Kathy Davis's ambivalence toward the success of intersectionality also registers in her consideration of Kimberlé Crenshaw's contributions to its development in terms that might be characterized as "begrudging"; "showing dissatisfaction with; *esp.* to envy [one] the possession of; to give reluctantly." She truncates and simplifies Crenshaw's arguments to report to her audience only what is similar to previous arguments and provides excuses why feminist scholars have not already addressed Crenshaw's other concerns (2008 79n1). She ignores how Crenshaw's arguments brought in precise intersectional analysis of specific court cases and created complex metaphors in order to break a long-standing impasse. Davis's summaries of Crenshaw's arguments (1989, 1991), are full of negativity and dismissal: "hardly a new idea," "by no means the first," and "not making a particularly new argument" (2008, 68, 72–73). Davis's ambivalence and begrudging language dramatically misrepresent Crenshaw's influence. Crenshaw's work led to rich scholarship across the disciplines retheorizing sameness and difference. Reprints aside, Google Scholar citations for the original articles of "Demarginalizing" (1989) reach more than 8,300, and for "Mapping" (1991) more than 13,200, as of May 10, 2018; both "Mapping" and Crenshaw's earlier "Retrenchment" (1988) appear among the top 100 "most-cited law review articles of all time" (Shapiro and Pearse 2012). Kathy Davis's rendition of these contributions as prosaic makes it hard to imagine how intersectionality could ever have become a theory interesting enough to write about!

Problems of disciplinarity infuse Kathy Davis's text. She establishes symbolic dominance by using an uninterrogated disciplinary structure of sociology as the proper standard to evaluate intersectionality. Her arguments do not reflect the interdisciplinary nature of feminist theory, instead treating sociology as the center of feminist scholarship, and one version of sociology's interests, exigencies, and research criteria as the unquestioned standard that all feminist theories must meet. These moves are particularly problematic given intersectionality's origins in feminist legal, literary, historical, and cultural studies as well as the social sciences. The result is a kind of symbolic domination over intersectionality, but also over interdisciplinary feminist scholarship and feminist scholarship in other fields. Davis's text controls the production of authority and value according to the interests of her version of feminist sociology, not the interests of scholars across the disciplines producing intersectionality, not the public constituencies they serve, and not a more general inter-, cross-, or multidisciplinary feminist studies. Ambivalence reveals itself as a crucial tool for powerblind rhetorics of domination.

ANXIETY AND THE COMPETITION FOR CATEGORICAL PRIMACY

As it began to gain interest and acceptance from the 1970s to the 1990s, intersectional analysis made important contributions not only to feminism but also to other social movements and theories by challenging the premise that one social contradiction was more crucial than any other as grounds for hierarchy and exploitation. It challenged the idea that the liberation of only one social group would produce the liberation of everyone. For feminists, the universal woman of feminism—like the universal worker of Marxism, the universal free-market actor of capitalism, and the universal rights-bearing subject of the law—had been seen as a privileged agent at a privileged site of struggle, destined to deliver freedom to everyone else by addressing what was assumed to be the core contradiction in society.

Thinking intersectionally disturbed these investments. It suggested that even oppositional discourses could contain traces of dominant ideologies, that white women might advance their interests at the expense of women who are not white, that Black men might make gains at the expense of Blacks who are not men, that triumphs by Black and white women and men in the Global North might come at the expense of people in the Global South. Challenges by multidimensional thinkers thus implicitly questioned feminists' investment in their own special political virtue. Such challenges undermined feminist scholars' certainty that they acted as pure and righteous agents of history. The result for some was anxiety about the potential loss of their investment in gender as the primary axis of oppression and a sense of competitiveness with regard to other categories.

Discursive anxiety and competitive affect emerge in white feminist critiques of intersectionality through powerblind discourses. For example, historian Nancy A. Hewitt criticizes intersectional analysis for its failure to identify which category—gender, race, or class—should be distinguished as "primary" (1992). (There are more than fifty citations in Google Scholar to the journal article as of May 10, 2018.) Hewitt complains: "The intersection model does not provide the path out of the jungle of primacy debates *that it once promised*. Instead, it simply leads back to it by a more circuitous route" (1992, 315, emphasis added). In a typical powerblind gesture, Hewitt unifies and corporatizes intersectional arguments from a range of viewpoints emerging for different disciplines into an "intersection model," an entity capable of making promises and then failing to keep them. As becomes evident in her argument, Hewitt apparently feels that she was promised a way that gender could maintain its particular importance for Hewitt and perhaps other feminists. But the question of which category is the most important was explicitly *not* of central importance for the scholars who introduced intersectionality, who were arguing *against* emphasis on single-axis categorization. While those promoting intersectional analysis are focused on hierarchies of social oppression, the hierarchies that concern Hewitt appear focused on hierarchies of scholarly importance—about who is to rule in the quest for "oppositional universalism" (rather than promoting "pluriversalism"). In Hewitt's imaginary, gender, race, and class are in a rivalry for supremacy. The problem of the "intersection model," in this argument, is that the "model" does not properly identify the winner, the category that should prevail as primary.

Rather than referring to published intersectional scholarship, Hewitt illustrates the failure of the promises she attributes to intersectionality by constructing a *personal* "intersection model," an image of intersectionality at work:

> My first intimation of this came when, a few years back, I took a self-conscious look at the image of "an intersection" *that I carried in my head.* Here came a middle-class woman, a white working-class man, and a Black man barreling down on each other from different directions. They reached the intersection simultaneously *and—CRASH— the one left standing won.* (1992, 315, emphasis added)

This instantiation of the metaphor of intersectionality decontextualizes it from arguments about subordination, interconnected multiple categories, and structures of social power—the context for which it was proposed. Having reified the multiplicity of intersectionality into a singular abstraction—"*the* intersection *model*"—Hewitt assumes that it can be represented by *whatever image* of "an intersection" comes to the critic's mind. There are substantial differences between Crenshaw's metaphor and Hewitt's. In Crenshaw's metaphor of intersectionality (see Chapter 3), the concern is with how *discriminations* flow along the streets to affect different individuals; in Hewitt's metaphor, differently oppressed people clash in violent competition, with only one "winner."

Hewitt's personal image of "the intersection model" is also notable for what it includes and what it doesn't: the middle-class woman has class and gender but not a race, the white working-class man has race, class, and gender; the Black man has race but not class. Black women are not present at all. Hewitt recognizes this disparity as a problem that is "disquieting" *but attributes the problem to "the model" itself,* which apparently asks too much: despite her training as a historian "steeped in race-class-and-gender," Hewitt indicates that she finds it difficult *not* to think that "women have more gender than other groups, that Blacks have more race, and that men have more class" (1992, 315). Hewitt is generous to share this difficulty with readers but fails to recognize that the difficulty stems not from a flaw in conceptions of intersectionality but from the difficulty all academics and activists face in trying to think against the dominant grain of separate social categories.

Hewitt finds the image she has created "disquieting" for other reasons also. She is concerned to find *her image reveals* that an "intersection model" assumes race, class, and gender to be *distinct elements of identity* which are variously mixed together under particular historical circumstances. Scholars can thus claim that at different historical crossroads, *different elements win out. Far from eradicating hierarchy, we just make primacy situational rather than universal.* And *who is left standing, who "wins"* at any particular moment, is dependent on which variable is stronger, *not only historically but theoretically.* (1992, 315–316, emphasis added)

Hewitt's argument here unwittingly reveals the shock, the provocation created by having to take seriously the challenge to think intersectionally. In the middle of making an argument about which separate and isolatable category—gender, race, or class—will surpass its rivals, Hewitt pauses to criticize the "intersectional model" for separating and isolating categories. Yet intersectional thinking challenges this dominant formulation of isolated social categories, while Hewitt's argument reinscribes it.

Competition among scholars remains central to this part of Hewitt's argument. The phrase "far from eradicating hierarchy" seems to conflate social hierarchies—which intersectionality is proposed to analyze—with hierarchies of categories in scholarly or social competition. Identifying primacy is so central to Hewitt's intellectual investment in gender that she sees little benefit in intersectionality's ability to analyze how gender, race, class, and other categories actually work together in uneven equilibrium. She frames as a problem, rather than an advantage, that intersectional analyses might reveal how different situations produce different categorical relations. In this argument, intersectionality fails to contribute to what appears to be Hewitt's most important goal: determining which category gets to be celebrated as significantly "stronger" in all situations, with an investment in having gender emerge the winner and anxiety that it will not. This is a foundationalist response to an antifoundationalist argument. Once we have done away with foundations, it asks, what will be the new foundation? This foundationalist response misses the point of intersectional arguments, which are not foundational. Crenshaw (1989) argues that, in the court cases she analyzes, gender and race *together* determine the outcome: the Black women are not discriminated against as women, nor as Blacks, but specifically as *Black women.* Neither category is more important because their effect results from their interconnection. Hewitt's fears about gender being displaced by such an analysis could be valid only if Black women can somehow be thought of as *other than* women.

Hewitt (1992) expresses concern that the widespread use of intersectional analysis will offer more possibilities for race or class to "win" over gender. She worries that gender scholars may not "win" in this competition because the categories of race and class might be stronger *"not only historically but theoretically"* (316). Hewitt's claim emphasizes that she is thinking in terms of competition among scholars' arguments, evidence, and theories, not in terms of countering subordination in lived experience. She argues:

> In attempting, then, to diversify and deconstruct, we women's historians *may* find gender as a motor of change overpowered by the more smoothly running engines of race and class. But more importantly, as long as we cling to an intersection model, we will find it impossible to grapple fully with the complexities of individual and group identities. (1992, 316)

Hewitt seems concerned that scholars of race and class have "more smoothly running engines" than scholars of gender but does not acknowledge that thinking intersectionally is a way of integrating theories and arguments about race and class *into* gender analyses. She argues that what scholars need is an approach sensitive to gender, race, and class, but that "clinging to" "an intersection model"—which is sensitive to gender, race, and class—is getting in the way. Hewitt's argument might seem contradictory, but at the scene of argument it is not: she has reduced intersectionality to a calculus of which static identity is more important. She condemns the stasis that her own misreading of the image she has invented actually produces. Hewitt positions intersectionality as about identity—and identities linked to scholars in competition—not social relations and larger structures of power. This blind spot can be a built-in contradiction in feminism itself, because its sphere of action is at one and the same time a social movement, an academic enterprise, and a personal consciousness-raising mode. These three elements have often been held together by the unity of the identity of an unmarked, undifferentiated "woman" as the universal sign of feminism, an identity that intersectionality challenges. Hewitt's framing of the "intersection model" is contradictory, both revealing and disavowing intersectionality's flexibility as a way of analyzing social relations.

Some critiques blame intersectionality for offering a heuristic that could produce unlimited numbers of categories, with scholars spinning into a chaos of division and difference, as if there were no political, practical, and theoretical constraints on research design. Hewitt does seem to envision "division gone awry," with scholars or subjects both insisting on diving into what might seem like an "abyss of atomistic identities" (319).[8] But she expresses particular anxiety about the potential of multidimensional thinking to reveal that subjects are more different from one another than scholars had imagined—that they form varied groups marked deeply by dynamics of difference. Hewitt argues:

> If each race/class/sex/sexual/regional/generational/ national/religious subgroup forges its own particular identity, then how do we analyze patterns or make comparisons, much less analyze change over time among and within various groups that cohabit any particular historical setting? (1992, 319)

Hewitt seems to worry that the plurality and diversity of human experience will outstrip scholars' capacity to study it and act on it. She is undoubtedly correct; this will always be the case. It is not the fault of intersectional analysis, nor can it be prevented by avoiding intersectional analysis; it is simply a problem of human intellectual capacities. Surely, if power dynamics in the world create such identities, it should be up to scholars to try to discover and analyze them, using tools such as intersectional analysis.

Hewitt's critique of intersectionality is not so much a counterargument as an expression of anxiety about the possible threat to white feminism posed by the assertions of new subjectivities, new analytic tools, and new political power in feminism voiced by those previously ignored because they possessed what Hewitt called "contested identities" (1992, 319). The raced identities of those who proposed intersectionality seem to permeate the unease of white feminists of the early 1990s, leading them to suffer from an anxiety of diminished overrepresentation. Even white feminists' presumption that those (white women) who have been dominant in feminism can and should determine the nature, pace, and purpose of feminism's diversification—also found in Hewitt's text—is an assertion of uninterrogated privilege.

CONDESCENSION, CONTEMPT, AND BAD VENTRILOQUISM

Condescension and contempt infuse white feminist critiques of intersectionality, often displayed through what I call "bad ventriloquism"—articulating a false and deeply inadequate representation of an intersectional metaphor or argument as if accurately repeating the original. The strategy of bad ventriloquism infuses Wendy Brown's critique of the multidimensional thinking of women of color in "The Impossibility of Women's Studies" (1997, 2005, 2008)—also discussed in Chapter 6⁹—most dramatically her depiction of Crenshaw's metaphor of "intersections." Brown's development of a specific counterargument to Crenshaw's metaphor of intersectionality is found in a peculiar but instructive note in the reprinted and slightly revised version of

"The Impossibility of Women's Studies" published in *Edgework* (2005): the major revision to the text appears to be an addition to note 3 that purports to represent Crenshaw's metaphor of intersectionality. (There are more than one thousand citations to *Edgework* in Google Scholar as of May 10, 2018.)

In the *Edgework* revision of note 3, Brown asks: "What happens if Crenshaw's notion of 'intersectionality' is used to explain the subject formation or even subject position of black women in the United States?" (2005, 152n3). Rather than answering the question she has posed, Brown instead devotes part of the note to create an imaginary scene that she labels "Crenshaw's notion of 'intersectionality.'" Brown yanks the term "intersection" out of its context in Crenshaw's argument, making no reference to Crenshaw's imagery of circulating discriminations. She then rather awkwardly constructs a different "intersection" metaphor by building an image that appears to represent the "opposite" of her own conception of power. However, the image she builds bears no resemblance to Crenshaw's argument and is as far from Crenshaw's conceptions of power as from her own. In effect, Brown attempts to defeat intersectionality by conjuring it as a lame horse that won't be able to compete and naming the horse "Crenshaw's metaphor of intersections." Proffering an illegitimate image that she holds in contempt and misattributing that image to Crenshaw is a powerblind move that serves to reinforce racial hierarchy through condescending treatment of the conceptions of scholars of color.

Crenshaw's metaphor of intersectionality, developed most elaborately in "Demarginalizing" (1989), illuminates the ramifications of multidirectional flows of traffic through intersections in a complex world of contestation and change where remedies often depend on categorization. I reiterate here several passages quoted earlier in Chapter 3 to allow comparison between Crenshaw's metaphor and Brown's bad ventriloquism of it. Crenshaw argues:

> Consider an analogy to traffic in an intersection, coming and going in all four directions. Discrimination, like traffic through an intersection, may flow in one direction, and it may flow in another. If an accident happens in an intersection, it can be caused by cars traveling from any number of directions and, sometimes, from all of them. Similarly, if a Black woman is harmed because she is in the intersection, her injury could result from sex discrimination or race discrimination. (1989, 149)

Crenshaw's metaphor is a *circulation network of identity-related events*, not simply a means of labeling people more complexly. Her concern is with the problems that result when the complexity of identities is not recognized by structural power:

> Providing legal relief only when Black women show that their claims
> are based on race or on sex is analogous to calling an ambulance for
> the victim only after the driver responsible for the injuries is identi-
> fied. . . . [In complex cases] the tendency seems to be that no driver
> is held responsible, no treatment is administered, and the involved
> parties simply get back in their cars and zoom away. (1989, 149)

Crenshaw's focus is on the ways in which the law's reliance on single-axis categories fails to take account of multidimensionality.

Brown makes no attempt to examine, counter, or comment on Crenshaw's actual metaphor. Instead, Brown constructs an entirely different metaphor using the word "intersection," attributing to Crenshaw a "metaphorical scene" of static location. Brown begins: "Imagine that someone lives in the country, and one day a set of roads is laid down adjacent to her house. One road is named Gender, the other is named Race, the woman's house is at their intersection" (2005, 152n3). Having argued that it is "impossible to extract the race from gender" (exactly Crenshaw's point), Brown's first sentences nonetheless insist that this metaphor she attributes to Crenshaw assumes that it *is* possible to extract race from gender (using "*her* house" and "the *woman's* house"): for Brown, the "black woman's" gender is primary and her race secondary (Brown does *not* state: "the *Black's* house is at their intersection" or "the *Black woman's* house is at their intersection").

Brown's scene opens with a subject, "someone," who exists prior to the workings of power—what Crenshaw, Brown, many intersectional scholars, and most poststructuralists would regard as a fiction of a nonraced, nongendered subject. Her spatial metaphor begins with an empty space not already permeated by politics, while raced scholars argue that the spatial is already racial. Brown's story treats as invisible the operations of power that decide how the "someone's" environment is to be changed: "One day a set of roads is laid down adjacent to her house." This phrasing presents the change as unmotivated by any considerations of structural social and political power, although inequality in location of roads, amenities, and toxic waste dumps are central problems for racialized communities. Brown's conjured intersectionality apparently overlooks operations of power at this site, but actual intersectional scholars cannot.

To continue her refutation of an argument that Crenshaw has never made, Brown deploys in this scene only two roads, treated as analytically distinct, "premade," "discrete units" of gender and race, units that are "separable in the subject itself." Brown has been proclaiming that "the forms of power that produce gender or class are themselves saturated with that production—they do not precede it" (2005, 124), but in Brown's story of Crenshaw's metaphor, these forms of power *do* precede it, so that the roads and their names appear from nowhere. Pounding home the limited view of power that she misattributes to Crenshaw, Brown continues:

> For purposes of having an address, she [the woman/black woman] is asked to choose which one [road] she lives on. Whether she chooses one or the other, or whether she insists that she lives at their intersection, these roads impose an address, and the address will have its consequences. (2005, 152n3)

Brown positions her figure—"the woman/black woman"—not as a politicized, racialized, gendered subject but rather a sovereign subject who gets to choose which street she lives on. In contrast to such a naïve claim, both intersectional and poststructuralist scholars know that subjects are not free to choose whether or not they cite dominant gender or racial norms, even if they insist. In Brown's story the roads themselves are positioned as the source of power, since they can impose an address on the woman. It would appear that in this story "the roads" serve as metaphor to disguise structural power that seems to work in a way resembling "top-down" or structural domination, the position Brown misattributes to Crenshaw. Brown does not deny that "the address will have its consequences," but she appears to have little concern for what these consequences are, which is Crenshaw's main point of departure.

Brown goes on to comment: "The woman . . . lives at an intersection of naming in the law, as do most people. . . . 'Intersectionality' describes a phenomenon of address and interpellation" (2005, 152n3). In the first claim here, Brown simply ignores the problem that Crenshaw considers: that while "most people" are indeed "named in the law," some are not named in the same way, are not named intersectionally, and in consequence are treated differently by the law. In fact, as discussed in Chapter 3, Crenshaw found that race and gender create dramatic differences in how "most people" live "at the intersection of the naming of the law" because of the courts' emphasis on single-axis analysis (as well as the courts' support of compound classes if they are composed of white males).

Brown's subsequent claim, that "'intersectionality' describes a phenomenon of address and interpellation" is a delegitimating move meant to support another part of her argument (2005, 152n3).[10] In fact, Crenshaw's argument is that the courts, feminists, and antiracists all have tended to "address and interpellate" people through single-axis categories, including unsatisfactory phrases such as "women and Blacks." Brown obscures rather than elucidates Crenshaw's argument and its challenge to structural power. She also evades the importance of structural power: who gets to name and what significance is given to names are central issues of power.

It would seem important in evaluating Brown's counterargument to note that Brown does not acknowledge, much less come to grips with the meta-phor of "intersectionality" that Crenshaw has developed, but simply imagines a simplistic claim, attributes it to Crenshaw, and then refutes her own imagi-nary construct. Brown reveals herself a *bad ventriloquist*: both the metaphori-cal model and the language usages she purports to be Crenshaw's *are not*.

Earlier I described Brown's note 3 in *Edgework* (2005), the location of this critique, as "peculiar but instructive." The note is peculiar in part because the primary revision in note 3 is the additional text developing what had been a rather casual and careless criticism of the term "intersection" in the 1997 ver-sion of "The Impossibility" (the version reprinted in an anthology in 2008). It is also peculiar because the additional argumentation in *Edgework* is even more contemptuous in its misrepresentation of what intersectional thinking might mean, and even more condescending in its specific misattributions to Crenshaw. It is instructive in its reflection of powerblind discursive strategies. Brown's patronizing condescension depends on the implicitly hierarchical re-lationship between the two scholars, the assumption that she need not be ac-curate about Crenshaw's stance or the specifics of her argument because she does not acknowledge Crenshaw as a significant interlocutor whose argument must be treated responsibly. Brown's argument, with its wide reception and citation, demonstrates that the shared social space of feminist scholarship also has no interest in ensuring either for its own sake or for Crenshaw's that Cren-shaw's arguments—available for any scholar to read and compare to Brown's claims—be accurately represented. The result is to wedge unacknowledged and unchallenged powerblind strategies at the center of feminist argumentation.

SUPERIORITY IN MASTERING INTERSECTIONALITY

The condescension and contempt evoked through bad ventriloquism are con-nected to other affects created by its deployment, specifically affects of hier-archy and superiority. Bad ventriloquism serves as an important component of the strategy I call "mastering intersectionality," a powerful tool for dele-gitimizing intersectionality. Brown and Hewitt—as well as West and Fenster-maker and also Weston (see Chapter 5)—all engage in the strategy of master-ing intersectionality, a systematic and affect-laden pattern of argumentation. Mastering intersectionality is a "schema" of discursive strategies deployed to delegitimize, suppress, control, and exploit the metaphor of intersectionality and related scholarship developed by women of color and their allies.

Through mastering intersectionality, critics (1) radically decontextualize the term "intersectionality" and reduce it to a singular restricted device (for example, "collisions," "static locations," or "geometry"); (2) treat the decontextualized word as superseding all previous arguments about intersectionality (regardless of sources, contexts of meaning, and histories of use); (3) render invisible previous discussions of intersectionality as complex, flexible, and strategic in order to present the critics' "charges" as new and decisive; (4) treat the meaning of the word "intersectionality" as "up for grabs"; and (5) frequently provide a new, "better" metaphor to "replace" intersectionality (Hewitt proposes "chemical compound"; West and Fenstermaker, "difference"; Weston, "rendition").

In deploying mastering intersectionality, critics adopt a stance of affective superiority over the terms developed by intersectional scholars of color, a stance congruent with that of Humpty Dumpty in Lewis Carroll's *Through the Looking Glass:*

> "When I use a word," Humpty Dumpty said, in rather a scornful tone,
> "it means exactly what I choose it to mean—neither more nor less."
> "The question is," said Alice, "whether you can make words mean
> so many different things." "The question is," said Humpty Dumpty,
> "which is to be master—that's all."[11]

Mastering intersectionality—"making a word mean exactly what you choose it to mean"—is a process of intertextual reference that relies on a set of academic conventions to both "center" and "displace" the texts being criticized. Even when alleged to be the work of a particular scholar, the arguments being criticized are often imaginary. If scholars are identified, their specific arguments are ignored, framed selectively, or "badly ventriloquized" to justify the critic's counterarguments.

Mastering intersectionality is thus a discursive practice of power to evade the challenges posed by intersectionality through reactionary strategies of denigration, displacement, suppression, and even appropriation. Paradoxically, these disturbing discursive patterns are both hidden and in plain sight. They are hidden because they are framed as legitimate conventional practices of counterargument often accepted as persuasive, yet they are readily available for careful reading and analysis at the scene of argument. The result is systematically to valorize white knowledge producers and their knowledge production while delegitimizing the knowledge production of intersectional scholars of color. Mastering intersectionality allows critics to ignore the resources that would be available to them if they acknowledged the supple nature of metaphor and the specific arguments presented by Crenshaw, Collins, and others proposing intersectional analysis—the focus on structures of power, the insistence on shifting and multiple categories, the contingency and flexibility, and the tension of *both/and.*

As my examples demonstrate, even accomplished scholars who have made valuable contributions to feminist ways of knowing have not been able to reckon sufficiently with the disturbance of race to avoid the practice of mastering intersectionality. Even the reviewers and editors of top journals and presses in the field—such as *Feminist Studies* (Hewitt), *Gender and Society* (West and Fenstermaker), Princeton University Press (Brown), and Columbia University Press (Weston)—have overlooked or accepted the terms of debate that allow decontextualized misrepresentations to stand.

DISCURSIVE DISAVOWAL AND THE EPISTEMIC MACHINE

Mastering intersectionality and the other powerblind strategies analyzed in these chapters have systematically reinscribed racial hierarchy at the scene of feminist argument, almost unchallenged until recent years. They work together to create as "fact" that Black feminists and other women of color created only limited and reified conceptions of intersectionality.

According to Bruno Latour, whether or not a scientific claim is considered to be a "fact" does not rest with the claim itself, but with later statements, when other authors modify or shape the claim for their own purposes: "The accepted statement is, so to speak, eroded and polished by those who accept it" (1987, 42–43). Eventually the claim may be transformed into a "black box"—no longer examined, abstracted from its circumstances of creation and origins in argumentative choices. The powerblind strategies examined in this book—including the affect-laden strategies examined in this chapter—work together to fold the origins of intersectionality into such a black box, a black box that positions the originators of intersectionality as rationally and ontologically deficient and occludes intersectionality's challenge to the ever-renewing "transparency" of the identity politics of white feminism.

The Epistemic Machine works through the socially shared practices I examine in this book. The practices I have described are currently found in innumerable introductions, articles, and footnotes that critique intersectionality. These examples—along with a phalanx of similar counterarguments—establish decontextualized critique as a legitimate, conventional, efficient, even desirable means to criticize intersectional arguments. Flawed critiques of decontextualized imaginary intersectionalities are continually re-cited as authoritative, re-establishing powerblind critiques as "fact" and evading the responsibility of accurately reframing the origins of intersectionality in feminist scholarship.

A representative example is found in Leslie McCall's much-cited article "The Complexity of Intersectionality" (2005), which cites Brown (1997) in its note 1. (There are nearly 4,500 citations to McCall's article in Google Scholar as of May 10, 2018.) McCall argues:

> Many scholars will not regard *intersectionality* as a neutral term, for it immediately suggests a particular theoretical paradigm based in identity categories (see, e.g., Brown 1997). This is not the only sense in which I use the term here; rather, I intend for it to encompass perspectives that completely reject the separability of analytical and identity categories. (McCall 2005, 1771n1)

McCall's comment demonstrates the citational power of Brown's de-contextualized critique: "many scholars" "immediately" think of Brown's critique when they see the term "intersectionality" and, it would appear, assume that the "identity politics" of women of color are what is criticized by Brown, even though the main focus of Brown's article—"The Impossibility of Women's Studies"—is on the identity politics of women. McCall represents herself as free of the theoretical paradigm based on identity categories criticized by Brown, but of course she is not: the main critique of Brown (1997) is on women's studies exactly because of its focus on *women* as an identity category; McCall's article appears in the journal *Signs: A Journal of Women in Culture and Society*. McCall's comment implicitly references the commonplace notion that it is raced subjects who are concerned with identity categories, while treating the position of white women as free from identity politics.

McCall's comment also demonstrates the most frequent argumentative move supporting the operation of the Epistemic Machine: discursive disavowal. She demonstrates a performed credulity that enables her to cite yet evade accountability for a claim that served to reinforce white disciplinary centrality. She makes no effort to challenge Brown's argument but merely declares her own use of intersectionality different from that which Brown critiques, as moving beyond and innocent of the alleged failures of the past that have been framed as the responsibility of women of color.[12] While Brown does not and would not endorse McCall's arguments (including the notion that scholarship can use "neutral" terms), McCall endorses Brown in a way that evades responsibility for repeating Brown's faulty critique in the service of the Epistemic Machine.

BEWILDERED AND SHAMED: THE EFFECTS OF THE EPISTEMIC MACHINE

Taken as a whole, white critiques of intersectionality are a peculiar genre. Critiques operating from entirely different premises repeat one another's criticisms rather than explaining how the premises and arguments of different critiques are incompatible. Though the critiques often contradict one another, they seldom criticize one another: rather, all criticisms of intersectionality, no matter how incongruous, are treated as grist for the Epistemic Machine to denigrate the intellectual work of women of color. Criticisms are radically underargued, often amounting to little more than an unsupported claim—"intersectionality is additive"—or a preference treated as an argument: "Many prefer the term *interlocking*." Lists of citations compress entire arguments, so that the same citational list will claim that intersectionality has both excessively limited categories and excessively infinite categories; both claims are treated as equally valid and not as contradictory. Claims about texts are frequently not merely misinterpretations but also factual misrepresentations. Intersectionality is treated as a corporate production, one that has failed to supply a book of directions to solve all the problems that might beset someone conducting research. Worst of all, intersectionality is criticized because it makes attention to difference inescapable; one can avoid studying categories scholars may feel to be potentially unpleasant—race, for example—but the very existence of intersectionality foregrounds the existence and intellectual production of women of color.

The Epistemic Machine created by the relentless critiques of intersectionality result in discursive affects of bewilderment and shame for those who wish to use intersectionality. Because specific criticisms are underargued, it is hard for scholars to understand exactly what they need to do to create a successful study: they know they must avoid many pitfalls, but it is not clear what these pitfalls are. They know that intersectionality has great potential, but it is also clear that using intersectionality exposes one to derision. Critiques often mention that feminist scholars find intersectionality confusing, but they do not acknowledge that much confusion stems directly from the contradictions and incongruities promoted by powerblind critiques of intersectionality.

Yvette Taylor, Sally Hines, and Mark E. Casey, for example, introduce their *Theorizing Intersectionality and Sexuality* (2011) with rhetorics of discursive bewilderment and shame, particularly focused on branding and temporality. They worry about whether their useful anthology of articles about intersectionality will be treated as outmoded and unnecessary. (There are more than 70 citations in Google Scholar to the introduction and nearly 162 to the book as of May 10, 2018.) Throughout their introduction the authors reply to what they frame as a *generally accepted climate of disparagement* of intersectionality, a climate so accepted as to need no direct citation. The authors muse:

> Does such attention amount *to a return to the past,* as a memorable celebration of what was enabled between then and now, or does it involve an *uneasy resurrection of what should be departed from?* . . . [S]ometimes invoking this term in the present risks casting the debate as *already passé, over and done with, where nothing useful can be added.* . . . [In the] *"mantra"* of race, class, and gender . . . this collection asks . . . *is there hope still for intersectionality? . . .* Indeed *its easy "buzzword" status* may serve to sideline continued interrogation of inequalities in the sweep of *"what we already know."* . . . Bearing in mind that "intersectionality" has been significantly critiqued within feminist theory and is *now even dismissively branded as "outmoded" and "outdated,"* the point is not simply to resurrect what may be a *void term,* but also to ask "Where do we go from here?" . . . The framing of identities and categories as "intersectional" *often pins down issues and debates as "old hat,"* a response which arguably misconstrues what intersectionality actually is, does, and enables, even if only as a "check and balance." (2011, 1–3, emphasis added)

The discursive confusion, bewilderment, and shame that infuse this introduction are evoked in many introductions to articles about intersectionality. Their source is not intersectionality itself—the heuristic tool and mid-level theory that can help counter social subordination—but the imaginary intersectionality that is the primary product of white critiques of intersectionality.

RECOGNIZING THE EPISTEMIC MACHINE

The Epistemic Machine has established itself by reciting rules that have been created for contingent political purposes to condemn the arguments of the women of color who developed the concept of intersectionality. The Epistemic Machine grinds out idealized and simplistic rules in the face of intersectionality's proposed flexible strategies focused on specific situations and disciplinary frames, leading critiques of intersectionality into stasis and contradiction. The machine requires amnesia about the dominance in scholarship and social life of single-axis categories that intersectionality challenges and refuses responsibility for developing antisubordination strategies with regard to race.

My claim is that powerblind critiques of intersectionality have failed to acknowledge the effects of power of their own argumentative strategies.[13] Part of the problem stems from the migration of concepts across disciplines, from the ways that reading and writing strategies developed inside particular disciplines can fail when applied to work crafted elsewhere. The hubris of interdisciplinarity encourages feminist scholars to read texts in other disciplines without knowing the argumentative strategies of that discipline. As a result, scholars, reviewers, and editors accept modes of argument that allow powerblind critics to assume sole authority over the meaning of the metaphor and argument including uninterrogated claims relying on the authority of scholars in other disciplines. Arguments about intersectionality are also haunted by the disciplines, by the degree to which some disciplines value or do not value the goals and resources of other disciplines. They are haunted by their willingness to ignore the problem of decontextualization. Mikhail Bakhtin argues that texts are always dialogic, that words do not have intrinsic properties but are social products, involving strategies and constraints (1986). In contrast, the assumptions involved in reifying the term "intersection" and underlying many powerblind strategies of criticizing intersectionality appear oddly similar to those of single-axis categorizing: critics assume there is one true meaning for a word, transparent to the critic. The nature of language undercuts the productivity of decontextualized critiques, yet increases their power.

As a discursive practice, the enduring and pervasive presence and power of the Epistemic Machine marks the continuing failure to recognize and move on from the point of a painful rupture—the moment when white women perceived they had lost control of feminism. It manifests a return of the repressed, a part of the past that will not go away, that impedes progress in the present. Critics and readers inhabit the discursive affects made available through the Epistemic Machine. The incessant grinding of the Epistemic Machine—central in critiques and prominent in commentaries, introductions, and footnotes—suggests that it has become part of the expected discursive practice of the scholar concerned with intersectionality. According to Latour, "The power of rhetoric lies in making the dissenter feel lonely" (1987, 44). What, then, is the cost to the dissenter of challenging the Epistemic Machine?

Richard Bauman and Charles L. Briggs, examining the role of language in the creation of modernity, note that modernity developed "ways of speaking and writing" that "make social classes, genders, races, and nations seem real and enable them to elicit feelings and justify relations of power, making subalterns seem to speak in ways that necessitate their subordination" (2003, 17). Bad ventriloquists make puppets of those who proposed intersectionality, making them appear to speak in "deficient" ways and therefore justify the condemnation or appropriation of intersectionality. Bad ventriloquism of the scholarship of women of color is not merely poor scholarship; it is a remarkable gesture of racial dominance delivered through the workings of the Epistemic Machine.

Delegitimizing intersectional metaphors and arguments while appropriating an intersectionality stripped of its radical antiracist imperatives advances the interests of an impoverished version of feminism. Critiques of a decontextualized and misrepresented metaphor serve a vital function for the racial recuperation of power that has reverberated throughout critiques of intersectionality to the present. The stakes of the acceptance of the Epistemic Machine are racial because there is racial inequality at the heart of what might seem a conventional practice. Intersectionality was proposed by women of color to address problems of racial subordination. Both in the 1980s and 1990s and in the present, most feminist scholars are white, most feminist critics are white, and most feminist readers are white. But feminism does not need to remain committed to whiteness rather than a larger vision of antisubordination.

TURNING OFF
THE EPISTEMIC MACHINE

The Epistemic Machine geared up to invalidate the intersectional theorizing of women of color functions through affect-laden revanchist moves
designed so white feminism can regain the territory perceived lost by the
displacement of white women and their concerns from the center of feminism
and feminist research. These critiques work from a position of dominance. I
argue that authors need not be white to produce powerblind white feminist
critiques of intersectionality. Whiteness in this case is not an embodied color
but an epistemological condition, a structured advantage, and an intellectual
cartel designed to monopolize discourse. The specific discursive strategies
analyzed in previous chapters are part of the Epistemic Machine for devalorizing the intellectual labor of women of color. They include the following:

incorporation
appropriation
erasure
bad ventriloquizing
arguing with straw persons
adopting imaginary allies
inclusion as a one-way street
neoliberal asset-stripping
rhetorics of rejection and replacement
errors of attribution

chains of fallacious citations
decontextualizing metaphors from their argumentative utility
treating the meaning of metaphor as unaffected by context
deploying the "mark of the plural"
creating a gulf between the critic and the criticized
"fixing" the "essential" nature of the women of color criticized
exploiting claimed differences for the benefit of the critic
rewriting the role of inclusiveness in the history of feminism
providing alibis for dominant white feminists
treating intersectionality as a singular "corporatized" entity
dissolving the concept of intersectionality into the history of white
    feminism
reinscribing white feminism as the center of the field's social analysis

The historical production, reiteration, and legacy of quotation and citation of these strategies as part of the Epistemic Machine persist in the present as powerful, yet largely unnoticed and uninterrogated obstacles to fulfilling feminism's potential as a force for social justice.

While revealing powerblind strategies requires analyzing particular examples from the texts of individual scholars, my target is the workings of the Epistemic Machine. The moves I describe in this book are made repeatedly by novices and by experts, by graduate students and by their most senior advisors. I have revealed the workings of this Epistemic Machine even in the work of scholars who have made significant and lasting contributions to feminism, such as Stephanie Shields, Wendy Brown, and Leslie McCall. Moreover, as I demonstrate, the pervasive rhetorical presence of powerblind critiques of intersectionality, such as Intersectionality Telephone, the Canyon of Echoes, practices of managing and mastering intersectionality, and problematical patterns of citation and quotation permeate present practices at the scene of feminist argument.

In this conclusion I examine several additional sources to delineate ongoing problems in contemporary feminist argument about intersectionality. First I turn to statements by the distinguished feminist socialist historian Linda Gordon (2016) and the prominent feminist literary critic and philosopher Toril Moi (2015).[1] I take issue with these writings not because they reveal Gordon and Moi to be any less accomplished as scholars but precisely because their handling of intersectionality produces arguments that are not worthy of scholars of such distinction. Their critiques demonstrate that the pervasive and unacknowledged power of the Epistemic Machine leaves even highly skilled and perceptive scholars confounded and adrift on issues of race and gender. I then turn to analyses of my own arguments made by European feminists in *NORA—Nordic Journal of Feminist and Gender Research* and other European sites to consider their responses and the opportunity they provide to outline a plan of work that can lead to more principled and more productive feminist engagement with intersectionality.

When Gordon provides her white feminist critique of intersectionality—"'Intersectionality,' Socialist Feminism and Contemporary Activism: Musings by a Second-Wave Socialist Feminist" (2016)—she unwittingly adopts the powerblind strategies and the carelessness and confusion that have so frequently characterized the rhetoric of powerblind critiques of intersectionality since the 1990s. (There are seven citations in Google Scholar to the journal article as of May 10, 2018.) Gordon's critique is suffused with an affect of benign condescension. She serves as a bad ventriloquist and makes gestures to "rescue" women of color from their primitive or unsophisticated thinking. She fails to provide citations for many arguments and provides false citations for other arguments. While Gordon states that she wishes to consider intersectional activism, she conflates sources from scholarly texts and from blogs produced from a variety of political positions with a range of levels of knowledge, treating them all as representative of this concept called "intersectionality." I suspect that Gordon would not be equally willing to rest claims about the nature of "socialist feminism" on the myriad popular arguments found in a variety of blogs and online sources, including misogynist sources and those opposed to socialism and to feminism. When Gordon does consider scholarship on intersectionality, she presents it inaccurately and tendentiously. I focus here on the problems of Gordon's misrepresentation of the arguments of Sirma Bilge, who has vigorously criticized white feminist critiques of intersectionality (2013, 2014). Gordon twice cites Bilge 2013 irresponsibly and inaccurately, representing Bilge's argument as its opposite, then reinforcing her misrepresentation by falsely claiming that another source "echoes" Bilge when it does not.

If Gordon wished to take a responsible, grounded stance toward intersectionality, a close reading of Bilge 2013 would be very useful. Gordon's title, for example, positions herself as an outsider "musing": gazing thoughtfully at or reflecting on intersectionality from her own socialist feminist position. Bilge provides a caution against the tendency of white critiques to "muse" about intersectionality rather than engage with its empirical grounding. According to Bilge, such musings provide

> a profusion of speculative and prescriptive declarations, sentences starting with "what intersectionality might or might not" be or do, and "what intersectionality should or should not" be or do. These musings fail to consider what intersectionality actually *does* in research, what

researchers *do* with intersectionality, and with what kind of outcomes. This strong tendency runs the risk of confining intersectionality to an overly academic contemplative exercise. (2013, 411)

Indeed, Gordon muses about intersectionality in just the terms that Bilge has challenged. Gordon does not provide evidence of thorough review of intersectional scholarship but bases her image of intersectionality on general public discussions (some two-thirds of her references are to blogs and other public sources about intersectionality, written from all sorts of knowledge bases and political positions). The paragraph in which Gordon first cites Bilge begins exactly as Bilge's argument about musing would suggest, with condescending advice about "'what intersectionality might or might not' be or do" and continues through a series of loosely linked and ungrounded claims made without context or citation. Gordon claims:

Perhaps intersectionality needs to homogenise categories to some degree, suggesting that, say, African-American women have some common interests. If these categories are to avoid essentialism, however, they have to rest on experience. Moreover, these categories must also register that common interests can be constructed, reconstructed or discovered, through group experience. But the metaphor of intersection sometimes suggests that *only* African-American women can understand their oppression, that, for example, *only* the disabled can understand disability. This claim appears in some recent criticism of white women's appropriation of intersectionality talk, suggesting that if whites talk this way they are denying women of colour the authority to define their own experiences. *Sociologist Sirma Bilge, for example, denounces the "whitening of intersectionality."* Surely one would not want to claim that it is impossible for those without a given experience to learn from those who have the experience. As many people of colour have had to point out to whites, deferring to any and every person of colour on the subject of race was just another form of racism. (2016, 347, emphasis added on sentence referring to Bilge)

Gordon's musings jump from one kind of argument to another, reflecting the swirl of discussion found across a range of blogs and websites and demonstrating her distance from a careful examination of contemporary academic arguments about intersectionality and racial categorization. She scolds women of color for their faulty ideas. She corrects what she presents as the limited thinking of women of color, advising them, for example, to notice that African American women may have common interests based on their group experiences.[2] She misinforms her readers by conflating the arguments of bloggers and intersectional scholars. An ungrounded claim that only disabled people can understand disability is immediately followed by the unrelated ungrounded claim that some criticize white women for denying women of color authority in using intersectionality to discuss their experiences.[3] Gordon implies that those who would make such an argument are engaging in "just another form of racism," and she knows this because she has listened to people of color. Gordon, having become aware of long-standing arguments about racial privilege in speaking and being heard, attributes these to "the metaphor of intersectionality," not the vexed terrains of racial dominance, resistance, recognition, and misrecognition.

The only person—scholar or blogger—cited in the paragraph is Bilge, cited as a person who "denounces the 'whitening of intersectionality'" (2016, 347). The use of "for example" is a grammatical signal to position what Gordon means in quoting Bilge. "For example" indicates that Bilge denouncing the "whitening of intersectionality" is to be understood as an *example* of the argument that "if whites talk this way [intersectionally] they are denying women of colour the authority to define their own experiences" (347). There is no grammatical signal connecting Bilge to the following sentence, but the principles of relevance in communication would suggest that Gordon also means to identify Bilge as a person who might claim that it is impossible for those without a given experience to learn from those who have the experience.

Gordon's context and quotation provide an astonishing misrepresentation of Bilge's argument. I quote Bilge at length here because her thoughtful argument presents a dramatic contrast to Gordon's simplistic arguments about race. Bilge criticizes rhetorical strategies used by what she calls "disciplinary feminism" that may work to "depoliticize" intersectionality through the "curatorship" of and for the benefit of white scholars. Contra Gordon's claim, Bilge is explicit that she is not limiting who should engage in intersectional analyses. She maintains:

> To make this argument [against disciplinary feminism] is not to say that White feminists should "move over" and leave intersectionality to feminists of color who will make it transformative and counter-hegemonic again. No! It is to argue that disciplinary feminists, whether White or of color, should stop doing intersectionality in ways that *undo* it. One way to undo intersectionality is to turn it into an overly academic exercise of speculative or normative musings. (2013, 411, emphasis in original)

Gordon's article would appear to be an example of speculative or normative musings, but *not* an "overly academic" one, given that it fails to distinguish adequately three categories of argument: the research writings of intersectional scholars addressed to other scholars; intersectional scholars' introductions designed for the general public; and public discussions in sources such as Internet blogs, newspaper articles, and political opinion pieces.

Rather than an example of the kind of argument Gordon alleges, Bilge's article demonstrates a series of sophisticated arguments about racial positioning that Gordon would have done well to digest and incorporate into her thinking. Bilge is explicit that she is not making claims about embodied identities: "What I mean by 'whitening intersectionality' does not refer to the embodiment, skin color or heritage of its practitioners" (2013, 412). Bilge is also explicit that she is not attempting "to police the boundaries of who can legitimately do intersectionality and who cannot" (412). Rather, Bilge analyzes several lines of argument particularly common in European scholarship, which she contends serve as political efforts to "whiten intersectionality." Bilge argues:

> I analyze these two argumentative strategies from an intellectual tradition that unties *whiteness* from skin color, physiology, or biology, and understands it as: a structurally advantaged position (race privilege); a (privileged) standpoint from which White people view themselves, others, and society; and a set of cultural practices that are considered "unmarked"—yet unmarked only if viewed from the perspective of normative whiteness (Frankenberg 1993). My problematizing of the whitening of intersectionality thus builds on an understanding of whiteness as a social formation that is conditioned, reproduced and legitimized by a racial habitus—*a White habitus*. . . . While hegemonic positions are never entirely stable, hegemonic "White" ways of knowing and "White" entitlements are fully implicated in the feminist struggles for meaning over intersectionality and the forced take-over of intersectionality from feminists of color. Such a critical understanding of whiteness also clarifies that whiteness and whitening are symbolic fields. To be explicit—one does not need to be White to "whiten intersectionality." (412–413)

Bilge provides a useful way of thinking of intersectionality and race that Gordon not only ignores but also flatly misrepresents.

Previously I indicated that Gordon cited Bilge 2013 twice in ways that were inaccurate and irresponsible. Gordon's second inaccurate citation of Bilge is openly false. It is a spurious claim that a blog "echoes" Bilge when it does not. The claim appears in the concluding section of the article on intersectionality and activism, which combines ungrounded claims with a plethora of citations to commentaries from blogs and newspapers. Gordon claims:

> The concept [intersectionality] is commonly narrowed to refer only to African Americans, or in the negative, to white racism, a narrowing that parallels some scholarly usage. This usage can take on an anti-highbrow slant: The "Rogue Feminist," echoing Silma [*sic*] Bilge's critique, argues that white women should not use the term at all, because whites don't experience "it": "once whiteness gets their grasp on something they love that Black people have created, they have to make it more and more inaccessible to Black people while also whitening it to be no longer noticeable as a Black creation."[4] (2016, 351)

It is hard to account for this misrepresentation on the part of a distinguished historian. In this sequence of sentences, Gordon does not explain who narrows "intersectionality" to African Americans or white racism and what that might mean, though she does implicate unnamed and uncited scholars in this move ("parallels some scholarly usage"). Then she claims that "this usage" (this scholarly usage?) can take on "an anti-highbrow slant," without explaining what this might mean. At this point Gordon provides her second citation of Bilge 2013, misspelling Bilge's first name. Examination of the blog "The Rogue Feminist" reveals it to be an informal and not very well-informed commentary by a white woman that uses the term "whitening" for a different purpose than Bilge does and *does not mention Bilge at all.* The second citation of Bilge reinforces the inadequacy of Gordon's earlier inaccurate citation of Bilge. While Gordon is willing to cite any number of blogs and informal discussions of intersectionality, she does not accurately reflect Bilge's scholarly argument but feels free to claim that Bilge is making an entirely different and deeply simplistic argument. Despite her scholarly credentials, Gordon falls into many of the traps encouraged by the rhetorical form of powerblind white critiques of intersectionality authorized by the Epistemic Machine.

Understanding the function of the political and conceptual tasks performed by powerblind white feminist critiques of intersectionality and their reiteration through the Epistemic Machine can improve the precision of feminist claims about intersectionality. For example, in a recent article in *New Literary History*, Moi uses "intersectionality theory" as an example to argue that feminist theory "has become abstract and overgeneralizing, operating at a vast remove from women's concrete experiences" (2015, 193).[5] (There are eight citations in Google Scholar to the journal article as of May 10, 2018.)

Moi's argument could provide more specificity and depth if she distinguished between intersectional conceptualization and analyses focused on antisubordination (such as the work of Crenshaw [1989], which Moi reports accurately, praises, and which does not illustrate the features Moi criticizes) and powerblind white feminist critiques of intersectionality (such as the work of Kathy Davis [2008], which demonstrates all the features that Moi criticizes).

Because Moi does not distinguish between intersectionality used as a tool to counter subordination and the powerblind strategies of white critiques of intersectionality, she attributes to a generalized "intersectionality theory" what are actually the operations of the Epistemic Machine deployed to control the unruly radical challenges of intersectional analysis. For example, Moi is critical of feminist theory's "craving for generality" that she sees as evident in three features: "(1) the tendency to require concepts to have clear boundaries; (2) the wish to emulate the natural sciences' understanding of what an explanation is; and (3) the demand for completeness" (2015, 196). This "craving for generality" does not characterize the work of antisubordination scholars such as Crenshaw (1989) and Collins (1991) but does characterize the work of many white critics of intersectionality discussed in previous chapters, such as Kathy Davis (2008), Nira Yuval-Davis (2006b), and Candace West and Sarah Fenstermaker (1995). These arguments stem from specific racialized and political counterarguments used for political purposes rather than from an inherent "craving for generality."

Moi situates her argument philosophically, but not historically or politically. She argues that "Wittgenstein spells out the reasons why the craving for generality breeds contempt for the particular case" (2015, 200). While this is true, it is not adequate for describing the specifically political debates surrounding intersectional theorizing. Overlooking the racial politics of these debates results in Moi generalizing about intersectionality *nonintersectionally,* without accounting for intersectionality's grounding as a tool for antisubordination. Those who have used intersectionality as a tool for antisubordination are often focused on particular cases. However, their analyses have received a barrage of negative commentary primarily from white critiques of intersectionality. To claim that there is a "craving for generality" in the case of intersectionality does not properly locate this craving as a move in the long history of powerblind white feminist critiques of intersectionality, claiming that the conception is limited, too focused on the "particular cases" of Black women, and must therefore be reformulated and expanded to become a "general" theory. If Moi was aware of the racialized history of these critiques, their intellectual moves would be more understandable to her.

Because Moi does not distinguish between intersectionality used as a tool of antisubordination and white feminist critiques of intersectionality, she does not recognize that there are two quite different "theories" of intersectionality at play in the contemporary academic feminism she surveys. Powerblind white feminist critiques of intersectionality use concepts of grand theory or general theory or disciplinary frames as a political tool to subordinate and appropriate the conceptualizations of women of color that have gained attention. It is these powerblind feminist critiques that make the kinds of arguments to which Moi objects. For example, Moi argues,

> a "theory of intersectionality" will set out to specify the concept of intersectionality in the hope that the concept so defined will subsume all past, present, and future cases under itself. This project inevitably pushes the theorist away from the particular case and towards the giddy heights of abstraction. In this way, theory itself becomes the attempt to produce rigidly bounded concepts. (2015, 200)

Moi is correct that *some* ways of theorizing intersectionality demand that intersectionality provide instructions to account for all cases. But these are the demands of powerblind feminist critiques of intersectionality, seeking to demonstrate that intersectionality as a tool for antisubordination "lacks" what is needed to count as a "real" theory, in order to dismiss the concepts developed by women of color so that the "more sophisticated" white critics can "correct" their thinking. Because grand or general theories are in some ways validated in the academy, because philosophy and some other disciplines refuse intimacy with the world (see C. Mills 2007), both Moi and the white critiques of intersectionality do not recognize the suitability of intersectionality's emergence as a "mid-level theory," in Gramsci's terms, connecting large concepts to specific situations (Hall 1986, 5; see also Gramsci 1971 and Chapters 1 and 2).

It is hard to step back and look at the scene of argument when one has been immersed in it one's whole career. But if white feminists don't insist on doing so, don't insist on transforming the terms of feminist reading and writing, the Epistemic Machine reproduces itself in perpetuity. People may understand critiques like mine and Vivian M. May's (2014, 2015) or Bilge's (2013, 2014) as if they are attempts to identify injured victims and malicious victimizers. But our focus is not on individuals. The examples we identify are not simply the production of individuals but are authorized by and contribute to a shared social discourse—a metadiscursive regime—that constitutes what feminism is and can be. It is feminist discourse, and therefore feminism itself, which is demeaned and defiled by the deployment of uninterrogated terms of reading and writing.

My own and other analyses of white critiques of intersectionality can serve an urgent function in alerting feminists to the ways that they and their colleagues have been unwittingly misreading, mishearing, and misrepresenting arguments about intersectionality in ways that systematically reinscribe racial hierarchy. Yet it is not evident that scholars have responded carefully to our concerns. Rather, analyses of white critiques of intersectionality appear to be *incorporated back into the Epistemic Machine,* misrepresenting and invalidating these arguments.

For example, reporting in an editorial on the 2013 *Signs* special issue on intersectionality, Kathy Davis and Dubravka Žarkov (2017) claim that my article in that issue—"To Tell the Truth and Not Get Trapped" (2013b)—expresses "worry" "that the term had become so 'trendy' that it was well on its way to becoming an 'asset for dominant disciplinary discourses'" (Davis and Žarkov 2017, 314, citing Tomlinson 2013b, 996). Davis and Žarkov dramatically misrepresent my argument in two ways. First they insert the term "trendy" in a whole-scale misrepresentation of my argument, which has nothing whatsoever to do with the popularity of or widespread use of the term "intersectionality." It is *Davis* (K. Davis 2008) who has mounted the argument that intersectionality is "trendy," and denigrates it through her disparaging term "buzzword" (see my criticism of Davis's argument in Chapter 9). Davis and Žarkov's second misrepresentation also works to protect white critiques of intersectionality: they present my claim as asserting that *because* the term intersectionality is in widespread use, it is a becoming an "asset for dominant disciplinary discourses." In fact, that article focuses on the problems presented by specific rhetorics and argumentative constructions—similar to what in this book I call "powerblind" strategies—and critics' assumption that "their task is *to critique intersectionality,* not *to foster intersectionality's ability to critique subordination*" (Tomlinson 2013b, 996). I argue that the *faulty methods of argument* of the rhetorical frameworks and tropes I examine "offer a deradicalized intersectionality as an asset for dominant disciplinary discourses" (2013b, 997) (the full text of the paragraph is found in the endnote here).[6] Davis and Žarkov's claim is the *opposite* of my precise argument: it is *problem-filled critiques* that are an asset for dominant disciplinary discourses.

Kirsten Hvenegård-Lassen and Pauline Stoltz (2014) report on my criticism of the critiques of Dorthe Staunæs and several other European feminists (Tomlinson 2013a; see Chapter 8) in an editorial in *NORA—Nordic Journal of Feminist and Gender Research.* Hvenegård-Lassen and Stoltz appear concerned that the context I provided in my article seemed to them to imply that there is no debate about "race, racism, and colonialism" in Europe, and "to generalize (white) European feminism in a way that is not fruitful for a nuanced debate" (2014, 167). My article neither implies nor states this. I present a discussion of the discursive context shaping discourse about race in

Europe for a specific purpose: to explain why openly colonizing discourses appear without criticism in three European critiques of intersectionality, and why those and many other European critiques systematically generalize about what they allege to be the limited thinking of Black U.S. feminist scholars of intersectionality (see Chapters 7 and 8). Hvenegård-Lassen and Stoltz—and other white European scholars, as is evident below—object to what they describe as my generalizations about their discursive context, but to this point I have not found evidence of any concern on their part with regard to their own generalizations about Black U.S. intersectional scholars, generalizations replete with powerblind rhetorics permeated by frequently dismissive, disparaging, and inaccurate comments. Statements of such generalizations are specifically quoted in the article (Tomlinson 2013a) and Chapter 8 (see also Chapter 7).

In fact, Hvenegård-Lassen and Stoltz's editorial illustrates exactly the point I was trying to make when they indicate that one critique that I analyzed—Staunæs 2003—has "consistently been among the top ten most-read articles" in *NORA* (2014, 167). Has the popularity of Staunæs's article been accompanied by notice of or criticism of her colonizing discourses and her large generalizations about U.S. intersectional scholars of color? My specific claims are not generalizations. It is not a generalization on my part to point out that Staunæs attributes to Patricia Hill Collins (1998) claims made by Audre Lorde (1980). It is not a generalization to reveal that her article folds together for criticism a mass of unidentified people from diverse political groups and incongruous theoretical positions: people in the "practical, political arena (for example, in nongovernmental organizations,) as well as in the theoretical field dominated by standpoint feminism and critical race theory" (Staunæs 2003, 103). It is not a generalization to quote and critique the article's inaccurate claim that U.S. intersectional scholars of color exhibit "a tendency toward fixing categories and identities and using the concepts in certain ideologically informed ways" (103). It is not a generalization to notice the article's repetition of the false claim that intersectionality in the U.S. context presumes that identities are fixed, when it asserts "The fixing of categories can be a useful strategy if you work in and against a system built upon the privileges and rights of certain fixed identities and categories and where 'the natural' and 'the given' can be converted into political activities" (103). It is not a generalization, but rather an exposure of generalizing, to note that the article claims—without a grounded review of research—that the intersectional thinking of U.S. intersectional scholars of color is not good enough for reckoning with the "complexity and changing nature of lived experience" because of its "underlying assumptions of determination, clear demarcations and fixed substance" (103). It is understandable that European scholars would prefer a more nuanced discussion of their own discourses; it is also understandable that I would prefer a more nuanced representation of the work of U.S. intersectional scholars of color that I have demonstrated to be subject to oversimplification, generalization, and misrepresentation in many European publications (see Chapters 6, 7, and 8).

In the text (2013a; see also Chapter 8) I provide a specific discussion of Albert Memmi's analysis of colonizing discourses and presented explicit quotations that demonstrated the congruent use of such discourse in white European critiques of intersectionality. Hvenegård-Lassen and Stoltz bypass this entire discussion in order to imagine what my "real problem" might be. They claim, "In this piece, it seems that Tomlinson believes all travel of the concept from its original location to be bad" (2014, 167). There is no evidence in the text to indicate that this is Tomlinson's belief—not least because I hold no such belief. I am convinced that there should be many opportunities to use intersectional theorizing productively in countering various kinds of subordination in the European context—if it is accurately represented. Yet so enthusiastic are Hvenegård-Lassen and Stoltz about Staunæs's theoretical framework that they ignore the reasons I give and the examples I quote, going on to imagine some other reason for my criticism of Staunæs's colonizing discourses. They argue that Tomlinson "is clearly not happy with the questioning of standpoint feminism from theoretical perspectives with a more poststructural leaning" (168). Particularly disturbing about this claim is the fact that it assumes that my demonstration of the use of colonizing discourses that disparage and confuse the arguments of U.S. intersectional scholars of color is not *itself* objectionable enough to justify my criticism. It is also disquieting that the claim ignores my own reliance on poststructural theory: the abstract and first paragraphs of the article state this theoretical position clearly, indicating that "in this article I use tools of critical and poststructural discourse analysis to examine a particular rhetorical frame" (2013a, 1, 2). I not only use poststructuralist theory; I argue that Crenshaw's "Demarginalizing" and other works also have points of connection with poststructuralism (see also Chapter 7). If the critics desire more nuanced discussions, it would help if they would answer the criticisms actually made rather than invent straw person critiques that they would prefer to answer by criticizing my ethos rather than my arguments (see Tomlinson 2010).

Concern with regard to my "generalizing" about the discourses of (white) European academic feminists also appears in a European interview with Moi and the accompanying commentary by other European scholars (Bergstrom 2015). Responding to Tomlinson 2013a and 2013b (see Chapter 8), Ida Irene Bergstrom indicates that Nina Lykke, for example, "just felt angry," and claimed: "I am not sure we should take Tomlinson's arguments seriously.

She applies the same yardstick to everybody; she is marginalizing and generalizing" (2015, n.p.). The stakes of academic arguments are high: we tend to have political and emotional investments in the arguments we make, so such reactions are not surprising. Since academic arguments must always go beyond the particular, perhaps we need to think carefully about what we mean by "generalizing" and "marginalizing," recognize when we do it, and consider when it may be useful and when it is not. Both of those articles cited—like Chapters 4–10 of this book—provide analysis of problematical rhetorical strategies that appear in specific texts that I cite and quote. These close analyses cannot properly be considered "generalizations." While I set them in discursive context (particularly in 2013a), I do not claim that the use of such strategies is the sole responsibility of individual authors, nor characteristic of all authors. But it is possible that thinking of my arguments as erroneously generalizing serves to distract from my central claims that specific rhetorical strategies such as colonizing discourses inappropriately denigrate the intellectual production of U.S. intersectional scholars of color, in effect marginalizing and generalizing their work.

According to Bergstrom, some European scholars read my arguments as claiming that "they use the concept [intersectionality] in a manner that makes the black feminist theorists who first came up with the theory invisible" (2015, n.p.). This is not my claim. Rather, I argue that feminist critical discourses make Black feminist scholars quite visible, but, by misrepresenting them in inappropriate ways, implying that they are intellectually deficient and their ideas limited, such discourses serve to justify moves to appropriate intersectionality on the basis of European claims of superior thinking. I do not argue that any specific scholar holds such an opinion, but that commonly accepted conventional discursive strategies *create this effect*. The solution, then, is to attend more carefully to how feminist scholars have created this effect in order to address it and prevent its continuing presence as a taken-for-granted method of criticizing intersectionality.

Bergstrom's article indicates that Staunæs is concerned about the emotions involved in this debate and also about the proper response. According to Bergstrom, Staunæs asserts that "this is a heated debate where a lot of emotions are involved. We've felt pushed into a corner. What are we doing here, and what can we do about it?" (2015, n.p.). I take the opportunity that Staunæs's question offers to provide some suggestions for transforming the terms of feminist reading and writing about intersectionality.

What would be the consequences of a critical awareness—a presence of mind—about the potential for unwitting use of powerblind strategies, of using what appear to be conventional rhetorics and arguments in ways that result in racially marked arguments that reinscribe racial hierarchy? What steps can feminists take at the scene of argument to nurture and sustain intersectional thinking as a force for social justice? I propose the following:

1. *Acknowledge the racial dynamics of white critiques of intersectionality.* Because the originating conception of intersectionality is a production of women of color and because white feminist critiques of intersectionality are written from a position of dominance, these critiques need to display awareness of their potential for reinscribing racial hierarchy at the scene of argument.

2. *Work in* accompaniment *with intersectional scholars of color.* Use intersectional theorizing and analysis to counter racial as well as other social subordinations; demonstrate how one's preferred methods might contribute to intersectionality's ability to critique subordination.

3. *Avoid framing arguments as competing with, intending to defeat, or taking over the claims made by intersectional scholars of color.*

4. *Read and write arguments* intersectionally. Assume that claims will be read differently by different audiences, that some audiences will notice that derogatory claims and argumentative shortcuts are inappropriate and inaccurate, even though they may go unnoticed by others.

5. *Avoid developing arguments for novelty or new branding that rely on inappropriate and inaccurate denigration of previous conceptions of intersectionality.*

6. *Avoid "bad ventriloquism."* Make sure that claims about the terms, metaphors, and arguments of intersectional scholars of color are accurate and reflect their full contexts.

7. *Avoid setting up "straw persons."* Work to make sure that critiques foreground the best version of intersectional arguments rather than presenting intersectional arguments as inaccurately weak.

8. *Avoid marshaling the authority of what are actually imaginary allies.*

9. *Avoid engaging in neoliberal asset-stripping.* Do not frame arguments as "rescuing" intersectionality from the alleged inadequate thinking of intersectional scholars of color.

10. *Avoid rhetorics of rejection and replacement.* Avoid rhetorics that work according to a unifying logic that attempts to close down multiple paths of feminist antiracist analysis and replace them with a single path to feminist knowledge. Working from a competitive, hierarchical, *either/or* perspective, these rhetorics shut down options—as if in a "zero-sum" game where one project can grow only at the expense of another, as though *multiple* fields of feminist antiracist analysis are not possible, as though any "promising" new category or analytic must be a *singular* path to feminist knowledge, a *singular* site of political investment.

11. *Do not make broad claims about the inability of "intersectionality" to account for some area of concern—"narrative" or "experience," for example—without a thorough review of research that includes the work of women of color and scholarship that uses intersectional conceptions without necessarily using the term "intersectionality."* If there is not time for such a review, simply do not make such a broad condemnation.

12. *Use citations in ways that are accurate and responsible.* Chains of citations that rest on arguments that are illegitimate, badly argued, inaccurate, and contradictory assume that authority is created through quantity rather than quality. Much confusion would be eliminated by citations that point to specific, accurate arguments.

13. *Do not rely excessively on a small and familiar group of careless critiques of intersectionality or "black-box" the arguments of outside authorities.* The constant repetition of claims drawn from a small set of critiques of intersectionality implies that those critiques represent fully the *best arguments* about intersectionality; restricting claims to *critiques* rather than other discussions of intersectionality insures that is not the case. Critics who "black-box" the arguments of outside authorities do not make those arguments available for their readers' inspection, allowing critics to modify the claims of those they cite, rendering them "false authorities."

14. *Rethink the life of feminist theoretical tools.* Conventional disciplinary practices place a premium on new, original, and generative contributions, but contemporary critiques often seem to assume that the primary way to make a contribution is not by using intersectionality in generative ways but by incorporating, replacing, erasing, or overturning the concept. All of these motivations for incorporating, replacing, erasing, or overturning intersectionality treat intersectionality as if it can be easily replaced by new tools. But no tool from the past has been totally superseded. Conceptual and theoretical tools need not be sacrificed to temporal imperatives of "progress."

15. *Avoid authorizing gestures such as a reflexive denigration of past scholarship in order to elevate a new view.* These moves are often done through assertion rather than rigorous argument. This "presentist" view of argument sacrifices both past and future for momentary gain. It is necessary to have "presence of mind," to see what tools were good for in the past and *what a tool is good for NOW.*

16. *Avoid "potted histories" of intersectionality as authorizing gestures.* Many critiques of intersectionality include pro forma "histories" of intersectionality. These narratives tend to *begin* with the subject of their critique—intersectionality. They pass lightly over or ignore explanations of the social and scholarly conditions instigating intersectionality's intervention. This small decision about temporality produces huge political effects. It unmoors intersectionality—the counterargument—from the argument with which it is in dialogue. The effect is to erase from the scene of argument the powerful dominant frameworks that intersectionality seeks to disrupt.

17. *Do not misconstrue the nature of metaphor.* Recognize that metaphors are heuristic and interpretive tools that rely on context for their meaning.

18. *Acknowledge the entrenched power and protean nature of dominant discourses and categories that complicate our challenging them.* Many critiques blame the term or metaphor of "intersectionality" for having failed to free feminists from the power of dominant categories. Others blame intersectional scholars for thinking according to dominant categories; still others blame feminist readers—implying that the metaphor of intersectionality should be jettisoned because feminist readers tend to think of it "literally." These moves rest on the faulty assumption that there is a perfect word, a perfect concept, an easier and more effective way for us to shake off the past. Framing the problem this way misapprehends the nature and power of social categorization. Regimes that use race to justify social hierarchy are, as Cedric Robinson argues, "hostile to their own exhibition" (2007, xii). These regimes do not operate in fixed and static ways: their formations of dominance and subordination coalesce around rhetorical moves, episodes, and patterns of events and arguments that are unstable, unpredictable, precarious, and contingent.

19. *Do not mount atemporal and acontextual critiques.* Academic texts are produced for particular purposes at particular moments, meeting specific exigencies. Subsequent criticism is also produced at particular moments from particular positions. Yet critiques of intersectionality frequently collapse such temporalities, treating original texts, subsequent criticism, and their own texts as if they shared the same historical time. They often refer to arguments by intersectional scholars of color from ten, twenty, even thirty years in the past, ignoring the recent work of these scholars. They make claims about the thinking of intersectional scholars of color by ignoring the context of arguments, conflating texts that range across disciplines and purposes and treating them as if they represented only one line of thinking.

20. *Acknowledge that "intersectionality" is a "term of art" that has come to have a variety of specialized meanings in contemporary argument.* Treating "intersectionality" as a term of art could focus attention on imagining what intersectionality *can* mean rather than condemning what critics falsely claim it *must* mean as an abstract and decontextualized term.

21. *Do not treat "intersectionality" as if its meaning could be closed down by exercises in logic.* Frequently critics assume that they can consider the validity of the term "intersectional" atemporally. They remove the word from its rhetorical contexts: its political temporality, its temporality of production, and its temporality within the course of the text. They then criticize the use of *the word "intersectionality" as if one can attribute meanings to it divorced from its contexts of use.* Most metaphors have many potential entailments, but not all possible entailments will be in play in every context. Discursive contexts determine which potentially relevant entailments are in play in an instance of language use. It is not useful to treat as propositions of logic what are really issues of politics.

22. *Do not disparage intersectionality in order to justify a preferred alternative research method.* Let arguments in favor of preferred methods stand on their own strengths.

23. Be mindful of the problematic temporalities of "origin stories." Many critiques include short "origin stories," attributing the origin of "intersectionality" to specific people or groups. Origin stories are inherently problematic (see, for example, Hemmings 2011; Wiegman 1999a; Foucault 1984). But the specific patterns of origin stories about academic intersectionality have significant political effects. For example, some critiques of intersectionality mention that women of color have a long tradition of thinking in terms of *multiple identities*, evident, for example, in the statements of Sojourner Truth and Anna Julia Cooper. These and other figures are important and mentioned by scholars such as Collins (1991) and Crenshaw (1989). But some critiques use these historical figures to undermine the conceptual work of more recent scholars responsible for the *academic concept of intersectionality*. To overemphasize these early "origins" can work to deny the *theoretical and analytic* work of intersectional scholars and to reinforce the position that African American women are *not capable of theorizing*, but merely "have experiences" (see Lewis 2009).

24. *Recognize intersectionality as a collaborative creation grounded in shared social struggles.* Attributing the "origins" of the academic concept of intersectionality to a few specific individuals is bound to be misleading, since theoretical and analytic concepts of intersectionality were developed multiply and in concert by a number of scholars of color in different disciplines through the 1980s and since. Yet, as in all scholarly conversations, key interlocutors have made especially original and generative contributions. Political purposes are served by identifying specific individuals as primary "originators" and designating others as "mere followers." Particularly dramatic is the repetitive reduction of Kimberlé Crenshaw's work to the mere "coining" of the term "intersectionality." The elevation of Cooper and Truth and the marginalizing of Crenshaw and Collins is a doubled move resonating with bad faith. Rather than honoring Cooper and Truth (who are generally not cited by the critics denigrating Crenshaw and Collins in any other contexts), the decision to focus on them in origin stories reflects a colonial logic positing an unchanging Black consciousness that is the parochial and private property of members of an aggrieved group. This locates Crenshaw and Collins as uncritical conveyers of folk wisdom rather than the original generative and critical scholars that they are. It hides the role of late twentieth-century antiracist movements in the development of intersectionality (see Chapter 4). The purpose of these critiques is not to join Cooper, Truth, Crenshaw, and Collins in accompaniment but rather to see their work as sites of raw material to be appropriated, refined, and advanced to build a new racially unmarked social theory.

25. *Acknowledge the specificity of social categories as tools for managing difference.* Critics of intersectionality often criticize examination of categories as if attending to categorical differences stems merely from scholars' individual choices. They are treated as individual, even when clearly concerned with social structures.

26. *Avoid folding together different people of color according to what Albert Memmi (1991) calls "the mark of the plural."*

27. *Recognize changing conceptions of women of color as well as of white women.*

28. *Do not misrepresent dominant feminism's history of exclusion.*

29. *Do not treat intersectionality as a singular "corporatized" entity.* As a mid-level theory, intersectionality has different versions and forms suitable for different purposes; do not confuse them or treat them as a singular entity capable of making and failing to keep promises, provide sets of instructions, and so forth.

30. *Avoid assuming that white women are the normative subjects of feminism.*

NOTES

CHAPTER 1

1. For example, the concept of intersectionality played a significant role in the 2001 UN World Conference against Racism, Racial Discrimination, Xenophobia and Related Intolerance held in South Africa (see, especially, Chan-Tiberghien 2004 and Falcón 2016; see also Chapter 6). The African American Policy Forum, among other organizations, supports U.S. and international projects focused on affirmative action and structural racism through intersectional analysis and action (see http://aapf.org/).

2. Intersectionality is discussed in popular activism and blogging. See, for example, "The Angry Black Woman" (http://theangryBlackwoman.com/2009/08/02/intersection ality/) and activist sites about intersectionality (http://www.slideshare.net/dustinkidd1/ intersectionaltheory).

3. Other challenges to dominant epistemologies that have been subjected to dramatically deficient misreadings include concepts of social construction and poststructuralism, and conceptions negatively labeled "cultural relativism."

4. Many scholars have argued that academic disciplines carry with them historically sedimented notions about how to think about social categories. For example, liberal Enlightenment thought generally treats the specific standpoints of women and people of color as parochial and provincial while defining Euro-American white masculinity as universally important and interesting (Noble 2002). The philosophy of the humanities and social sciences encourages a discomfort with analyses of power, particularly racial power (Robinson 2007). Studies of language help structure social relations along hierarchical lines to control social disorder (Bauman and Briggs 2003). A long tradition of sociological research treats social problems as aberrant interruptions of fundamentally just prevailing values, norms, and structures, promoting reformist rather than radical critiques of racism and sexism while rendering the discipline more focused on race and gender *relations* than race and gender *justice* (Lyman 1993). An emphasis on classification in the biological and social sciences originated in overtly racist frameworks rooted in assumptions about the superiority of some

classes of people over others (Bonilla-Silva and Zuberi 2008; Guthrie 2003; Wallerstein 1996). Charles W. Mills (1997) argues that the absence of race from philosophical discourse is not aberrant or accidental, but constitutive of the discipline. Intimacy with the world is not seen as theoretical; philosophy reduces practical injustice to a lower level of thought and elevates discussion of ideal categories to a higher level.

5. Spelman develops these metaphors elsewhere in her text also. At one point she notes: "One's gender identity is not related to one's racial and class identity as the parts of *pop-bead necklaces* are related, separable and insertable in other strands with different racial and class 'parts'" (1988, 15, emphasis added). She also comments: "In much [white middle-class] feminist theory, we have chopped women up metaphysically into parts: the part of me in virtue of which I have a particular gender identity, the part of me in virtue of which I am of a particular race, and so on—as if a person's identity were like a patchwork quilt, made up of separable pieces, each with an identity, a history, and a meaning all its own; or, as mentioned earlier, as if identity were like a tootsie roll, or a pop-bead necklace, made up of detachable parts" (1988, 185–186).

CHAPTER 2

1. Some critics abstract the terms from the arguments in which they appear and treat them in isolation. So, for example, critics allege that the meaning of the "intersect" can be *only* that of a crossing of geometrical lines. Since geometrical lines in diagrams are constructed as separate from one another, the critics may argue, the term "intersect" ineluctably requires categories to be the equivalent of geometrical lines: separate thin marks representing things that are "discrete," "pure," "pre-existing." Rather than resisting binary thinking, such claims deploy it. The artificial conditions that the critics set for interpreting the term "intersect" require that categories be framed dichotomously: either "discrete" or not, either "pure" or not, either "pre-existing" or not. Such claims evade the arguments of intersectional scholars to think flexibly about categories in terms of *both/and.* It is possible to think of categories "intersecting" without necessarily presupposing "discrete" and "pure" categories. The terms "intersect" and "categories" have a whole range of literal and metaphorical meanings that can be deployed for a whole range of purposes; intersectional scholars use them as part of arguments about political and social construction of categories and categorical flexibility, fluidity, and change.

2. Crenshaw (1988, 1373) quotes a passage of Derrida pointing out that thinking in terms of binaries seems natural because it is a characteristic structure embedded in Western ways of thinking: "Western thought . . . has always been structured in terms of dichotomies or polarities: good vs. evil, being vs. nothingness, presence vs. absence, truth vs. error, identity vs. difference, mind vs. matter, man vs. woman, soul vs. body, life vs. death, nature vs. culture, speech vs. writing. These polar opposites do not, however, stand as independent and equal entities. The second term in each pair is considered the negative, corrupt, undesirable version of the first, a fall away from it. . . . In other words, the two terms are not simply opposed in their meanings, but are arranged in a hierarchical order which gives the first term *priority*" (1981, viii, emphasis in original). Hélène Cixous wants to counter the binary by exposing its hierarchical nature (1980). Audre Lorde (1984) wants to explicitly recognize the dissimilarities, distinctions, and particularities of the people and groups lumped together into the disfavored secondary term of the binary. According to Anne Cranny-Francis and colleagues (2003, especially 39–60), Lorde's politics of difference demands relational, rather than oppositional, thinking. By placing the secondary term of the binary at the heart of the dominant term, this relational thinking deconstructs not only the power relation in which the terms are engaged but also the meaning of each term—the dominant term (why is it

defined in certain ways?) and also the absent secondary term (whom does this term refer to? how is it related to their actual conditions of being?).

3. Blacks became eligible for citizenship in 1868 with the Fourteenth Amendment, followed by the 1870 revision of the Naturalization Act.

4. Federal and state laws were passed to prevent immigration and ownership of agricultural land by nonwhites in states on the West Coast (Chan 1991; Takaki 1989).

5. The a priori imperative of the ideological category of race *presupposes* racial homogeneity that fits patterns of racial hierarchy. What appear to be generalizations inferred from specific cases are actually the converse: presumptions of the category filtering observations. Creation of the ideological category creates the illusion of homogeneity out of diversity. For example, the Africans initially brought to the United States did not belong to one racial category but were of diverse ethnic groups: "Twi, Agante, Fulani, Yoruba, and Ibo, who spoke different languages, practiced different customs, and were not necessarily even on peaceful terms with one another" (Almaguer and Jung 1998, 6n6). Tómas Almaguer and Moon-Kie Jung trace the development of the category "Asian" or "Asian American" from the very different national groups such as Chinese, Japanese, Korean, Hmong, Thai, and Filipino.

CHAPTER 3

1. Zoltán Kövecses argues: "The production and comprehension of utterances, that is, the construction of meaning, is always influenced by and emerges in a larger context as well. The larger context involves, in addition to the speaker and addressee, the circumstances under which the utterance is made (including who communicates, with whom, when, where), the circumstances of the action of which the utterance is a part (the intentions and other mental states that provide the motivation for making the utterance, i.e., that respond to the question of why communication takes place), as well as the background knowledge attaching to the topic of communication (i.e., answering the question of "about what")" (2015, x).

2. According to Kövecses, "context is never predetermined and objectively existing; it must be created (and recreated) in the course of the communicative process. This view of the nature of context implies that meaning construction is heavily context dependent and that even the formally same utterance may have very different meanings in different contexts" (2015, x).

3. In "Demarginalizing" Crenshaw examines three Title VII cases: *DeGraffenreid v. General Motors, Moore v. Hughes Helicopter,* and *Payne v. Travenol.* She argues:

1. In *DeGraffenreid,* five Black women brought suit against General Motors, alleging that the employer's seniority system perpetuated the effects of past discrimination against Black women. . . . The district court granted summary judgment for the defendant, rejecting the plaintiffs' attempt to bring a suit not on behalf of Blacks or women, but specifically on behalf of Black women. (1989, 141)

2. In *Moore,* the plaintiff alleged that the employer, Hughes Helicopter, practiced race and sex discrimination in promotions to upper-level craft positions and to supervisory jobs. . . . The court rejected Moore's bid to represent all females apparently because her attempt to specify her race was seen as being at odds with the standard allegation that the employer simply discriminated "against females." (1989, 143, 144)

3. [In *Payne v. Travenol*] two Black female plaintiffs alleging race discrimination brought a class action suit on behalf of all Black employees at a pharmaceutical plant. The court refused, however, to allow the plaintiffs to represent Black males and granted the defendant's request to narrow the class to Black women only. (1989, 147)

4. Briggs argues: "Even if they are produced and received at particular historical moments, acts of production and reception create intertextual links with both previous and subsequent discursive formations. Rather than reify the products of these historical junctures as autonomous objects, we should investigate the history of their production and reception, focusing particularly on the social relations that have shaped who gains what types of rights to produce and receive texts, and how, when, and to what effect this occurs" (1993, 420).

5. Bauman and Briggs are concerned about the divisions between nature, society, tradition, and language as they engage in dialogue with Brian Stross 1999 and particularly Bruno Latour 1993. I contend that their arguments are useful for considering the problems of heterogeneous categories treated as homogeneous by enduring histories of dominant discourses, as is the case with race, gender, and sexuality.

6. Charles R. Hale argues for close analysis of the political ramifications of such metaphors in specific contexts. According to Hale, "The newly imbued theoretical meanings of hybridity and *mestizaje* do not travel very well to Guatemala, where Mayas are mobilizing to demand rights and contest oppression. But this barely scratches the surface of the issues raised by the disjuncture. In Chimaltenango, the dilemma seems to be that 'multiple subjectivities' and other notions that new theories of identity bring to the fore are both salutary and dangerous" (1999, 312).

7. The game can be played in various ways. Typically, "the sticks are bundled and taken in one hand that touches the table/ground. The release creates a circular jumble. Now one stick after another should be taken up without moving/touching others. The take away could be by hand, possibly through pressing on a stick's tip or if one has already picked up a special stick (Mikado/Mandarin), it could be used as a helper, possibly to throw up another stick." Apparently the highest scoring stick is sometimes labeled the Mikado, or the Emperor of Japan. "Mikado (Game)," Wikipedia, accessed August 10, 2017.

CHAPTER 4

1. The note does not mention the work of a number of intersectional scholars of color working on multidimensionality during that period, even those who are sociologists. Particularly evident is the failure to mention the foundational work of Patricia Hill Collins (1986, 1989, 1991), president of the American Sociological Association in 2009, though a more recent article (P. Collins 2000b) is later cited.

2. Aileen Moreton-Robinson argues, "What is interesting in West and Fenstermaker's analysis is that, although white women are identified as such, they are not racialized; instead the category white is a subordinate additive to class or gender. The category 'race' refers to all those who are non-white. Failing to racialize white women as such means white racial privilege remains uninterrogated as a source of oppression and inequality" (2000, 344–345).

3. The article "Doing Difference" does not identify the anthology, but does criticize Margaret L. Andersen and Patricia Hill Collins's preface (1992a) to their anthology *Race, Class, and Gender* (Andersen and Collins 1992b). When West and Fenstermaker publish their article as a chapter in their book (Fenstermaker and West 2002) they cite the second edition of the anthology (1994). (The ninth edition of the anthology was published in 2015.) It is not clear why West and Fenstermaker would expect unity in use of metaphors and methods in an introductory anthology for undergraduates that is more than 570 pages in length.

4. West and Fenstermaker do not explain why a general comment about ranking oppressions should be tied to the word "intersect." The metaphor of "intersection" does not entail calculable, countable, measurable, or quantitatively "amassing a specific quantity of oppression" or assuming one should rank number of oppressions to determine the "amount" of oppression. In fact, such assumptions are *countered* by thinking intersectionally.

5. See Chapter 5 for more detailed quotations from Collins's text.

6. The critics cite *This Bridge Called My Back* (1981) as the source of their quotation of Moraga; they do not cite its appearance in the first pages of the compilation of essays that they say impelled their critique (apparently Andersen and Collins 1992b or 1994).

7. The critics cite *On Call: Political Essays* (1985) as the source of their quotation of Jordan; they do not cite its appearance in the first pages of the compilation of essays that they say impelled their critique (apparently Andersen and Collins 1992b or 1994).

8. Bronwyn Davies and Sue Saltmarsh, examining the impact of neoliberal discourses and strategies in Australian universities, argue, "Neo-liberal policy espouses 'survival of the fittest' and unleashes competition among individuals, among institutions, and among nations, *freeing them from what are construed as the burdensome chains of social justice and social responsibility* " (2007, 3, emphasis added). In another essay Davies argues that neoliberalism "*whips up a small-minded moralism that rewards the attack of each small powerless person on the other.* . . . It draws on and exacerbates a fear of difference and rewards a rampant, consumerist, competitive individualism" (2005, 7, emphasis added). I follow Stuart Hall's lead in recognizing that although neoliberalism is not a singular and completely uniform process, neoliberal rhetorics have "enough common features" to justify "a *provisional* conceptual identity," and that naming them "is *politically* necessary to give the resistance to its onward march content, focus and a cutting edge" (Hall 2011, 706, emphasis in original).

CHAPTER 5

1. Both texts deploy a familiar but destructive architecture of argument using *rhetorics of rejection and replacement* that work according to a unifying logic that attempts here to close down multiple paths of feminist antiracist analysis and replace them with a single path to feminist knowledge (see Tomlinson 2013a). Rhetorics of rejection and replacement work explicitly to eliminate heterogeneity in theory and method. Working from a competitive, hierarchical, *either/or* perspective, they shut down options—as if in a "zero-sum" game where one project can grow only at the expense of another, as though *multiple* fields of feminist antiracist analysis are not possible, as though any "promising" new category or analytic must be a *singular* path to feminist knowledge, a *singular* site of political investment. Commonplace in critiques of intersectionality, rhetorics of rejection and replacement illustrate the very problems with difference that intersectional theorizing challenges: the insistence that difference must be positioned as *better than* or *worse than*, not just *different from*. The result is a discursive technology of power structured in dominance, working to reinstall the unified subject of feminism, framing decisions about the central methods of feminist scholarship in terms of a "contest" for supremacy within the terms of capitalism and modernity.

2. Ethnomethodology seeks to understand how people within a culture understand the world (ethno = folk; methodology = methods) (Silverman 2011). According to Keith Punch: "The fundamental assumption of ethnomethodology is that people within a culture have procedures for making sense of their daily life. For ethnomethodologists, culture thus consists not of a stable set of things that members are supposed to know, but of processes for figuring out or giving meaning to the actions of members. The primary focus is on how central features of a culture, its shared meanings and social norms, are developed, maintained, and changed, rather than on the content of these meanings and norms (Feldman 1995, 8). . . . With so much of social life mediated through written and especially spoken communication, the study of language is at the heart of ethnomethodology" (2013, 189–190).

3. West and Fenstermaker recommend that feminist studies turn to ethnomethodology, which, they indicate, examines gender, race, and class as "ongoing interactional

accomplishment[s]" (1995, 8). Ethnomethodology is one of a panoply of research methods that provides useful insights into power and social life, a valuable tool for understanding social identities and social relationships. It connects cultural practices to social structures by emphasizing how social identities and categories are recreated constantly through everyday interactions, processes, and discourses. West and Fenstermaker offer ethnomethodology to replace virtually *all* of the kinds of intersectional analysis of structural power, no matter what the specific goals, without explaining why any field of research would be best served by uniform methods and language. Ethnomethodology, West and Fenstermaker promise, will be able to reveal the "*actual mechanisms* that produce social inequality" (13, emphasis added). But ethnomethodology, like other methods of social inquiry, can never reveal an unmediated social "reality" of *actual mechanisms*. In fact, the *reflexivity* that is a central tenet of ethnomethodology also applies to the language activities of scholars themselves: for ethnomethodologists, like other people, "to describe a situation is at the same time to create it" (Marshall 1998a, 204). Ethnomethodology depends vitally on the intellectual labor of the analyst to create an impression of coherence, to create an impression that the scholar's interpretations and constructions might possibly be the "*actual mechanisms* that produce social inequality" (see Mehan and Wood 1983). Further, ethnomethodology's core principles and obligations include *indexicality,* which situates the meaning of words always in reference to other words and contexts, always subject to further understanding (Marshall 1998a, 203). Yet determining and condemning what they argue to be the final and inescapable meaning of words such as "interlocking" and "intersecting" is, in fact, the key to West and Fenstermaker's critique. The critique is *all about* words decontextualized and treated in isolation from "reference to other words and to the context in which the words are spoken" (Marshall 1998a, 203).

4. West and Fenstermaker claim to be motivated in part by their reading of a recent anthology for undergraduate students that provided an overview of research on gender, race, and class (apparently Andersen and Collins 1992b or 1994); they claim to have found the lack of uniform terminology, methods, and theoretical assumptions among the various articles to be "confusing" (West and Fenstermaker 1995, 8). They propose to solve this problem of "difference" in research by promoting instead one method, one theory. It is unclear why the critics argue that *any field of research* is best served by uniform methods and language. The words they mention—"intersecting systems," "interlocking categories," "multiple bases," "distinct axes," "concentric axes" (9)—bear a strong "family resemblance," in Wittgenstein's terms (Wittgenstein 1953; see discussion in Mehan and Wood 1983, 31–32, 139). The different words and arguments have many features in common, forming an overlapping and crisscrossing network of concepts; Wittgenstein likens such relationships to family members who resemble one another through different combinations of partly shared features rather than sharing a single common feature. It is unclear why the critics argue that the term they propose—"difference"—is capable of representing the meanings needed for such a variety of studies.

5. West and Fenstermaker could have criticized the metaphors without evoking a sexist stereotype. They could have used the deft deployment of "mathematical" and "geometric" metaphors by feminist scholars to demonstrate the stereotype to be invalid. They could have pointed out that the stereotype does not predict the "femininity" of the many women sociologists with quantitative skills. They could have evoked numerous research studies about the social construction of gender and stereotypes, the role of schooling in shaping girls' response to mathematics (Sadker and Sadker 1995; Sadker and Zittleman 2009), and even the role of school mathematics texts in constructing girls' subjectivity (Dowling 1991). They could have acknowledged many vigorous contemporaneous feminist arguments that girls and women are fully capable of work in mathematics, engineering, and the sciences (see, for example, Rosser 1990, 1995; Tobias [1978] 1995; Walkerdine 1989). They could have

referenced research from the 1970s and 1980s (including that published in *Signs*) indicating that, in fact, girls do well in math, but suffer from lack of confidence caused in part by the repetition of the very stereotype the critics evoke (Eccles and Jacobs 1986; Fennema and Sherman 1977; Linn and Hyde 1989). Subsequent research has demonstrated that "stereotype threat" impairs the math performance of girls and college women (Good, Aronson, and Harder 2008; Lindberg et al. 2010; Spencer, Steele, and Quinn 1999; Steele 1997).

6. In referencing those who have cited the authors whose work I analyze here, I follow a tactic employed by Clare Hemmings throughout *Why Stories Matter* (2011), identifying citers not by name but by *source*—journal and year—to emphasize citation's work of repetition as part of scholarly communities. Hemmings argues: "This tactic is intended to emphasize the role of journal communities—editors, boards, peer reviewers, and responses to publishing conventions and expectations—in the establishment of feminist (and broader academic) knowledge practices. . . . Taking the authors out of the citation frame is thus a way of focusing attention on repetition instead of individuality and how collective repetition actively works to obscure the politics of its own production and reception" (21–22). Many citers do not question or criticize any of West and Fenstermaker's arguments. One citer echoes them, calling it "peculiar" that feminists "rely so heavily on mathematical metaphors" (*Science, Technology, and Human Values* [2006]). Another citer adds "science" to the argument, claiming that feminists rely on them "in spite of stereotypes of women as uncomfortable with math and the sciences" (*Race, Gender and Class* [1999]). A third citer interprets the argument as chastising feminists who use mathematics because it is "a linear, discrete, and traditionally masculinist domain" (*Affilia: Journal of Women and Social Work* [2010]).

7. Paul Dowling argues: "The constitutions of subjectivity [of school mathematics texts] are not contingent upon cognitive styles: they are part of what it means to be male or female. School mathematics texts do not cause girls to fail: they reproduce and augment what it means to be a girl. Whatever their actions, girls must either be confirmed in their femininity and therefore as lacking anything more than moderate "ability" in mathematics, or they must be labelled as gender-freaks" (1991, 4).

8. Particularly useful in understanding the flexible thinking generated through geometry and knot theory is the video *Not Knot*. *Not Knot* is a guided tour into computer-animated hyperbolic space that works on the premise that it may be easier to understand something by looking at what it is *not*. It starts with the realm of knots and goes on to examine their "complementary spaces—what's not a knot. Profound theorems of recent mathematics show that most known complements carry the structure of hyperbolic geometry, a geometry in which the sum of three angles of a triangle always is less than 180 degrees" (*Not Knot* 1991). Metaphors like "intersect" are examples of "Euclidean geometry" (where lines remain at a constant distance from each other); Borromean rings and Venn diagrams are examples of "non-Euclidean geometry" (where lines curve away or curve toward each other).

9. This is an example of what mathematicians call a "link with three strands." The study of such links is part of knot theory, a mathematical topic that studies the forms of knots and links. In knot theory, the Borromean rings are a simple example of a Brunnian link: although each pair of rings is unlinked, the whole cannot be unlinked.

10. West and Fenstermaker are, in fact, recommending the second Venn diagram, despite it being "geometrical," a move contrary to their entire argument against thinking with geometry. It is perhaps for this reason that their position has proved ambiguous for the politics of citation. Some citers incorrectly assume that the critics are "rejecting" Venn diagrams (*Gender and Society* [1995]; *Race, Gender and Class* [1999]; *Professional Geographer* [2007]).

11. *Professional Geographer* (2007).

12. For discussions of difference, see Crenshaw 2010; Lowe 1996; Melamed 2011; Sandoval 2000; Wiegman 1999b.

13. For example, Baca Zinn 1990; Beale 1970; Dill 1988; Glenn 1985; hooks 1981, 1984; Hull, Scott, and Smith 1982; Lorde 1984; P. Williams 1991.

14. West and Fenstermaker are cited as refuting previous conceptions, which posited fixed or stable categories, in *Professional Geographer* (2007) and *Sociology* (2010). They are cited as establishing simultaneity in *European Journal of Women's Studies* (2011).

15. *Render Me, Gender Me* did important work in many ways. It played a vital role in revealing the differential consciousness, hybridity and heterogeneity of lesbian lives and in revealing how people tell stories and make meaning for themselves in the face of negative social ascription. Weston's work also played an important role in opening the door to subsequent generative studies of gender and sexuality. Weston weaves together the narratives that her interview protagonists provided about their lived experiences and their negotiations of gender in a quest to make the complexities of individuals' lives "come alive." Given that analysis of life narratives is a common method of research, these ends could have been achieved without making any reference at all to intersectionality.

16. Weston's bibliography includes Anzaldúa 1987; P. Collins 1991; Crenshaw 1995a; Hammonds 1994; Lugones 1994; Moraga and Anzaldúa 1981; P. Williams 1991, 1995.

CHAPTER 6

1. Much of the passion of Brown's polemic appears to stem from her frustration with the ways of talking about multidimensionality adopted by graduate and undergraduate students at her campus, the University of California, Santa Cruz.

2. In a 2015 interview Brown reiterates that intersectionality was an important legal concept but limited as a theoretical and historical understanding of subject formation (Cruz and Brown 2016). The interview does not indicate the degree that feminist scholarship ranges far beyond the focus on subject formation that Brown promulgated in 1997.

3. Collins also criticizes earlier standpoint theories further, arguing: "One implication of standpoint approaches is that the more subordinated the group, the purer the vision of the oppressed group. This is an outcome of the origins of standpoint approaches in Marxist social theory, itself an analysis of social structure rooted in Western either/or dichotomous thinking. Ironically, by quantifying and ranking human oppressions, standpoint theorists evoke criteria for methodological adequacy characteristic of positivism" (1991, 207).

4. Collins also argues: "As epistemological stances, both positivist science and relativism minimize the importance of specific location in influencing a group's knowledge claims, the power inequities among groups that produce subjugated knowledges, and the strengths and limitations of partial perspective (Haraway 1988)" (1991, 235).

5. Collins argues, for example: "The overarching matrix of domination houses multiple groups, each with varying experiences with penalty and privilege that produce corresponding partial perspectives, situated knowledges, and, for clearly identifiable subordinated groups, subjugated knowledges" (1991, 234). She goes on to suggest the benefits of bringing together a variety of partial perspectives: "Those ideas that are validated as true by African-American women, African-American men, Latina lesbians, Asian-American women, Puerto Rican men, and other groups with distinctive standpoints, with each group using the epistemological approaches growing from its unique standpoint, thus become the most "objective" truths. Each group speaks from its own standpoint and shares its own partial, situated knowledge. But because each group perceives its own truth as partial, its knowledge is unfinished. Each group becomes better able to consider other groups' standpoints without

relinquishing the uniqueness of its own standpoint or suppressing other groups' partial perspectives. . . . Partiality and not universality is the condition of being heard; individuals and groups forwarding knowledge claims without owning their position are deemed less credible than those who do" (1991, 236).

6. Dhamoon closely paraphrases what Yuval-Davis provides as block text but does not identify the source. Since her citations include Crenshaw 1989 and 1994, which do not include the block text, and Yuval-Davis 2006b, which does and implies that it is Crenshaw's, one would presume that Dhamoon's source is Yuval-Davis 2006b.

7. Yuval-Davis's incorrect attribution of the block text to what she calls "Mapping the Margins" (2001) [sic], may not be an isolated incident but reflects systematic misattribution and confusion that should cast considerable doubt on the validity of her arguments about the conceptions of other scholars. The block text falsely attributed to Crenshaw's "Mapping the Margins" (2001) [sic] appears at the bottom of page 196. At the top of page 198 Yuval-Davis provides two short quotes that she attributes to Crenshaw. Yuval-Davis indicates that Crenshaw describes "structural intersectionality" as "the ways in which the location of women of colour at the intersection of race and gender makes our actual experience of domestic violence, rape, and remedial reform qualitatively different than that of white women" (Crenshaw, 1993: 3) [sic], and "political intersectionality" as related to how "both feminist and antiracist politics have functioned in tandem to marginalize the issue of violence against women of color" (Crenshaw, 1993: 3) [sic]. Yuval-Davis cites the source of these short quotations as page 3 of Crenshaw's "Beyond Racism and Misogyny" (1993) in *Words That Wound*. Once again, Yuval-Davis's attribution is false. Page 3 of *Words That Wound* is not Crenshaw's article "Beyond Racism and Misogyny." Rather, it is part of the jointly authored introduction to the volume and discusses Critical Race Theory, not intersectionality or violence against women. In fact, both short passages that Yuval-Davis quotes are from the *actual* article "Mapping the Margins" (1994, 95). Some errors are inevitable in scholarly work, but it is reasonable to ask whether this degree of inaccuracy and misattribution has been tolerated because it serves to undermine the conceptual work of intersectional scholars of color.

8. The complications of audience at conferences such as WCAR are sharply different from those involved in academic discourses. WCAR involved more than 10,000 governmental delegates attending the UN WCAR and 8,000–10,000 delegates attending the parallel nongovernmental forum (the majority women) (Blackwell and Naber 2002; Falcón 2016). Those attending represented and reported back to governments, nongovernmental organizations, and a wide range of groups concerned with human rights. They represented multiple stakeholders seeking to influence decision makers, and included decision makers themselves, all with a wide range of knowledges and opinions (Falcón 2016). Workshops on gender were often marginalized, but WCAR helped create "dialogue around shared oppressions in an international context and broadened our definition of racism and how racism intersects in its complexities with multiple forms of oppression" (Blackwell and Naber 2002, 245). WCAR was infused with arguments about language, concepts, and politics. Maylei Blackwell and Nadine Naber argue about broad issues: "In order to understand the complex maneuvering in Durban, it is crucial to realize that at the core of WCAR was a discursive struggle, or a struggle over representation and the power to define, which has been a central feature of colonial domination and legitimation throughout history" (2002, 239). As Jennifer Chan-Tiberghien discloses, at WCAR the concept of "gender as intersectionality" marked a "paradigm shift" in international human rights frameworks. This move put "the issue of diversity among women at the forefront," marking "the beginning of a new phase of transnational feminist mobilization" (2004, 454; see also Falcón 2016).

9. The roads (in this version of the metaphor) are racism, colonialism, and patriarchy. The *identity* of the minority woman is *not* racism, colonialism, and patriarchy. Those are

forces that may impinge on her identity and affect her experiences and trajectory. It is Vakulenko and other critics making similar claims who have slid from the discriminations found in the actual metaphor to what is their *trigger*: gender and race, in Vakulenko's case.

CHAPTER 7

1. Randi Gressgård (2008) also cites and repeats Knapp's misrepresentation of the Case of the Et Cetera as criticizing theories of specifically "predicated" subjects, as a condemnation of the illegitimacy of "too many" demands for difference. Gressgård also adopts without question Knapp's characterization of the history of feminist argumentation, with all the feminist positions it renders invisible. She agrees with Knapp that there is a fundamental problem at the heart of feminism specifically *because of* the "clash between identitarian (political) articulations of difference and radical questioning of the epistemological and political foundations of feminism" (n.p.). Such uncritical repetitions of previous critiques infuse critiques of intersectionality, resulting in what I call in Chapter 6 the "Canyon of Echoes."

2. In "Contingent Foundations" Butler argues: "Within feminism, it seems as if there is some political necessity to speak as and for *women,* and I would not contest that necessity. . . . [L]obbying efforts are virtually impossible without recourse to identity politics. . . . Identity categories are never merely descriptive, but always normative, and as such, exclusionary. This is not to say that the term "women" ought not be used. . . . To deconstruct the subject of feminism is not, then, to censure its usage, but, on the contrary, to release the term into a future of multiple significations . . . and to give it play as a site where unanticipated meanings might come to bear" (1995, 49–50).

3. This problem is deftly explored by William Connolly. Connolly argues that the postmodernist or poststructuralist sees political danger in current conditions of closure, while the modernist fears the openness that poststructuralists advocate: "So . . . we have a subterranean conflict over the nature of language, discourse, and identity that issues in an overt conflict over where the political danger is located in the late-modern period. One side seeks to open up discourses that are too closed and self-righteous and the other to protect established truths it considers threatened. But this ethicopolitical conflict . . . is hardly ever thematized by the modernist in overtly political terms. The opponent is treated as if she shared (or must share, if she is a rational, responsible thinker) the modernist's political starting points and the ethicopolitical difference is unconsciously translated into a universal philosophical issue with one rational response" (1991, 60).

4. Butler questions categories in order to free them for "rethinking," not to flatly deny, denigrate, or eliminate their use. She reiterates this point throughout her work. For example, discussing challenges to the concept of "the subject," Butler argues: "To take the construction of the subject as a political problematic is not the same as doing away with the subject; to deconstruct the subject is not to negate or throw away the concept; on the contrary, deconstruction implies only that we suspend all commitments to that which the term, "the subject," refers, and that we consider the linguistic functions it serves in the consolidation and concealment of authority. To deconstruct is not to negate or dismiss, but to call into question and, perhaps, most importantly, to open up a term, like the subject, to a reusage or redeployment that previously has not been authorized" (1995, 48–49).

CHAPTER 8

1. Discussions of the politics of the European reception and development of intersectional analysis can be found in K. Davis 2011; Ferree 2011; and Yuval-Davis 2006b. These

articles make claims about general discourses and politics rather than examining the scene of argument.

2. European scholars have good reasons to resist the importation of theoretical concepts and investigative categories from the United States. The global hegemony of U.S.-based media conglomerates, the rise of English as a global business language, and decades of covert and overt funding of scholarly institutions in Europe by U.S. government agencies combine to exert undue and unjust pressures that suppress and marginalize local European perspectives. Scholars of color in the United States may feel purely oppositional to this hegemony, yet they also access the privileges that accrue to them from settler colonialism at home and imperialism abroad. So it is legitimate for European scholars to distrust an uncritical application of U.S. concepts to European realities. Racism's specific history in Europe and in its colonies should provoke situated theories and critiques. There are empirical differences between the racial orders of Europe and the United States that can be productive for theoretical work if their diversity is recognized and acknowledged. Neither U.S. nor European scholarship on race is monolithic or uniform. Yet there is a clear pattern evident in the white critiques of intersectionality that I discuss here that illuminates both the specifics of racial europeanization (Goldberg 2006) and the general problems of how traveling theories are misrepresented at the scene of argument.

3. The Holocaust was a cataclysmic event in world history that obligates scholars to acknowledge and analyze its horrible origins and effects. Yet if they view all world racism through the specific lens of the Holocaust, scholars can commit the error of confusing the dominant particulars of Europe with universally true principles. In addition, by granting priority to the Holocaust at the expense of the broader history of racist brutality and exploitation of which it is a part, scholars can unwisely come to argue that the loss of only European lives matters.

4. There is a significant body of scholarship examining the continuing contemporary influence of race and racisms in European life, inflected by national histories. With regard to the Netherlands, for example, Philomena Essed and Kwame Nimako (2006) and Gloria Wekker (2016) describe specific strategies deployed to deny racisms and delegitimize research on race, while Wekker (2004) also describes the erasure of Dutch colonialism from schools and public discussion. With regard to France, Trica Danielle Keaton (2010) examines the difficulties of discourses of "race-blindness" in the face of anti-Blackness (see also Keaton, Sharpley-Whiting, and Stovall 2012). With regard to the Nordic countries, Kristin Loftsdóttir and Lars Jensen (2012) examine how ideologies associated with colonialism underpin Nordic identities. Robert Stam and Ella Shohat (2012) provide a comparative analysis of the discourses of race in France, the United States, and Brazil.

5. European scholars who critique intersectionality for its alleged shortcomings miss an opportunity here to draw productively on similarities between Europe and North America. Black feminist writings on intersectional analysis respond directly to the ways in which laws purporting to oppose racial subordination (especially the Fourteenth Amendment to the U.S. Constitution) became distorted into bans against racial recognition.

6. According to the text, during the 1970s, "frustrated about the way the Dutch government had betrayed their parents, young Moluccans engaged in violent protests," including train hijackings, taking hostages, and killings (Prins 2006, 283). Prins grants that there were "strained relations" between the two racial groups but goes on to praise the success of white paternalism: in "the longer run . . . the hijacking had beneficial effects" (283) because the Moluccans were forced to set aside their political goals and the Dutch were forced to begin policies of multiculturalism.

7. For example, of forty-eight classmates, three had died, all Moluccans (Prins 2006, 283). One Moluccan "suffered a psychotic breakdown" (287). Of twenty-two Dutch class-

mates, twenty live in or near the town where they attended high school; of fourteen Moluc-can classmates, one lives locally, eight in the north of the Netherlands, the rest elsewhere. Prins notes that the Moluccan classmates appear more interested in their "origins" but overlooks her own description of the social relations of power that lead her Dutch classmates to be less interested: "We are part of clearly delineated family networks, our grandparents and other relatives lived close to our homes and at school we learned proud stories about the Dutch, the Frisians and even the Stellingwarfs, as people that bravely and successfully fought for their freedom and independence" (287).

8. The narratives Prins quotes indicate that "social problems" occur even in the lives of people she describes as "ordinary," including the two classmates she uses as her main examples. A male Dutch classmate sought to differentiate himself from his family's reputa-tion for "antisocial behavior and backwardness" (2006, 284). Prins praises this subject's use of class and masculinity to intimidate, to make "a—barely—concealed threat" (284). A female Moluccan classmate left town at the age of sixteen after being sexually assaulted by her stepfather, who also beat her mother. "The stories of her private life . . . revolve around violence" (285). She went on to live with a Dutch heroin addict and herself "perpetuated violence" in the relationship (286).

9. For example, Prins cites Crenshaw's "Mapping the Margins" (1994) without ac-knowledging the text's argument that a gendered position alone is not possible but must account also for race, class, and citizenship status.

10. Nothing in the arguments of Foucault or Gramsci authorizes the notion that citing them is required for productive discussions of power. Nonetheless, both theorists are cited by U.S. intersectional scholars of color more than Prins claims, even in these older texts: see Collins's use of Gramsci and Foucault (1991); Prins ignores Crenshaw's arguments about Gramsci and hegemony (1988). Significantly, when she turns to her classmates' narratives, Prins adopts an analytic frame that is *neither Foucauldian nor Gramscian* but simply a liberal humanist celebration of the individual.

11. All three U.S. intersectional scholars discuss white racism. The racialized subjects they discuss include not only Blacks (P. Collins 1991, 1998) but also Latinas, Filipinas, and immigrant women (Crenshaw 1991), and Asian American and Native American women (Matsuda 1991). Crenshaw (1991) also discusses how whites are disadvantaged by their own racism: she argues that their attachment to racial privilege ultimately exacerbates inequali-ties to their detriment.

12. For example, the arguments of both Staunæs (2003) and Prins (2006) are not criti-cized by Nina Lykke (2010, 74–75) or Kathy Davis (2011, 49), whose powerblind rhetorics I examine in Chapter 7 (and in the case of Davis, also Chapters 6 and 9). Myra Marx Ferre (2011, 56) and Nancy A. Naples (2009, 568–569) do not criticize the arguments of Prins (2006).

CHAPTER 9

1. My attention was drawn to this argument by Charles L. Briggs 2007.

2. This definition and all subsequent definitions are from the *Oxford English Diction-ary* (2018).

3. Kathy Davis does not provide citations to texts arguing that intersectionality is "sci-entifically unsound," nor does she provide relevant criteria for readers to make such a judg-ment. She indicates that "by soundness I am referring to the scientific conventions for good theory" (2008, 80n5). Such a claim evades responsibility both to the intersectional scholars she denigrates and to other readers, who surely deserve to know the explicit grounds for disparaging intersectionality. Also see notes 6 and 7 below on theory.

4. Kathy Davis also calls intersectionality *"catchy* and complex" (2008, 76, emphasis added) and quotes Ann Phoenix using the term "handy catchall phrase": "Intersectionality addresses precisely the issue of differences among women by providing *'a handy catchall phrase* that aims to make visible the multiple positioning that constitutes everyday life and the power relations that are central to it'" (Davis 2008, 70, quoting Phoenix 2006, 187, emphasis added).

5. Of course, like any term of art, "intersectionality" can be used in a casual, perfunctory fashion, but Kathy Davis's superficial gloss attends to only that potential use, not to the substantive work that the term performs in scholarship and civic life.

6. Murray Davis argues: "Students who follow to the letter all the injunctions of current textbooks on 'theory-construction,' but take into account no other criterion in construction of their theories [like interestingness for audiences], will turn out work that will be found dull indeed. Their impeccably constructed theories will go unnoted—or more precisely, unfootnoted—by others" (1971, 310).

7. According to the *Oxford Dictionary of Sociology:* "A theory is an account of the world which goes beyond what we can see and measure. It embraces a set of interrelated definitions and relationships that organizes our concepts of and understanding of the empirical world in a systematic way. . . . Generally speaking there are three different conceptions of theory in sociology. Some think of theory as generalizations about, and classifications of, the social world. The scope of generalization varies from theorizing about a particular range of phenomena to more abstract and general theories about society and history as a whole. Others believe that theoretical statements should be translated into empirical, measurable, or observable propositions, and systematically tested. . . . Finally, yet others argue that theory should explain phenomena, identifying causal mechanisms and processes which, although they cannot be observed directly, can be seen in their effects" (Marshall 1998b, 666).

8. Interestingly, Hewitt recommends poststructuralist arguments that meanings are relational and multiple and that identities are multivalent. She also demonstrates as "nonintersectional" work that demonstrates how identities change in specific material and historical settings. In fact, all of these conceptions are part of intersectional thinking.

9. In Chapter 6, I analyze Brown's discussion of Aída Hurtado and Patricia Hill Collins; in this chapter I consider Brown's argument about Crenshaw's metaphor of intersections.

10. Brown is also very concerned about usage with regard to the metaphor of "intersection." She argues, "The woman is not an intersection, nor is she intersectional. . . . Black women as such are not 'intersectional'; rather, their legal position is" (2005, 152n3). Such usage is found in neither Collins's *Black Feminist Thought* (1991) nor Crenshaw's "Demarginalizing" (1989). However, despite Brown's strictures, describing oneself or other women as "intersectional" in order to emphasize multiple categorization has become part of U.S. popular and political culture, often used in productive ways.

11. Lewis Carroll, *Through the Looking Glass,* quoted in Hubbard, Henifin, and Fried 1979, and subsequently quoted by Haraway. The Lewis Carroll quotation and the following definition of "master" appear in Haraway 1981, 469, 470. Haraway defines "master" as the following: *"Master*—a person with the ability or power to use, control, or dispose of something; male head of a household; a victor or conqueror; a man eminently skilled in something; one holding this title." Haraway's definition is from the *Random House Dictionary of the English Language.*

12. Scholars undertaking an intersectional analysis frequently begin by citing past critical arguments, some based on mastering intersectionality; they take the criticisms of such arguments for granted, contrasting those alleged failures to their own more perspicacious approaches with disclaimers such as: "They [the women of color who proposed intersection-

ality] saw categories as fixed and static, but I see them as fluid and flexible." (An example of this distinction is found in Ferree 2009.)

13. Foucault argues that scholars must examine how "effects of power circulate among scientific statements, what constitutes, as it were, their internal regime of power" (1980b, 112).

CHAPTER 10

1. Linda Gordon is the only person to win the prestigious Bancroft Prize twice. The Bancroft Prize is awarded each year by the trustees of Columbia University for books about diplomacy or the history of the Americas. Gordon received the prize in 2010 for *Dorothea Lange: A Life beyond Limits* (2009) and in 2000 for *The Great Arizona Orphan Abduction* (1999).

2. Gordon's argument advising African American women to consider that they might "have some common interests" displays a profound lack of familiarity with the history of thought of African American women as well as the intersectional arguments discussed in Chapter 1 and the arguments about race discussed in Chapter 2. Gordon does not cite classic sources on intersectional thinking that would give her a much stronger grounding in the arguments of African American women, such as Patricia Hill Collins's *Black Feminist Thought* (1991).

3. Gordon does not acknowledge that over centuries whites have used racial dominance to deny women of color the right to define their own experiences.

4. Accompanying citation: Iphis, "If You're White, don't Call Yourself an 'Intersectional Feminist' and don't Use 'Intersectionality' for White People," the rogue feminist, 5 December 2013, http://theroguefeminist.tumblr.com/post/69108181677/if-youre-white-dont-call-yourself-an.

5. Moi's argument would be more precise if she recognized the interrelationship of intersectional theorizing by women of color and the powerblind white counterarguments that attempt to find that work experiential, clumsy, and in other ways cognitively deficient. Claims of the need for greater theoretical sophistication are argumentative tools deprecating the conceptual skills of women of color and indicating that needed theoretical advances can be supplied by the perspicacious thinking of white critics. Moi's argument would also be more precise if she distinguished the line of the argument she criticizes from the large body of work that engages in intersectional analyses without seeking to critique intersectionality and sometimes does not even use the term "intersectional."

6. At the point that Davis and Žarkov (2017) identify, I (2013b) state: "Many critics approach intersectionality carelessly, however, through metacommentary and complaint and through recommendations to bring its radical critique under control by advocating recourse to specific disciplinary methods—without acknowledging that such methods may have long been criticized for their service to dominant discourses. Critics assume that their task is *to critique intersectionality,* not *to foster intersectionality's ability to critique subordination.* The rhetorical frameworks and tropes examined here misrepresent the history and arguments of intersectionality, treat it as a unitary entity rather than an analytic tool used across a range of disciplines, distort its arguments, engage in presentist analytics, reduce intersectionality's radical critique of power to desires for identity and inclusion, and offer a deradicalized intersectionality as an asset for dominant disciplinary discourses" (996–997, emphasis in original).

REFERENCES

Ahmed, Sara. 2000. "Whose Counting?" *Feminist Theory* 1.1:97–103.

———. 2004. *The Cultural Politics of Emotion*. New York: Routledge.

———. 2011. "Problematic Proximities: Or Why Critiques of Gay Imperialism Matter." *Feminist Legal Studies* 19:119–132.

———. 2012. *On Being Included: Racism and Diversity in Institutional Life*. Durham, NC: Duke University Press.

Alcoff, Linda Martín. 2007a. "Fraser on Redistribution, Recognition, and Identity." *European Journal of Political Theory* 6.3:255–265.

———. 2007b. "Mignolo's Epistemology of Coloniality." *CR: The New Centennial Review* 7.3:79–101.

Alexander-Floyd, Nikol. 2012. "Disappearing Acts: Reclaiming Intersectionality in the Social Sciences in a Post-Black Feminist Era." *Feminist Formations* 24.1:1–25.

Almaguer, Tómas, and Moon-Kie Jung. 1998. "The Enduring Ambiguities of Race in the United States." University of Michigan, Ann Arbor, Department of Sociology, Center for Research on Social Organization. Working Paper Series No. 573.

Althusser, Louis. 1971. "Ideology and Ideological State Apparatuses." In *Lenin and Philosophy and Other Essays*, 127–187. New York: Monthly Review.

Andersen, Margaret L., and Patricia Hill Collins. 1992a. "Preface." In *Race, Class and Gender*, ed. Margaret L. Andersen and Patricia Hill Collins, xii–xvi. Belmont, CA: Wadsworth.

———, eds. 1992b. *Race, Class and Gender*. Belmont, CA: Wadsworth.

———, eds. 1994. *Race, Class and Gender*. 2nd ed. Belmont, CA: Wadsworth.

Anthias, Floya, and Nira Yuval-Davis. 1983. "Contextualizing Feminism: Gender, Ethnic, and Class Divisions." *Feminist Review* 15:62–75.

———. 1992. *Racialized Boundaries: Race, Nation, Gender, Colour and Class and the Antiracist Struggle*. London: Routledge.

Anzaldúa, Gloria. 1987. *Borderlands/La Frontera: The New Mestiza*. San Francisco, CA: Spinsters/Aunt Lute.

————, ed. 1990. *Haciendo Caras: Making Face, Making Soul: Creative and Critical Perspectives by Feminists of Color.* San Francisco, CA: Aunt Lute Books.

Armstrong, Nancy. 1990. *Desire and Domestic Fiction: A Political History of the Novel.* New York: Oxford University Press.

————. 2005. *How Novels Think: The Limits of Individualism from 1719–1900.* New York: Columbia University Press.

Asia Pacific Forum on Women, Law and Development (APWLD). 2003. "What Does the WCAR Mean for Asia Pacific Women?" University of New South Wales, Center for Refugee Research, Sidney. Available at http://iknowpolitics.org/sites/default/files/women_human20rights_apwld_part1.pdf.

Asylum Aid. 2002. "Romani Women from Central and Eastern Europe: A 'Fourth World,' or Experience of Multiple Discrimination." Refugee Women's Resource Project, Asylum Aid, London. Available at https://www.asylumaid.org.uk/wp-content/uploads/2013/02/Romani-Women-from-Central-and-Eastern-Europe-A-Fourth-World.pdf.

Australian Human Rights and Equal Opportunity Commission. 2001. "HREOC and the World Conference against Racism." Available at www.hreoc.gv.au/worldconference/aus_gender.html.

Australian National Committee on Refugee Women (ANCORW) Annual Report. 2001–2002. Dir. Eileen Pittaway. Centre for Refugee Research, New South Wales. Available at http://ancorw.org.au/wp-content/uploads/2017/12/2001-2002.pdf.

Aydemir, Murat. 2009. "In Queer Street." *FRAME* 22.2:8–15.

————. 2012. "Dutch Homonationalism and Intersectionality." In *The Postcolonial Low Countries: Literature, Colonialism, and Multiculturalism,* ed. Elleke Boehmer and Sarah De Mul, 187–202. Lanham, MD: Lexington Books.

Baca Zinn, Maxine. 1990. "Family, Feminism and Race in America." *Gender and Society* 4:68–82.

Bailey, Alison. 2009. "On Intersectionality, Empathy, and Feminist Solidarity: A Reply to Naomi Zack." *Journal for Peace and Justice Studies* 19.1:14–36.

————. 2011. "On Intersectionality and the Whiteness of Feminist Philosophy." In *The Center Must Not Hold: White Women Philosophers on the Whiteness of Philosophy,* ed. George Yancy, 51–71. Lanham, MD: Lexington Books.

Bakhtin, Mikhail M. 1981. *The Dialogic Imagination.* Ed. Michael Holquist. Trans. Caryl Emerson and Michael Holquist. Austin: University of Texas Press.

————. 1986. *Speech Genres and Other Late Essays.* Ed. Caryl Emerson and Michael Holquist. Trans. Vern W. McGee. Austin: University of Texas Press.

Balibar, Etienne. 1991. "Is There a 'Neo-Racism'?" In *Race, Nation, Class: Ambiguous Identities,* ed. Etienne Balibar and Immanuel Wallerstein, 17–28. London: Verso.

————. 2009. "Europe as Borderland." *Environment and Planning D: Society and Space* 27:190–215.

Barkley-Brown, Elsa. 1992. "What Has Happened Here? The Politics of Difference in Women's History and Feminist Politics." *Feminist Studies* 18:295–312.

Barnes, Trevor. 1992. "Reading the Texts of Theoretical Economic Geography: The Role of Physical and Biological Metaphors." In *Writing Worlds: Discourse, Text and Metaphor in the Representation of Landscape,* ed. Trevor Barnes and James S. Duncan, 118–135. New York: Routledge.

Barskanmaz, Cengiz. 2010. "Intersectionality as a Fetish." Paper presented at the 4th Annual Critical Race Studies Symposium, Los Angeles, March 13.

Barvosa, Edwina. 2008. *Wealth of Selves: Multiple Identities, Mestiza Consciousness, and the Subject of Politics.* College Station: Texas A&M University Press.

Bauman, Richard, and Charles L. Briggs. 1990. "Poetics and Performance as Critical Perspectives on Language and Social Life." *Annual Review of Anthropology* 19:59–88.

———. 2003. *Voices of Modernity: Language Ideologies and the Politics of Inequality.* New York: Cambridge University Press.

Beale, Frances M. 1970. "Double Jeopardy: To Be Black and Female." In *The Black Woman: An Anthology,* ed. Toni Cade Bambara, 90–100. New York: Signet.

Becker, Howard S. 1996. "The Epistemology of Qualitative Research." In *Ethnography and Human Development: Context and Meaning in Social Inquiry,* ed. Richard Jessor, Anne Colby, and Richard A. Shweder, 53–71. Chicago: University of Chicago Press.

Bereswill, Mechthild, and Anke Neuber. 2011. "Marginalized Masculinity, Precarization and the Gender Order." Trans. Gerard Holden. In *Framing Intersectionality: Debates on a Multi-faceted Concept in Gender Studies,* ed. Helma Lutz, Maria Teresa Herrera Vivar, and Linda Supik, 69–87. Burlington, VT: Ashgate.

Bergstrom, Ida Irene. 2015. "Toril Moi: Feminist Theory Needs a Revolution." Available at http://kjonnsforskning.no/en/2015/09/toril-moi-feminist-theory-needs-revolution.

Berlant, Lauren. 2007. "On the Case." *Critical Inquiry* 33.4:663–672.

———. 2011. *Cruel Optimism.* Durham, NC: Duke University Press.

Bilge, Sirma. 2013. "Intersectionality Undone: Saving Intersectionality from Feminist Intersectionality Studies." *Du Bois Review* 10.2:405–424.

———. 2014. "Whitening Intersectionality. Evanescence of Race in Current Intersectionality Scholarship." In *Racism and Sociology: Racism Analysis Yearbook 5–2014,* ed. Wulf D. Hund and Alana Lentin, 175–205. Berlin: Lit Routledge Verlag.

Blackwell, Maylei. 2011. *Chicana Power! Contested Histories of Feminism in the Chicano Movement.* Austin: University of Texas Press.

Blackwell, Maylei, and Nadine Naber. 2002. "Intersectionality in an Era of Globalization: The Implications of the UN World Conference against Racism for Transnational Feminist Practices—a Conference Report." *Meridians: Feminism, Race, Transnationalism* 2.2:237–248.

Blee, Kathleen M. 2003. *Inside Organized Racism: Women in the Hate Movement.* Berkeley: University of California Press.

Bonilla-Silva, Eduardo. 2001. *White Supremacy and Racism in the Post–Civil Rights Era.* Boulder, CO: Lynne Rienner.

———. 2003. *Racism without Racists: Color Blind Racism and the Persistence of Racial Inequality in America.* Lanham, MD: Rowman and Littlefield.

Bonilla-Silva, Eduardo, and Tukufu Zuberi. 2008. "Toward a Definition of White Logic and White Methods." In *White Logic, White Methods: Racism and Methodology,* ed. Eduardo Bonilla-Silva and Tukufu Zuberi, 3–27. Lanham, MD: Rowman and Littlefield.

Borges, Jorge Luis. 1999. "The Exactitude of Science." In *Collected Fictions,* 325. Trans. Andrew Hurley. New York: Penguin.

Botman, Maayke, Nancy Jouwe, and Gloria Wekker, eds. 2001. *Caleidoscopische Visies: De Zwarte, Migranten en Vluchtelingenvrouwenbeweging in Nederland.* Amsterdam: Koningklijk Instituut voor de Tropen.

Bourdieu, Pierre. 1977. *Outline of a Theory of Practice.* Trans. Richard Nice. New York: Cambridge University Press.

Bourdieu, Pierre, and Loïc J. D. Wacquant. 1992. *Invitation to Reflexive Sociology.* Cambridge: Polity.

Bowker, Geoffrey C., and Susan Leigh Star. 1999. *Sorting Things Out: Classification and Its Consequences.* Cambridge, MA: MIT Press.

———. 2000. "Invisible Mediators of Action: Classification and the Ubiquity of Standards." *Mind, Culture, and Activity* 7.1–2:147–163.

Bowleg, Lisa. 2008. "When Black + Lesbian + Woman ≠ Black Lesbian Woman: The Methodological Challenges of Qualitative and Quantitative Intersectionality Research." *Sex Roles* 59:312–325.

———. 2012. "The Problem with the Phrase Women and Minorities: Intersectionality—an Important Theoretical Framework for Public Health." *American Journal of Public Health* 102.7:1267–1273.

Brattain, Michelle. 2005. "Miscegenation and Competing Definitions of Race in Twentieth-Century Louisiana." *Journal of Southern History* 71.3:621–658.

Brick by Brick . . . A Civil Rights Story. 2007. Dir. Bill Kavanagh. Kavanagh Productions. Film. Available at www.brick-by-brick.com.

Briggs, Charles L. 1993. "Metadiscursive Practices and Scholarly Authority in Folkloristics." *Journal of American Folklore* 106.422:387–434.

———. 2007. "Mediating Infanticide: Theorizing Relations between Narrative and Violence." *Cultural Anthropology* 22.3:315–356.

Briggs, Charles L., and Richard Bauman. 1992. "Genre, Intertextuality, and Social Power." *Journal of Linguistic Anthropology* 2.2:131–172.

Brown, Richard Harvey. 1977. *A Poetic for Sociology: Toward Logic of Discovery in the Human Sciences.* Chicago: Chicago University Press.

Brown, Wendy. 1995. *States of Injury: Power and Freedom in Late Modernity.* Princeton, NJ: Princeton University Press.

———. 1997. "The Impossibility of Women's Studies." *differences: A Journal of Feminist Cultural Studies* 9.3:79–101.

———. 2005. "The Impossibility of Women's Studies." In *Edgework: Critical Essays on Knowledge and Politics,* 116–135. Princeton, NJ: Princeton University Press.

———. 2008. "The Impossibility of Women's Studies." In *Women's Studies on the Edge,* ed. Joan Wallach Scott, 17–38. Durham, NC: Duke University Press.

Buhle, Mary Jo. 1998. *Feminism and Its Discontents.* Cambridge, MA: Harvard University Press.

Butler, Judith. 1990. *Gender Trouble: Feminism and the Subversion of Identity.* New York: Routledge.

———. 1993. *Bodies That Matter: On the Discursive Limits of "Sex."* New York: Routledge.

———. 1995. "Contingent Foundations: Feminism and the Question of 'Postmodernism.'" In *Feminist Contentions: A Philosophical Exchange,* ed. Seyla Benhabib, Judith Butler, Drucilla Cornell, and Nancy Fraser, 35–57. New York: Routledge.

———. 1997. *Excitable Speech: A Politics of the Performative.* New York: Routledge.

Butler, Judith, Stanley Aronowitz, Ernesto Laclau, Chantal Mouffe, and Cornel West. 1992. "Discussion." The Identity in Question. *October* 61:108–120.

Calmore, John O. 1995. "Critical Race Theory, Archie Shepp, and Fire Music: Securing an Authentic Intellectual Life in a Multicultural World." In *Critical Race Theory: The Key Writings That Formed the Movement,* ed. Kimberlé Crenshaw, Neil Gotanda, Gary Peller, and Kendall Thomas, 315–329. New York: New Press.

Carastathis, Anna. 2016. *Intersectionality: Origins, Contestations, Horizons.* Lincoln: University of Nebraska Press.

Carbado, Devon. 2009. "Yellow by Law." *California Law Review* 97.3:633–692.

———. 2013. "Colorblind Intersectionality." *Signs: A Journal of Women in Culture and Society* 38.4:811–845.

Carbin, Maria, and Sara Edenheim. 2013. "The Intersectional Turn in Feminist Theory: A Dream of a Common Language?" *European Journal of Women's Studies* 20.3:233–248.

Carby, Hazel V. 1982. "White Women Listen! Black Feminism and the Boundaries of Sisterhood." In *The Empire Strikes Back: Race and Racism in Seventies Britain,* ed. Centre for Contemporary Cultural Studies, 212–235. London: Hutchinson.

Center for Women's Global Leadership. 2001. "A Women's Human Rights Approach to the World Conference against Racism." Available at https://www.google.com/url?sa=t&rct =j&q=&e src=s&source=web&cd=1&cad=rja&uact=8&ved=0ahUKEwil8dOWl5_bAhXJ5oMKH dvrDlYQFggpMAA&url=http%3A%2F%2Fwww.cwgl.rutgers.edu%2Fdocman%2Fcsw-2001%2F83-women-s-human-rights-approach-to-the-world-conference-against-racism&u sg=AOvVaw0HPXwoZpwDvCfiUsfyVO9N. Accessed May 10, 2018.

Chan, Sucheng. 1991. *Asian Americans: An Interpretive History.* Boston: Twayne.

Chan-Tiberghien, Jennifer. 2004. "Gender-Skepticism or Gender Boom? Poststructural Feminists, Transnational Feminisms and the World Conference against Racism." *International Feminist Journal of Politics* 6.3:454–484.

Cho, Sumi. 2009. "Post-racialism." *Iowa Law Review* 94.5:1589–1645.

———. 2013. "Post-intersectionality: The Curious Reception of Intersectionality in Legal Scholarship." *Du Bois Review* 10.2:385–404.

Cixous, Hélène. 1980. "Sorties." In *New French Feminisms,* ed. Elaine Marks and Isabelle de Courtivron, 90–98. Amherst: University of Massachusetts Press.

Cohen, Cathy J. 1997. "Punks, Bulldaggers, and Welfare Queens: The Radical Potential of Queer Politics?" *GLQ* 3.4:437–465.

Collins, Patricia Hill. 1986. "Learning from the Outsider Within: The Sociological Significance of Black Thought." *Social Problems* 33.6:S14–S32.

———. 1989. "The Social Construction of Black Feminist Thought." *Signs: A Journal of Women in Culture and Society* 14.4:745-773.

———. 1991. *Black Feminist Thought: Knowledge, Consciousness and the Politics of Empowerment.* New York: Routledge.

———. 1998. "It's All in the Family: Intersections of Gender, Race and Nation." *Hypatia* 13.3:62–82.

———. 2000a. *Black Feminist Thought: Knowledge, Consciousness and the Politics of Empowerment.* Rev. 10th anniv. 2nd ed. New York: Routledge.

———. 2000b. "It's All in the Family: Intersections of Gender, Race, and Nation." In *Decentering the Center: Philosophy for a Multicultural, Postcolonial, and Feminist World,* ed. Uma Narayan and Sandra Harding, 156–176. Bloomington: Indiana University Press.

Collins, Patricia Hill, and Sirma Bilge. 2016. *Intersectionality.* Malden, MA: Polity Press.

Collins, Patricia Hill, Lionel A. Maldonado, Dana Y. Takagi, Barrie Thorne, Lynn Weber, and Howard Winant. 1995. "Symposium on West and Fenstermaker's 'Doing Difference.'" *Gender and Society* 9.4:491–494.

Collins, Randall. 2000. "Situational Stratification: A Micro-Macro Theory of Inequality." *Sociological Theory* 18.1:17–43.

Combahee River Collective. 1983. "Combahee River Collective Statement." In *Home Girls: A Black Feminist Anthology,* ed. Barbara Smith, 264–274. New York: Kitchen Table: Women of Color Press.

Connolly, Clara, and Pragna Patel. 1997. "Women Who Walk on Water: Working across 'Race' in Women against Fundamentalism." In *The Politics of Culture in the Shadow of Capital,* ed. Lisa Lowe and David Lloyd, 375–395. Durham, NC: Duke University Press.

Connolly, William. 1991. *Identity, Difference: Democratic Negotiations of Political Paradox.* Minneapolis: University of Minnesota Press.

Cooper, Anna Julia. 1892. *A Voice from the South: By a Black Woman of the South.* Xenia, OH: Aldine.

Cooper, Brittney. 2015. "Intersectionality." In *The Oxford Handbook of Feminist Theory,* ed. Lisa Disch and Mary Hawkesworth, 385–406. New York: Oxford University Press.

Cranny-Francis, Anne, Wendy Waring, Pam Stavropoulos, and Joan Kirby. 2003. *Gender Studies: Terms and Debates*. Houndmills, UK: Palgrave Macmillan.

Crenshaw, Kimberlé Williams. 1988. "Race, Reform, and Retrenchment: Transformation and Legitimation in Antidiscrimination Law." *Harvard Law Review* 101.7:1331–1387.

———. 1989. "Demarginalizing the Intersection of Race and Sex: A Black Feminist Critique of Antidiscrimination Doctrine, Feminist Theory and Antiracist Politics." *University of Chicago Legal Forum* 14:139–167.

———. 1991. "Mapping the Margins: Intersectionality, Identity, and Violence against Women of Color." *Stanford Law Review* 43:1241–1299.

———. 1992. "Whose Story Is It Anyway? Feminist and Antiracist Appropriations of Anita Hill." In *Race-ing Justice, Engendering Power*, ed. Toni Morrison, 402–440. New York: Pantheon.

———. 1993. "Beyond Racism and Misogyny: Black Feminism and 2 Live Crew." In *Words That Wound: Critical Race Theory, Assaultive Speech, and the First Amendment*, ed. Mari Matsuda, Charles R. Lawrence III, Richard Delgado, and Kimberlé Williams Crenshaw, 111–132. Boulder, CO: Westview Press.

———. 1994. "Mapping the Margins: Intersectionality, Identity Politics, and Violence against Women of Colour." In *The Public Nature of Private Violence*, ed. Martha Albertson Fineman and Roxanne Mykitiul, 93–120. New York: Routledge.

———. 1995a. "Mapping the Margins: Intersectionality, Identity Politics, and Violence against Women of Color." In *After Identity: A Reader in Law and Culture*, ed. Dan Danielsen and Karen Engle, 332–354. New York: Routledge.

———. 1995b. "Mapping the Margins: Intersectionality, Identity Politics, and Violence against Women of Colour." In *Critical Race Theory: The Key Writings That Formed the Movement*, ed. Kimberlé Crenshaw, Neil Gotanda, Gary Peller, and Kendall Thomas, 357–383. New York: New Press.

———. 2000. "The Intersection of Race and Gender Discrimination." Background paper prepared for the Expert Group Meeting, Zagreb, Croatia, November 21–24.

———. 2001. "The Intersectionality of Race and Gender Discrimination." Presentation, World Conference against Racism, Durban, South Africa, August–September.

———. 2003. "Traffic at the Crossroads: Multiple Oppressions." In *Sisterhood Is Forever: The Women's Anthology for a New Millennium*, ed. Robin Morgan, 43–57. New York: Washington Square Press.

———. 2010. "Close Encounters of Three Kinds: On Teaching Dominance Feminism and Intersectionality." *Tulsa Law Review* 46.1:151–189.

———. 2011a. "The Curious Resurrection of First Wave Feminism in the U.S. Elections: An Intersectional Critique of the Rhetoric of Solidarity and Betrayal." In *Sexuality, Gender and Power: Intersectional and Transnational Perspectives*, ed. Anna G. Jónasdóttir, Valerie Bryson and Kathleen B. Jones, 227–242. New York: Routledge.

———. 2011b. "Postscript." In *Framing Intersectionality: Debates on a Multi-faceted Concept in Gender Studies*, ed. Helma Lutz, Maria Teresa Herrera Vivar, and Linda Supik, 221–233. Burlington, VT: Ashgate.

———. 2011c. "Twenty Years of Critical Race Theory: Looking Back to Move Forward." *Connecticut Law Review* 43.5:1253–1352.

Crenshaw, Kimberlé, Neil Gotanda, Gary Peller, and Kendall Thomas. 1995. "Introduction." In *Critical Race Theory: The Key Writings That Formed the Movement*, ed. Kimberlé Crenshaw, Neil Gotanda, Gary Peller, and Kendall Thomas, xiii–xxxii. New York: New Press.

Crenshaw, Kimberlé, Luke Harris, Daniel HoSang, and George Lipsitz, eds. 2018. "Introduction." In *Seeing Race Again: Countering Colorblindness across the Disciplines,* ed. Kimberlé Crenshaw, Luke Harris, Daniel HoSang, and George Lipsitz. Berkeley: University of California Press.

Cruz, Katie, and Wendy Brown. 2016. "Feminism, Law, and Neoliberalism: An Interview and Discussion with Wendy Brown." *Feminist Legal Studies* 24:69–89.

Davies, Bronwyn. 2005. "The (Im)possibility of Intellectual Work in Neoliberal Regimes." *Discourse: Studies in the Cultural Politics of Education* 26.1:1–14.

Davies, Bronwyn, and Sue Saltmarsh. 2007. "Gender Economies: Literacy and the Gendered Production of Neo-liberal Subjectivities." *Gender and Education* 19.1:1–20.

Davis, Angela. 1971. "Reflections on the Black Women's Role in the Community of Slaves." *The Black Scholar* 3.4:2–15.

———. 1981. *Women, Race, and Class.* New York: Vintage Books.

———. 1997. "Reflections on Race, Class, and Gender in the United States." Interview with Lisa Lowe. In *The Politics of Culture in the Shadow of Capital,* ed. Lisa Lowe and David Lloyd, 303–323. Durham, NC: Duke University Press.

———. 2005. *Abolition Democracy: Beyond Empire, Prisons, and Torture.* New York: Seven Stories Press.

———. 2009. "Feminist Methods and Contemporary Quests for Social Justice." Lecture given at Syracuse University, Syracuse, New York, October 19.

Davis, Kathy. 2008. "Intersectionality as Buzzword: A Sociology of Science Perspective on What Makes a Feminist Theory Successful." *Feminist Theory* 9.1:67–85.

———. 2011. "Intersectionality as Buzzword: A Sociology of Science Perspective on What Makes a Feminist Theory Successful." In *Framing Intersectionality: Debates on a Multifaceted Concept in Gender Studies,* ed. Helma Lutz, Maria Teresa Herrera Vivar, and Linda Supik, 43–54. Burlington, VT: Ashgate.

Davis, Kathy, and Dubravka Žarkov. 2017. "*EJWS* Retrospective on Intersectionality." *European Journal of Women's Studies* 24.4:313–320.

Davis, Murray S. 1971. "That's Interesting! Towards a Phenomenology of Sociology and a Sociology of Phenomenology." *Philosophy of the Social Sciences* 1:309–344.

———. 1986. "'That's Classic!' The Phenomenology and Rhetoric of Successful Social Theories." *Philosophy of the Social Sciences* 16:285–301.

Dawson, Michael C. 2003. *Black Visions: The Roots of Contemporary African-American Political Ideologies.* Chicago: University of Chicago Press.

De Lauretis, Teresa. 1988. "Displacing Hegemonic Discourses: Reflections on Feminist Theorizing in the 1980s." *Inscriptions* 3/4:127–144.

Derrida, Jacques. 1978. *Writing and Difference.* Trans. Alan Bass. Chicago: University of Chicago Press.

———. 1981. *Dissemination.* Trans. Barbara Johnson. London: Athlone Press.

Dhamoon, Rita Kaur. 2011. "Considerations on Mainstreaming Intersectionality." *Political Research Quarterly* 64.1:230–243.

Dill, Bonnie Thornton. 1988. "Our Mothers' Grief: Racial Ethnic Women and the Maintenance of Families." *Journal of Family History* 13:415–431.

Dotson, Kristie. 2011. "Tracking Epistemic Violence, Tracking Practices of Silencing." *Hypatia* 26.2:236–257.

Dowling, Paul. 1991. "Gender, Class, and Subjectivity in Mathematics: A Critique of Humpty Dumpty." *For the Learning of Mathematics* 11.1:2–8.

Dreger, Alice. 1998. "'Ambiguous Sex'—or Ambivalent Medicine? Ethical Issues in the Treatment of Intersexuality." *Hastings Center Report* 28.3:24–36.

Eccles, Jacquelynne S., and Janis E. Jacobs. 1986. "Social Forces Shape Math Attitudes and Performance." *Signs: A Journal of Women in Culture and Society* 11.2:367–380.

Erel, Umut, Jin Haritaworn, Encarnación Gutiérrez Rodríguez, and Christian Klesse. 2011. "On the Depoliticisation of Intersectionality Talk: Conceptualising Multiple Oppressions in Critical Sexuality Studies." In *Theorizing Intersectionality and Sexuality*, ed. Yvette Taylor, Sally Hines, and Mark E. Casey, 56–81. Houndmills, UK: Palgrave Macmillan.

Essed, Philomena, and Kwame Nimako. 2006. "Designs and (Co)incidents: Cultures of Scholarship and Public Policy on Immigrants/Minorities in the Netherlands." *International Journal of Comparative Sociology* 47:281–312.

European Union Race Equality Directive. 2000. Council Directive 2000/43/EC of 29 June 2000. *Official Journal L 180, 19/07/2000 P. 0022–0026.* Available at http://eur-lex.europa.eu/LexUriServ/LexUriServ.do?uri=CELEX:32000L0043:en:HTML.

Falcón, Sylvanna M. 2016. *Power Interrupted: Antiracist and Feminist Activism inside the United Nations.* Seattle: University of Washington Press.

Feagin, Joe R. 2001. *Racist America: Roots, Current Realities, and Future Reparations.* New York: Routledge.

Feldman, Martha S. 1995. *Strategies for Interpreting Qualitative Data.* Thousand Oaks, CA: Sage.

Fennema, Elizabeth, and Julia Sherman. 1977. "Sex-Related Differences in Mathematics Achievement, Spatial Visualization and Affective Factors." *American Educational Research Journal* 14.1:51–71.

Fenstermaker, Sarah, and Candace West, eds. 2002. *Doing Gender, Doing Difference: Inequality, Power, and Institutional Change.* New York: Routledge.

Ferguson, Roderick A. 2013. *Aberrations in Black: Toward a Queer of Color Critique.* Minneapolis: University of Minnesota Press.

Ferree, Myra Marx. 2009. "Inequality, Intersectionality and the Politics of Discourse: Framing Feminist Alliances." In *The Discursive Politics of Gender Equality: Stretching, Bending and Policy-Making*, ed. Emanuela Lombardo, Petra Meier, and Mieke Verloo, 86–101. New York: Routledge.

———. 2011. "The Discursive Politics of Feminist Intersectionality." In *Framing Intersectionality: Debates on a Multi-faceted Concept in Gender Studies*, ed. Helma Lutz, Maria Teresa Herrera Vivar, and Linda Supik, 55–66. Burlington, VT: Ashgate.

Fish, Julie. 2008. "Navigating Queer Street: Researching the Intersections of Lesbian, Gay, Bisexual and Trans (LGBT) Identities in Health Research." *Sociological Research Online* 13.1:n.p. Available at www.socresonline.org/13/1/12.html.

Flax, Jane. 1991. "The End of Innocence." In *Disputed Subjects: Essays on Psychoanalysis, Politics and Philosophy*, 131–147. New York: Routledge.

Foucault, Michel. 1972. *The Archaeology of Knowledge.* New York: Pantheon Books.

———. 1980a. *The History of Sexuality.* Vol. 1, *An Introduction.* Trans. Robert Hurley. New York: Vintage.

———. 1980b. "Truth and Power." In *Power/Knowledge: Selected Interviews and Other Writings, 1972–1977*, ed. Colin Gordon, 109–133. New York: Pantheon.

———. 1980c. "Two Lectures." In *Power/Knowledge: Selected Interviews and Other Writings 1972–1977*, ed. Colin Gordon, 78–108. New York: Pantheon.

———. 1984. "Nietzsche, Genealogy, History." In *The Foucault Reader*, ed. Paul Rabinow, 76–100. New York: Pantheon Books.

———. 1988. "Practicing Criticism." Interview with Didier Eribon. Trans. Alan Sheridan. In *Politics, Philosophy, Culture: Interviews and Other Writings, 1977–1984*, ed. Lawrence D. Kritzman, 152–156. New York: Routledge.

Frankenberg, Ruth. 1993. *White Women, Race Matters: The Social Construction of Whiteness.* Minneapolis: University of Minnesota Press.

Fraser, Nancy. 1997. *Justice Interruptus: Critical Reflections on the "Postsocialist" Condition.* New York: Routledge.

Fregoso, Rosa Linda. 2003. *MeXicana Encounters: The Making of Social Identities on the Borderlands.* Berkeley: University of California Press.

Fujino, Diane C. 2005. *Heartbeat of Struggle: The Revolutionary Life of Yuri Kochiyama.* Minneapolis: University of Minnesota Press.

Gabel, Peter. 1980. "Reification in Legal Reasoning." In *Research in Law and Sociology,* vol. 3, ed. Steven Spitzer, 25–51. Greenwich, CT: JAI Press.

Gallagher, Charles A., ed. 1999. *Rethinking the Color Line.* New York: McGraw-Hill.

Garry, Ann. 2012. "Who is Included? Intersectionality, Metaphors, and the Multiplicity of Gender." In *Out from the Shadows: Analytical Feminist Contributions to Traditional Philosophy,* ed. Sharon L. Crasnow and Anita M. Superson, 493–530. New York: Oxford University Press.

Gibbs, Raymond W., Jr., ed. 2008. *The Cambridge Handbook of Metaphor and Thought.* New York: Cambridge University Press.

Giddings, Paula. 1984. *When and Where I Enter . . . The Impact of Black Women on Race and Sex in America.* New York: William Morrow.

Glass, Kathy L. 2012. *Courting Communities: Black Female Nationalism and "Syncre-Nationalism" in the Nineteenth Century North.* New York: Routledge.

Glenn, Evelyn Nakano. 1985. "Racial Ethnic Women's Labor: The Intersection of Race, Gender and Class Oppression." *Review of Radical Political Economics* 17.3:86–108.

———. 2002. *Unequal Freedom: How Race and Gender Shaped American Citizenship and Labor.* Cambridge, MA: Harvard University Press.

Goatly, Andrew. 2011. *The Language of Metaphors.* 2nd ed. New York: Routledge.

Goldberg, David Theo. 2006. "Racial Europeanization." *Ethnic and Racial Studies* 29:331–364.

Good, Catherine, Joshua Aronson, and Jayne Ann Harder. 2008. "Problems in the Pipeline: Stereotype Threat and Women's Achievement in High-Level Math Courses." *Journal of Applied Developmental Psychology* 29:17–28.

Gordon, Colin. 2008. *Mapping Decline: St. Louis and the Fate of the American City.* Philadelphia: University of Pennsylvania Press.

Gordon, Linda. 1999. *The Great Arizona Orphan Abduction.* Cambridge, MA: Harvard University Press.

———. 2009. *Dorothea Lange: A Life beyond Limits.* New York: W. W. Norton.

———. 2016. "'Intersectionality,' Socialist Feminism and Contemporary Activism: Musings by a Second-Wave Socialist Feminist." *Gender and History* 28.2:340–357.

Gramsci, Antonio. 1971. *Selections from the Prison Notebooks.* New York: International.

Green, Joyce, ed. 2007. *Making Space for Indigenous Feminism.* London: Zed Books.

Gressgård, Randi. 2008. "Mind the Gap: Intersectionality, Complexity and 'the Event.'" *Theory and Science* 10.1. Available at http://theoryandscience.icaap.org/content/vol10.1/Gressgard.html.

Grosfoguel, Ramón, and Eric Mielants. 2006. "Introduction: Minorities, Racism and Cultures of Scholarship." *International Journal of Comparative Sociology* 47.3–4:179–189.

Guha, Ranajit. 1988. "The Prose of Counter-insurgency." In *Selected Subaltern Studies,* ed. Ranajit Guha and Gayatri Chakravorty Spivak, 45–86. New York: Oxford University Press.

Guthrie, Robert V. 2003. *Even the Rat Was White: A Historical View of Psychology.* 2nd ed. Boston: Pearson.

Guy-Sheftall, Beverly, ed. 1995. *Words of Fire: An Anthology of African-American Feminist Thought.* New York: New Press.

Hage, Ghassan. 2016. "Towards an Ethics of the Theoretical Encounter." *Anthropological Theory* 16.2–3:221–226.

Hale, Charles R. 1999. "Travel Warning: Elite Appropriations of Hybridity, *Mestizaje,* Antiracism, Equality, and Other Progressive-Sounding Discourses in Highland Guatemala." *Journal of American Folklore* 112.445:297–315.

Hall, Stuart. 1985. "Signification, Representation, Ideology: Althusser and the Post-structuralist Debates." *Critical Studies in Mass Communication* 2.2:91–114.

———. 1986. "Gramsci's Relevance for the Study of Race and Ethnicity." *Journal of Communication Inquiry* 10.2:5–27.

———. 1990. "Cultural Identity and Diaspora." In *Identity: Community, Culture, Difference,* ed. Jonathan Rutherford, 222–237. London: Lawrence and Wishart.

———. 1992. "What Is This 'Black' in Black Popular Culture?" In *Black Popular Culture,* ed. Gina Dent and Michelle Wallace, 21–33. Seattle, WA: Bay Press.

———. 1996. "Introduction: Who Needs 'Identity'?" In *Questions of Cultural Identity,* ed. Stuart Hall and Paul du Guy, 1–17. Thousand Oaks, CA: Sage.

———. 2011. "The Neo-liberal Revolution." *Cultural Studies* 25.6:705–728.

Hall, Stuart, Chas Critcher, Tony Jefferson, John Clarke, and Brian Roberts. 2013. *Policing the Crisis: Mugging, the State, and Law and Order.* 2nd ed. Houndmills, UK: Palgrave Macmillan.

Hallyn, Fernand, ed. 2000. *Metaphor and Analogy in the Sciences.* New York: Springer.

Hammonds, Evelynn. 1994. "Black (W)holes and the Geometry of Black Female Sexuality." *differences* 6.2/3:126–145.

Hancock, Ange-Marie. 2013. "Empirical Intersectionality: A Tale of Two Approaches." *University of California Irvine Law Review* 3:259–296.

———. 2016. *Intersectionality: An Intellectual History.* New York: Oxford University Press.

Haney López, Ian. 2006. *White by Law: The Legal Construction of Race.* Rev. ed. New York: New York University Press.

———. 2014. *Dog Whistle Politics: How Coded Racial Appeals Have Reinvented Racism and Wrecked the Middle Class.* New York: Oxford University Press.

Haraway, Donna J. 1981. "In the Beginning Was the Word: The Genesis of Biological Theory." *Signs: A Journal of Women in Culture and Society* 6.3:469–481.

———. 1988. "Situated Knowledges: The Science Question in Feminism and the Privilege of Partial Perspective." *Feminist Studies* 14.3:575–599.

———. 1991. *Simians, Cyborgs, and Women: The Reinvention of Nature.* New York: Routledge.

Harnois, Catherine E. 2013. *Feminist Measures in Survey Research.* Thousand Oaks, CA: Sage.

Harper, Frances Ellen Watkins. 2012. *Iola Leroy, or Shadows Uplifted.* London: Forgotten Books.

Harris, Anita. 2004. *Future Girl: Young Women in the Twenty-First Century.* New York: Routledge.

Harris, Cheryl I. 1993. "Whiteness as Property." *Harvard Law Review* 106.8:1707–1791.

Harris, Marvin. 1964. *Patterns of Race in the Americas.* New York: W. W. Norton.

Hartsock, Nancy. 1983. "The Feminist Standpoint: Developing Grounds for a Specifically Feminist Historical Materialism." In *Discovering Reality: Feminist Perspectives on Epistemology, Metaphysics, Methodology, and Philosophy of Science,* ed. Sandra Harding and Merrill Hintikka, 283–310. Dordrecht: Riedel.

Hawkesworth, Mary. 2003. "Congressional Enactments of Race-Gender: Toward a Theory of Raced-Gendered Institutions." *American Political Science Review* 97.4:529–550.

Hemmings, Clare. 2011. *Why Stories Matter: The Political Grammar of Feminist Theory.* Durham, NC: Duke University Press.

Hernández, Kelly Lytle. 2010. *Migra! A History of the U.S. Border Patrol.* Berkeley: University of California Press.

Hewitt, Nancy A. 1992. "Compounding Differences." *Feminist Studies* 18.2:313–326.

Higginbotham, Elizabeth. 1983. "Laid Bare by the System: Work and Survival for Black and Hispanic Women." In *Class, Race, and Sex: The Dynamics of Control,* ed. Amy Swerdlow and Helen Lessinger, 200–215. Boston: G. K. Hall.

———. 1985. "Race and Class Barriers to Black Women's College Attendance." *Journal of Ethnic Studies* 13:89–107.

Holyoak, Keith J., and Paul Thagard. 1996. *Mental Leaps: Analogy in Creative Thought.* Cambridge, MA: MIT Press.

hooks, bell. 1981. *Ain't I a Woman: Black Women and Feminism.* Boston: South End.

———. 1984. *Feminist Theory: From Margin to Center.* Boston: South End.

Hubbard, Ruth, Mary Sue Henifin, and Barbara Fried, eds. 1979. *Women Look at Biology Looking at Women: A Collection of Feminist Critiques.* Piscataway, NJ: Transaction Publishers.

Hull, Gloria T., Patricia Bell Scott, and Barbara Smith, eds. 1982. *All the Women Are White, All the Blacks Are Men, but Some of Us Are Brave.* Old Westbury, NY: Feminist Press.

Hurtado, Aída. 1989. "Relating to Privilege: Seduction and Rejection in the Subordination of White Women and Women of Color." *Signs: A Journal of Women in Culture and Society* 14.4: 833–854.

———. 1996. *The Color of Privilege: Three Blasphemies on Race and Feminism.* Ann Arbor: University of Michigan Press.

Hvenegård-Lassen, Kirsten, and Pauline Stoltz. 2014. "Editorial." *NORA—Nordic Journal of Feminist and Gender Research* 22.3:165–169.

James, Joy. 1996. *Resisting State Violence: Radicalism, Gender and Race in U.S. Culture.* Minneapolis: University of Minnesota Press.

Jay, Nancy. 1981. "Gender and Dichotomy." *Feminist Studies* 7.1:38–56.

Jibrin, Rekia, and Sara Salem. 2015. "Revisiting Intersectionality: Reflections on Theory and Praxis." *Trans-Scripts* 5:7–24.

Johnson, Mark. 1990. *Body in the Mind: The Bodily Basis of Meaning, Imagination, and Reason.* Chicago: University of Chicago Press.

Johnston, Claire. 1976. "Women's Cinema as Counter Cinema." In *Movies and Methods,* vol. 1, ed. Bill Nichols, 208–224. Berkeley: University of California Press.

Jordan, June. 1985. "Report from the Bahamas." *On Call: Political Essays,* 39–49. Boston, MA: South End Press.

———. 1992. "Report from the Bahamas." In *Race, Class and Gender,* ed. Margaret L. Andersen and Patricia Hills Collins, 28–37. Belmont, CA: Wadsworth.

Kaplan, Elaine Bell. 1997. *Not Our Kind of Girl: Unraveling the Myths of Black Teenage Motherhood.* Berkeley: University of California Press.

Kapur, Ratna. 2001. "Imperial Parody." *Feminist Theory* 2.1:79–88.

Keaton, Trica Danielle. 2010. "The Politics of Race-Blindness: (Anti)Blackness and Category-blindness in Contemporary France." *Du Bois Review* 7:103–131.

Keaton, Trica Danielle, T. Denean Sharpley-Whiting, and Tyler Stovall, eds. 2012. *Black France/France Noire: The History and Politics of Blackness.* Durham, NC: Duke University Press.

Keller, Evelyn Fox. 1996. *Refiguring Life: Metaphors in Twentieth-Century Biology.* New York: Columbia University Press.

Kermode, Frank. 1983. *The Classic: Literary Images of Permanence and Change.* Cambridge, MA: Harvard University Press.

King, Deborah K. 1988. "Multiple Jeopardy, Multiple Consciousness: The Context of a Black Feminist Ideology." *Signs: A Journal of Women in Culture and Society* 14:42–72.

Kittay, Eva Feder. 1987. *Metaphor: Its Cognitive Force and Linguistic Structure.* New York: Oxford University Press.

Knapp, Gudrun-Axeli. 1999. "Fragile Foundations, Strong Traditions, Situated Questioning: Critical Theory in German-Speaking Feminism." In *Adorno, Culture, and Feminism,* ed. Maggie O'Neill, 119–140. London: Sage.

———. 2005. "Race, Class, Gender: Reclaiming Baggage in Fast Travelling Theories." *European Journal of Women's Studies* 12.3:249–265.

Kövecses, Zoltán. 2015. *Where Metaphors Come From: Reconsidering Context in Metaphor.* New York: Oxford University Press.

Lakoff, George, and Mark Johnson. 1980. *Metaphors We Live By.* Chicago: University of Chicago Press.

Lakoff, Robin. 1975. *Language and Woman's Place.* New York: Harper and Row.

Lalander, Rickard. 2016. "Gendering Popular Participation: Identity-Politics and Radical Democracy in Bolivarian Venezuela." In *Multidisciplinary Latin American Studies: Festschrift in Honor of Martti Pärssinen,* ed. Harri Kettunen and Antti Korpisaari, 149–173. Helsinki: University of Helsinki.

Latour, Bruno. 1987. *Science in Action: How to Follow Scientists and Engineers through Society.* Cambridge, MA: Harvard University Press.

———. 1993. *We Have Never Been Modern.* Trans. Catherine Porter. Cambridge, MA: Harvard University Press.

Lawrence, Charles R., III. 2008. "Unconscious Racism Revisited: Reflections on the Impact and Origins of 'The Id, the Ego, and Equal Protection.'" *Connecticut Law Review* 40:931.

Leary, David E., ed. 1994. *Metaphors in the History of Psychology.* New York: Cambridge University Press.

———. 1995. "Naming and Knowing: Giving Forms to Things Unknown." *Social Research* 62.2:267–298.

Lee, Chana Kai. 2000. *For Freedom's Sake: The Life of Fannie Lou Hamer.* Urbana: University of Illinois Press.

Lee, Sharon Heijin. 2008. "Lessons from 'Around the World with Oprah': Neoliberalism, Race, and the (Geo)Politics of Beauty." *Women and Performance: A Journal of Feminist Theory* 18.1:25–41.

Lewis, Gail. 2009. "Celebrating Intersectionality? Debates on a Multi-faceted Concept in Gender Studies: Themes from a Conference." *European Journal of Women's Studies* 16:203–210.

———. 2013. "Unsafe Travel: Experiencing Intersectionality and Feminist Displacements." *Signs: A Journal of Women in Culture and Society* 38.4:869–892.

Lezra, Esther. 2014. *The Colonial Art of Demonizing Others: A Global Perspective.* New York: Routledge.

Lindberg, Sara M., Janet Shibley Hyde, Jennifer L. Petersen, and Marcia C. Linn. 2010. "New Trends in Gender and Mathematics Performance: A Meta-analysis." *Psychological Bulletin* 136.6:1123–1135.

Linn, Marcia C., and Janet S. Hyde. 1989. "Gender, Mathematics, and Science." *Educational Researcher* 18.8:17–27.

Lipsitz, George. 1994. *Dangerous Crossroads: Popular Music, Postmodernism and the Poetics of Place.* New York: Verso.

————. 1998. *The Possessive Investment in Whiteness: How White People Profit from Identity Politics*. Philadelphia: Temple University Press.

Lloyd, Moya. 2005. *Beyond Identity Politics: Feminism, Power and Politics*. Thousand Oaks, CA: Sage.

Loftsdóttir, Kristin, and Lars Jensen, eds. 2012. *Whiteness and Postcolonialism in the Nordic Region: Exceptionalism, Migrant Others and National Identities*. Burlington, VT: Ashgate.

Lorde, Audre. 1980. "Age, Race, Class, and Sex: Women Redefining Difference." Paper delivered at the Copeland Colloquium, Amherst College, Amherst, MA, April.

————. 1984. *Sister Outsider: Essays and Speeches*. Freedom, CA: Crossing Press.

Lowe, Lisa. 1991. "Heterogeneity, Hybridity, Multiplicity: Marking Asian American Differences." *Diaspora: A Journal of Transnational Studies* 1.1:24–44.

————. 1996. *Immigrant Acts: On Asian American Cultural Politics*. Durham, NC: Duke University Press.

Ludvig, Alice. 2006. "Differences between Women? Intersecting Voices in a Female Narrative." *European Journal of Women's Studies* 13:245–258.

Luft, Rachel E. 2010. "Beyond Disaster Exceptionalism: Social Movement Developments in New Orleans after Hurricane Katrina." In *In the Wake of Hurricane Katrina: New Paradigms and Social Visions,* ed. Clyde Woods, 73–101. Baltimore, MD: Johns Hopkins University Press.

Lugones, María. 1994. "Purity, Impurity, and Separation." *Signs: A Journal of Women in Culture and Society* 19.2:458–479.

————. 2007. "Heterosexualism and the Colonial/Modern Gender System." *Hypatia* 22.1:186–209.

————. 2010. "Toward a Decolonial Feminism." *Hypatia* 25.4:742–759.

Lugones, María C., and Elizabeth V. Spelman. 1983. "Have We Got a Theory for You! Feminist Theory, Cultural Imperialism, and the Demand for 'The Woman's Voice.'" *Women's Studies International Forum* 6.6:573–581.

Lukács, Georg. 1971. *History and Class Consciousness: Studies in Marxist Dialectics*. Trans. Rodney Livingstone. Boston, MA: MIT Press.

Lutz, Helma, Maria Teresa Herrera Vivar, and Linda Supik, eds. 2011. *Framing Intersectionality: Debates on a Multi-faceted Concept in Gender Studies*. Farnham, UK: Ashgate.

Lykke, Nina. 2010. "Theorizing Intersectionalities: Genealogies and Blindspots." In *Feminist Studies: A Guide to Intersectional Theory, Methodology and Writing,* 62–86. London: Routledge.

————. 2011. "Intersectional Analysis: Black Box or Useful Critical Feminist Thinking Technology?" In *Framing Intersectionality: Debates on a Multi-faceted Concept in Gender Studies,* ed. Helma Lutz, Maria Teresa Herrera Vivar, and Linda Supik, 207–220. Burlington, VT: Ashgate.

Lyman, Stanford M. 1991. "The Race Question and Liberalism: Casuistries in American Constitutional Law." *International Journal of Politics, Culture, and Society* 5.2:183–247.

————. 1993. "Race Relations as Social Process: Sociology's Resistance to a Civil Rights Orientation." In *Race in America: The Struggle for Equality,* ed. Herbert Hill and James E. Jones, 370–401. Madison: University of Wisconsin Press.

Maira, Sunaina. 2000. "Henna and Hip Hop: The Politics of Cultural Production and the Work of Cultural Studies." *Journal of Asian American Studies* 3.3:329–369.

Marchetti, Sabrina. 2014. *Black Girls: Migrant Domestic Workers and Colonial Legacies*. Leiden, Netherlands: Brill.

Marshall, Gordon, ed. 1998a. "Ethnomethodology." *Oxford Dictionary of Sociology,* 203–205. 2nd ed. New York: Oxford University Press.

———, ed. 1998b. "Theory, Social Theory." *Oxford Dictionary of Sociology,* 666. 2nd ed. New York: Oxford University Press.

Marx, Karl, with Friedrich Engels. 1973. *The German Ideology.* New York: International Publishers.

Massey, Doreen. 1993. "Politics and Space/Time." In *Place and the Politics of Identity,* ed. Michael Keith and Steve Pile, 139–159. New York: Routledge.

———. 2008. *For Space.* Los Angeles: Sage.

Massey, Douglas S. 2007. *Categorically Unequal: The American Stratification System.* New York: Russell Sage Foundation.

Matsuda, Mari. 1991. "Beside My Sister, Facing the Enemy: Legal Theory Out of Coalition." *Stanford Law Review* 43:1183–1192.

Maxwell, Jill. 2006. "Sexual Harassment at Home: Altering the Terms, Conditions, and Privileges of Rental Housing for Section 8 Recipients." *Wisconsin Women's Law Journal* 21:223–261.

May, Vivian M. 2012. *Anna Julia Cooper, Visionary Black Feminist.* New York: Routledge.

———. 2014. "'Speaking into the Void'? Intersectionality Critiques and Epistemic Backlash." *Hypatia* 29.1:94–112.

———. 2015. *Pursuing Intersectionality: Unsettling Dominant Imaginaries.* New York, Routledge.

McCall, Leslie. 2001. *Complex Inequality: Gender, Class, and Race in the New Economy.* New York: Routledge.

———. 2005. "The Complexity of Intersectionality." *Signs: A Journal of Women in Culture and Society* 30.3:1771–1800.

McCloskey, Donald N. 1995. "Metaphors Economists Live By." *Social Research* 62.2:215–237.

McKinney, Karyn. 2004. *Being White: Stories of Race and Racism.* New York: Routledge.

McKittrick, Katherine, ed. 2015. *Sylvia Wynter: On Being Human as Praxis.* Durham, NC: Duke University Press.

Mehan, Hugh, and Houston Wood. 1983. *The Reality of Ethnomethodology.* Malabar, FL: Krieger.

Melamed, Jodi. 2011. *Represent and Destroy: Rationalizing Violence in the New Racial Capitalism.* Minneapolis: University of Minnesota Press.

Memmi, Albert. 1991. *The Colonizer and the Colonized.* Exp. ed. Trans. Howard Greenfield. Boston, MA: Beacon Press. Originally published as *Portrait du colonisé précédé du portrait du colonisateur.* Paris: Editions Buchet/Chastel, Corrêa, 1957.

Mignolo, Walter D. 2011. *The Darker Side of Western Modernity: Global Futures, Decolonial Options.* Durham, NC: Duke University Press.

Mills, Charles W. 1997. *The Racial Contract.* Ithaca, NY: Cornell University Press.

———. 2007. "White Ignorance." In *Race and Epistemologies of Ignorance,* ed. Shannon Sullivan and Nancy Tuana, 11–38. Albany: State University of New York Press.

Mills, Sara. 1995. "Gender and Reading." *Feminist Stylistics,* 66–79. New York: Routledge.

Mirón, Louis F., and Jonathan Xavier Inda. 2000. "Race as a Kind of Speech Act." *Cultural Studies: A Research Annual* 5:85–101.

Mitchell, Juliet. 1974. *Psychoanalysis and Feminism.* New York: Pantheon.

Moglen, Seth. 2007. *Mourning Modernity: Literary Modernism and the Injuries of American Capitalism.* Stanford, CA: Stanford University Press.

Mohanty, Chandra Talpade. 1988. "Under Western Eyes: Feminist Scholarship and Colonial Discourses." *Feminist Review* 30:61–88.

Moi, Toril. 2015. "Thinking through Examples: What Ordinary Language Philosophy Can Do for Feminist Theory." *New Literary History* 46.2:191–216.

Molina, Natalia. 2010. "'In a Race All Their Own': The Quest to Make Mexicans Ineligible for U.S. Citizenship." *Pacific Historical Review* 79.2:167–201.

Moraga, Cherríe. 1981. "The Güera." In *This Bridge Called My Back: Radical Writing by Women of Color,* ed. Cherríe Moraga and Gloria Anzaldúa, 27–34. New York: Kitchen Table Press.

———. 1983. *Loving in the War Years.* Cambridge, MA: South End Press.

———. 1992. "The Güera." In *Race, Class and Gender,* ed. Margaret L. Andersen and Patricia Hills Collins, 27–34. Belmont, CA: Wadsworth.

Moraga, Cherríe, and Gloria Anzaldúa, eds. 1981. *This Bridge Called My Back: Writings by Radical Women of Color.* Watertown, MA: Persephone Press.

———. 1984. *This Bridge Called My Back: Writings by Radical Women of Color.* 2nd ed. New York: Kitchen Table Press.

Moreton-Robinson, Aileen. 2000. "Troubling Business: Difference and Whiteness within Feminism." *Australian Feminist Studies* 15.33:343–352.

———. 2002. *Talkin' Up the White Woman: Indigenous Women and Feminism.* St. Lucia, Australia: University of Queensland Press.

———. 2015. *The White Possessive: Property, Power, and Indigenous Sovereignty.* Minneapolis: University of Minnesota Press.

Morning, Ann. 2011. *The Nature of Race: How Scientists Think and Teach about Human Difference.* Berkeley: University of California Press.

Mullings, Leith. 1986. "Uneven Development: Class, Race and Gender in the United States before 1900." In *Women's Work, Development and the Division of Labor by Gender,* ed. Eleanor Leacock and Helen Safa, 41–57. South Hadley, MA: Bergin and Garvey.

Mulvey, Laura. 1975. "Visual Pleasure and Narrative Cinema." *Screen* 16.1:6–18.

Nadasen, Premilla. 2009. "'We Do Whatever Becomes Necessary': Johnnie Tillmon, Welfare Rights, and Black Power." In *Want to Start a Revolution? Radical Women in the Black Freedom Struggle,* ed. Dayo F. Gore, Jeanne Theoharis, and Komozi Woodard, 317–338. New York: New York University Press.

Naples, Nancy A. 2009. "Teaching Intersectionality Intersectionally." *International Feminist Journal of Politics* 11:566–577.

Nayak, Suryia. 2015. *Race, Gender and the Activism of Black Feminist Theory: Working with Audre Lorde.* New York: Routledge.

Noble, David W. 2002. *Death of a Nation: American Culture and the End of Exceptionalism.* Minneapolis: University of Minnesota Press.

Not Knot. 1991. University of Minnesota Geometry Center. Video. Available at http://www.geom.uiuc.edu/video/.

Novkov, Julie. 2002. "Racial Constructions: The Legal Regulation of Miscegenation in Alabama, 1890–1934." *Law and History Review* 20.2:225–277.

Nussbaum, Martha. 1999. "The Professor of Parody." *New Republic* 22 (February 22): 37–45.

Ortony, Andrew, ed. 1996. *Metaphor and Thought.* 2nd ed. New York: Cambridge University Press.

Oxford English Dictionary (OED). 2018. Oxford: Oxford University Press.

Palmer, Bruce. 1980. *"Man over Money": The Southern Populist Critique of American Capitalism.* Chapel Hill: University of North Carolina Press.

Pascoe, Peggy. 1991. "Race, Gender, and Intercultural Relations: The Case of Interracial Marriage." *Frontiers* 12.1:5–18.

———. 1996. "Miscegenation Law, Court Cases, and Ideologies of 'Race' in Twentieth-Century America." *Journal of American History* 83.1:44–69.

———. 2010. "Seeing Like a Racial State." In *What Comes Naturally: Miscegenation Law and the Making of Race in America,* 131–159. New York: Oxford.

Patel, Indira. 2001. Report of the WCAR Meeting at London seminar of Women's International League for Peace and Freedom (WILPF) UK, November.

———. 2002. "What the Hell Is Intersectionality?" *NAWO UPDATE* 23:12.

Patterson, Orlando. 1982. *Slavery and Social Death: A Comparative Study.* Cambridge, MA: Harvard University Press.

Peterson, Carla L. 1998. *"Doers of the Word": African-American Women Speakers and Writers in the North (1830–1880).* New Brunswick, NJ: Rutgers University Press.

Petzen, Jennifer. 2012. "Queer Trouble: Centring Race in Queer and Feminist Politics." *Journal of Intercultural Studies* 333:289–302.

Pfeifle, Jason. 2012. "Rethinking Race, Recognition, and the Politics of Education after Judith Butler's *Gender Trouble.*" Ph.D. diss., Department of Political Science, University of California at Santa Barbara.

Phoenix, Ann. 2006. "Editorial: Intersectionality." *European Journal of Women's Studies* 13.3:187–192.

Piven, Frances Fox, and Richard Cloward. 1977. *Poor People's Movements: Why They Succeed, How They Fail.* New York: Vintage.

Prins, Baukje. 2006. "Narrative Accounts of Origins: A Blind Spot in the Intersectional Approach?" *European Journal of Women's Studies* 13:277–290.

Prins, Baukje, and Sawitri Saharso. 2008. "In the Spotlight: A Blessing and a Curse for Immigrant Women in the Netherlands." *Ethnicities* 8:365–384.

Punch, Keith F. 2013. *Introduction to Social Research: Quantitative and Qualitative Approaches.* 3rd ed. Thousand Oaks, CA: Sage.

Race, the Power of an Illusion. 2003. Part 3, *The House We Live In.* California Newsreel. Film.

Radin, Margaret J. 1982. "Property and Personhood." *Stanford Law Review* 34.5:957–1015.

Reddy, Chandan. 2011. *Freedom with Violence: Race, Sexuality, and the U.S. State.* Durham, NC: Duke University Press.

Richardson, Marilyn, ed. 1987. *Maria W. Stewart, America's First Black Woman Political Writer.* Bloomington: Indiana University Press.

Riesman, David. 1950. "Listening to Popular Music." *American Quarterly* 2.4:359–371.

Roberts, Dorothy. 1998. *Killing the Black Body: Race, Reproduction, and the Meaning of Liberty.* New York: Vintage.

———. 2011. *Fatal Invention: How Science, Politics, and Big Business Re-create Race in the Twenty-First Century.* New York: New Press.

———. 2012. "Prison, Foster Care, and the Systematic Punishment of Black Mothers." *UCLA Law Review* 59.6:1474–1500.

Robinson, Cedric J. 1996. "Manichaeism and Multiculturalism." In *Mapping Multiculturalism,* ed. Avery F. Gordon and Christopher Newfield, 116–124. Minneapolis: University of Minnesota Press.

———. 2007. *Forgeries of Memory and Meaning: Blacks and Regimes of Race in American Theater and Film before World War II.* Chapel Hill: University of North Carolina Press.

Rodríguez, Juana María. 2003. *Queer Latinidad: Identity Practices, Discursive Spaces.* New York: New York University Press.

Roediger, David R. 1991. *The Wages of Whiteness: Race and the Making of the American Working Class.* London: Verso.

Rollins, Judith. 1985. *Between Women, Domestics and Their Employers.* Philadelphia: Temple University Press.

Rose, Tricia. 2008. *Hip Hop Wars: What We Talk about When We Talk about Hip Hop—and Why.* New York: Basic Civitas.

———. 2013. "Public Tales Wag the Dog: Telling Stories about Structural Racism in the Post–Civil Rights Era." *Du Bois Review* 10.2:447–469.

Rosser, Sue V. 1990. *Female-Friendly Science: Applying Women's Studies Methods and Theories to Attract Students to Science.* New York: Pergamon Press.

———, ed. 1995. *Teaching the Majority: Science, Mathematics, and Engineering Teaching That Attracts Women.* New York: Teachers College Press, Columbia University.

Sadker, David, and Karen R. Zittleman. 2009. *Still Failing at Fairness: How Gender Bias Cheats Girls and Boys in School and What We Can Do about It.* New York: Scribner.

Sadker, Myra, and David Sadker. 1995. *Failing at Fairness: How Our Schools Cheat Girls.* New York: Scribner.

Samuels, Shirley. 1992. *The Culture of Sentiment.* New York: Oxford University Press.

Sandoval, Chela. 1991. "U.S. Third World Feminism: The Theory and Method of Oppositional Consciousness in the Postmodern World." *Genders* 10:1–24.

———. 2000. *Methodology of the Oppressed.* Minneapolis: University of Minnesota Press.

Saunders, Peter. 1989. *Social Class and Stratification.* New York: Routledge.

Scott, John. 1996. *Stratification and Power: Structures of Class, Status, and Command.* Cambridge: Polity.

Semino, Elena. 2008. *Metaphor in Discourse.* New York: Cambridge University Press.

Shah, Nayan. 2001. *Contagious Divides: Epidemics and Race in San Francisco's Chinatown.* Berkeley: University of California Press.

Shapiro, Fred R., and Michelle Pearse. 2012. "The Most Cited Law Review Articles of All Time." *Michigan Law Review* 110.8:1483–1520.

Shapiro, Michael J. 1985–1986. "Metaphor in the Philosophy of the Social Sciences." *Cultural Critique* 2:191–214.

Sharma, Sarah. 2014. *In the Meantime: Temporality and Cultural Politics.* Durham, NC: Duke University Press.

Shields, Stephanie A. 2008. "Gender: An Intersectionality Perspective." *Sex Roles* 59:301–311.

Silber, Ilana Friedrich. 1995. "Space, Fields, Boundaries: The Rise of Spatial Metaphors in Contemporary Sociological Theory." *Social Research* 62.2:323–355.

Silverman, David. 2011. *Interpreting Qualitative Data: Methods for Analyzing Talk, Text, and Interaction.* Thousand Oaks, CA: Sage.

Smith, Andrea. 2006. "Heteropatriarchy and the Three Pillars of White Supremacy: Rethinking Women of Color Organizing." In *Color of Violence: The INCITE! Anthology,* 66–73. Cambridge, MA: South End Press.

Smith, Barbara, ed. 1983a. *Home Girls: A Black Feminist Anthology.* New York: Kitchen Table—Women of Color Press.

———. 1983b. "Introduction." *Home Girls: A Black Feminist Anthology,* ed. Barbara Smith, xxi–lvi. New York: Kitchen Table–Women of Color Press.

Spelman, Elizabeth V. 1988. *Inessential Woman: Problems of Exclusion in Feminist Thought.* Boston, MA: Beacon Press.

Spencer, Steven J., Claude M. Steele, and Diane M. Quinn. 1999. "Stereotype Threat and Women's Math Performance." *Journal of Experimental Social Psychology* 35:4–28.

Stam, Robert. 1988. "Mikhail Bakhtin and the Left Cultural Critique." In *Postmodernism and Its Discontents,* ed. E. Ann Kaplan, 116–145. London: Verso.

Stam, Robert, and Ella Shohat. 2012. *Race in Translation: Culture Wars around the Postcolonial Atlantic.* New York: New York University Press.

Staunæs, Dorthe. 2003. "Where Have All the Subjects Gone? Bringing Together the Concepts of Intersectionality and Subjectification." *NORA: Nordic Journal of Feminist and Gender Studies* 11.2:101–110.

Steele, Claude M. 1997. "A Threat in the Air: How Stereotypes Shape Intellectual Identity and Performance." *American Psychologist* 52.6:613–629.

Steinberg, Stephen. 2007. *Race Relations: A Critique.* Stanford, CA: Stanford University Press.

Sternberg, Robert J. 1990. *Metaphors of Mind: Conceptions of the Nature of Intelligence.* New York: Cambridge University Press.

Strathern, Marilyn. 1988. *The Gender of the Gift: Problems with Women and Problems with Society.* Berkeley: University of California Press.

Stross, Brian. 1999. "The Hybrid Metaphor: From Biology to Culture." *Journal of American Folklore* 112.445:254–267.

Taimina, Daina. 2009. *Crocheting Adventures with Hyperbolic Planes.* Wellesley, MA: A K Peters.

Takaki, Ronald. 1989. *Strangers from a Different Shore: A History of Asian Americans.* Boston: Little, Brown.

Talisse, Robert, and Scott F. Aikin. 2006. "Two Forms of the Straw Man." *Argumentation* 20:345–352.

Tannen, Deborah. 1990. *You Just Don't Understand: Men and Women in Conversation.* New York: HarperCollins.

Tapia, Ruby C. 2011. *American Pietàs: Visions of Race, Death, and the Maternal.* Minneapolis: University of Minnesota Press.

Tarrow, Sidney. 2013. "Repertoires of Contentious Language." In *The Language of Contention: Revolutions in Words, 1688–2012*, 8–34. New York: Cambridge University Press.

Taylor, Yvette. 2011. "Complexities and Complications: Intersections of Class and Sexuality." In *Theorizing Intersectionality and Sexuality,* ed. Yvette Taylor, Sally Hines, and Mark E. Casey, 37–55. Houndmills, UK: Palgrave Macmillan.

Taylor, Yvette, Sally Hines, and Mark E. Casey. 2011. "Introduction." In *Theorizing Intersectionality and Sexuality,* ed. Yvette Taylor, Sally Hines, and Mark E. Casey, 1–12. Houndmills, UK: Palgrave Macmillan.

Terdiman, Richard. 1985. *Discourse/Counter-discourse: The Theory and Practice of Symbolic Resistance in Nineteenth-Century France.* Ithaca, NY: Cornell University Press.

———. 1993. *Present Past: Modernity and the Memory Crisis.* Ithaca, NY: Cornell University Press.

Terrell, Mary Church. 2005. *A Colored Woman in a White World.* Amherst, NY: Humanity Books.

Thompson, Robert Farris. 1984. *Flash of the Spirit: African and Afro-American Art and Philosophy.* New York: Vintage.

Tilly, Charles. 1983. "Speaking Your Mind without Elections, Surveys, or Social Movements." *Public Opinion Quarterly* 47:461–478.

Tobias, Sheila. (1978) 1995. *Overcoming Math Anxiety.* New York: W. W. Norton.

Tomlinson, Barbara. 2010. *Feminism and Affect at the Scene of Argument: Beyond the Trope of the Angry Feminist.* Philadelphia: Temple University Press.

———. 2013a. "Colonizing Intersectionality: Replicating Racial Hierarchy in Feminist Academic Arguments." *Social Identities: Journal for the Study of Race, Nation and Culture* 19.2:254–272.

———. 2013b. "To Tell the Truth and Not Get Trapped: Desire, Distance, and Intersectionality at the Scene of Argument." *Signs: A Journal of Women in Culture and Society* 38.4:993–1017.

Tomlinson, Barbara, and George Lipsitz. 2013a. "American Studies as Accompaniment." *American Quarterly* 65.1:1–30.

———. 2013b. "Insubordinate Spaces for Intemperate Times: Countering the Pedagogies of Neoliberalism." *Review of Education, Pedagogy, and Cultural Studies* 35.1:3–26.

———. 2019. *Insubordinate Spaces: Improvisation and Accompaniment for Social Justice.* Philadelphia: Temple University Press.

Topp, Michael Miller. 2001. *Those without a Country: The Political Culture of Italian American Syndicalists.* Minneapolis: University of Minnesota Press.

Truscan, Ivona, and Joanna Bourke-Martignoni. 2016. "International Human Rights Law and Intersectional Discrimination." *Equal Rights Review* 16:103–131.

Tuider, Elisabeth. 2014. "Ansätze der Geschlechterforschung in Beratung und Coaching" [Approaches to gender studies in counseling and coaching]. In *Gender und Beratung. Auf dem Weg zu mehr Geschlechtergerechtigkeit in Organisationen* [Gender and counseling: Toward a greater gender equality in organizations], ed. Heidi Möller and Ronja Müller-Kalkstein, 137–154. Göttingen, Germany: Vandenhoeck and Ruprecht.

Turner, Charles. 2010. *Investigating Sociological Theory.* Los Angeles: Sage.

Vakulenko, Anastasia. 2012. "Gender and International Human Rights Law: The Intersectionality Agenda." In *Research Handbook on International Human Rights Law,* ed. Sarah Joseph and Adam McBeth, 196–214. Cheltenham, UK: Edward Elgar Publishing.

Valdes, Francisco, and Sumi Cho. 2011. "Critical Race Materialism: Theorizing Justice in the Wake of Global Neoliberalism." *Connecticut Law Review* 43:1513–1572.

Verloo, Mieke. 2006. "Multiple Inequalities, Intersectionality and the European Union." *European Journal of Women's Studies* 13.3:211–228.

Vives, Luna. 2010. "One Journey, Multiple Lives: Senegalese Women in Spain." *ENQUIRE* 5:19–38.

Walkerdine, Valerie, and The Girls and Mathematics Unit. 1989. *Counting Girls Out.* London: Virago.

Wallerstein, Immanuel, ed. 1996. *Open the Social Sciences: Report of the Gulbenkian Commission on the Restructuring of the Social Sciences.* Stanford, CA: Stanford University Press.

Walter, Jochen, and Jan Helmig. 2008. "Discursive Metaphor Analysis: (De)Construction(s) of Europe." In *Political Language and Metaphor: Interpreting and Changing the World,* ed. Terrell Carver and Jernej Pikalo, 119–131. New York: Routledge.

Warner, Michael. 2002. *Publics and Counterpublics.* New York: Zone.

Wekker, Gloria. 2004. "Still Crazy after All Those Years . . . : Feminism for the New Millennium." *European Journal of Women's Studies* 11:487–500.

———. 2016. *White Innocence: Paradoxes of Colonialism and Race.* Durham, NC: Duke University Press.

Wertheim, Christine. 2006. "To Be or Knot to Be." *Cabinet Magazine* 22. www.cabinet magazine.org/issues/22/Wertheim2.php.

West, Candace, and Sarah Fenstermaker. 1995. "Doing Difference." *Gender and Society* 9.1:8–37.

Weston, Kath. 1996a. "Me, Myself, and I." In *Render Me, Gender Me: Lesbians Talk Sex, Class, Color, Nation, Studmuffins . . . ,* 125–147. New York: Columbia University Press.

———. 1996b. *Render Me, Gender Me: Lesbians Talk Sex, Class, Color, Nation, Studmuffins. . . .* New York: Columbia University Press.

Whiteman, Roberta Hill. 1996. "Preguntas." In *Philadelphia Flowers: Poems by Roberta Hill Whiteman,* 89–91. Duluth, MN: Holy Cow! Press.

Wiegman, Robyn. 1999a. "What Ails Feminist Criticism? A Second Opinion." *Critical Inquiry* 25.2:362–379.

———. 1999b. "Whiteness Studies and the Paradox of Particularity." *boundary 2* 26.3:115–150.

———. 1999–2000. "Feminism, Institutionalism, and the Idiom of Failure." *differences: a Journal of Feminist Cultural Studies* 11.3:107–136.

———. 2005. "The Possibility of Women's Studies." In *Women's Studies for the Future: Foundations, Interrogations, Politics,* ed. Elizabeth Lapovsky Kennedy and Agatha Beins, 40–60. New Brunswick, NJ: Rutgers University Press.

———. 2010. "The Intimacy of Critique: Ruminations on Feminism as a Living Thing." *Feminist Theory* 11.1:79–84.

Wilkins, A. C. 2012. "Becoming Black Women: Intimate Stories and Intersectional Identities." *Social Psychology Quarterly* 75:173–196.

Williams, Fannie Barrier. 1987. "The Colored Girl." In *Invented Lives: Narratives of Black Women 1860–1960,* ed. Mary Helen Washington, 150–159. Garden City, NY: Anchor Press.

Williams, Patricia J. 1991. *The Alchemy of Race and Rights.* Cambridge, MA: Harvard University Press.

———. 1995. *The Rooster's Egg: On the Persistence of Prejudice.* Cambridge, MA: Harvard University Press.

Williams, Rhonda Y. 2004. *The Politics of Public Housing: Black Women's Struggles against Urban Inequality.* New York: Oxford University Press.

Winter, Steven L. 2001. *A Clearing in the Forest: Law, Life, and Mind.* Chicago: University of Chicago Press.

Wittgenstein, Ludwig. 1953. *Philosophical Investigations.* London: Basil Blackwell and Mott.

Woods, Clyde. 2010a. "Les Misérables of New Orleans: Trap Economics and the Asset Stripping Blues, Part 1." In *In the Wake of Hurricane Katrina: New Paradigms and Social Visions,* ed. Clyde Woods, 343–370. Baltimore, MD: Johns Hopkins University Press.

———. 2010b. "The Politics of Reproductive Violence: An Interview with Shana Griffin by Clyde Woods, March 12, 2009." In *In the Wake of Hurricane Katrina: New Paradigms and Social Visions,* ed. Clyde Woods, 157–165. Baltimore, MD: Johns Hopkins University Press.

Yuval-Davis, Nira. 2006a. "Belonging and the Politics of Belonging." *Patterns of Prejudice* 40.3:197–214.

———. 2006b. "Intersectionality and Feminist Politics." *European Journal of Women's Studies* 13.3:193–209.

———. 2007. "Intersectionality, Citizenship and Contemporary Politics of Belonging." *Critical Review of International Social and Political Philosophy* 10.4:561–574.

———. 2011. "Beyond the Recognition and Re-distribution Dichotomy: Intersectionality and Stratification." In *Framing Intersectionality: Debates on a Multi-faceted Concept in Gender Studies,* ed. Helma Lutz, Maria Teresa Herrera Vivar, and Linda Supik, 155–170. Burlington, VT: Ashgate.

INDEX

BARBARA TOMLINSON is a Professor of Feminist Studies at the University of California, Santa Barbara, where she received the Academic Senate Distinguished Teaching Award. She is the author of *Authors on Writing: Metaphors and Intellectual Labor*; *Feminism and Affect at the Scene of Argument: Beyond the Trope of the Angry Feminist*; and (with George Lipsitz) *Insubordinate Spaces: Improvisation and Accompaniment for Social Justice*.